Exceptional Music Pedagogy for Children with Exceptionalities

D1695192

Exceptional Music Pedagogy for Children with Exceptionalities

International Perspectives

Edited by Deborah VanderLinde Blair
and Kimberly A. McCord

OXFORD
UNIVERSITY PRESS

OXFORD
UNIVERSITY PRESS

Oxford University Press is a department of the University of
Oxford. It furthers the University's objective of excellence in research,
scholarship, and education by publishing worldwide.

Oxford   New York
Auckland   Cape Town   Dar es Salaam   Hong Kong   Karachi
Kuala Lumpur   Madrid   Melbourne   Mexico City   Nairobi
New Delhi   Shanghai   Taipei   Toronto

With offices in
Argentina   Austria   Brazil   Chile   Czech Republic   France   Greece
Guatemala   Hungary   Italy   Japan   Poland   Portugal   Singapore
South Korea   Switzerland   Thailand   Turkey   Ukraine   Vietnam

Oxford is a registered trademark of Oxford University Press
in the UK and certain other countries.

Published in the United States of America by
Oxford University Press
198 Madison Avenue, New York, NY 10016

Library of Congress Cataloging-in-Publication Data
Exceptional music pedagogy for children with exceptionalities : international perspectives / edited by
Deborah VanderLinde Blair and Kimberly A. McCord.
    pages cm
Includes bibliographical references and index.
ISBN 978–0–19–023456–0 (hardcover : alk. paper) — ISBN 978–0–19–023457–7
(pbk. : alk. paper)   1. Children with disabilities—Education.   2. Music—Instruction and
study.   I. Blair, Deborah (Deborah V.)   II. McCord, Kimberly.
MT17.E94 2015
371.9′04487—dc23
2015010523

9 8 7 6 5 4 3 2 1
Printed in the United States of America
on acid-free paper

CONTENTS

FOREWORD

Sam looks everywhere but at the music teacher, who is describing how to play the mallet instrument in front of her. His body movements are irregular; he lies down and rolls back and forth. Sam's typical classmates have seen this before and neither they nor their teacher are distracted or concerned. They seem to know what will happen next. With the first sounds of the instrument, two notes played with a steady pulse, Sam sits up, looks in the direction of the teacher, and imitates playing the instrument, and in perfect time.

There are many children like Sam throughout the world. And there are others to whom we have given any number of labels as a result of their unique physical, behavioral, or learning characteristics. Does Sam have a disability? If so, when, where, and under what conditions? Will music become an important part of his life? How should we approach a music education for Sam, or for any child for that matter? Where do we go for ideas?

For decades now, since I have worked as a choral and instrumental music teacher and as a music therapist in hospital settings, I have been a strong advocate for quality music experiences for all children. I am only one of the many hundreds of advocates worldwide who share a common goal: to create music environments in homes, schools, and communities where every child can develop skills, deepen understanding, and cultivate independence in a culture of accomplishment and joy.

My early experiences shaped my philosophy of inclusive education, guiding my work in higher education where I now teach eager, bright-eyed undergraduates and inquisitive graduate students. My goal is for my students to learn skills for successful music teaching but also, importantly, to learn how to *think* as a teacher encountering children from diverse backgrounds; who vary considerably in their capabilities, interests, and levels of motivation; and who present a variety of learning challenges. They will need to learn how to think about Sam and how to create a music classroom where Sam and all his classmates will learn. And as they continue their path as teachers, as they think about what worked and what did not, I want them to rely on past wisdom and explore new ideas and new perspectives.

Earning a degree is not the end of thinking and learning; it's a point on a continuum of growing awareness about ourselves and ways to work collaboratively to bring the joy of music to all children. Many of us continue to think of ourselves as learners, and it is books such as this one by Deborah VanderLinde Blair and Kimberly McCord that make thinking and learning so rewarding, even for those of us who have been "learners" for some time.

Blair and McCord are household names for those in the global community who have attended meetings of the International Society for Music Education Commission on Music in Special Education, Music Therapy and Music Medicine. Others know of these highly regarded professionals from their clinics and conference presentations, and many have benefited from the wisdom found in their engaging articles and books. Blair and McCord are the ideal individuals to bring together a collection of chapters written by internationally prominent experts in their fields, all dedicated to improving the musical lives of children with disabilities worldwide.

For many teachers, attendance at international and national conferences is not possible. It is well past time for a book that brings teachers international perspectives regarding a variety of pedagogical approaches, programs, strategies, and technologies.

There is much to like about this book. Here you have a unique collection of scholarly chapters by knowledgeable authors on a wide range of topics unified in purpose and style, each supported by research, each with practical applications for pedagogy and inclusive classrooms. The descriptions of programs and practices in other countries are intriguing. From this book, I am vividly reminded of how much there is to know and the importance of talking with one another, whether in spoken conversation or through written words.

Collective efforts have resulted in conferences and commissions that led to important documents such as the first UNESCO document on special needs education in 1994 and others to follow on arts education in 2006 and inclusion in 2009. In a fitting, concluding chapter, Kim McCord directs our thoughts to worldwide policies, providing important information about developments concerning the Convention on the Rights of Persons with Disabilities (2006) and how the United States and other countries have responded to its ratification. Also included in this chapter is information about special education policies and music education programs in the countries of contributing authors.

Years of advocacy, litigation, and legislation in many countries have led to dramatic reforms that affect deeply the lives of children with disabilities, their teachers, and their families. Sam and millions of children now benefit from inclusion in regular music classes with their typically developing peers, and many benefit from increased music experiences with skilled, caring pedagogues.

The challenges of working with widely diverse populations are many. The issues are complex. This volume benefits from an international perspective, a wide range of appealing topics, a variety of pedagogical approaches, and numerous strategies. I applaud the editors and authors for their passion, their knowledge, and their generosity. This book will be a valuable resource for teachers, offering yet more ideas to ponder and strategies to implement in their pursuit of bringing quality music experiences to all children of the world.

Judith A. Jellison, PhD
Mary D. Bold Regents Professor in Music and Human Learning
University Distinguished Teaching Professor
Sarah and Ernest Butler School of Music
The University of Texas at Austin

Author of *Including Everyone: Creating Music Classrooms Where All Children Learn*, Oxford University Press, 2015

PREFACE

Deborah VanderLinde Blair

Throughout the past few decades, legislation has spurred the ways education is experiencing the move toward fully inclusive classrooms for the benefit all students. Intentionally inclusive schools and community organizations celebrate this diversity; advances in the practice of music and arts therapies inform teachers as they seek to use music as a vehicle for learning across the curriculum (Adamek & Darrow, 2010). The concurrent surge in technology has propelled the ways learners with exceptionalities interact with music, peers, and the world around them.

Sociocultural manifestations of inclusion have paralleled this move, with attitudes shifting from tolerance toward the *celebration* of difference; in addition, increased public awareness of disabilities such as autism and revisions of legislation have propelled the support needed for learners with exceptionalities in school settings. However, issues of access to appropriate education, particularly music education, remain a lingering inequity for education communities. Jellison (2012) offers: "Even as each country clarifies inclusive education in its laws and educational policies, the fundamental premise of inclusion—equity of educational opportunity for children with disabilities—is supported worldwide" (p. 66).

Inspiration for this collection of chapters comes from the International Society for Music Education (ISME) Commission on Music in Special Music Education and Music Therapy. The commission meets every two years before the ISME World Conference and is the only group that includes international representation from both fields. The researchers and teachers who share their work have influenced changes in the way we engage and teach children from many different cultures and abilities around the world. Through the years, we have learned about the possibilities of instruments like the Soundbeam, developments in cochlear implants for individuals who are deaf including deaf musicians, and alternative methods of teaching music notation such as Figurenotes.

Teachers and researchers from the United States often forget to look beyond their own borders for brilliant strategies that can engage and unlock even the most difficult-to-reach children. In addition to music in special education, the dialogue that occurs between the two fields of special music education and music therapy is valuable and important. With so much new research using brain imaging and neuroscience, educators and therapists can hardly keep up with newly emerging information on how the brain works in individuals with disabilities. The commission, founded in 1974, is now celebrating 40 years of bringing together teachers and researchers who have developed exceptional pedagogies for children with exceptionalities who have a passion for expressing themselves through music.

This book aims to explore musical possibilities for children with exceptionalities, offered by leaders around the globe who work to develop inclusive environments and pedagogical strategies for the teaching and learning of music for all. Throughout this text, the reader will find connections of research and practice, the ways that legislation drives change and support for learners, the collaborative nature of professional teaching, the continual search for and sharing of creative modifications and accommodations, the nature of universal design for learning with implications for curriculum, locating opportunities for self-determination, and a stance of care and advocacy for the children whose musical lives are represented in these chapters.

What is a child? To see a child is to see possibility, someone in the process of becoming. (van Manen, 1991, p. 1)

A stance of care (Noddings, 1984/2003) has emerged as a pervasive theme throughout the words offered by the authors of the chapters that follow. Legislated requirements impact the field of special education in certain ways, but the implementation of any pedagogy is unsuccessful without the teacher's ethically humble stance of empathy and compassion. This is coupled with an attitude of "recognition of and longing for relatedness that forms the foundation of our ethic, and the joy that accompanies fulfillment of our caring enhances our commitment to the ethical ideal that sustains us as one-caring" (p. 6). The chapters that follow exemplify the work of educators who not only seek the best for the learner but also seek to know the learner and to support the learner's quest for being and becoming, for belonging, and for enabling the learner's best musical self. Perhaps this ethical stance is what drives legislation along with research and pedagogy. It calls the teacher to the classroom every day—to figure out how to meet the child and to find and build upon interests, ideas, and skills that celebrate the child. Van Manen (1991) speaks to the heart of this:

> Every child is unique and exhibits inclinations, sensitivities, modalities of being which soon express themselves in certain choices, interests, and desires. Any pedagogical intention needs to respect the child for what he or she is and what he or she can become. Pedagogical intent is aimed at strengthening as much as possible any positive intentions and qualities of the child. (p. 19)

As teachers and learners—with their peers, families, and other professionals—work toward fostering inclusive musical communities, learners move closer toward the place of being and becoming, toward feeling included and knowing that their musical contributions and roles are part of a valued musical experience. Noddings (1984/2003) suggests that a child feels included when one moves beyond acceptance and is "made to feel a partner in the enterprise. . . . More important than anything else, however, is whether the child is welcome, whether he is seen as a contributing person" (pp. 64, 65).

The teacher has a pedagogical interest in the life of the child. He stands in pedagogical relationship to her, and he cannot help but see the child as a unique and whole human being involved in self-formative growth. (van Manen, 2002, p. 25)

In his chapter, "Music for All: Everyone Has the Potential to Learn Music," Markku Kaikkonen challenges the music educator with an ethical pledge to *promise to teach musical knowledge and skills to all, and to promise to foster everyone's musicianship diversely*. A teacher who has made the ethical pledge will constantly strive to develop his or her professional ability and to improve the learning environment so that all who yearn to engage in musical experiences may to do so. Kaikkonen suggests that the key to teaching is discovering an individually optimal way for each learner to engage in learning. Teachers must not settle for busy work or secondary musical activity on the part of anyone, as it is their obligation to seek and discover an artistically significant musical task for each learner that respects his or her level of skill and point of departure.

Alice Hammel explores a narrative approach (Clandinin & Connelly, 2000) in her poignant account of caring and learning as she lives and relives, tells and retells her daughter's extraordinary educational journey. Twice exceptional—a child with learning challenges combined with areas of giftedness—is an intriguing and moving description of a child experiencing school with a wide range of abilities and disabilities, of managing school work and finding the appropriate school setting and educational supports, and ultimately of finding one's own path. For this narrative, the words of Lamott (2013) find resonance as the parent or educator takes one step (or one stitch) at a time:

> To me, teaching is a holy calling, especially with students less likely to succeed. It's the gift not only of not giving up on people, but of even figuring out where to begin.
>
> You start wherever you can. You see a great need, so you thread a needle, you tie a knot in your thread. You find one place in the cloth through which to take one stitch, one simple stitch, nothing fancy, just one that's strong and true. The knot will anchor your thread. Once that's done, you take one more stitch. . . . (p. 93)

The challenge for music education is to provide appropriate educational opportunities for all children in a variety of educational and social settings, so that children will participate happily and successfully in quality music experiences throughout their lives. (Jellison, 2006, p. 257)

Shirley Salmon and Ryan Hourigan offer their respective chapters as models of specific pedagogies designed for learners with exceptionalities. Salmon, in "How the Orff Approach Can Support Inclusive Music Teaching," describes her use of the Orff teaching method to connect with and support young learners in musical experiences. The essence of care is personified in the narratives of the young children in the vignettes and the way the pedagogical strategies that Salmon delineates are developed with the child at the center of the activity.

Hourigan, in "Lessons Learned from the Prism Project," offers the music teacher educator a glimpse into an innovative program that provides first and foremost a musical environment for learners with autism—a space that is not otherwise provided in that area's educational landscape. Second, the program provides preservice music educators with opportunities to learn and teach within this setting in an apprenticed context. Hourigan describes the musical activities designed to engage learners in authentic musical roles and explores the layers of interaction and musical interaction among peers, teacher-learners, experienced music educators, and families.

As music educators, our challenge is to put our inclusive ideals into practice by exploring new and innovative instructional strategies, and by serving as models of acceptance and appreciation for student diversity. (Darrow & Adamek, 2012, p. 93)

The ways that teachers reflect upon their practice and, subsequently, modify their practice—in, after, and perhaps before teaching scenarios (Schön,

1983, 1987)—is a testament to the ethical care that pervades a teacher's professional life. As a teacher notices an unmet need in a child's experience of the music classroom and seeks to mediate the need, the teacher may turn to assistive technologies (complex or simple) to enable the multiplicity of musical processes in which children will engage (whether alone or with peers). Emily Watts, Kimberly McCord, and Deborah VanderLinde Blair offer an overview of the role and nature of assistive technologies and services that are central to the many ways music educators design accommodations and modifications to their music curriculum.

Grainne McHale, in "SoundOUT: Examining the Role of Accessible Interactive Music Technologies Within Inclusive Music Ensembles in Cork City, Ireland," provides a compelling account of SoundOUT—a community-based organization that provides music-making and learning opportunities for approximately 400 young people with and without disabilities. The term *accessible interactive music technology* in this chapter refers to electronic music devices that facilitate access to music making regardless of physical limitations. McHale examines the role of accessible interactive music technology in facilitating participation and progression within inclusive music making and learning, which is a complex and largely unexplored element of music education research in Ireland.

Liza Lee explores the use of Soundbeam technology in her chapter, "Music Activities for Children with Disabilities: An Example from Taiwan." Lee's account of the use of Soundbeam for learners with extensive challenges is a demonstration of her caring commitment to this special group of children and to the teachers she mentors in this process of collaborative teaching. Lee's extensive research—synthesized in her chapter—supports her perspective on the benefits of Soundbeam; in addition, she provides a framework for curriculum and music activities incorporating Soundbeam technology for children with special needs, as well as examples of ongoing assessment tools.

Denied educational opportunities for decades, children with disabilities are now learning alongside "typical" classmates, interacting with them, developing musically, and becoming independent, competent, and self-confident. By doing so, they are more fully enjoying the varied and rich musical experiences that life has to offer. (Jellison, 2012, p. 77)

Teachers—novice and veteran alike—may be stymied when working with learners with exceptionalities. In the chapters offered by Alice Ann Darrow and Mary Adamek, Kimberly McCord, and Christine Lapka, readers have the opportunity for mentorship by these exceptional educators and researchers who have spent their professional lives in caring and supportive roles for learners and their teachers. These next chapters provide the much-needed "application to practice" that reflective teachers are seeking when developing their own practice. Palmer (1998) describes the role of educational mentors; paradoxically, this relationship may also resonate with us as teachers who interact with learners:

> Mentors and apprentices [or teachers and students] are partners in an ancient human dance, and one of teaching's great rewards is the daily chance it gives us to get back on the dance floor. It is the dance of the spiraling generations, in which the old empower the young with their experience and the young empower the old with new life, reweaving the fabric of the human community as they touch and turn. (p. 250)

Darrow and Adamek explore what often seems to be one of the most challenging aspects of working with children with exceptionalities in their chapter, "Behavioral Issues in the Music Classroom: Promoting the Successful Engagement for All Students." They include a discussion of classroom management and its connection to learner motivation and engagement, with a focus on how teachers might work to prevent students' challenging behaviors. The second half of their chapter focuses on the needs of students with identified behavioral disorders, with specific information about characteristics of differing diagnoses and suggestions to support students' successful participation in the music class. Darrow and Adamek also provide information regarding applied behavioral analysis and positive behavioral supports that are used in many US schools to support students' behavioral and learning needs.

McCord offers music educators specific information about and tools for teaching in her chapter, "Specified Learning Disabilities and Music Education." McCord delineates what constitutes a learning disability and offers her expertise in the areas of dyslexia, dyscalculia, dysgraphia, and dyspraxia. McCord's discussion of learning disabilities will enable teachers to better identify challenges when working with students; likewise, McCord's suggested strategies offer teachers proactive ways to engage learners with the highest-incidence disability, specified learning disabilities.

Lapka's chapter focuses specifically on strategies for inclusion in instrumental music ensembles. Drawing on her expertise as an inclusive music teacher educator, Lapka uses universal design for learning as the fundamental premise when designing curriculum, exploring accommodations and modifications, seeking ways to support learner self-reliance, and providing an inclusive learning environment for all learners.

By definition, children who are "special" in one way or another will be in the minority, but I believe that, far from being on the periphery, their concerns should be at the heart of music education research. (Ockelford, 2012, p. 8)

The complex work of Alan Gertner and Lyn Schraer-Joiner, Elaine Bernstorf, and Kimberly VanWeelden contributes to the multiple layers of ethical care that is demonstrated by the authors throughout this book. Their chapters offer readers information that is thorough in scope and includes research-supported strategies for learners with exceptionalities. The care in their extensive research is infused with pedagogical thoughtfulness— "a multifaceted and complex mindfulness toward children" (van Manen, 1991, p. 8) that is evident in the depth of information they provide to teachers, parents, and ultimately learners.

Gertner and Schraer-Joiner present a comprehensive resource to teachers and teacher educators in their chapter, "Music for Children with Hearing Loss." The information regarding hearing loss will benefit teachers as they come to understand the medical issues surrounding hearing loss and implications for the learner in the classroom, particularly in music classrooms. The innovative lesson ideas that Gertner and Schraer-Joiner provide are a wonderful resource for teachers and serve as a model for future curriculum design.

Bernstorf draws on her literacy expertise in "Reading Acquisition Frameworks for Music and Language: Layering Elements of Literacy for Students with Exceptionalities." Bernstorf presents a framework of literacy acquisition as it relates to reading acquisition within music pedagogy contexts for children with exceptionalities. Bernstorf notes that in meeting the continuum of learner needs, it is important to explore not only proven methods of music education but also how these methods intersect with the needs of exceptional learners at both ends of and throughout the learning continuum. An understanding of music literacy development from a conceptual framework for reading literacy requires many points of access for individual learners in our inclusive music learning environments.

VanWeelden provides a thorough description of an important part of US special education law in her chapter, "Understanding the Individualized Education Program Model Within the United States." The creation and implementation of an Individualized Education Program (IEP) serves to provide each student with appropriate modifications and accommodations that are designed to support students with services appropriate for their success. VanWeelden's caring commitment to music educators and their students is demonstrated in her detailed outline of the IEP. VanWeelden includes critical information for teachers as they seek to use the material in each child's IEP to better support all learners in their classrooms.

We acknowledge that these chapters contain extensive information regarding special education law in the United States. In a closing chapter,

McCord provides the reader with information about special education law in Austria, Finland, Ireland, and Taiwan—the countries represented by the international authors in this text. Framed by the Convention on the Rights of Persons with Disabilities, this brief overview may serve to inform educators regarding the scope of laws and educational policies within which these authors frame their ideas and pedagogy.

Most importantly, I learn that my gift as a teacher is the ability to dance with my students, to co-create with them a context in which all of us can teach and learn, and that this gift works as long as I stay open and trusting and hopeful about who my students are. (Palmer, 1998, p. 72)

In closing, we invite readers to reconsider their professional lives—to see each child anew as someone who seeks to belong and to fully participate in his or her blossoming musical life as lived out in music classrooms. We are grateful for the authors who have generously contributed their work to this text and to the teachers with whom they work, who collaboratively embody a pedagogical intent "to strengthen the child's contingent possibility for 'being and becoming'" (van Manen, 1991, p. 17).

REFERENCES

Adamek, M., & Darrow, A. A. (2010). *Music in special education* (2nd ed.). Silver Spring, MD: American Music Therapy Association.

Clandinin, D. J., & Connelly, F. M. (2000). *Narrative inquiry: Experience and story in qualitative research*. San Francisco, CA: Jossey-Bass.

Darrow, M., & Adamek, A. A. (2012). Preparing for the future: Music students with special education needs in school and community life. In G. E. McPherson & G. F. Welch (Eds.), *The Oxford handbook of music education* (Vol. II, pp. 81–96). New York, NY: Oxford University Press.

Jellison, J. (2006). Including everyone. In G. McPherson (Ed.), *The child as musician: A handbook of musical development* (pp. 257–272). New York, NY: Oxford University Press.

Jellison, J. A. (2012). Inclusive music classrooms and programs. In G. E. McPherson & G. F. Welch (Eds.), *The Oxford handbook of music education* (Vol. II, pp. 65–80). New York, NY: Oxford University Press.

Lamott, A. (2013). *Stitches: A handbook on meaning, hope and repair*. New York, NY: Riverhead Books.

Noddings, N. (1984/2003). *Caring: A feminine approach to ethics and moral education* (2nd ed.). Berkley and Los Angeles, CA: University of California Press.

Ockelford, A. (2012). Commentary: Special abilities, special needs. In G. E. McPherson & G. F. Welch (Eds.), *The Oxford handbook of music education* (Vol. II, pp. 7–10). New York, NY: Oxford University Press.

Palmer, P. (1998). *The courage to teach: Exploring the inner landscape of a teacher's life*. San Francisco, CA: Jossey-Bass.

Schön, D. A. (1983). *The reflective practitioner: How practitioners think in action.* New York, NY: Basic Books.

Schön, D. A. (1987). *Educating the reflective practitioner.* San Francisco, CA: Jossey-Bass Publishers.

Van Manen, M. (1991). *The tact of teaching: The meaning of pedagogical thoughtfulness.* London, Ontario: Althouse Press.

van Manen, M. (2002). *The tone of teaching: The language of pedagogy.* London, Ontario: Althouse Press.

CONTRIBUTORS

Mary Adamek, **PhD, MT-BC**, is the Director of the Music Therapy Program at the University of Iowa. She is a coauthor of the textbook *Music in Special Education*, published by the American Music Therapy Association. She has extensive professional experience as a music therapist and music educator with expertise in the area of music in special education.

Elaine Bernstorf, **PhD, CCC-SLP,** is Professor of Music Education at Wichita State University, Kansas, and served as Associate Dean of Fine Arts (2000–2009). Her specializations include elementary and special music education; arts integration; and voice, child language, and literacy. Dr. Bernstorf coauthored *The Music and Literacy Connection* and serves as KSMEA Special Learners cochair.

Alice-Ann Darrow, **PhD, MT-BC,** is an Irvin Cooper Professor of Music in the College of Music at Florida State University. Before coming to Florida State University in 2003, she taught at the University of Kansas for 20 years where she held courtesy appointments in the Departments of Speech and Hearing and Special Education and also worked with students at the Kansas School for the Deaf in Olathe, KS. She has been the recipient of over 25 federal, corporate, or university grants related to music and deafness, and inclusive education. Other areas of research and clinical specialization include nonverbal communication in music education and music therapy, and integrated groups in clinical practice. She is coauthor of *Music in Special Education* and *Music Therapy and Geriatric Populations* and editor of *Introduction to Approaches in Music Therapy*. She has been the recipient of research and clinical practice awards from the American Music Therapy Association.

Alan Gertner is a Professor in the School of Communication Disorders and Deafness at Kean University. He is the Attending Audiologist at Monmouth Medical Center and Consulting Audiologist to the Monmouth Medical Center Regional Cleft Palate Team.

Alice M. Hammel is currently affiliated with James Madison and Virginia Commonwealth Universities. She is also an Autism Spectrum Disorder Music Intervention Specialist for ASSET. She is a well-known author, teacher, and clinician whose primary goal is to become a better teacher every day. Several of her resources are available through Oxford University Press.

Ryan Hourigan holds degrees from Eastern Illinois University (BM) and Michigan State University (MM, Wind Conducting) and a PhD in Music Education from the University of Michigan. Dr. Hourigan currently teaches music education and is the Associate Director of the School of Music at Ball State University.

Markku Kaikkonen, **MMus**, works as a Director at the Special Music Centre Resonaari (Finland). He is a coauthor and editor of dozens of music education books and articles. Kaikkonen is a guest lecturer on continuing education programs in Finland and abroad. He is a board member of the Finnish Society for Music Education and is the chair-elect of the Commission on Music in Special Education, Music Therapy, and Music Medicine of the International Society for Music Education.

Christine Lapka, Professor of Music Education at Western Illinois University, guides teacher education candidates and previously taught kindergarten through grade 12 music, where she found her two undergraduate degrees (music education and music therapy) valuable resources. While completing a doctorate (University of Illinois), she was inspired to look for positive models of inclusion.

Liza Lee is Professor of Early Childhood Development and Education at the Chaoyang University of Technology in Taiwan. She is a graduate of Teachers College, Columbia University, where she received her doctoral degree in music and music education. Dr. Lee conducts research in both early childhood music education and music therapy in the treatment of special needs children.

Gráinne McHale, **BAMus, BMus** (University College Cork), MA (Community Music, York), is a PhD student and lecturer at the University College Cork School of Music and Theatre. She is also the Director of SoundOUT, an inclusive music education initiative in Ireland. She received a PhD scholarship from University College Cork to research the use of accessible interactive music technology within inclusive music education in Ireland.

Shirley Salmon has taught children and adults with different abilities and disabilities for over 30 years. She has served as lecturer at the Orff-Institute in Salzburg since 1984 and at the Universities of Teacher Education in

Graz, Austria, since 2001. Salmon teaches and lectures nationally and internationally and has published books and numerous articles in journals.

Dr. Lyn Schraer-Joiner is Assistant Professor of Music Education at Kean University. She has chaired the International Society for Music Education Commission on Music in Special Education, Music Therapy, and Music Medicine and is the founder of PROJECT REACH: The Kean University Concert Series for the Deaf.

Dr. Kimberly VanWeelden is Professor of Music Education at Florida State University. Her research in the area of music and special education has been presented at national and international conferences and published in leading music education and music therapy journals.

Emily H. Watts is an Associate Professor Emeritus from Illinois State University. She holds a PhD in Special Education from the University of Illinois, Urbana-Champaign. She has conducted research in assistive technology and teacher education.

*Exceptional Music Pedagogy for Children
with Exceptionalities*

CHAPTER 1

Music for All

Everyone Has the Potential to Learn Music

MARKKU KAIKKONEN

Enjoying, learning, and making music are essential to human life and, consequently, a basic right of all people (Lubet, 2011, p. 57). Music is an integral and powerful part of our everyday lives and soundscape (DeNora, 2000; Turino, 2008). It is a social experience, and for everyone to be able to fully participate in it, the physical barriers and social and cultural restraints related to music making, experiencing, and learning must be eliminated. The issues of accessibility and educational equality in music learning are profound: professional and goal-oriented music education should be available to everyone.

Media, Internet, and games, for instance, are prolific sources of everyday musical experiences; music listening, too, has been expanded through new technologies. Community music-based activities and informal ways of learning music reinforce formal music education. However, technologies are not available to everyone, and participation in community music is not always possible due to challenges or barriers caused by illness, disability, or aging. It becomes the community's responsibility to provide equal opportunities for diverse learners and the necessary support services to reach a wide continuum of music making and learning. Music educators make a commitment to teach music for all, and the following ethical promise can serve as the foundation to drive both practice and teacher–student relationships: "I promise to teach musical skills and knowledge to all students and strive to enhance every student's growth as a musician" (Darrow, 2009, pp. 29–31; Kaikkonen, 2013).

This ethical promise obligates the teacher to continuously develop his or her professional capabilities and establish learning environments that meet all students' educational needs. The promise necessitates sensitive and quality music education for all students; the teacher must recognize every student's musical ability and learning potential. Wide-range pedagogy, the ability to interact with compassion, the carefully considered use of new methods and applications, and continuous training are required to fulfill the ethical requirements. In addition to having comprehensive professionalism and versatile approaches and curriculums, the teacher must reconsider his or her own perspective and strive to minimize attitudinal barriers within the learning environment and school communities (Darrow, 2009, pp. 29–31; Unkari-Virtanen & Kaikkonen, 2007).

Irrespective of the student's special needs or features, he or she may have strong musical capabilities and various capacities to learn. The music teacher's aim is to identify the student's strengths and, above all, to appreciate this potential by creating individualized ways to participate in music learning (Bernstorf, 2001, p. 36; Ruokonen, Pollari, Kaikkonen, & Ruismäki, 2012, p. 406). The teacher cannot be satisfied with secondary musical activities or busy work; he or she must have the capacity to offer musical tasks that meet the student's present skill level. The tasks should also be challenging for the student while significant to the artistic whole. Everyone in the particular learning situation should have a purposeful musical task and an experience of full participation. The music teacher's ethical promise is deeply rooted in practice and the design of meaningful musical experiences.

The professional capabilities of a music teacher include knowledge of different methods and approaches of learning and teaching. When teachers are working with students with special educational needs (SENs), strictly organized models and methods may not necessarily serve everyone well. In the process of interaction, the teacher must be able to truly interact with the student and be sensitively present during the entire activity. Furthermore, the teacher should be able to promptly modify the mode of interaction so that it enriches the situation and enhances the student's learning. It is the teacher's responsibility to acknowledge the student's individual features and needs in interactive situations and then operate to meet those challenges. The most significant factor is the motivation of the student, and the teacher should remember that the most befitting way to teach is not necessarily the most suitable way to learn.

To productively respond within dynamically interactive situations and to teach very diverse learners require a wide range of pedagogical knowledge and capabilities. Teacher training and continuing education that focuses on special music education provide teachers with in-depth methodological and practical knowledge. As a result, all learners may be provided opportunities to participate in quality music education that fosters musical learning (Kaikkonen, 2005; McCord & Fitzgerald, 2006; McCord & Watts, 2006; Pontiff, 2004; Walter, 2006).

ACCESSIBILITY

Every person is unique. Diverseness and diversity are defined through the surrounding mainstream culture. In some societies, differences are diagnosed, while in others, the same features are entirely ignored. Because definitions of diversity vary according to the specific culture, solutions to create accessibility also differ. Regardless of the cultural or social differences, it is essential that the local culture strives for accessibility and promotes participation for all.

People are also diverse as learners. The special features of people create richness, but they also generate unpredictable challenges to learning situations. Student diversity can prove to be either a constructive pedagogical challenge or a serious strain for the teacher. If the teacher does not have the appropriate education or readiness to encounter students and meet their special needs, these diverse challenges can become an encumbrance for the teacher. On the other hand, good will and vocational competence are not enough if there are shortages in financial resourcing or in educational policy in general. The main support services for the teacher are continuing education, a supportive organizational culture, possibilities to utilize special needs assistance, and consultations with the specialists working in the related fields of education. The curriculum should be flexible enough to offer possibilities for differentiation. Even more significant is cooperation with parents and other professionals who provide services for the student.

In general, taking care of all learners and engaging in educational equality are acknowledged as desirable values. The appreciation of individuality is encouraged at all levels of (music) education, and the curriculum should be geared toward inclusion. Accessibility allows full participation irrespective of the individual's special features, needs, or background. In an accessible society, the respectful response afforded to the special needs of people is the customary action that transpires as a matter of course and thus increases the well-being of all. Accessibility that furthers inclusion is also an essential objective of the United Nations' conventions on disability rights and the Salamanca agreement of UNESCO (1994).

Unfortunately, good will and respected principles are not enough. Strategies that may increase full participation and accessibility in music learning include careful observation, thorough analysis, and effective practices. Often the most significant barrier may be the lack of awareness of what accessibility is and can be in a particular learning environment. In some cases, the attitudinal environment or lack of financial resources prevents accessibility. It is critical for the teacher to acknowledge and realize his or her personal responsibility toward creative and inclusive education—this becomes a continuous challenge for every teacher. It is equally important to understand that accessible learning environments generate and reinforce learning and musical growth of all students (Hagedorn, 2004; Savolainen, 2009, p. 128).

The music learning environment should be evaluated as a whole. Accessibility consists of the following areas: *attitudinal, physical, sensory, informational, social and cultural,* and *financial* accessibility. Also noteworthy is the accessibility connected with *decision making* (Anttalainen & Tapaninen, 2009; Ekholm, 2009; Lampinen, 2011). Table 1.1 presents the dimensions of accessibility as issues related to workspace (physical), to the teacher (attitudinal and informational), and to the school system and society (financial and decision making).

Based on the previous classifications, the main objective in music education is to establish learning environments that are designed to meet the

Table 1.1 ACCESSIBILITY IN MUSIC EDUCATION

Underlying Factors		Objectives	Outcomes
Workspace	Physical accessibility	Functionality	MUSIC
	Sensory accessibility	Differentiation	FOR ALL
	Financial accessibility		
Teacher	Informational accessibility	Attitudes	MUSIC
	Attitudinal accessibility	Interaction skills	FOR ALL
		Differentiation	
		Pedagogical capabilities	
		Readiness for development	
		Education and continuing education	
		Coteaching	
		Organizational culture	
		Curriculum	
School system and society	Accessibility in decision making	Budgeting	MUSIC
	Financial accessibility	Curriculum	FOR ALL
	Social and cultural accessibility	Education	
		Policies	

needs of all students. This means that students are able to move and act, see, hear, and understand without any limiting factors. It is important to note that practices and support services are not evaluated until they are used in the educational setting. The basis for accessible learning environments is a continuous dialogue among the students, teachers, and administrators that arrange the teaching and learning processes. This empowering cooperation is also part of accessibility in decision making.

ACCESSIBILITY TO FOSTER PARTICIPATION

The physical learning environment should be organized in a way that contributes to the desired behavior. To establish safe and functional musical learning environments, teaching, lighting, suitable acoustical solutions (for students with SENs related to hearing), air conditioning, and even scents are features to design. Moreover, physical accessibility is often connected with informational accessibility. Customized instruments, for example, often make playing and music learning possible. These instruments might include the Skoog, the MagicFlute, the use of push buttons, the Figurenotes Guitar, or technology-based applications like Soundbeam, Brainfingers, and mobile devices. Materials in plain language or in a large font size also can be extremely useful.

For example, Figurenotes notation[1] is an innovation that creates educational equality (Kaikkonen, 2005). Figurenotes is a system of notating music in a concrete way, by means of colors and shapes. It gives learners all of the same musical information as conventional notation, such as pitches, note values, rests, sharps, flats, octaves, and chords, and colors and shapes indicate the keys or frets of an instrument. Therefore, Figurenotes notation is a concrete way of notating music that also serves learners who have difficulty understanding abstractions.

Figurenotes notation presents musical information in an uncomplicated manner and may become a significant tool and a key approach for a student in elementary music studies. With Figurenotes, the use of notation is possible in learning situations, which results in pedagogical solutions also becoming more versatile. It is important to understand that all of the same musical information that can be offered with Figurenotes can be shown with conventional notation, allowing differentiation among students for inclusive music making. It is also possible for a student to shift from Figurenotes to conventional notation if he or she has the ability and motivation.

If the teacher considers it purposeful to apply notation in instruction, Figurenotes can be a remarkable pedagogical tool for enhancing the student's learning and commitment. Applications and approaches like

Figurenotes can be highly beneficial for students with SENs. For students with some developmental and/or cognitive disabilities, Figurenotes can facilitate participation in goal-oriented music education.

Differentiation

Like physical accessibility, informational accessibility requires differentiation. To create and enhance learning, the teacher must have pedagogical capabilities—technologies are merely *assistive*. Music education has multiple modes of experience (playing, singing, moving, listening, creating) that give endless opportunities for students to reflect their personal learning styles and present their capabilities as musicians. It is important to consider that the functionality of the musical tasks is a relevant basis for the differentiation process. In music education, it is possible to plan and adapt individual learning tasks (for instance, by modifying the arrangements) so that the tasks have some recognizable amount of connection with the acquired skills and meanings learned earlier (Kivijärvi, 2012, p. 422). It is of critical importance that the teacher has the ability to differentiate the musical tasks.

Sensory accessibility is taken into account intuitively in quality music education. This may include multiple ways of providing verbal instructions (adapting information), the manner of speaking and listening (auditive perceiving), observational or model learning (imitation, echo, playing by ear), movements and postures, and written instructions (visual perceiving, graphic and traditional notation). The teacher must acknowledge the meaning of nonverbal interaction (facial expressions, eye contact, touching, movements, positions, postures); likewise, the teacher must understand that the physically accessible workspace must also be considered to transfer the sensory information.

Sensory and informational accessibility are realized with widely grounded pedagogical solutions and necessary support services. When working with students with special needs, it is essential to understand that learning occurs, even if it does take time. Pedagogical courage and strong belief in everyone's learning potential are even more important than the external resources.

FROM EXPERIENCE OF SELF-CONTROL TO ACTUAL LEARNING

Keeping the ethical promise is a challenge for the teacher. One must continuously and carefully evaluate, with all students, how to create learning and how the barriers limiting learning can be removed. There are several factors that influence education for learners with special needs as even the actual learning situation and environment can seem strange or scary. For learners with SENs, the experience of being able to organize one's behavior in the current environment and learning situation is of special importance. The student cannot necessarily understand where he or she is, who the people involved in the situation are, and what the items are in the environment. The problems are in perceiving and in the sense of being: the requirements are often difficult to find and all circumstances can seem chaotic. Therefore, the teacher must seek to organize the chaos. To create a safe learning environment and atmosphere, the teacher must find a way to help students understand the meaning of the present structures, including the activities, so that learners can easily comprehend them.

Music teachers have multiple tools to apply to potential problems in perceiving, as music in itself is full of structures. As Uusitalo (2005) notes:

> Music is filled with structures. In musical activities, the following phenomena can be recognized: basic pulse, timbre, even the vibration. Everything that enhances [an] individual's comprehension of structures stabilizes his or her worldview. It is also significant if the student adopts something so strongly that she or he is able to independently start the activity, continue with it and even create variations. The achieved knowledge and skills and more organized behaviour can also shed light on new appealing situations. (pp. 67–69)

In extreme cases, assessing if the student understands the activities and is able to take part in them is less problematic. However, sometimes it is challenging for the teacher to recognize how the student comprehends instructions and the meanings of the activity. Sometimes learning elementary skills will start from the very basics; the requirements are relatively modest and the progress is slow. However, all purposeful musical tasks generally enhance the student's learning potential and capabilities (Kaikkonen & Kivijärvi, 2013).

Even though a task might seem simple, it can be significant for a sense of the musical whole. Still, the teacher should aim to be goal oriented but at the same time emphasize the utilization and pleasure of the skills the student has already learned. The teacher should also acknowledge what the next step in the learning process is and, equally, what the purpose is of the current task. Timing poses a challenge to pedagogical arrangements: all of the tasks should be aligned with the long-term objectives. The aim is that gradually the students themselves will take responsibility of the tasks and artistic wholeness. When the players manage their own parts fluently and musical skills develop, the actual musical interaction, sharing, and artistic work take place (Kivijärvi, 2012, p. 422).

Providing structure in the activities and learning situations can build an atmosphere of safety, but the teacher should also ensure that the student's role in the activity is not superficial (for instance, playing a rhythmic instrument that has no musical purpose or value to the composition). Pedagogical sensitivity also includes the capability to recognize whether the student fully understands what he or she is doing.

Step by step, students will grow to adopt more complex musical tasks, take part in joint playing, and manage performances. The pleasure derived from music making deepens when the student starts to realize that he or she is an important part of the artistic process and the entire community (Alvin & Warwick, 1992, p. 2). The student's identity and roles grow to be more versatile. At best, music learning has considerable effects on other areas of the student's life. Box 1.1 shows how organized behavior, learning, and musical participation are connected.

Box 1.1

FROM EXPERIENCE OF SELF-CONTROL TO ACTUAL LEARNING

1. **Problems in perceiving and in self-control**
   What is this situation I am in?
   Who are these people in the situation?
   What is expected from me?
   What do the given instructions mean?
   → Chaotic worldview
2. **Advancing organized behavior**
   Clear and comprehendible tasks
   Lots of recursion
   → Music is a multidimensional device to gain order
3. **Learning creates order**
   "I know what I am doing."
   "I know why I am doing this."
   "I know when the piece begins and ends."
   "I can play"; "I recognize this piece."
   "I am part of the group."
4. **Experience of self-control**
   New challenging tasks and situations
   → Joint playing
   → Performing
   New standards of activity
   → Improvisation
   → Composing

The foundations of learning are similar with all humans, even though the process can sometimes appear different externally. Some learners adopt new situations and complete tasks through analysis, logical thinking, and reasoning, whereas others learn easily by doing or may be described as spatial or kinesthetic learners. Some students are musically or linguistically more capable. Some learners may enjoy using their skills in collaboration (interpersonal intelligence), whereas others prefer to work individually (intrapersonal intelligence; Gardner, 1993). In addition to a deep knowledge about the theories and approaches of learning, the ability to recognize the learning styles of students is an essential skill for successful teaching. Interaction skills are fundamental in recognizing students' current situations, prevailing circumstances, and experiences as learners, as well as in supporting students' experience of self-control.

In some cases, acknowledging the student's diagnosis or special features may help in building purposeful teaching and learning strategies. However, preconceptions and expectations can also disorient the teacher. A student with developmental disabilities not only has special needs but also is living through his or her own identity and background. The student's family situation or expectional mother tongue may also affect his or her development and learning as much as the medically defined impediments do. Identity is greater than the sum of a learner's noted exceptionalities, and it is never merely characterized by special needs (Ikonen, 1999, p. 30; Uusikylä & Atjonen, 2000, pp. 84–85).

Learning occurs when the student's learning potential is fully discovered and used to the student's advantage. In this process, diagnoses are irrelevant. Of most importance are the student's strengths, even though the special features or factors limiting the learning should be acknowledged. It is essential to respect the student and treat him or her equally with other students: high expectations and challenges should be given (Adamek & Darrow, 2005, p. 57).

When music making takes place, new capabilities are achieved and weaker areas of students' development are supported. Teachers must be able to vary the challenge level of the tasks and provide multiple entry points in multisided musical experiences to meet a wide range of students' abilities. Students commit comprehensively to the working process when the given task is motivating and meaningful; the adoption of a new musical piece and the sharing of it are intrinsically rewarding.

CYCLE OF LEARNING

Music listening, creating, and playing are pleasurable and exciting activities. For young learners in the music classroom, music playing is an extremely multifaceted and challenging activity that requires continuous commitment and hard work. A student's enthusiasm to learn and practice new music does not last if the experience of learning and practicing is not rewarding. The teacher should offer experiences that foster success to create motivation.

The experience of success can be described as the "big smile" phenomenon. Smiling reflects motivation and orientation toward new events (Anttila & Juvonen, 2006, p. 33). A motivated person works actively to achieve a goal. A "big smile" experience generates motivation and propels it toward music and music making, commitment, and further practicing. Practicing creates learning, and learning enables the experience of success. Consequently, the cycle of learning begins again.

The phases of the cycle of learning must be aligned with the student's capabilities and include tasks that are manageable. The "big smile" can be achieved through specific experiences or simply by completing tasks that to some may seem very unambitious at first (playing rhythm instruments, for instance). These experiences can be significant and exciting and should be enjoyable for the learner. Still, the teacher must be prepared and willing to continually utilize the motivation. The "big smile" should not remain a separate experience but should lead to learning that perpetuates the subsequent phases of the cycle (Kaikkonen, 2005, pp. 85–87).

The phases of cycle of learning are as follows:

1. "Big smile"
2. Motivation
3. Commitment
4. Practice
5. Learning

Optimistic attitudes toward learners, knowledge, skills, education, equipment, a supportive organizational culture, resources, and cooperative networks are conditions that generate the cycle of learning (see Hammel, 2004, pp. 33–37). However, students with SENs are often underestimated. Sometimes the limiting factor is the lack of high expectations in the learning process. Within the field of education, some teachers are satisfied when learners with SENs are superficially active or peripherally engaged, which results in the learning potential of these students remaining undiscovered (Kivijärvi, 2012, p. 423). A strong trust in students' learning potential is significant above all else for teachers. Confidence and motivation are at the core of the teacher's ethical promise.

Learning supports and develops an individual's capability to regulate his or her behavior and immediate surroundings. Learning is of the utmost importance for an individual as it may further affect life management skills and quality of life in general. In music learning, the student may be able to interact with just the teacher at first, gradually move to a small group, and, finally, manage actual joint playing and even performances. When playing as part of a group, the student can use the skills already attained and experience the meanings of his or her own actions as a part of the learning community.

The experience of success and the skills to interact and play with others positively affects a person's self-efficacy and self-image as a learner (Ala-Harja, 2010). Bandura (1997, p. 19) notes that self-efficacy influences almost every area of a person's life—how he or she thinks, reflects, and reasons; how he or she sees him- or herself and others; and how he or she feels and behaves. Self-efficacy is connected to motivation, mental schemas, behavioral patterns, and reactions in different (social) situations (Bandura, 1997, p. 279).

Self-efficacy is crucial in learning. "Big smiles" support self-efficacy, while learning and commitment support resiliency (Dillon, 2006). Music learning and musical activities can be considered as broad educative experiences; learning improves self-efficacy and, consequently, the sense of life management. Thus, individuals recognize their own potential capabilities and opportunities, and a strengthened sense of self-esteem contributes to social participation.

Box 1.2 summarizes the meanings and effects of music learning for the student, his or her immediate surroundings, and society as a whole.

Box 1.2

SUMMARY OF THE MEANINGS AND EFFECTS OF MUSIC LEARNING

1. **Individual**
   Working skills and the capability to adopt new skills
   Self-efficacy
   Resilience
   Holistic development
   Interaction skills
   Commitment to a group
2. **Immediate surroundings**
   Active role in the community
   Community realizes the potential of the individual
   Token of appreciation in the community
   Networking
   Effects on the family's life management and quality of life
   More efficient cooperation between the parents and the network
3. **Society**
   Diverse leaners as active members in the cultural field
   Diverse learners as active members in the society
   General understanding of the importance and benefits of music and arts education
   → Effects on health and well-being

SPECIAL MUSIC EDUCATION AND THE EQUAL CULTURAL REVOLUTION

It is important for a teacher to remember that music is central to the entire process. Learning, making, and enjoying music are the most significant goals and values in music education in general. To guarantee the success of these goals within all areas of music education, teacher training and research must support the development of novel approaches and pedagogical applications that define the process of special music education.

Special music education makes active learning possible for new groups of people. Because the learning potential and prospects of students are esteemed regardless of their SENs, special music education allows very diverse learners to achieve anticipated goals, musical knowledge, and skills. Among the most successful and recognized achievements is that musicians with developmental disabilities can work as appreciated professionals among other artists. Pedagogical work creates opportunities for advancing the changes in the musical scene where new groups of active members—musicians with SENs—have recently appeared (Poutiainen, Kivijärvi, & Kaikkonen, 2013). Special music education is the key to inclusive music education.

The student's growth as a musician is affected by the community's attitudes toward diversity. It is essential that the teacher works without hesitation as a change agent to promote respectful attitudes among students and the entire learning community. The reciprocal effect is that the teacher's attitude and the values that undergird it are recognized by others. This influences how the students' capabilities as professional artists are acknowledged and whether the general attitude toward these performers is depreciatory or celebratory. Hagman (2004) describes the key elements of arts education for people with special needs: "We do not make disability theatre, but theatre where the actors have developmental disabilities" (p. 125).

As change makers, teachers must make an ethical promise. This promise, like the one noted earlier, affirms that the teacher values the student's learning potential and establishes learning environments and circumstances (experience of self-control) that enable the cycle of learning. Playing and collaborating create opportunities for learning and create the transfer effects to the student's immediate surroundings and to society as a whole. Educational and social change are possible when the teacher ensures that everyone participates.

This ongoing change can be defined as the equal cultural revolution through which cultural life becomes more inclusive. Westerlund (2002, p. 33) suggests that action and culture are interdependent in a musical experience—experience that is generated by action. The holistic, socio-cultural approach to music education considers individual and collective experience as highly connected and, consequently, emphasizes broader educative objectives. Active people can affect their own worldviews and their social environment. This perspective on music and music education also influences the definitions of professionalism in music and the equaliza-tion of the entire cultural field (Dal Maso, 2004, p. 24; Kaikkonen, 2005, p. 104; Kurki, 2002, p. 14).

Special music education has the potential to more fully impact attitudes toward diversity and enhance learning about equality and humanity. As music and music learning serve as comprehensive tools between the indi-vidual and society, the idea of special music education as an environment for a stable and inclusive society must continue to be fostered (Kaikkonen, 2011; Westerlund, 2002).

ACKNOWLEDGMENTS

My sincere gratitude to Sanna Kivijärvi, who assisted with translation, and Nancy O'Neill, who proofread this text.

NOTE

1. See also: Figurenotes © Kaarlo Uusitalo, 1996; Figurenotes applications © Markku Kaikkonen and Kaarlo Uusitalo, 1998; http://www.figurenotes.com.

REFERENCES

Adamek, M. S., & Darrow, A. A. (2005). *Music in special education.* Silver Spring, MD: American Music Therapy Association.

Ala-Harja, A. (2010). *"Mä haluun soittaa." Erityistukea tarvitsevien oppilaiden musiikkitoimin-nan vaikutusten ja merkitysten tarkastelua elämänhallinnan näkökulmasta ["I wanna play:" Examination of the effects and meanings of musical activities from the point of view of control over life of students with special needs]* (Master's thesis, University of Helsinki).

Alvin, J., & Warwick, A. (1992). *Music therapy for the autistic child.* New York, NY: Oxford University Press.

Anttalainen, H., & Tapaninen, R. (2009). *Liikkumis-ja toimimisesteisille soveltuvat perusopetuk-sen tilat, kalusteet ja varusteet [Physically accessible learning environments in comprehensive school].* Vammala, Finland: Finnish National Board on Education.

Anttila, M., & Juvonen, M. (2006). *Musiikki koulussa ja nuoren elämässä. Kohti kolmannen vuosi-tuhannen musiikkikasvatusta [Music in school and in the youth's life: Toward the music edu-cation of third generation].* Joensuu, Finland: Joensuu University Press.

Bandura, A. (1997). *Self-efficacy: The exercise of control.* New York, NY: W. H. Freeman & Co.

Bernstorf, E. D. (2001). Paraprofessionals in music settings. *Music Educators Journal, 87*(4), 36–41.

Dal Maso, R. (2004). Kolme ajankuvaa [Three pictures of the times]. In A. Jämsén & T. Kukkonen (Eds.), *Voimavirtaa arkeen. Taide ja kulttuuri sosiaalialan työssä [Powering everyday life: Art and culture in social welfare work]*. Joensuu, Finland: Karelia University of Applied Sciences, 23–27.

Darrow, A. A. (2009). Barriers to effective inclusion and strategies to overcome them. *General Music Today, 22*(3), 29–31.

DeNora, T. (2000). *Music in everyday life.* New York, NY: Cambridge University Press.

Dillon, S. (2006). Assessing the positive influence of music activities in community development programs. *Music Education Research, 8*(2), 267–280.

Ekholm, E. (2009). *Monimuotoisuus ja esteettömyys: Näkövammaisten asiantuntijoiden työelämäkokemuksia [Diversity and accessibility: Working life experiences of people with visual impairments]*. Espoo, Finland: Ennora.

Gardner, H. (1993). *Multiple intelligences: The theory in practice.* New York, NY: Basic Books.

Hagedorn, V. S. (2004). Including special learners: Providing meaningful participation in the music class. *General Music Today, 17*(3), 44–50.

Hagman, A. (2004). Ilmaisun iloa: Draaman mahdollisuudet kehitysvammatyössä. In A. Jämsén & T. Kukkonen (Eds.), *Voimavirtaa arkeen. Taide ja kulttuuri sosiaalialan työssä [Powering everyday life: Art and culture in social welfare work]* (pp. 121–131). Joensuu, Finland: Karelia University of Applied Sciences.

Hammel, A. M. (2004). Inclusion strategies that work. *Music Educators Journal, 90*(5), 33–37.

Ikonen, O. (1999). Sietäminen ja suvaitseminen ovat avainasioita tulevaisuuden yhteiskunnassa [Appreciation is the core value in the future's society]. In O. Ikonen (Ed.), *Kehitysvammaisten opetus* (pp. 17–37). Helsinki, Finland: Kehitysvammaliitto.

Kaikkonen, M. (2005). Musiikinopetuksen ja kuntoutuksen risteyksessä [Music education and music therapy]. In M. Kaikkonen & K. Uusitalo (Eds.), *Soita mitä näet: Kuvionuotit opetuksessa ja terapiassa [Play what you see: Figurenotes in education and therapy]* (pp. 75–114). Helsinki, Finland: Kehitysvammaliitto.

Kaikkonen, M. (2011). Special music education as a positive cultural revolution. In H. Ruismäki & I. Ruokonen (Eds.), *Design learning and well-being: 4th International Journal of Intercultural Arts Education Conference* (pp. 125–133). Research Reports 331. Helsinki, Finland: University of Helsinki.

Kaikkonen, M. (2013). Kohti inklusiivista musiikinopetusta [Towards inclusive music education]. In P. Jordan-Kilkki, E. Kauppinen, & E. Korolainen-Viitasalo (Eds.), *Musiikkipedagogin käsikirja: Vuorovaikutus ja kohtaaminen musiikinopetuksessa [Music teacher's manual: Interaction and encountering in music teaching]* (pp. 28–36). Helsinki, Finland: Finnish National Board on Education.

Kaikkonen, M., & Kivijärvi, S. (2013). Interaction creates learning: Engaging learners with special educational needs through Orff-Schulwerk [Special Issue]. *Approaches: Music Therapy and Special Music Education, 5*(2), 1–32. Retrieved from http://approaches.primarymusic.gr

Kivijärvi, S. (2012). Project disabled people as musicians: A systemic approach. *Procedia: Social and Behavioral Sciences, 45*, 416–427.

Kurki, L. (2002). *Sosiokulttuurinen innostaminen [Sociocultural approach]*. Tampere, Finland: Vastapaino.

Lampinen, R. (Ed.). (2011). *Helsingin vammaispoliittinen selvitys [Report on disability policies in the City of Helsinki]*. Helsinki, Finland: City of Helsinki.

Lubet, A. (2011). Disability rights, music, and the case for inclusive education. *International Journal of Inclusive Education, 15*(1), 57–70.

McCord, K., & Fitzgerald, M. (2006). Children with disabilities playing musical instruments. *Music Educators Journal, 92*(4), 46–52.

McCord, K., & Watts, E. H. (2006). Collaboration and access for our children: Music educators and special educators together. *Music Educators Journal, 92*(4), 26–33.

Pontiff, E. (2004). Teaching special learners: Ideas from veteran teachers in the music classroom. *Teaching Music, 12*(3), 52–58.

Poutiainen, A., Kivijärvi, S., & Kaikkonen, M. (2013). Music for all for music: Special music education equalizing concert society. In K. Tirri, E. Hanhimäki, & E. Kuusisto (Eds.), *Interaction in educational domains. Finnish Educational Research Association Publications, 62*, pp. 56-66. Sense Publishers.

Ruokonen, I., Pollari, S., Kaikkonen, M., & Ruismäki, H. (2012). The Resonaari Special Music Centre as the developer of special music education between 1995-2010. *Procedia: Social and Behavioral Sciences, 45*, 401–406.

Savolainen, H. (2009). Erilaisuuden huomioimisesta hyviin oppimistuloksiin [From accounting for dissimilarity to good learning results]. *Kasvatus: The Finnish Journal of Education, 40*(2), 121–130.

Turino, T. (2008). *Music as social life: The politics of participation.* Chicago, IL: University of Chicago Press.

UNESCO. (1994). *The Salamanca statement and framework for action.* Salamanca, Spain: World Conference on Special Needs Education: Access and Quality.

Unkari-Virtanen, L., & Kaikkonen, M. (2007). Läsnäolon, huomion ja kunnioituksen musiikkipedagogiikka [Sensitive presence, respect, and music education]. *Musiikkikasvatus: Finnish Journal of Music Education, 10*(1–2), 23–33.

Uusikylä, K., & Atjonen, P. (2000). *Didaktiikan perusteet [Basics of didactics].* Juva, Finland: WSOY.

Uusitalo, K. (2005). Väriä musiikkiterapiaan [More colours for music therapy]. In M. Kaikkonen & K. Uusitalo (Eds.), *Soita mitä näet. Kuvionuotit opetuksessa ja terapiassa [Play what you see. Figurenotes in Education and Therapy]* (pp. 62–75). Helsinki, Finland: Kehitysvammaliitto.

Walter, J. S. (2006). The basic IDEA: The Individuals with Disabilities Act in your classroom. *Teaching Music, 14*(3), 22–26.

Westerlund, H. (2002). *Bridging experience, action, and culture in music education. Studia Musica, 16.* Helsinki, Finland: Sibelius Academy.

CHAPTER 2

Twice Exceptional

ALICE M. HAMMEL

She was six weeks old as I held her and she instinctively grasped my finger with her hand.

I looked at her beautiful face and suddenly had a deep feeling that this child was going to need more and better from me than I ever thought I could provide.

HOLLIE

When our first daughter was born, we thought the "what your baby will do this month" books were extraordinarily cautious with skills they predicted she would display each month. Her older sister, Hannah,[1] easily breezed past each expectation and was months ahead of the expected benchmarks by the time she was 4 months old. Because of this experience, we were unprepared for the struggle we witnessed as our younger daughter worked herself to exhaustion to achieve each milestone. We began reading the books again with new eyes and took note of each small achievement made, almost always after great energy and practice had enervated her in the process. It was at Hollie's eight-month well-baby appointment that I first voiced our concerns and requested a referral to a developmental pediatrician.

After months of providing data and documentation and delivering increasingly distressed pleas for assistance, we were finally referred to a developmental pediatrician and placed on the waiting list for an appointment. Hollie was 13 months old when we began the rounds of developmental and medical testing to discern the cause of the developmental delays my daughter was experiencing. Two months later, we received a diagnosis of pervasive developmental disorder (PDD) and began occupational, speech, and sensory integration therapies. It was then that the work really started.

Our lives began to revolve around regular trips to the children's hospital for therapy. Therapists also visited our home each week to monitor her progress. I knew we were racing against time to make gains because each month of delays let the sand sift further underneath Hollie's developmental feet. It was during this time that we began to notice her uncanny sense of timing and comedy as she drew everyone who knew her into her world with her bright eyes and silly faces. These abilities confused doctors and therapists, who were looking for a simple diagnosis; our daughter was anything but simple.

In preschool, Hollie loved being a part of the classroom and enjoyed silly songs and games, as well as arts and crafts projects. We were concerned, however, when, at age 4, Hollie brought home a painting with her friend Emily's name on it insisting she had drawn it. Hollie finally admitted switching pictures because "Emily was a good drawer"—she wanted me to be proud of the drawings that came home from preschool. This began our introduction into the world of a child who is twice exceptional.

INTELLECTUAL GIFTEDNESS AND TWICE EXCEPTIONAL

This chapter will focus on the needs of students who are intellectually or musically gifted and present unique challenges that must be met within the music classroom. Teacher qualities necessary for successful educational experiences, as well as specific needs and issues that can arise when teaching students who are twice exceptional, will be addressed. Research and best practice will be framed within the narrative of a family experiencing the daily challenges posed by a child who is intellectually and musically gifted and who has other special needs.

Intellectual Giftedness

Testing to determine speed of cognition and processing began in the late 1800s. Alfred Binet (1894) designed a test to determine whether children were considered educable. Children who did not score well were then considered unsuitable for formal education. Lewis Terman standardized the intelligence test created by Binet that became known as the Stanford-Binet Intelligence Scale (Winner, 1996). Through this process, Terman determined that intelligence is fixed, and he defined intellectual giftedness as the top 1% of scores on the Stanford-Binet scale (Terman & Oden, 1947).

In the past, schools utilized an IQ testing process that included group and/or individual testing of students in schools with results often used to determine the children eligible for gifted programs in schools. Most schools established the initial level of giftedness as those students with an IQ of at least 125; however, students from diverse backgrounds traditionally scored lower on these tests. As a result, tests of nonverbal language ability began to be used in addition to IQ testing to identify students who may have otherwise gone unnoticed (Webb, Meckstroth, & Tolan, 1994).

Some schools request individual testing for students. This can be time consuming and expensive; however, it is often more accurate than group testing (Winner, 1996) at finding a precise level of giftedness. The use of augmented teacher narratives, standard achievement testing scores, and products created by a child are now utilized (Walker, 1991). Intellectual giftedness, when thinking in quantitative terms, occurs according to the universal bell curve (Figure 2.1).

Most students in school, as with most of the general population, demonstrate IQs between 85 and 115, whereas those most often identified as having intellectual giftedness possess an IQ between 125 and 200 (Hollingsworth, 1975). Issues sometimes arise when students who are exceptionally or profoundly gifted are found within an inclusive population of students (Table 2.1). These can include underperformance, a need for perfection, behavioral issues, and a feeling of disrespect by these students because their intellectual needs are not being met. While school systems use a multiple-method approach to finding students in need of gifted services, the presence of giftedness in the general population does fall along a universal curve.

Some researchers have determined that students with exceptionally high IQs may "waste" most of their time in school because they have already learned the material being taught (Hollingsworth, 1975; Silverman, 1993;

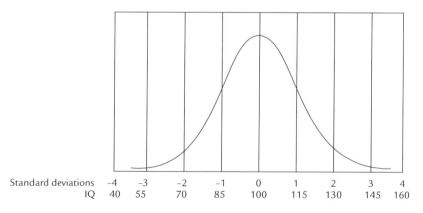

| Standard deviations | −4 | −3 | −2 | −1 | 0 | 1 | 2 | 3 | 4 |
| IQ | 40 | 55 | 70 | 85 | 100 | 115 | 130 | 145 | 160 |

Figure 2.1. Giftedness ratios within the universal bell curve.

Table 2.1 INTELLECTUAL GIFTEDNESS
CATEGORIES USING IQ SCORES

Intellectual Giftedness Categories	I.Q. Score
Mildly (or basically) gifted	115–129
Moderately gifted	130–144
Highly gifted	145–159
Exceptionally gifted	160–179
Profoundly gifted	180+

Winner, 1996). When students who have IQs of 120 are offered the same educational differentiation as students who have IQs of 160, the inequity is painfully apparent. A glance at the commensurate differentiation for students who have IQs of 40 to 80 creates an educational paradox. (Van Tassel-Baska, 1998).

Definitions and common practices regarding the identification of students who are gifted have varied. For example, the Marland Report (Marland, 1971/1972) defines students who are gifted as those who score in the 95th percentile or above on an IQ test or demonstrate achievement or potential for achievement in one or more of these areas:

- General intellectual ability
- Specific academic aptitude
- Creative or productive thinking
- Leadership ability
- Visual and performing arts
- Psychomotor ability

Their recommendation was that students be evaluated according to objective measures and professional evaluation. A few years later, Renzulli (1977) posited a theory of giftedness. His markers for giftedness include above-average ability, creativity, and task commitment. This theory began to be applied in identification procedures in some school systems and is still highly regarded by some. Others have posited further conceptions regarding giftedness, and scholars in the field are still somewhat in disagreement on the matter.

Some in the field recommend that students be identified through a demonstration of exceptional performance or the potential for exceptional performance. Others contend that truly intellectually gifted students often refuse to display their true ability in an environment that is not intellectually or creatively stimulating (Tolan, 1999). Through use of the Torrence Tests of Creative Thinking and the Structure of Intellect

Learning Abilities Tests, students have been identified as creatively talented by school systems. These tests, however, have not been proven to show high correlation with subsequent creative production by students (Silverman, 2013).

The widespread use of various markers to identify students who are intellectually gifted began in the 1990s. This shift led to the inclusion of some or all of the following indicators by some school systems when identifying students who are gifted (Silverman, 2013):

- Top 10% of the school population
- Domain-specific giftedness
- Achievement or the potential for achievement
- Motivated
- External manifestations of giftedness apparent
- Observable in adolescents and/or adults
- IQ scores used as partial evidence of giftedness

This current thinking is disputed somewhat by another group of researchers and thinkers in the field of giftedness who counter that children who are intellectually gifted are inherently different and that giftedness (Gallagher, 2000):

- Can be identified through developmental differences in abstract reasoning, emotional sensitivity, and intensity
- Can be observed in very young children
- Can be documented on measures of IQ
- Is lifelong
- Encompasses 2% to 3% of the population
- Creates qualitative different life experiences
- Leads to a set of unique life situations
- Requires early intervention and accommodation

In my experience with my daughter and with other intellectually gifted children, the Gallagher premise has been the most useful.

Twice Exceptional

It can be difficult to identify students who have learning differences and are intellectually gifted because strengths and deficits often mask each other. Silverman (2013) notes, "When IQ testing is abandoned, when children are only deemed gifted on the basis of demonstrated performance, when they are not qualified as disabled unless they are performing significantly below grade level, and when psychologists are left out of the process, most twice exceptional children are imperceptible" (p. 13). In addition, Merrill (2012) finds that "highly gifted is not the same as high achieving. Highly gifted is how a person is wired, not what a person produces" (p. 8). Through a combination of testing, teacher narratives, parental input, and student achievement, it is difficult, yet possible, to accurately identify students who are twice exceptional.

If a student has been identified as being intellectually gifted and also has a 504 Plan or Individualized Education Program (IEP), the designation of twice exceptional may be utilized. Researchers have found that 2% to 5% of students who are intellectually gifted also have a disability (Dix & Schafer, 2005; Whitmore, 1980). A child who is twice exceptional may have a more difficult time being admitted into a program for students who are intellectually gifted. If a student has significant gaps in knowledge and/or moderate to severe differences in attention, standardized testing may not accurately measure the cognitive abilities of that student (Bisland, 2004). The gaps may occur because of a specific learning disability or other difference that does not correctly measure the overall achievement levels of a student who is twice exceptional.

The identification of students who are gifted and have learning differences is problematic and may require new or revised methods for identification (Karnes, Shaunessy, & Bisland, 2004). Observations, portfolios, and anecdotal data provide invaluable information to supplement standardized testing (Silverman, 1989). Moreover, a comprehensive evaluation that includes multiple quantitative and qualitative measures and allows students to demonstrate both their strengths and their challenges is the most reliable way to appropriately identify students who are twice exceptional.

HOLLIE: ELEMENTARY SCHOOL

Before Hollie entered kindergarten, we endured another round of psychological and educational testing that included IQ and achievement measures, video and photographic data, and two visits by the public school special education teacher to the preschool classroom. We learned that Hollie was highly gifted intellectually; however, we were told that she would probably never test to her actual aptitude level because of her differences.

Other deficits including low muscle tone and gross motor problems surfaced. Sensory integration therapy did much to improve these conditions; when funding for this ended, we enrolled Hollie in a gymnastics class.

While she had some obvious gross motor development differences from her classmates, she was an affable and energetic little girl who loved nothing more than to spring unannounced into the arms of her teachers to display her unbridled affection. I applauded her early use of social charms to mask difficult tasks.

Music was an early and important part of Hollie's life. Growing up in a house with parents who are professional musicians and music educators facilitated this early interest. I will never forget the day I first heard Hollie babble. She had struggled to say "mama" and "dada" and was working very hard in speech therapy to learn to talk. While teaching a flute lesson, I began to hear a very musical set of babbling from across the room. I asked my student to stop playing, and we listened to Hollie literally sing before she could speak. Her expressive language soon began to increase rapidly and was almost always preceded by vocal explorations and improvisatory singing. As a result, we sang many words and phrases to her, and her sister began to create "Baby Hollie Songs" to sing to Hollie.

Hollie possessed a social awareness far beyond that of many of her friends. With the reality of kindergarten looming large the summer after preschool graduation, I revisited the idea of enrolling Hollie in another year of preschool. Her understanding that most children would advance to kindergarten but those not ready would be held back kept me focused toward kindergarten. She had set kindergarten as an immediate goal.

I was grateful for the opportunity to have Hollie enter kindergarten with an IEP in place and a caring kindergarten teacher who collaborated well with the special education teacher. Social issues became more apparent as Hollie became tired and distracted during the day and was sometimes unable to make and sustain friendships. Hollie met academic goals on time yet struggled with testing and long-term summative assessments. An example is the time-honored "count to 100" that kindergarten students experience each spring. Hollie was able to count to 100 but was not able to do it "in the moment" when the teacher was there with her. She eventually succeeded when allowed to go to a quiet hallway without the distractions of other students in the classroom. This difference widened as timed math tests, multiplication tables, Virginia history state-standardized testing, and multistep science experiments became realities during elementary school.

Musically, Hollie excelled. Her singing voice was always on pitch, and she loved to express herself through song. In second grade, she scored in the 98th percentile for her grade level on the Primary Measures of Music Audiation (PMMA; Gordon, 2012). It was a liberating moment to have her aptitude revealed free of qualifiers. Hollie began piano lessons and continued to sing almost as much as she spoke.

The moments of greatest happiness for Hollie in elementary school often involved music. We were all thrilled when she was chosen to sing at various school events, and we beamed with pride from the front row of the audience when she sang with the All-Virginia Elementary School Choir in the fifth grade. Hollie resisted learning to read music, and memorization was difficult. She played the flute in the school band and easily learned everything she performed by ear. Her flute lessons with me were similar because she had heard the melodies and exercises for years. Hollie auditioned for a summer choral camp and used word rhythms to read a portion of her entrance exam. The examiner asked why she had used unusual words for her rhythms ("puppy puppy cat cat" for "ta-ti ta-ti ta ta"). Hollie's response was that she liked animals better than vegetables. Her sense of humor and aptitude for antics increased as her personality began to bloom.

Elementary school was also the time when Hollie worked her way out of her PDD diagnosis and into three new diagnoses—developmental delay, severe attention deficit hyperactivity disorder (ADHD) combined (hyperactivity/impulsivity and inattention), and generalized anxiety disorder. We spent two years trying to find the correct medication and dosage to assist Hollie with attention while maintaining a balance emotionally. The frightening reality came to us suddenly as we were watching our home video of Hollie in the third-grade PTA program. She was the sun in the production and was responsible for striking a large drum on cue. As we watched the video, we could see her holding her breath for lengthy periods followed by a quick exhalation and another held inhalation. After speaking to her doctor, we realized that she was attempting to slow her heart rate because the medication was causing it to race.

In general, we were very fortunate that Hollie attended an outstanding elementary school with a caring staff and an approachable administration. Hollie thrived during those years and we were satisfied with her academic progress. Socially, Hollie struggled because her peers did not always understand her behavior. We continued to help make connections with peers and provide happy play dates when friends would visit our home.

CHARACTERISTICS OF STUDENTS WHO ARE TWICE EXCEPTIONAL

Students who are twice exceptional often display the characteristics shown in Table 2.2 (L. D. Higgins & Nielsen, 2000). The following characteristics

Table 2.2 CHARACTERISTICS OF STUDENTS WHO ARE TWICE EXCEPTIONAL

Strengths	Challenges
Superior Vocabulary	Poor Social Skills
Advanced ideas and opinions	High sensitivity to criticism
High levels of creativity and problem-solving ability	Lack of organizational and study skills
Extremely curious, imaginative, and questioning	Discrepant verbal and performance skills
Wide range of interests not related to school	Poor performance in one or more academic areas
Penetrating insight into complex issues	Difficulty with written expression
Specific talent or consuming interest area	Stubborn, opinionated demeanor
Sophisticated sense of humor	High impulsivity

are also common among a student who is twice exceptional (D. Higgins, Baldwin, & Pereles, 2000; Weinfeld, Barnes-Robinson, Jeweler, & Roffman Shevitz, 2006):

- Has high verbal ability with some language used in an inappropriate way and at inappropriate times
- Displays strong observation skills with difficulty in memorization
- Has excellent problem-solving skills when posed with "real world" issues
- Possesses outstanding critical thinking and decision-making skills, particularly if compensatory skills have been developed
- Has attention issues (however, hyperfocus is obvious in an area of interest)
- Has a strong questioning attitude that may appear (or be) disrespectful (questions may include facts or other information presented by authority figures)
- Possesses an unusual imagination with a high level of originality and a divergent thought process
- Shows lack of risk taking in academic settings but a high level of risk taking in creative or nonacademic situations
- Has an outstanding ability to use humor to deflect, deflate, and defuse situations that may include a lack of academic understanding
- Appears immature and will sometimes use behaviors common in much younger students when stressed or tired
- Constantly asks for support and assurance in area of deficit; may also appear defiant and angry when challenged
- Is highly critical of self and others
- Has difficulty with peer and social groups; may frequently shift friend groups
- May be removed from a friend group by peers if level of intellectual giftedness does not match performance or if social skills are considered inappropriate or immature

- Is often a leader of nontraditional students or of students with lesser cognitive ability who have accepted the student in their peer circle and recognize the leadership skills present in the student
- Demonstrates a wide range of interests but often must choose based on area of strength rather than the interest that is strongest
- May have a strong area of interest that consumes time and energy
- Has difficulty following directions and exhibiting executive function skills in a "step by step" fashion
- Has great difficulty when communicating via written language
- Has difficulty understanding tasks based on written directions due to cognitive functioning and processing delays
- May appear to lack basic language and mathematical skills because of cognitive processing issues
- May excel in music, art, theater, and dance
- Often demonstrates outstanding higher-order thinking skills while being unable to process discrete information

Because of dichotomous behaviors and learning characteristics, students who are twice exceptional are often misdiagnosed or undiagnosed. This complicated learning profile can flummox many teachers, who may resort to labels of behaviors and things that irritate them rather than a thoughtful consideration of the whole child and what he or she brings to the class-room. Moreover, the longer a child traverses a public school system without receiving appropriate services to meet his or her needs, the higher the like-lihood of failure, disappointment, decreased self-esteem, and depression.

Behavior

The already complicated behavior profile of students who are intellectually gifted becomes increasingly murky when learning differences are present. Students who are gifted and have learning differences can be exponentially frustrated because they are aware of the standard or level of competence expected but are not able to communicate their level of understanding or the desired response. Attention-seeking behaviors or behaviors that seem rude can occur, resulting in misunderstandings between teachers and stu-dents. These developmentally asynchronous events are disruptive to the classroom routine and to the learning process of all students. Moreover, the frustration felt by a student who is twice exceptional can appear to be aggressive, careless, and/or off-task.

An awareness of the asynchronous characteristics of students who are intellectually gifted can lead to an even greater awareness of the compounding asynchronicity inherent within a student who has learning differences. For example, a student who is chronologically 10 years old may have an IQ of 150, thus placing his cognitive age at 15 years. On the other hand, if this student has a learning difference in mathematics that places his calculating and processing abilities at 7 years old, he will demonstrate a compounded asynchronous profile that can be debilitating in an elementary classroom created for students who are neurotypical. Frustration, anxiety, and tension may present in a vicious cycle that leads to behavioral outbursts (Benito, 2003).

The music classroom can be a place of respite and joy for a student who struggles in a traditional classroom. By utilizing multimodal teaching techniques, music educators can increase the potential for every student to obtain competence and demonstrate musical understanding. Many behavioral outbursts and disruptive occurrences can be diminished through choice of modality in expression of understanding, chunking of assignments to decrease anxiety, and an atmosphere of inquiry that encourages freedom to explore through multilevel opportunities. Improvisation and composition are excellent musical activities for differentiation as each student may choose his or her own specific level of comfort in a process-oriented approach (Benito, 2003).

Learning

"Street smart versus school smart" is a phrase used by some students who are twice exceptional to describe themselves. They may be able to expertly travel city streets at an early age, know the exact change necessary to complete almost any transaction, and be able to talk their way out of any number of possibly difficult situations, yet these same students struggle with academic tasks that include memorization, organization of materials, study habits, and use of executive function skills to titrate long-term assignments. The lack of cognition speed to quickly absorb global information becomes debilitating when instruction and expectations become task and sequence oriented (Hannah & Shore, 1995).

Many students who are twice exceptional must process information several times before making a conclusion or stating a final response. This often causes anxiety and frustration, which leads students to stop processing because of the time it takes to produce an answer or to problem solve a situation. They sometimes find themselves offering an incorrect response after having labored to express it. This, over time, can lead teachers to add another label to this child: lazy.

A student who is twice exceptional can appear lazy, disinterested, and disengaged. With a studied and compassionate approach, a teacher can increase the potential for a student to achieve *and* demonstrate understanding at a level closer to his or her aptitude. Creating an atmosphere of collegial inquiry using open-ended questioning and a structure for responses that is clearly organized will benefit students who struggle to acquire and demonstrate knowledge.

Creativity

Students who are intellectually gifted can possess an almost limitless amount of creative potential in their area of giftedness. Likewise, students who have differences in learning may also be extraordinarily creative in one or more areas of scholarly pursuit. With strict guidelines or expectations removed, all students are able to create at a level that is comfortable for them and to fully utilize their creative gifts and strengths.

The music classroom can provide students with many opportunities to create music that demonstrates their level of creativity and their ability to present divergent thought within a musical context. The capacity of a music educator to cultivate creativity can translate to other academic settings. Works created by a student can also be a powerful indicator of creativity that may not be seen in other classrooms. By creating meaningful partnerships with other faculty and staff, evidence of creativity in the music classroom may be shared with everyone who interacts with the student.

Emotion

For students who have been identified as intellectually gifted, the possibility that their giftedness may be "taken" from them can cause significant frustration. Some students will do almost anything to mask their areas of difficulty. The higher the level of intelligence is, the longer a student may succeed in school while not really understanding or mastering certain subject material. Conversely, a student who has a learning difference may never be identified as also possessing a high level of intelligence. This situation can be equally difficult because the student may never know his or her true intellectual potential and, more important, may never understand the way his or her brain processes information. This can also lead to depression, despair, and even suicide.

Music is filled with complex emotions and understandings that are multidimensional. By exploring emotion and its relationship to music, students can become familiar with complex and abstract processes inherent in music. Students who struggle yet are also highly capable may benefit from opportunities to search for meaning within masterworks, new creations, compositions, and performances.

General Intellectual Ability and Specific Academic Aptitude

Until recently, many educators assumed that students who are intellectually gifted are equally capable in every academic situation. This premise is only appropriate for some students. Many students are gifted in only one subject area or in a small number of areas. This is also true for students who are twice exceptional. For example, a high level of potential in verbal and written communication does not necessarily transfer to the music classroom. It may be mitigated by a learning difference in syntax, grammar, or other subset of learning. We do not yet know enough about specific connections within the brain to understand exactly how to teach all students, but we do know that each child is different and some children must work harder to learn in certain ways.

Students who are musically gifted may not always demonstrate a global pattern of high performance in the music classroom. This is particularly true for students who are musically gifted and who also have one or more learning differences. Music teachers who use objective data for identifying musical giftedness, as well as music teachers who rely on subjective data, will be most successful if they measure achievement according to the individual profile of a student, rather than an aptitude score or portfolio of process/product accomplishments.

HOLLIE: MIDDLE SCHOOL

We were fortunate to live in a diverse, urban school district with many school choice options. Hannah was selected to attend an International Baccalaureate (IB) school program for the 50 top-scoring fifth-grade students from around the city. Hollie soon stated that the IB program was her goal as well. As part of their application process, students took standardized tests to measure aptitude and achievement levels. As a result, not many students with learning differences were admitted. Hollie, however, was admitted, and we spent the next three years advocating for her and traveling almost daily to the school to make sure her academic, social, and emotional needs were being met. The teachers in the program were not accustomed to accommodating students with IEPs and 504 Plans. They also were only practiced in accelerating and compacting courses for students who were simply intellectually gifted. The conundrum of a child with multiple areas of gifts and differences was not an opportunity some of the teachers were prepared to accept.

The middle-school-girl carousel of emotions was heightened for Hollie. Her social and emotional development was also uneven, as the "sorting hat" of cliques was confusing and frustrating for her. We had less control over her peer group because middle school is, well, middle school. We continued to support Hollie as much as possible as parents and consoled her when the social sorting made her feel inferior.

During parent/teacher conferences, we would hear of the impulsive, disruptive, and immature behaviors exhibited by our daughter. We would also be told, repeatedly, that her handwriting was unacceptable and her organization skills were lacking. No amount of gentle reminders from us would assuage the blame and judgment in the voices of these teachers. I am convinced our phone number was on speed dial as it rang, almost daily, with new recitations of Hollie's transgressions during school. We had a running agreement with the girls—if they told us what happened at school first, the punishment would be lessened. I lost count of the number of days they flew off the school bus and into the house to explain what happened at school before a teacher had the opportunity to call.

A disappointing accompaniment to the environment of intellectually elite academic situations is that the parents are sometimes more competitive than the children. The totality of this environment included a number of inappropriate assumptions made about Hollie by parents of the peers in her classes. I found myself retreating from volunteer activities and committees at school as I began to see judgment in the eyes of other parents and teachers. Hollie was definitely seen as different in this highly achieving academic environment, and I struggled to not verbally eviscerate anyone who dared counsel me regarding my daughter's behavior and work ethic. In retrospect, choosing an academically elite school for her may have been a mistake; however, I shudder to consider how her intellectual giftedness would have fared in a local neighborhood middle school.

These years were not as musical as her elementary school years. An unfortunate incident with a children's choral director who physically punished Hollie for humming along with a choir singing onstage caused Hollie to stop singing for three years. Her middle school band director constantly compared Hollie to Hannah and shook his head while laughing when we walked in the band room for a parent/teacher conference. Hollie quit the flute soon after this. She also stopped taking piano lessons because reading music using a grand staff was still so difficult for her. Lastly, she stopped ballet classes and cited "too many rules" as her rationale. I allowed her to stop her after-school activities because she was already exhausted from all the requirements of preadolescence, and I could see the daily wear caused by anxiety, frustration, and tension. We did not want to add more to the stresses of her daily life.

Specific Strategies for Engaging Students Who Are Twice Exceptional

Students who are twice exceptional benefit from flexible groups that change according to the situation. Chamber music, music theory, composition and improvisation, and music listening can all be accomplished within flexible groupings that take into account the intellectual, musical, and emotional needs of students who are twice exceptional.

Table 2.3 describes other grouping options (adapted from Tomlinson, 1999).

Table 2.3 GROUPING OPTIONS FOR INSTRUCTION

Strategy	Description	Benefits for students who are Twice-Exceptional
Flexible Skills Grouping	Students are placed in groups according to their musical and intellectual needs. Movement among groups is common, based on readiness according to a specific objective.	Students are not expected to perform at the highest musical or intellectual level at all times. They are able to learn in appropriate groups that change according to the task. For students with uneven learning profiles, this allows a label-free and organic system that honors their needs.
Compacting	A three-step process that (1) assesses what a student knows about material to be studied and what the student still needs to master, (2) plans for learning what is not known and excuses a student from what is known, and (3) plans for additional time to spend in enriched or accelerated study.	Students who are twice exceptional often understand the 'whole' of a concept far before the 'part' of a concept. This can create difficulty in the classroom because a student may appear to understand the entire topic or be able to 'talk around' an area without really mastering the concept or skill. Compacting allows the student to pretest for current knowledge and then ameliorate elements that are unclear.
Most Difficult First	Students can demonstrate mastery of a concept by responding to a small number of the most difficult tasks with 85% accuracy (scale, key signature, rhythm, composition). Students who can demonstrate mastery do not need to practice anymore.	Students who struggle with attention, discrete steps, detailed assignments, and memorization will appreciate only being asked to do the most difficult portions of composition, memorization, and series of specific direction activities.

(*continued*)

Table 2.3 (CONTINUED)

Strategy	Description	Benefits for students who are Twice-Exceptional
Orbital Study	Independent projects that are long term. They orbit, or revolve, around some facet of the curriculum. Students select their own topics for orbital, and they work with guidance and coaching from the teacher to develop more expertise on the topic and the process of becoming an independent investigator. Musical examples could include studies of historical performance styles, composers, music concepts, and performance projects.	Individual rather than group projects are often preferred. An opportunity to choose the topic, depth, and breadth for study without the forced community and social issues that arise in a group project can create a true creative and differentiated project. The time to spend studying a musical topic of interest can also lead to a process and product that closely aligns with the intellectual or musical aptitude of the student because she is able to learn and create according to her strengths.
Independent Projects, Group Investigations	Teacher directed individual and group projects allow students the opportunity to demonstrate skills and understandings through verbal, written, aural, and kinesthetic activities.	Student interest and independence can both be encouraged through these active opportunities. The addition of a specific timeline with many checkpoints provides a structure for students who need small chunks of accountability frequently.
Problem Based Learning	Active and 'real world' situations that require inferential learning.	Students who are twice exceptional often tire of exercises they consider meaningless. By providing a 'real world' situation and asking students to use brainstorming and problem solving to resolve an issue, they can see the applicability of the issue to their musical lives.
Agendas	A task analysis or sequence of events necessary to complete and assignment.	Metacognition and executive functioning are often compromised with students who are twice exceptional. Frustration can ensue when specific directions are not provided. An agenda levels the playing field for students who struggle moving from whole to part.
Learning Centers, Interest Centers, Choice Boards	Offer options that include improvisation, composition, singing, playing instruments, listening, and movement.	Student choice is a powerful motivator for students who are often passive in their own learning. Students who are twice exceptional often crave depth of understanding.

(*continued*)

Table 2.3 (CONTINUED)

Strategy	Description	Benefits for students who are Twice-Exceptional
Portfolios/ Assessment	Provide a multi-dimensional opportunity to demonstrate knowledge acquisition over time. Assessment procedures are ongoing and do not depend on performance on one day.	Students who vary widely in their readiness to learn appreciate the opportunity to add their best work performed on their best days to their portfolios or assessment charts. This also levels the playing field for students who sometimes have a 'bad day.'

HOLLIE: HIGH SCHOOL

Hannah decided in the sixth grade that she wanted to attend the Regional Governor's School for the Arts and Technology; Hollie soon decided that she also wished to attend the same school. Aware of the application process, point distribution for applicants, and competition within each of the seven art areas, I began to search frantically for the area that would best display Hollie's innate talents and gifts. Our local school system had approximately 9 to 14 slots each year for eighth-grade students who wished to attend this school, and the vetting process could be fierce. We chose musical theater and soon after enrolled Hollie in a local class that I knew was taught by the program director of musical theater at the Governor's School.

She did not do well in her first musical theater classes, and I began to see and hear the same familiar weariness from these teachers. Her father and I began engaging in cognitive rehearsal each day after school to help Hollie comprehend her behaviors and the way they were viewed by others. She had a difficult time understanding that her words could be misunderstood and that people around her had their own independent reactions to her language and behavior choices. We began to see improvement within a few months and also began private voice lessons with one of the teachers from the musical theater class. I began to fervently hope we had found the opportunity for excellence Hollie desperately needed.

I continued to remind myself that what Hollie says and what Hollie means are often dissimilar. Through the cognitive rehearsals each day, she began to develop an increased theory of mind and become slightly less impulsive when queried or challenged by someone. The voice lessons went very well and the teacher easily prepared Hollie for an audition at the Governor's School. The audition required singing, dancing, and improvisatory acting. Her father took her to the audition and dawdled afterward hoping to "run into" the director of the program. When he did, he learned that Hollie had received a perfect score on her audition. The combination of her interview, audition, and academic record secured her a space at the prestigious school.

High school began with a flurry of meetings, carpool lists, and orientation activities. Hollie was very excited to be starting a new school and made friends easily with other rising freshmen who were interested in musical theater. In the first round of auditions, Hollie was cast in a touring show opportunity that would end with a statewide competition for awards at the end of the fall. Academically, she did not struggle because much of the coursework had already been introduced during her middle school program. Her stagecraft teacher contacted me in late September with some of the same concerns we had heard during middle school. A notable difference was that this teacher seemed to be contacting me to inform her teaching rather than judge my parenting. The relief in my voice was palpable.

Hollie began to struggle socially and academically in the spring of her freshman year. The unsettled schedule of a musical theater student did not fit her need for consistency and a quiet space each day to complete assignments and study for classes. Hollie's grades began to drop, and she became annoyed with some of the other students who could easily dance, sing, act, and excel in the classroom without seeming to work at any of it. Hollie asked to return to ballet, even with the rules, and then wanted to change her focus area from musical theater to dance. I considered the difference between the daily schedule of an actor and a dancer. The consistency of classes and rehearsals offered at her ballet school would better suit her temperament and anxiety level. Hollie easily convinced the dance department chair to allow her to enter as a sophomore, and we started a new schedule.

Sophomore year was a train wreck. Hollie was doing poorly in her honors trigonometry class and also did not understand the mathematics portions of her chemistry course. Her anxiety worsened and she began experiencing symptoms of panic and distress on days she had assignments due. We asked for a complete re-evaluation including psychological and educational testing to determine the cause of these issues. After months of testing, we learned that Hollie had two learning disabilities in mathematics (processing and computation), as well as chronic depression and acute anxiety. Her functional mathematics achievement levels were at the early fourth-grade level. After receiving the diagnosis of the learning disabilities in math, we met with Hollie at home to talk about it. I expected a dramatic scene that would require reassurance and consolation. Instead, her reaction was "Oh my God! This is awesome! I'm not stupid. I'm LD!" She immediately ran upstairs to post the diagnosis on Facebook. It was such a relief to her to know that her giftedness was not in danger. She was not floundering in math because she was not intelligent enough to understand; she had learning disabilities. We addressed the depression and anxiety through a new psychiatrist, new medication, and new rounds of 24-hour-a-day monitoring for side effects.

We found an excellent math tutor who managed to teach Hollie as she pirouetted and sang around the dining room table. John became a close family friend during the three years he guided Hollie through high school math, through the PSAT and SAT (tests for US college admittance), and into college. He was also willing to attend case study meetings and a tension-filled discussion we had with the school administrators and Princeton about accommodations during SAT testing. We were so very fortunate to find John; I now offer his name to anyone who needs a lifeline!

Hollie's junior year was filled with emotional pain. She was acutely aware that the year was very important for college applications and became paralyzed at times with fear and panic during the school day. We received a call one day from school stating that Hollie was underneath a table in the library sobbing. The school nurse called frequently to talk about Hollie or to let me know she was in the clinic again asking to come home for the day. We began allowing Hollie to take days off when she felt overwhelmed with school. She stopped taking dance classes, dropped out of the church band, refused to audition for musicals or other theater activities, and spent a lot of time sleeping and listening to music. Her voice teacher moved to Italy, and her sister was four states away in college.

In an attempt to reach Hollie, I began spending most afternoons watching television with her. We did not do homework or talk about school. We made snacks, snuggled on the couch with blankets, and watched television. I reminded myself of a statement I had made in a case study meeting when she was in the third grade: "I don't care if she ever graduates high school. I just want my child to be happy." I repeated that mantra many times during that difficult year.

Hollie's friends dropped by the wayside during junior year, and a former friend in her dance group orchestrated a "shun" just before the spring dance performances. I kept buying flowers, listening to her music, watching television, and making snacks. Her psychiatrist was helpful, and thankfully, her innate intelligence buoyed her through the coursework. My relationship with my child was the most important thing in the world to me, and as a result, we watched every single episode of the television show *House.*

By the end of the school year, Hollie had qualified to be a lifeguard and spent her summer saving three lives at our local pool. She decided she wanted to major in music in college; however, commercial/popular voice was her route. We began identifying schools and preparing applications.

Hollie was heartily accepted at a top university in the area of commercial music. We were elated and terrified at the same time.

Suggested Adaptations and Accommodations for Students Who Are Twice Exceptional

Some common themes permeate the literature regarding best practice for students who are twice exceptional (Baum & Owen, 2004; Silverman, 2013). Students who are highly capable and need assistance benefit from:

- Completing only the most difficult questions or examples
- Testing out of an area of study or unit
- Receiving extended time to complete assignments and projects
- Having preferential seating
- Receiving nonverbal cues to signal inappropriate behavior
- Having copies of visuals for study and use during class
- Using repeated self-talk during difficult and stressful tasks (academic and emotional)
- Highlighting areas of music and text
- Using organizational aids to assist with complicated information and large assignments
- Using mnemonics for memorization of notes, keys, circle of 5ths, musical terms, and historical performance practice
- Modeling (by teacher) and reviewing organizational skills and techniques
- Making to-do lists—prioritized and possibly color-coded according to musical subject or task
- Having additional copies of materials, instruments, and supplies
- Using a computer or notation software for lengthy written work
- Chunking concepts and skills into small parts

Students who are twice exceptional often understand an assignment but lack the necessary metacognitive skills to allow them to complete an assignment within the allotted time. Some examples are naming notes on a staff, playing key signature games, marking musical terms and definitions, playing several scales in a short period of time, and memorizing music. Frustration can occur rapidly and behavioral outbursts often follow. By understanding the characteristics of students who are twice exceptional and applying adaptations and accommodations in advance, these episodes can be lessened in duration and frequency.

Teacher Qualities That Foster Learner Success

Some common successful teacher qualities have been noted in research and the literature. They include:

- Teachers who design high-level projects with open-ended product expectations
- Teachers who include a multisensory approach to all objectives
- Teachers who demonstrate and advocate brainstorming opportunities
- Teachers who respect creative thinking
- Teachers who design safe classroom and rehearsal environments that encourage risk taking
- Teachers who recognize achievement before aptitude
- Teachers who reinforce success as effort=success)
- Teachers who provide opportunities to develop leadership skills
- Teachers who are flexible in response style expected from students
- Teachers who encourage all students to be aware of the gifts (academic, social, emotional) of every student
- Teachers who are active members of the team of professionals who work with students who are twice exceptional (including the parents/guardians)

Students can be difficult to diagnose and label. Creating differentiated assignments for music classrooms and ensembles can be exhausting. The process is sometimes made more difficult when students have intellectual and musical gifts and comorbid learning challenges. The task is to be the best teacher possible for every child in every class and ensemble.

Knowing your students and their needs can be far more important than the specific labels included in their paperwork, if they are even listed. The music teacher may be the first professional to notice the difference between aptitude and achievement, ability and performance, and motivation and executive function skills. When the profile is apparent to you, make the adaptations and accommodations you consider most appropriate for the student. If the student improves, you have made good choices. If the student does not improve, keep applying different strategies until the student begins to improve in musical and academic skills and understanding.

The reward of this process is to know you have done your very best. By providing your very best each day, you are increasing the possibility that you are creating an environment that will meet the needs of every student. In the end, we teach the students—music is our vehicle.

HOLLIE: COLLEGE

Hollie will start college next week. Letting go is never easy, and letting go when a child is twice exceptional can be complicated. Her school is 10 hours from home, and the commercial music students will be talented and focused. Hollie has prepared organizational tools, taken responsibility for finding a job on campus, delivered her college credit courses for transfer consideration, and emailed her voice teacher in advance. We will always be on speed dial, and I imagine there will be some frequent flier miles with my name on them. She is still the beautiful baby who looked meaningfully into my eyes to tell me this wasn't going to be easy, and her journey is partly also my journey. I hope her teachers know that she is loved, valued, and supported. I hope Hollie knows that we love her for who she is rather than the enumeration of her successes. If she can recognize her challenges and utilize her abilities, her life will be happy and whole. I hope those who read this derive a renewed sense of the individual personhood of each young person and the charge we have as educators to meet the needs of every student we teach.

The efficacy of our pedagogy depends on our ability to understand our individual students and to apply teaching and learning experiences that will lead to meaningful musical experiences for them. Our students require individual approaches that are based on research, best practice, and the uniqueness of each person. By continuing to purposefully learn about our students' strengths and challenges, we ensure that their musicianship, divergent thinking abilities, and sense of self will be increased throughout their musical lives.

NOTE

1. Hollie's and Hannah's names are used with permission.

REFERENCES

Baum, S. M., & Owen, S. V. (2004). *To be gifted & learning disabled: Strategies for helping bright students with LD, ADHD, and more.* Mansfield, CT: Creative Learning Press.

Benito, Y. (2003). Intellectual giftedness and associated disorders: Separation anxiety disorders or school phobia. *Gifted and Talented International, 18*(1), 27–35.

Binet, A. (1894). *Psychologie des grandes calculateurs (et de jouers d'echecs)* [Psychology of large computers (and players of chess)]. Paris, France: Hachette.

Bisland, A. (2004). Using learning-strategies instruction with students who are gifted and learning disabled. *Gifted Child Today, 7*(3), 52–58.

Dix, J., & Schafer, S. (2005). From paradox to performance: Practical strategies for identifying and teaching gifted/LD students. In S. K. Johnson & J. Kendrick (Eds.), *Teaching gifted students with disabilities* (pp. 153–159). Waco, TX: Prufrock Press.

Gallagher, J. J. (2000). Unthinkable thoughts: Education of gifted students. *Gifted Child Quarterly, 44,* 5–12.

Gordon, E. E. (2012). *Learning sequences in music: Skill, content, and patterns.* Chicago, IL: GIA Publications.

Hannah, C. L., & Shore, B. M. (1995). Metacognition and high intellectual ability: Insights from the study of learning-disabled gifted students. *Gifted Child Quarterly, 39,* 95–106.

Higgins, D., Baldwin, L., & Pereles, D. (2000). *Comparison of characteristics of gifted students with or without disabilities.* Unpublished manuscript.

Higgins, L. D., & Nielsen, M. E. (2000). Responding to the needs of twice-exceptional learners: A school district and university's collaborative approach. In K. Kay (Ed.), *Uniquely gifted: Identifying and meeting the needs of the twice-exceptional student* (pp. 287–303). Gilsum, NH: Avocus Publishing.

Hollingsworth, L. S. (1975). *Children above 180 IQ.* New York, NY: Arno Press.

Karnes, F. A., Shaunessy, E., & Bisland, A. (2004). Gifted students with disabilities: Are we finding them? *Gifted Child Today, 27*(4), 16–21.

Marland, S. P. (1971/1972). *Education of the gifted and talented: Report to the Congress of the United States by the U.S. Commissioner of Education, Volume 1.* Pursuant to Public Law 91–230, Section 806. Washington DC: US Government Printing Office.

Merrill, J. (2012). *If this is a gift, can I send it back? Surviving in the land of the gifted and twice exceptional.* Ashland, OR: GHF Press.

Renzulli, J. S. (1977). *The enrichment triad model: A guide for developing defensible programs for the gifted.* Mansfield, CT: Creative Learning.

Silverman, L. K. (1989). Invisible gifts, invisible handicaps. *Roeper Review, 12*(1), 37–42.

Silverman, L. K. (1993). *Counseling the gifted and talented.* Denver, CO: Love Publishing Company.

Silverman, L. K. (2013). *Giftedness 101.* New York, NY: Springer Publishing Company.

Terman, L. M., & Oden, M. H. (1947). *Genetic studies of genius: Vol. 4. The gifted child grows up.* Stanford, CA: Stanford University Press.

Tolan, S. (1999). Self-knowledge, self-esteem, and the gifted adult. *Advanced Development, 8,* 147–150.

Tomlinson, C. A. (1999). *The differentiated classroom. Responding to the needs of all learners.* Alexandria, VA: ASCD.

Van Tassel-Baska, J. (1998). *Excellence in educating gifted and talented learners.* Denver, CO: Love Publishing Company.

Walker, S. Y. (1991). *The survival guide for parents of gifted kids.* Minneapolis, MN: Free Spirit Publishing.

Webb, J. T., Meckstroth, E. A., & Tolan, S. S. (1994). *Guiding the gifted child.* Scottsdale, AZ: Gifted Psychology Press.

Weinfeld, R., Barnes-Robinson, L., Jeweler, S., & Roffman Shevitz, B. (2006). *Smart kids with learning difficulties: Overcoming obstacles and realizing potential.* Waco, TX: Prufrock Press.

Whitmore, J. F. (1980). *Giftedness, conflict and underachievement.* Boston, MA: Allyn and Bacon.

Winner, E. (1996). *Gifted children: Myths and realities.* New York, NY: Perseus Books Group.

CHAPTER 3

How the Orff Approach Can Support Inclusive Music Teaching

SHIRLEY SALMON

The Orff Approach to music learning and teaching can provide models of differentiated instruction and can support inclusive teaching in a multitude of ways. In this chapter, I will present thoughts on Orff-Schulwerk and inclusive pedagogy and play songs and illustrate some of the possibilities based on a particular song and examples from work with three children. I will include descriptions of how the Orff Approach enables one topic—here, "The Owl Song"—to be developed through many activities and on different levels, thereby realizing the aspects of inner differentiation and cooperation on a joint theme that are essential in inclusive teaching.

Children between the ages of 4 and 10 form a "train" that, with their teacher, enters the classroom at the Carl Orff Institute at Mozarteum University in Salzburg, Austria, for a weekly music and movement lesson. Each child is an individual with his or her own background, experiences, interests, needs, and potential. The constellation of the group changes each school year, with some children staying for just one year and others remaining for several years. In the last school year, there were eight children between the ages of 4 and 10. Katie, Simon, and Maria[1] are three children who take part in this lesson and who have been attending the class for different lengths of time.

Katie has been coming to the weekly sessions for four years and is now 10 years old. Katie is a joyful child with learning difficulties who has a small active vocabulary but a large passive vocabulary. She has an exceptional ability to look after and help younger children. Her progress in understanding, participating, and learning has improved continuously, as have her speech and singing. At the beginning, she was unable to stay within group activities for any length of time. Now she rarely leaves the circle or group activity, is keenly interested, and participates in nearly all activities. Movement or dancing in a circle is sometimes still a problem. In her first year, she rarely used her voice, but gradually she has been able to recognize a number of songs and to sing or say keywords, and now she can usually sing the whole song.

Simon is now 9 and first attended the group with his mother five years ago when it was a group for parents and their children. After two years, it was appropriate that the children attended the group alone. Simon, who has Down syndrome, needed one more year with his mother in the group before it was possible for him to attend alone with the other children and a few student teachers. Simon has a good feeling for pulse and rhythm, is interested in many instruments, and is especially keen on drumming; he also enjoys experimenting with a variety of materials such as scarves, feathers, or sticks in connection with music and movement. He speaks very little during the lessons and sometimes sings parts of songs. He is not particularly interested in learning a dance with the group but has great ability for his own spontaneous expressive movements to music.

Maria is 5 and has been in the group for one year. She has a twin brother who also attended; sometimes their mother or aunt attended with them. Maria has Williams-Beuren-Syndrome which her twin brother does not have. Because of her motor difficulties, Maria cannot walk far on her own. It is necessary for someone (a parent or a student of the institute) to hold her hand. Maria is exceptional in her quick learning and memory for songs, her singing on pitch, and her feeling for pulse and rhythm. Because she has limited mobility, she can walk with support but not yet run, skip, or jump. She cannot yet move freely in the room using her whole body, but she enjoys activities with movement and finds ways of joining in.

The challenge of teaching this group is to support diverse interests, experiences, and abilities and to choose appropriate contents and methods so that each child can not only understand the tasks, take part, and learn at his or her own level but also be emotionally involved, use his or her imagination and creativity, enjoy the activities, and increase self-confidence. The planning of the sessions and the specific activities must meet the needs, interests, and levels of all the children.

In the last decades, Europeans have seen significant steps in the rights of people with disabilities to education and participation in and access to all areas of social and cultural life (see endnotes for further information). These include the following:

1. The UNESCO Salamanca Statement and Framework for Action on Special Needs Education Statement was adopted by the World Conference on Special Needs Education: Access and Quality in 1994.[2]

2. The International Classification of Functioning, Disability and Health (of the World Health Organization) in 2005 put the notions of "health" and "disability" in a new light.[3]

3. The UN Convention on the Rights of Persons with Disabilities, an international human rights instrument of the United Nations intended to protect the rights and dignity of persons with disabilities, came into force in Austria in 2008.[4]

4. In Austria, the Federal Ministry of Labour, Social Affairs and Consumer Protection developed the National Action Plan on Disability 2012–2020 (NAP), which views inclusion as a human right and mandate.[5]

THE CARL ORFF INSTITUTE

The children's group that Katie, Simon, and Maria take part in is held once a week. I serve as the teacher, and it is one of the many practice teaching groups available for students studying at the institute taught by faculty members. In 1961, Carl Orff established the Orff Institute as a center for elemental education in music and dance at the Mozarteum University in Salzburg, Austria. The Orff Institute (http://www.orffinstitut.at) is devoted to the training of teachers for Elemental Music and Dance/Movement Education in schools and as freelance teachers on all educational levels and with all age groups. It offers bachelor and master study programs in Elemental Music and Dance Pedagogy, as well as further development courses, international summer courses, and symposia. The main characteristics of its study programs are:

- Integration of music and dance within artistic areas and pedagogical transmission
- Combining experiential "hands on"-oriented teaching with theoretical support in reflection and analysis
- Practical orientation by observing and participating in groups that have been set up at the Orff Institute for people of different age groups and of differing abilities, as well as working together in social and special pedagogical establishments and general training schools
- Individual arrangement of studies with diverse optional choices and possibilities for concentrated studies in one area

During the full term of their studies, all students at the Orff Institute first observe and later plan, teach, and reflect in various practice teaching groups. Most of the classes are taught in the institute, but some are held in other institutions in Salzburg. The practice teaching classes enable students of the institute to work during the course of studies as closely as possible with a variety of age groups and abilities; it also enables children, teens, adults, and seniors from the Salzburg area to participate in qualified Elemental Music and Dance classes.

THE ORFF APPROACH

Elemental Music and Movement Education was conceived by Carl Orff and Gunild Keetmann and is also referred to as Orff-Schulwerk. (These are not to be confused with the printed volumes *Music for Children* by Orff/Keetmann that were written as models for teachers at that time, 1950–1954.) The word *Schulwerk* does not refer to "school" (German: *Schule*) but to "learning" (*Schulwerk*) and was originally conceived for work with children (C. Orff, 1978). Its significance and implementation in areas such as pre-school, special and inclusive education, therapy, and community work and with the elderly was recognized early on. From the 1960s, the use of Orff-Schulwerk in these areas was developed and documented by colleagues who took the fundamental ideas of Orff-Schulwerk and adapted them for their particular target groups. These developments were and are still a logical progression because of the humanistic orientation and because the idea of working with people of all ages and abilities is inherent in Orff's and Keetman's concept. Wilhelm Keller, the pioneer of music and movement in inclusive education and community work in German-speaking countries, recognized that for Orff, the development of the whole person was central and referred to this as "musica humana" (Salmon, 2012).

Gertrud Orff (1914–2000) was involved in developing Orff-Schulwerk during the time she was married to Carl Orff and worked as a music teacher with children with and without disabilities in Germany and later in the United States. In 1970, she developed Orff Music Therapy at the Children's Centre in Munich, Germany, an active multisensory therapy based on the elements of Orff-Schulwerk (using many senses, creative and spontaneous music making, play, and specific instruments). Gertrud Orff established a training course in Orff Music Therapy in Munich, and her work is documented in two books (G. Orff, 1980, 1989) and numerous articles by both her and her students.[6]

A Humanistic Approach

In Orff-Schulwerk, each individual—whether an infant, a young child, an adolescent, or an adult, and with his or her own development, background, culture, interests, abilities, and needs—is to be the center of our attention.

The human being is the touchstone of Orff-Schulwerk pedagogy, which contributes to experiencing and furthering our humanity and being human through the bringing forth of original music and dance contributions (cf. Widmer, 2011). The humanistic orientation recognizes the creative potential that each human being has and considers it one of the tasks of the teacher to foster this potential. Or, as Ulrike Jungmair writes: "The central focus of teaching is first to sense individual potential, to put this into action, to realize it. The whole person is the focus of our attention" (2008, p. 13).

From a humanistic point of view, Elemental Music and Dance Education is an anthropocentric approach in that the human being with his or her human attributes and individual characteristics is the starting point—not musical works, dance choreographies, or music and dance as subjects to be learned. The person is the center of the music making and dancing and is the reference point for the goals, contents, methods, and media including, for example, the use of special instruments or musical scales (cf. Cubasch, 1999). It is a concept of active and creative music practice for everybody— "the realization of an original, central musical potency anchored in each individual" (Keller, 1984, p. 801, transl. S. Salmon). It exists independently from any determined age or special talents or disabilities. It is, rather, the musical interactivity of persons with their individual capabilities. As each player of the ensemble receives an individual suitable role or assignment, he or she can take part as a full-fledged member of the group. It enables people of all abilities to play together in one group without any participant being under- or overchallenged. Tasks and roles can be adapted to suit the capabilities of the individuals, instead of the group having to adapt to a fixed form (Keller, 1996). Carl Orff stressed the importance of developing the whole personality.

The imagination must be stimulated at primary school age, and opportunities for emotional development, which contains experiences of the ability to feel and the power to control the expression of that feeling, must also be provided. Everything that a child of this age experiences, everything in him or her that has been awakened and nurtured, is a determining factor for the whole of his or her life. Much can be destroyed at this age that can never be regained (C. Orff, 1964/2011, cited in Haselbach, 2011, p. 154).

Schumacher (1999) notes that our feeling for self and the opportunities for being creative are, in today's world, more relevant than ever. The influence of too many technical media for too much of the time and the need for perfection of recordings can mean that students are shy when producing and expressing themselves through music and movement. Overstimulation from the (technical) environment may also produce difficulties in stimulus processing and the ability to select or dampen self-activity. It is important that at least one other person in the learning environment shows appropriate joy and recognition when students are active and productive; otherwise, self-activity may be lost or forgotten. Orff-Schulwerk emphasizes the value of self-activity and the necessary motivation and space for playing (Salmon, 2012).

Principles of Orff-Schulwerk

Orff-Schulwerk can be described as an open system in relation to working with the printed models, in relation to the target group and new sound sources, and in relation to music and dance, interdisciplinarity, and contemporary music and art (Haselbach, 2013).

Orff-Schulwerk has a number of principles that play an important role in its music educational concept (Haselbach, 2011, Haselbach & Hartmann, 2013; Jungmair, 1992; Keller, 1974, 1996; Widmer, 2011), including the following:

- The child is at the center: Orff-Schulwerk is not primarily about specialist music or dance training, but about the enrichment of the whole person through experience and expression with music and dance.
- The social dimension: The processes of learning, working, and creating are primarily experienced in the group and demand and develop appropriate behavior and attitudes.
- Music as an integral concept: In ancient Greek, *Musiké* means singing, dancing, playing instruments, and language but also includes the integrating proximity to other artistic forms. Orff saw this as the basis of the Schulwerk.
- The instruments: By providing instruments that can be experienced playfully, that do not have technical obstacles, and that are body aligned (do not position the players too far away from the instrument or from each other), the possibility of playing at many different levels is possible. These instruments are suitable for solo and group work—not only for interpreting pieces but also for experimentation, improvisation, and composition. Carl Orff encouraged the constant search for new sound possibilities and suitable material for elemental, physically related music making.
- The form of teaching as a *process:* The students are creatively involved in the work process and thereby also determine the direction and the result. In Orff-Schulwerk, the work process and the artistic results have the same importance.
- Creativity in improvisation and composition (including dance composition): The teaching creates opportunities for students to experience themselves as creators and co-creators.

• Adaptability of Orff-Schulwerk: Orff-Schulwerk sees itself as an "open pedagogy" that is applicable in its principles in all educational fields of work and can also be assimilated in different cultures.

INCLUSIVE PEDAGOGY

Excellent pedagogy is by nature inclusive. Fundamental, child-centered inclusive education involves teaching children and adolescents who are at different developmental levels and have different degrees of competencies in perception, cognition, and behavior. It recognizes the individuality of each person (in the sense of his or her unique past experiences) and thus the heterogeneity of every human group (Feuser, 1997, 2001).

Teaching the group in which Katie, Simon, and Maria take part involves, as with teaching any other group, being aware of factors such as individual learning styles and modes, speed of learning, level of learning, and motivation and concentration (IQSH, 2011). Teaching should be concerned with identifying the achievements of each child and, from there, identifying the next steps in learning for each individual child. It should include all learners in the group and appropriate strategies to support learning and teaching (Feuser, 1997; Goodkin, 2012). The aim should be to activate each child's abilities in every learning process in the best possible way. By extending and enhancing the learning environment—and the other students with their diverse competences contribute to this—a positive development is more likely to be achieved than with teaching methods that aim to speed up the learning process based on the deficits diagnosed (Athey, 1990, p. 76).

The building up of *self-confidence and self-awareness* can also be supported in group work and is an important requisite for learning and living. Self-confidence can be seen as "a necessary but still not adequate precondition for the maintenance and revival of the joy of discovery and desire to create and thereby for the search for creative and innovative solutions" (Hüther, 2008). Katie has been able to build up her confidence by being given specific musical tasks that she can accomplish—for example, playing a drone accompaniment or singing the song with the teacher or peer. She has also learned to be more aware of her body by joining in activities that call for free improvised movements, moving with a partner, and joining in simple dance forms. Simon has become more aware of the musical form and his role in a piece. This works especially well when Simon improvises an interlude between verses of a song. His awareness and confidence have been supported by the use of materials such as scarves or paintbrushes within movement activities. These give him support and motivate him to develop new and imaginative movements. Maria has gradually gained more confidence in movement activities. She works with a student teacher who gives her support by holding one hand but allowing Maria to join in as many of the activities as she can in her own way. Maria's confidence in playing instruments has increased with practice in eye-hand coordination—playing a frame drum with one hand or holding a mallet to play one or two resonator bars.

It has been necessary in this children's group to build up *security and trust* as well as *self-awareness and self-confidence*. Neurobiologist Gerald Hüther (2008) emphasizes the importance of security and trust, explaining that children and adults try to connect every new perception and every new experience to something that is familiar. The readiness to try out something new depends on how *secure* one is and how much *confidence* one has to confront the world. Hüther stresses that every kind of insecurity, fear, and pressure produces a spreading excitation and agitation in the brain. It is under these conditions that the incoming perceptual patterns cannot be collated with the memories already stored there from the sense channels. The result is that nothing new can be learned and lodged in the brain. Brain research has shown that trust is the only antidote to insecurity and fear. Those who want to be creative need to trust in themselves and in their own capabilities, knowledge, and skills (cf. Hüther, 2008).

As the teacher for Katie, Simon, and Maria, I have had to first find activities and methods with which they feel secure and in which their contribution is valued so that they then trust themselves to try something new. The repetition of activities, finding extensions and variations, is very important, as is the teacher's ability to notice children's spontaneous, unplanned responses (with the voice, an instrument, or movement) and to include these within the form. Research supports the observations and experiences we make as teachers when we see how much trust, repetition, and support individual students need to join in, try out and learn new things, play and dance together, or invent their own ostinatos, drones, melodies, accompaniments, or movement sequences (Salmon, 2012).

In this group, *social learning* can be seen in two ways: first, learning to become more social, where the content of our teaching and learning is social development, and second, learning socially, that is, learning a subject, song, dance, or rhyme with the help of others. The range of abilities in a group can be seen not as something difficult but as an important means of motivation, stimulation, and support for each individual.

One of the most important contributions of Orff-Schulwerk can be seen in the social learning made possible by working in different social constellations. Here, encounters on different levels and of many kinds can be made possible. With skilled teaching, *social resonance* and *social sensibility* can be encouraged and supported in all participants whatever their skills or needs.

Different social constellations form an important part in Orff-Schulwerk teaching. Singing, playing, dancing, and reciting with the whole group are complemented by working alone, with a partner, or in small groups and are usually a natural part of every class or session. Group work—whether this be practicing given parts or creating one's own—includes everyone in the small group and guards against isolation, separation, and exclusion while fostering togetherness. The wider the range of abilities in the group is, which of course calls for differentiated teaching, the more possibilities there may be for social learning.

Vygotsky's (1978) *zone of proximal development* (ZPD) is particularly relevant in groups of mixed ability. The ZPD is "the distance between the actual developmental level, as determined by independent problem solving, and the level of potential development as determined through problem solving under adult guidance, or in collaboration with more capable peers" (p. 86). The *zone of actual development* refers to tasks that the learner can do on his or her own. The zone of proximal development refers to functions and abilities that have not yet matured. These tasks may be strenuous or challenging but can be achieved—first with help and then independently (IQSH, 2011).

When learners of different abilities are in a group together, the proximity of others who are at a slightly higher level of development creates possibilities for imitation, support, and cooperation. This enables learners to successfully complete tasks and gain confidence while furthering intrinsic motivation. Elemental Music and Dance Education can give children and adults experiences within their zones of proximal development, thereby encouraging their individual learning.

Inclusive teaching is not a matter of analyzing every disability as a disability. It is primarily a question of using the *appropriate didactics* and is not a question of any particular child's abilities or challenges (Feuser, 2008). According to Feuser's *principles of inclusive education,* lessons should include all students in a class or group while taking into account their individual abilities, interests, and needs. From a pedagogical point of view, this means that all participants (including those who have a disability or complex learning difficulties) play, learn, and work together at their respective developmental levels (taking into consideration their present levels of competence in perception, cognition, and behavior), in cooperation with one another on a theme, activity, or task within a shared curriculum (project/ subject matter/topic; Feuser, 2001, p. 27).

In the realization of inclusive teaching, the two factors *individualization* and *cooperation on a joint topic* are essential. Elemental Music and Dance Education as offered in this children's group provides teaching that is centered on each individual child. A wealth of activities can be offered that enable all students to encounter and work on a joint topic. Nobody is excluded, and the subject, task, or theme is made available to all students at their own developmental level. Differentiated tasks appropriate for each child are planned that are part of the cooperation within one theme and include working in different social constellations. *Inner differentiation* (Feuser, 1997) is made possible when the teacher enables each student to experience and understand the topic on his or her own level and where individual tasks can be set that play a part within the *common topic, theme, or project.*

PLAY SONGS

Play songs offer preschool- and primary school–aged children many possibilities and can be particularly useful in inclusive groups. In a multisensory approach such as in Orff-Schulwerk, play songs can motivate, encourage, and inspire a variety of activities that involve music, movement, language, play materials, and objects. Several objectives can be the aim within these activities to focus on different needs, interests, and abilities. Playing, moving, speaking, singing, and creating can be experienced in a variety of ways. This multisensory approach offers a broad spectrum of experience and expression that supports the children's general development (Salmon, 2008).

In the play song, the music, movement, and certain elements of drama are combined and integrated. Music, movement, language, and play(ing) are closely related and mutually supportive. Play songs have been sung and played by children for centuries and have a long tradition in musical education. Carl Orff considered the traditional repertoire of children's songs as the basis for Orff-Schulwerk and also emphasized the importance of *play:* "The drive to play initiates the satisfying activity, and following from this the practice, and out of these the achievement" (C. Orff, 1932/2011, p. 74). Orff stressed that it is important that the child be allowed to play "undisturbed, expressing the internal externally. Word and sound must arise simultaneously from improvisatory, rhythmic play" (p. 68). Playing and experimenting are important parts of the creative process and should be part of every lesson.

Play songs are especially valuable and can link to and sometimes support and develop earlier games played with a parent. Schumacher (2003) notes:

> All early mother-child games are elemental music, movement and language games that connect to prenatal experiences. They represent a multi-sensory option, which has an effect on the child through the mother's emotional participation. The lullaby, the cradle- and rocking song, the clapping game and knee rides all offer sensory-emotional

stimulation. They support the child's emotional and cognitive abilities that are a basic necessity for establishing a relationship to the environment. The senses of balance, touch, of hearing and seeing (but surely also the olfactory sense) are simultaneously stimulated and in play lead to the establishment of contact and the development of a relationship between mother and child. (p. 14)

The use of play songs in both family and educational contexts supports the child's emotional and cognitive abilities.

Songs that inspire movement, dance, role-play, playing with language, use of emotional expression, and imagination can be an important part of the curriculum. The teacher may consider a variety of focal elements contained in the individual play song that may be effective alone but may be especially useful when combined, especially in groups of mixed ability.

In addition, the focus on one or more elements can be useful when planning single lessons, as well as when working on more long-term, interdisciplinary projects. The song and its various aspects can be stimulating and motivating, with possible extensions for each element (Figure 3.1). The final choice of activities corresponds with the content of the song and with the current abilities and needs of the children and the group (Salmon, 2008).

Play songs can be the starting point for activities that will focus on the needs and levels of each individual child and can inspire teachers to extend the specific theme in many directions (Salmon, 2007).

Sensory awareness may involve activities concentrating on sight, touch, vibration, taste, smell, kinesthetic experience, and balance.

Movement could include playful warmups; movement experiments; Rudolf von Laban's basic body activities: locomotion, rotation, elevation,

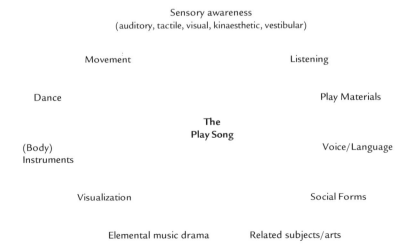

Figure 3.1. Focal points of play songs.

gesture, position; (Preston-Dunlop, 1990); movement sequences, forma-
tions, and paths; parameters such as tempo, dynamics, form, and space; and
accompaniment.

Dance may use preparatory exercises, traditional dance forms, popular
dance forms, narrative dance, improvisation, and composition.

Voice and language can focus on breathing, posture, physical exercises,
sounds, syllables, words, phrases, chants, rhymes, poems, and storybooks.

Play materials such as natural objects, toys, scarves, balls, spinning tops,
household objects, sounding objects, and instruments can be useful.

Instruments may include body instruments, voice, sounding objects,
found and elemental instruments, Orff instruments, homemade instruments, and classical instruments.

Listening could focus on sounds, noises, sounds of nature, live sounds,
recorded sounds, sounds of voices, instruments, songs related to the topic,
pieces of music related to the topic, poems or stories, and different styles of
music related to the theme.

Visualizing could involve using movement with one's own body or with a
partner—drawing, painting, using signs or symbols, forms of graphic notation, and traditional notation.

Social forms are particularly relevant in groups of mixed ability. They may
include relationship play, playing individually, working next to or with a
partner, working in a small group, working with the whole class, leading,
following, communicating, and cooperating.

Elemental music drama incorporates music, movement, and language, as
well as reciting, pantomime, acting out the song, making props and cos-
tumes, and using poems, pictures, and storybooks.

Providing time and space for playing, experimenting, and creating is
important in Elemental Music and Dance Education, especially when working with play songs. A certain amount of freedom is necessary so that children can (re)discover and develop their delight and passion for spontaneous
play. It is not enough to offer a secure place. The room, the space, and the
lesson must all have a playful atmosphere and must be familiar and inviting.
Providing space for play does not mean giving total freedom—accepting
the general setup and the rules is important (Jungmair, 1992). The feeling
for time is very individual, especially in groups of mixed ability. Children
need time to develop their activity and be completely absorbed in it, time
to experiment (alone, with a partner, or in a small group), and time to have
flow experiences (Csikszentmihalyi, 1990).

Play songs provide a particularly well-suited basis for diverse activities
involving music and movement in groups of mixed ability focusing on
different objectives. This work can be interdisciplinary in its concept and
inclusive in its realization provided the topics in question are prepared with
the appropriate level of differentiation.

"The Owl Song"

Gerda Bächli (1922–2013) was a Swiss music teacher and composer of songs for children of all ages and abilities. The image of "The Owl Song" (Figure 3.2) is that every night when it was dark and everyone was asleep, an owl flew through the town with its enormous wings. When he touched a church tower, the bells started to play (Bächli, 1977). For the activities during the song, the children stand around the room. In the middle there is a glockenspiel with two mallets. One child accompanies the song on a low xylophone or two chime bars. Another child plays the time of day and speaks quietly: "1, 2, 3" (practice in counting). During the counting, the children close their eyes and the owl flies through the room. It touches one child, who opens her eyes and goes quietly to the glockenspiel in the middle. She is allowed to improvise freely while the others listen with their eyes closed. The child who played becomes the new owl.

Bächli (1977) described the goals for the play song: the secret nighttime atmosphere attracts and calms many children and encourages them to listen to the child who is improvising. Because of the stillness while waiting for the owl with their eyes closed, the children are often more receptive than usual.

Planning Activities

Planning activities for my group would include a series of lessons looking at many aspects. "The Owl Song" was a good starting point for these children and involved considering the following:

- The musical material (melody, rhythm, harmony, form, key)
- The words
- Nonmusical themes and contents (the story, drama, setting, atmosphere, pictures, materials)

The Owl Song

Music: G. Bächli   Text: S. Salmon

Figure 3.2. "The Owl Song" (music: Gerda Bächli; English text: Shirley Salmon).

- The types of intelligence (linguistic, logical-mathematical, spatial, musical, bodily-kinesthetic, interpersonal, intrapersonal, naturalist) that may be involved
- Different media (movement, dance, voice, instruments, visual arts)
- Different types of participation: perceiving, exploring, experimenting, playing, recognizing, remembering, imitating, varying, depicting, differentiating, inventing, deciding, practicing, communicating, creating
- Social aspects and possibilities for cooperation and interaction
- The experience and levels of the children and individual objectives

The concept of *didactic reduction* (Jungmair, 2013) enables the teacher to concentrate on the elements of a song, which is useful in planning. Didactic reduction may not only lead us to creative and lively teaching but also show us a way to discover hidden movement in a score. Didactic reduction distinguishes between quantitative and qualitative reduction. Quantitative reduction, meaning to make less, to decrease, or to diminish, is also used in a sense to simplify. For Katie or Simon, this means simplifying rhythmical accompaniments; for Maria, it means simplifying the melody, playing at first just the first four bars. Qualitative reduction goes back to the original meaning of the word *reduce* (Latin: *re-ducere*), meaning "to lead back," in that every product is a result of a process and can be pursued to a suspected beginning (Jungmair, 2013). The idea of a bell and game (in Gertrud Orff 1980) and "The Owl Song" with a different activity (Bächli 1977) inspired me to develop the ideas further for my particular group of children.

Divergent thinking (Siegenthaler & Zihlmann, 1988) is especially important in groups where the abilities are very different. One task may be set for the whole group and there may be many different possible solutions. The teacher does not tell the children which solution to find, although they may need help in understanding the task. Each child finds his or her solution with the capabilities he or she has at his or her disposal at that time. The different solutions are not compared against each other and each contribution is considered of value.

For Wilhelm Keller (1996), *upgrading "minor roles"* is important in groups of mixed ability: a simple action or task is given a pivotal part; for example, Simon, who often cannot accompany in time, can master playing three strokes on a gong to introduce the piece or song. Other children, who cannot play or accompany rhythmically but can create the effect of wind blowing through the trees on their instruments, are given the task of improvising parts of a rondo while other students sing and play different accompaniments. In improvising, students produce that which is momentarily possible at their moment of individual development. While some students may be able to invent, remember, and notate a melody using a five-note scale, others may spontaneously play their melody on the given notes, while still others accompany perhaps by playing a drone (Salmon, 2007, 2008).

ACTIVITIES

The following examples of activities are a collection for Katie, Simon, and Maria's group and could be thought of as a mind map for these and other students. They are listed according to their central focus; the list is not hierarchical and should best be thought of as a circle (Figure 3.1). Work on this song and its extensions extended over many lessons, with activities being chosen from this pool of ideas according to specific objectives for each child without aiming to include all the activities. With many of these activities, the song needs to be sung more than once. If the melody is too high for some of the children, it could also be sung well in E minor. In some activities other music would be used, and some activities are without music.

In practice, activities usually combine one or more of these focal points, placing an emphasis on one or more intelligences. Within one activity—for example, working with the voice—individual tasks on different levels can be set. Katie and Maria can sing the whole song and Maria can make suggestions for new verses using different animals. Simon does not often sing in class but sings the songs to his mother at home. He enjoys using his voice to make sounds and can be encouraged to be part of an introduction or intermezzo using voices to imitate the call of the owl, the sounds in the woods at night, and so forth. He enjoys playing instruments but cannot yet imitate or remember ostinatos. He can play certain effects (the wind or the sound of the owl's wings) that can be used as an introduction or intermezzo.

Another child who has already learned an instrument was given a task on her level: playing the melody or improvising to it, or playing or inventing a second part. Other children may play different accompaniments on small percussion or barred instruments.

There are many ways of introducing songs: with something hidden, with a game, with an unusual instrument, with movement, with a story, by listening with closed eyes, with gestures, with lyrics, with the melody, with the harmony, with a strange sound, or by humming any many more. Here, we started with an owl hand puppet, who greeted all the children musically, allowed itself to be stroked, and showed the children various movements and other ideas. The pool of activities included the following:

Sensory Awareness
- Close your eyes and listen to the owl's sounds (played by the teacher moving around the room) and point to the owl.
- Listen to other sounds of the woods at night (rustling, wind, animals moving).
- Show the flight of the owl with a colored scarf (one child); follow the movement with your eyes and then your fingers (the other children).
- Paint the flight of the owl on the floor with your fingers or hand.

- Paint the flight of the owl on your partner's back.
- Use your arms to fly with the melody. Fly on the spot with your eyes closed.
- Imagine you are a tree (sitting, kneeling, or standing). Sway gently with the wind while keeping your balance.
- Show the flight of the melody with one hand or both hands.

Movement
- Fly away from your nest while the melody is being played or sung (with one repeat) and return at the end.
- Use the movements of different types of birds using your hands and arms to this melody or to different music.
- Use different routes when flying: straight line, curve, circle, spiral, tri- angle, zigzag.
- Try to fly a route that takes a lot of space or a little space.
- Fly behind your partner following the same route. Change roles and fly a new route.
- Space many objects to represent trees in the room. Fly around the room to the music without bumping into any trees.

Dance
- Learn different steps going forward, sideways, and backward. Experiment with fitting them to the melody.
- Learn different ways of holding hands and doing steps with a partner or in a small group.
- Experiment with the steps that different birds might make.
- Invent a dance just with your arms and hands.
- Invent and learn a simple group dance to the melody.
- Learn a folk dance related to the theme of birds, nighttime, and forests.

Voice and Language
- Experiment with sounds the owl might make. Listen and try other chil- dren's sounds.
- Make a pattern by combining two sounds. Teach your pattern to a partner.
- Sing the melody using different syllables.
- Use words about sounds in the woods. For example: "In the woods are many sounds. And the owl flies round and round. Come to me, let me play when it's (4) o'clock."
- Choose a different animal and think of ways of changing the words. Invent your own text.

- Learn and work with a poem about owls, for example:
  - "The Owl and the Pussycat" (Edward Lear)
  - English nursery rhyme: "A wise old owl lived in an oak. The more he saw the less he spoke. The less he spoke the more he heard. Why can't we all be like that wise old bird?"

Instruments

- Use instruments to create different effects (the wind, nighttime, bells, the flight of the owl).
- Choose an instrument to represent the church bell (triangle, cymbal, bell). Experiment with playing different times (8 o'clock, 5 o'clock, etc.).
- Get to know and play various simple wind instruments (top of the recorder, slide whistle, ocarina).
- Accompany the song with A minor drone (A–E) on barred instruments (see Fig 3.3.)
- Accompany with the moving drone A minor, G major (A–E, G–D).
- Learn or invent rhythmic ostinatos using words from song, for example:
  - Church bells sound ●●● –
  - Round the houses ●●●●
  - Owls fly ●– ● –
- Learn the first two bars of the melody on a barred instrument.
- Play two bar phrases from the melody as melodic ostinatos.
- Learn and play ostinatos as accompaniments (see Fig. 3.3.)
- Accompany on the guitar, alternating A minor with G major and/or E7.

Listening

- Close your eyes and listen to where the owl is in the room (teacher or child plays a slide whistle or the head piece of a recorder). Point in the direction of the owl.
- Listen to where the church bell is with your eyes closed. Can you count the chimes?
- Try to follow the pitches of the melody with your hand. Show when the owl is flying high or low.

Figure 3.3. Examples of ostinatos.

- With your partner, choose one instrument (small percussion or resonator bell). One of you close your eyes and listen to where the partner is playing. When the sounds stop, point to your partner. Try this many times and then swap roles.
- There are instruments (small percussion or resonator bells and mallets) far apart all over the room which represent the houses in the town. Fly with a few friends to the instruments, trying them all out. When everyone has had a turn, choose one instrument (as the "house") and sit or stand beside it. One of you is the owl and flies to the houses. When the owl is very close to a house, the house "sounds."
- One of you leads a partner, whose eyes are closed, through the town. When you are near a house, it "sounds."
- Listen to pieces of music (or parts of them) related to the topics of birds, night, or bells, for example, "Blackbird" (The Beatles), "The Firebird" (Stravinsky), "Dies Irae from Symphonie Fantastique" (Berlioz), "La cathédrale engloutie" (Debussy), and "Night on Bare Mountain" (Mussorgsky).

Visualization
- Show the flight of the owl with one hand, painting in the air.
- Paint the journey on a large piece of paper with a brush (without color).
- Paint using chalk, crayons, or pens. Swap papers with someone and see if you can follow his or her flight.
- Listen to different church chimes and find a way to notate them.
- Notate your own number of chimes to be played by you or others in your own way.
- Look at different ways of notating the melody.
- Look at a picture of a scene with an owl. How could this be played?

Social Forms
- Take over different roles for the music and/or movement: the owl, the clock bell, the "night music."
- Lead your partner (whose eyes are closed) holding hands.
- Lead your partner (whose eyes are closed) playing an instrument to guide him or her, making sure he or she does not bump into anything.
- Improvise spontaneously with the other children playing the "night music."
- With a partner or in a small group, choose instruments and decide and practice your own "night music" or "flying music."

Elemental Music Drama
- Create a story around the song.
- Using the elements of reciting, speaking, singing, moving, and dancing, create a piece on the story.

- Choose a children's book and create an elemental music drama piece:
  Owl Babies (Waddell & Benson, 1992)
  The Littlest Owl (Pitcher & MacNaughton, 2008)
  The Owl Who Was Afraid of the Dark (Tomlinson & Howard, 2004)

CONCLUDING THOUGHTS

While important for all teaching, including everyone in any group is essential to foster participation and for children to be able to learn at their own levels. The Orff Approach focuses on the individual and provides options for differentiated instruction while working on a common topic, and in this way it supports inclusive teaching of all age groups and abilities. It is an exciting, open, and flexible way to guide learning that calls for the teacher's own imagination, flexibility, and creative abilities. It means that we, as teachers, work in a wide scope of media, understand each child's learning style, simplify or extend parts, compose and choreograph on many levels, allow children to create at their own level of skill and understanding, recognize the dignity of each contribution, create opportunities for talent, and create challenges for discovery (Goodkin, 2012). Teaching Katie, Simon, and Maria means providing possibilities for them and us to discover their talents, develop their individual ideas and solutions, practice their parts, encourage their individual expression and creativity, and provide ways for them to develop socially and, especially, for them to experience the joy of being totally involved in music and dance.

NOTES

1. Pseudonyms were used for children's names.
2. The UNESCO Salamanca Statement and Framework for Action on Special Needs Education Statement (adopted in 1994 by the World Conference on Special Needs Education: Access and Quality) states that every child has a basic right to education and every child has unique characteristics, interests, abilities, and learning needs (http://www.unesco.org/education/pdf/SALAMA_E.PDF).
3. The International Classification of Functioning, Disability and Health (ICF; of the World Health Organization, 2005) put the notions of "health" and "disability" in a new light. It acknowledges that every human being can experience a decrement in health and thereby experience some degree of disability (http://www.who.int/classifications/icf/en/). Disability is not something that only happens to a minority of humanity. The ICF "mainstreams" the experience of disability and recognizes it as a universal human experience. Furthermore, the ICF takes into account the social aspects of disability and does not see disability only as a medical or biological dysfunction. It also recognizes the impact of the environment on the person's functioning.
4. The UN Convention on the Rights of Persons with Disabilities (http://www.un.org/disabilities/convention/conventionfull.shtml) is an international human rights instrument

of the United Nations intended to protect the rights and dignity of persons with disabilities and came into force in Austria in 2008. Its purpose is to promote, protect, and
ensure the full and equal enjoyment of all human rights and fundamental freedoms by
all persons with disabilities and to promote respect for their inherent dignity. It states,
"all human rights are universal, indivisible, interdependent and interrelated." It emphasizes the right to participation in political and public life (Article 29) and cultural life,
recreation, and sport (Article 30) and the right to inclusive education at all levels, regardless of age, without discrimination, and on the basis of equal opportunity. It intends to
enable persons with disabilities to have the opportunity to develop and utilize their creative, artistic, and intellectual potential, not only for their own benefit, but also for the
enrichment of society.

5. In Austria, the Federal Ministry of Labour, Social Affairs and Consumer Protection developed the National Action Plan on Disability 2012–2020 (NAP), which views inclusion
as a human right and mandate (http://www.bmask.gv.at/cms/site/attachments/7/4/9/
CH2092/CMS1359980335644/nap_behinderung-web_2013-01-30_eng.pdf).

It is a strategy of the Austrian federal government for the implementation of the UN
Disability Rights Convention and to also support the objectives and contents of the EU
Disability Strategy 2010–2020. The National Action Plan describes the current situation in each special field, formulates policy objectives, and contains 250 measures with
corresponding timelines and responsibilities. In line with disability mainstreaming,
the measures have to be applied by the individual federal ministries according to their
responsibilities, because the rights of people with disabilities are human rights, and they
cover all areas of life. Its key principles include inclusion and participation, accessibility,
disability mainstreaming, equal opportunities and equal treatment, financial security,
self-determination, self-advocacy, involvement, and awareness raising.

6. See http://www.orff-musiktherapie-gesellschaft.de/

REFERENCES

Athey, C. (1990). *Extending thought in young children: A parent-teacher partnership.* London: Paul
Chapmann Publishing.
Bächli, G. (1977). *Der Tausendfüßler. 2 x 11 Lieder für Vorschulkinder, Heimkinder, behinderte
Kinder.* [The Millipede. 2 x 11 songs for pre-school children, children in care and dis-
abled children]. Zürich, Switzerland: Musik Hug Verlage.
Csikszentmihalyi, M. (1990). *Flow: The psychology of optimal experience.* New York, NY:
Harper & Row.
Cubasch, P. (1999). Elementares Musizieren oder leibhaftige Bildung mit Musik und Bewegung.
[Elemental music-making and the human being]. *Orff-Schulwerk-Informationen, 62,*
19–24. Retrieved from http://bidok.uibk.ac.at/library/cubasch-musizieren.html
Feuser, G. (1997). *Thesis: Inclusive education: Education of all children and young people together
in preschool establishments and schools.* Retrieved from http://bidok.uibk.ac.at/library/
feuser-thesis-e.html
Feuser, G. (2001). Prinzipien einer inklusiven Pädagogik. [Principles of Inclusive Education.]
In: *Behinderte in Familie, Schule und Gesellschaft* [Disabled people in the family, in school and in society]. Retrieved from http://bidok.uibk.ac.at/library/
beh2-01-feuser-prinzipien.html
Feuser, G. (2008). All men will become brothers: Time and rhythm as basic processes of life
and understanding. In S. Salmon (Ed.), *Hearing, feeling, playing: Music and movement
with deaf and hard-of-hearing children.* pp. 41–62 Wiesbaden, Germany: Reichert Verlag.

Goodkin, D. (2012). No child left out: The Orff approach to differentiated educa- tion. *Orff-Schulwerk Informationen*, *87*, 38–40. Retrieved from http://www. orff-schulwerk-forum salzburg.org/english/orff_schulwerk_informationen/issues.html

Haselbach, B. (Ed.). (2011). *Orff-Schulwerk Basistexte: Studientexte zu Theorie und Praxis des Orff-Schulwerks* [*Basic texts: Texts on theory and practice of Orff-Schulwerk*] (Vol. 1). Mainz, Germany: Schott.

Haselbach, B. (2013). Orff-Schulwerk: Origins and development. In S. Hennessy (Ed.), *Reflections on Orff-Schulwerk* (pp. 10–18). London: Schott Music.

Haselbach, B., & Hartmann, W. (2013). *Notes for the convention of the Orff-Schulwerk Forum 2013, Salzburg.* Unpublished manuscript.

Hüther, G. (2008). The neurobiological preconditions for the development of curiosity and creativity. In H. von Seggern & J. Werner (Eds.), *Grosse-Bächle* [Creating knowledge] (pp. 125–137). Berlin, Germany: Jovis Verlag. Retrieved from http://www.gerald-huether.de/pdf/neurobiological_preconditions.pdf

IQSH (Institut für Qualitätsentwicklung an Schulen Schleswig-Hollstein) (Ed.). (2011). *Umgang mit Heterogenität im Musikunterricht* [Dealing with diversity in music teach- ing] (Vol. 1). Kronshagen, Germany: Institut für Qualitätsentwicklung an Schulen Schleswig-Holstein.

Jungmair, U. (1992). *Das Elementare: Zur Musik- und Bewegungserziehung im Sinne Carl Orff's. Theorie und Praxis.* [The Elemental: On music and movement education according to Carl Orff. Theory and Practice]. Mainz, Germany: Schott Music.

Jungmair, U. (2008). *"elementar" oder "Elementar"? Eine Annäherung an den in der Elementaren Musikpädagogik verwendeten Begriff zwischen Phänomen, pädagogischer Konzeption und pädagogischer Professionalität.* ["Elemental" or "Elemental"? Approaching the concepts used in elemental music – phenomena, pedagogical conception and pedagogical pro- fessionalism.] Paper presented at the EMP Symposium, July 9–11, 2008, Feldkirchen, Kärtnen, Austria.

Jungmair, U. (2013). Putting theory into practice. In S. Hennessy (Ed.), *Reflections on Orff-Schulwerk* (pp. 34–36). London, England: Schott Music.

Keller, W. (1974). Ziele und Aufgaben des Instituts für Musikalische Sozial und Heilpädagogik am Mozarteum in Salzburg. [Goals and tasks of the institute for musical social and spe- cial education at the Mozarteum in Salzburg.] In *Orff-Schulwerk Informationen 13*, 2–4

Keller, W. (1984). Elementare Musik von und mit Behinderten. [Elemental music – from and with the disabled]. *Musik und Bildung*, *16* (12), 797–802.

Keller, W. (1996). *Musikalische Lebenshilfe.* (Life enhancement through music). Mainz, Germany: Schott Music.

Orff, C. (1932). Gedanken über Musik mit Kindern und Laien. [Thoughts about music with children and non-professionals.] In: Schuster, Bernhard (ed.): *Die Musik* 24, 668 – 673 Berlin (Reprinted from *Texts on theory and practice of Orff-Schulwerk*, Vol. 1, pp. 66–76, by B. Haselbach, Ed., 2011, Mainz, Germany: Schott Music).

Orff, C. (1978). *The Schulwerk<. Carl Orff—His life and works, documentation* (Vol. 3, M. Murray, Trans.). New York, NY: Schott.

Orff, C. (1964). Orff-Schulwerk: Past and future. In *Orff-Institut, Jahrbuch* 1963 (Orff Institute Yearbook 1963) Mainz, Germany: Schott (Reprinted from *Texts on theory and practice of Orff-Schulwerk*, M. Murray, Trans., Vol. 1, pp. 134–159, B. Haselbach, Ed., 2011, Mainz, Germany: Schott).

Orff, G. (1980). *Orff music therapy. Active furthering of the development of the child* (M. Murray, Trans.). London, England: Schott Music.

Orff, G. (1989). *Key concepts in Orff music therapy: Definitions and examples* (J. Day & S. Salmon, Trans.). Mainz, Germany: Schott Music.

Pitcher, C., & Macnaughton, T. (2008). *The littlest owl*. Intercourse, PA: Good Books.

Preston-Dunlop, V. (1990). *Modern educational dance.* Boston, MA: Plays.

Salmon, S. (Ed.). (2008). *Hearing, feeling, playing: Music and movement with deaf and hard-of-hearing children.* Wiesbaden, Germany: Reichert

Salmon, S. (2007). *Hello children: A collection of songs and related activities for children aged 4-9.* New York, NY: Schott Music.

Salmon, S. (2012). Musica humana: Thoughts on humanistic aspects of Orff-Schulwerk. In B. Haselbach (Ed.), *Orff-Schulwerk Informationen 87,* 13–19. Retrieved from http://www.orff-schulwerk-forum-salzburg.org/english/orff_schulwerk_informationen/issues.html

Schumacher, K. (1999). Die Bedeutung des Orff-Schulwerkes für die musikalische sozial- und Integrationspädagogik und die Musiktherapie. [The importance of Orff-Schulwerk for community work, special needs and music therapy]. *Orff Schulwerk-Informationen, 62,* 6–11. Retrieved from http://bidok.uibk.ac.at/library/schumacher-orff.html

Schumacher, K. (2003). Frühe Mutter-Kind-Spiele und ihre Bedeutung für die zwischenmenschliche Beziehungsfähigkeit. [Early mother-child games and their importance fort he development of interpersonal relationships]. *Der Vierzeiler: Zeitschrift für Musik, Kultur und Volksleben, 23,* 13–16.

Siegenthaler, H., & Zihlmann, H. (1988). *Rhythmische Erziehung* (3rd ed.) [Rhythmics Education]. Hitzkirch, Switzerland: Comenius.

Tomlinson, J., & Howard, P. (2004). *The owl who was afraid of the dark.* London, England: Egmont.

Vygotsky, L. S. (1978). *Mind in society: Development of higher psychological processes* (14th ed.). Cambridge, MA: Harvard University Press.

Waddell, M., & Benson, P. (1992). *Owl babies.* London: Walker.

Widmer, M. (2011). *Die Pädagogik des Orff-Instituts: Entwicklung und Bedeutung einer einzigartigen kunstpädagogischen Ausbildung.* [The pedagogy of the Orff Institute: the development and importance of a unique artistic-educational training]. Mainz, Germany: Schott Music.

CHAPTER 4

Lessons Learned from the Prism Project

Pedagogical Viewpoints in Music Education
for Teaching Students
with Autism Spectrum Disorder

RYAN M. HOURIGAN

As of the summer of 2014, 1 in 68 births in the United States results in a diagnosis of autism (Autism Society of America, 2014). In May of 2013, the American Psychological Association released the fifth edition of the *Diagnostic and Statistical Manual of Mental Disorders* (DSM-V). With the release of this manual, substantive changes were made to the diagnosis criteria for persons with autism spectrum disorder (ASD).

According to the previous edition of the DSM, the DSM-IV, patients could be diagnosed with four separate disorders: autistic disorder, Asperger disorder, childhood disintegrative disorder, or the catch-all diagnosis of pervasive developmental disorder not otherwise specified. Researchers found that these separate diagnoses were not consistently applied across different clinics and treatment centers. Anyone diagnosed with one of the four disorders from the DSM-IV should still meet the criteria for ASD in the DSM-V or another, more accurate DSM-V diagnosis.

Asperger syndrome is now under the umbrella of ASD. With these changes in diagnosis and the ability of medical professionals to detect ASD in a more accurate way, more and more children are receiving special education services. Therefore, more children with ASD are being included in music classrooms. The Prism Project was founded in 2009 to provide an opportunity for children with autism to explore the performing arts, as well as to prepare future teachers at Ball State University (BSU). The Prism Project also provides awareness to the community regarding the power of the arts for students with special needs.

THE PRISM PROJECT

The Prism Project[1] is a program using the performing arts as a medium to explore and develop appropriate social skills, lasting relationships, and skills and understanding in the arts for children ages 6 to 16 with disabilities. The program runs for 12 weeks from January until April each year and is a pedagogical space for preservice educators to learn to include students with disabilities in future classrooms and clinical environments. The Ball State Prism Project[2] also provides university students an opportunity to collaborate on, plan, and implement learning initiatives in the arts for children with special needs, many of whom have ASD. I cofounded the Prism Project with Michael Daehn (Department of Theatre and Dance faculty member) and Amy Hourigan, MT-BC (School of Music faculty member). The following section examines each component of the program in detail.

Community Need for the Prism Project

Several of the performers with special needs who were served in this project either have no experience in the arts or have been excluded completely from the arts programs at their schools. Their exclusion has been due to many factors. First, in this geographical area consisting of roughly 10 school districts, many self-contained special education classes (those that contain only students with special needs) are not part of the regular rotation for music class. In other words, a music educator may only be required to teach all of the students at an elementary school *except* self-contained classes for students with disabilities (many of the performers come from this category). This has been reported by both the parents of the students in the project and music educators in the area. In addition, because of preparation and professional development gaps, music educators may lack the ability to provide meaningful opportunities in music for successful inclusion of students with disabilities, as noted by the many music teachers who have reached out for assistance. There have been several instances where, at their home schools, performers from the Prism Project have music class but they are not included in special events like the winter or spring all-school music program or in ensembles such as band, choir, or orchestra. Many of the performers' parents have commented that the Prism Project performance is the first time they have ever seen their child on stage participating in the arts. It is hoped that through this process, we can provide not only training but also awareness of the possibilities for audience members who are music educators or special education professionals in the field.

The Prism Project annually serves approximately 32 performers with special needs (ages 6 to 14) and approximately 50 Ball State students who serve as "buddies." The program was initially funded through a grant from the university and since then has been solely funded by donations that are given at the final capstone performance. The combination of donations and tuition completely funds the project. Funding is discussed later in the chapter.

The Collaborative Process: Building Appropriate Musical Content

The Prism Project presents capstone "informances" of the music, theater, and dance scenes that are created, written, and composed during the semester "from scratch" by the university students and the performers in the project. The process of creating content for the show begins by faculty selecting a theme that will give all of the educators the flexibility within the arts to find and arrange content based on the theme and the skill sets of the performers. For example, our 2012 theme was built around the children's book *Ish* by Peter Reynolds (2004). This book is based on the idea that you do not need to be perfect at the things you like to participate in and enjoy them. With this theme in mind, Ball State students went to work assessing the skill sets of the students to design "ish" experiences for them to encounter in the arts. The scenes included "ballroom dance-ish," "rock band-ish," and other involvements that were, in the end, not perfect, but good experiences for the performers and that also contained appropriate skills and understanding in the arts for them to gain.

In some cases, students have their own ideas on a piece or topic. For example, in 2013, a performer wanted to tell a story about a pirate treasure hunt. With the assistance of the theater student directors, a play was written in collaboration with the student to be performed at the "informance." This segment was highly successful and gave the student playwright an excellent opportunity to share his ideas. More information regarding the collaborative relationship will be explored later.

Most of the material for the show is decided upon before we enter into our first rehearsal. However, we often get things wrong by under- or overestimating what the performers can accomplish within our rehearsal schedule. This requires all of the musicians, actors, and dancers that are part of the project to spend the week between rehearsals adjusting content or accommodations for the performers. In some cases, we have thrown a song out and started over. In other cases, we have supplemented a song by adding choreography or having students play instruments.

Preparation for Rehearsal (Ball State University "Buddy Training")

As mentioned earlier, many Ball State University students from a variety of units across campus take part in the Prism Project. It is important to point out that the "buddies" attend training sessions that are designed by the faculty directors and behavior specialists that consult on our project. These behavior specialists are special educators from the public schools who also have a background in applied behavior analysis (ABA)[3] and have at least a bachelor's degree in special education. These consultants were added after the first year (2009), when we realized that we needed some support in this area. We found that we were spending most of our time on behavior and self-help issues and not enough time on music, theater, and dance. Therefore, we contract two special educators each year to attend rehearsals and assist us with challenges.

The behavior consultants discuss potential scenarios that could happen and instruct the students on positive reinforcement ideas and protocols that allow for a smooth rehearsal. These constructs can be generalized to a classroom or clinical setting. An example of this kind of behavioral support is examined later with Tommy's social story. In addition, we have a music therapist as a codirector (and cofounder) who also assists with items that may fall within the overlap between music education and music therapy. Our music therapist has an extensive background with children and adults with autism and has both a music education and music therapy expertise that provides a unique perspective. We consider this component to be an invaluable part of the program. More about the role of these consultants will be discussed as we progress through this examination.

After training, each buddy is assigned a performer, given a binder to keep notes, and given a color-coded T-shirt for his or her student buddy (red, yellow, or green). This also serves as a safety precaution for us to keep track of students. As directors, we attempt to assign BSU students based on application information provided by both the performer and the BSU student. For example, if a BSU student has experience at a special education camp or has been with us before, we may assign that student to a performer who has more profound needs. The buddies are allowed time to discuss any concerns they may have with the directors or consultants.

Rehearsals at Prism

The weekly rehearsals at Prism start with a full-group warmup/attention-getting activity. This is usually a song or dance that requires simple imitation. The students are then split into three groups (red, yellow, and green). Each group has students who are at similar functioning levels, and we also consider their age—to encourage social interaction—when making these decisions. This procedure is not perfect; however, it seems to work well. There is usually a range of abilities even within the groups, which helps us with modeling and peer assistance.

Although some of the music, theater, and dance segments are chosen before the start of rehearsal, the first two weeks of rehearsal are usually exploratory in nature to gain understanding of the students' interests, skill levels, communication abilities, and cognitive function. The buddies take notes of these items to plan for the next week. The content is adjusted and usually starts to take shape in week four.

Once the final music is chosen, lesson plans are developed, accommodations for each group and each student are discussed, and the buddies are assigned music segments to teach. Each of the three music rehearsals runs roughly 25 minutes, with a 5-minute transition between sections (e.g., music to dance, etc.). After the rehearsal is complete and the students have left with their caregivers, we have a debriefing meeting to discuss any large-scale concerns with rehearsal. This is when the special education consultants also discuss any overall behavior or learning environment concerns. The buddies are also encouraged to ask questions or bring any concerns they may have. After this segment is complete, students break into groups by discipline (music, dance, theater) to discuss plans for the next week.[4]

Communication with Parents

Communication with parents is essential. After each rehearsal, it is imperative to let the parents know what transpired and if there were any breakthroughs, successes, or challenges. Like many adolescents, students with ASD, even when high functioning, may not let their parents know about the day's events. We often learn about challenges in the students' lives or about motivating factors of which we have been unaware.

At the Prism Project, we insist that all of the college student "buddies" have conversations with the parents of the performers. We also insist that they keep the conversation positive and include things that the student enjoyed or did well. Many parents of children on the autism spectrum only hear about all of the things their children cannot do or behavior problems. The Prism Project is a place for students on the spectrum to find out about the things at which they can be successful.

The Performance or "Informance"

At the end of the sequence of rehearsals, we provide a performance that we call an "informance." The students perform their theater, dance, and music scenes for an audience of parents, family, and a very large contingent of Ball State University students. The goal of the performance is not only to show the product of the 10 weeks but also to discuss the process and to celebrate our wonderful performers. Michael Daehn (a theater major at BSU) narrates a script that attempts to tie together the theme of the show with each segment to create a seamless story where possible. We also interject video clips of rehearsals. There are many moments in which the performers are honored with applause and shown how much we appreciate their hard work and artistry. In 2014, over 700 people attended the capstone performance.

The Prism Project as Part of a University Learning Initiative

This project is part of a curricular initiative by Ball State University to encourage *immersive learning*, which is defined by the university as that which "pull(s) together interdisciplinary student teams guided by expert faculty to create unique, high-impact learning experiences that result in real-world solutions" and will "synthesize disciplinary knowledge with application. Students and faculty turn knowledge into judgment and judgment into action through projects and programs that benefit business, community, and government partners across the state and around the world."[5] Each project must carry credit, involve at least two units or departments, engage with a community partner, and produce a final product such as a play, book, report, or DVD.

In our case, the community partner is twofold. We consider east central Indiana and area not-for-profit agencies to be our community partners. We charge a small tuition fee that amounts to $7 per session as an incentive to be consistent with attendance. Some of the area not-for-profits supplement tuition ($75 per semester) for students who cannot otherwise afford to attend. This allows all students to have access to the program regardless of need. The Ball State students receive credit in many different ways such as clinical or observation credit or elective credit. As discussed later, our capstone performance serves as our tangible outcome for the project and is also used on our website and converted to a DVD. The program is a formal partnership between the School of Music and the Department of Theatre and Dance at Ball State University and Interlock (http://www.interlockin. org); Prism has also been awarded external funding from Autism Advocates of Indiana and from community member donations.

The Future of Prism

So far, the Prism Project has expanded to other cities including New Orleans, Louisiana, and the University of Northern Iowa. In each instance of expansion, a different demographic has added complexities to pedagogy. For example, in New Orleans, many of the students who are challenged with autism are also struggling with poverty and considered socioeconomically at risk. However, in working with students on the autism spectrum, much of what we do at the original site has been successful at other sites. In our work with the performers of the Prism Project, we have learned much about group and individual music making and children with ASD; it is the aim of this chapter to share what we have learned.

Research and the Prism Project

Initially, we noticed that some of the conditions that we set up for the performers seemed to work very well. We also wanted to see if our performers were indeed learning within the 10-week rehearsal cycle. We sought to move beyond anecdotal evidence and thus conducted a study based on these research questions: What are the conditions that facilitate music learning among students with special needs? Do conditions that facilitate music learning have an effect on the musical ability of students with special needs?

We found that many of the constructs mentioned previously *did* indeed impact music learning in a positive way. This research (Gerrity, Hourigan, & Horton, 2013), along with six years of experience with the project, has led to the following findings about music pedagogy, best practice, and students with autism spectrum disorder. The next section of this chapter will provide an in-depth look at the research-informed pedagogy of the Prism Project.

TEACHING AND LEARNING MUSIC
WITH STUDENTS ON THE AUTISM SPECTRUM

This section will examine many of the underlying traits or characteristics of autism through the lens of research-formed practice and pedagogy of the Prism Project. These examples will include both broad and individual accommodations, as well as the theoretical constructs based on the literature.

The Environment

Based on our interactions with the students of the Prism Project, the first order of business for all educators who teach students with ASD is to examine the learning environment. It is important to look at this space through the eyes of the students. Many people with autism have sensory sensitivities to lights, sounds, textures, and other items that may be uncomfortable for them. In fact, research shows that 42% to 80% of people with autism demonstrate unusual sensory responses (Kientz & Dunn, 1997). Therefore, when inspecting the learning environment, look for bright lights, potential loud sounds (e.g., drums that could be hit loudly by another student), distractions, and other items that could induce anxiety or interrupt the teaching and learning relationship. If these things exist, consult with the special education team to find alternatives. In addition, there may need to be a sensory space to retreat to when a child becomes overstimulated. This can also just be a bench or a place to walk to when anxiety or overstimulation occurs.

Another crucial piece concerning the learning environment is the support that a child with ASD receives. Gerrity, Hourigan, and Horton (2013) note that music teachers cannot teach students with ASD without the proper support mechanisms in place. Often there are extraneous behaviors, sensory needs, communication demands, and physical requirements that accompany a student with autism. As mentioned earlier, the Prism Project provides each student with a "buddy," and there is a special education consultant involved to look for improvements to how we provide instruction to all students. This would be similar to what a child with ASD needs in the school classroom. Many children with ASD require not only one-on-one support but also collaborative efforts between the music educator, the special educator, the paraprofessional or one-on-one assistant, and sometimes the parents (when possible) to be successful.

Establishing Trust

We have found in the Prism Project that once a teacher establishes a form of communication, trust must also be established. Children with autism, at whatever level of functioning, can be anxious. In fact, research shows that people with ASD show considerably more challenges with social anxiety (White, Bray, & Ollendick, 2011). This comes from years of expressive language and self-advocacy challenges and can also lead to depression. Imagine not being able to tell someone that you are scared, sick, or upset. Some students on the spectrum go years without having the language to be able to advocate for themselves (and some not at all). Establishing trust with a child on the spectrum can be the most important part of relationship building.

According to our experiences, lack of trust comes from not understanding the extent by which children with autism calculate things such as time and order. We often assume that because children cannot specifically tell time or know the days of the week, they do not have an internal clock of some kind. We suggest that one should "say what you mean and mean what you say" in the simplest language possible from the very beginning when working with a child with autism. It is always vital to accurately share information about the schedule and then to make every effort to stick to the plan. Equally important is the need to anticipate transitions to different or new activities. Playing the same piece of recorded music every time there is a transition to new material or placing some sort of visual aid in plain view that indicates transitions can alert learners of upcoming changes in their schedule. We also write the schedule on the board of each classroom along with a picture schedule. Each student has a binder with his or her own picture schedules (if needed) and a simplified version of his or her schedule. The student buddy is instructed to talk through the schedule with each student in a way that the student understands.

When there is an upcoming event—unexpected or planned—the buddy will talk through the event in advance. This allows children to learn to self-regulate their emotions, which is a very important skill set for children. For example, if the fire alarm goes off during a music lesson, the buddy will take the time to talk about why there was a loud noise, what to expect the next time, and how the student can help him- or herself talk through the event ("It's okay," "hand over ears," or "follow directions").

As mentioned, in the Prism Project, university student buddies are assigned to student performers. They learn to spend time exploring the anxiety level of the student and how to establish trust and communication strategies with each other. This process may start all over again when a buddy needs to miss a rehearsal/class meeting or is sick—with the substitute or when the university student returns. Communication strategies are shared in the Prism Project with binders that contain notes about anxiety and communication challenges. This is typically established by the first buddy during the first few rehearsals and then passed on if needed. Finding familiar interests, giving accurate information (telling the truth), and anticipating reactions often assists with smooth transitions between new buddies and the performers. This is a procedure that also should be followed with teachers and students with autism. Music teachers should spend time gathering information from other teachers and professionals to begin to establish trust and communication.

Communication

One of the pillars of an autism diagnosis is the challenges people with ASD face regarding communication (Prizant & Wetherby, 2005). Specifically, children with ASD often struggle with the social and functional use of language. Unfortunately, there is a direct correlation between social communication, behavior, and learning. Establishing functional communication between a teacher and a student with autism should be the first priority. Prizant and Wetherby state that "functional communication abilities have been considered to be of the highest priority in the efforts to improve communication" (p. 926). Without clear, functional communication between a student and a music teacher, a child will not have positive learning experiences in the music classroom. In addition, teaching a child to communicate effectively with peers will enhance their experience.

Receptive and Expressive Language Challenges

Communication can be broken down into two threads, receptive and expressive language. Receptive language refers to the student's ability to receive and decode language. People with autism can have trouble in this area. Joint attention plays a part here as well; the more turns you take in a conversation, the longer the joint attention will expand. For example, if a child shows you something he or she is interested in, ask about it. Johnny may show you his Star Wars action figure. You ask: "What is his name?" He responds: "Darth Vader." You keep extending the conversation loop as long as possible. This will assist in Johnny's overall engagement and joint attention skills.

At the Prism Project, we attempt to simplify our language and use multiple ways to reinforce our instructions. This may require both written and verbal communication, picture icons, or assistive communication devices.

Finding out how a student best communicates will not only enhance instruction but also help establish the trust needed to develop a strong teaching and learning relationship.

Joint Attention

To establish trust and to communicate with students on the autism spectrum, it is important to establish joint attention. Joint attention refers to a shared interest in an object or activity. Students on the spectrum often have difficulty with the desire to share interests as their own interests are placed above all else (Charman, 2003).

In the Prism Project, discussions with parents enabled us to learn what might spark the students' attention. It could be a stuffed animal, a movie, or a piece of music. We have found that if we know this information ahead of time, it eases the anxiety and starts the expansion of attention and joint attention. Participants might begin by asking students (who are verbal) a simple question about the item of interest. For example, questions such as "Who is your favorite character?" or "What are you drawing?" are great ways to start. In the beginning, one should keep the focus on the students' interests. After some time, students can be encouraged to become aware of others by asking peers about their interests. This will help with their overall joint attention.

Music as a Means of Expression

As autism is a spectrum disorder, verbal communication can also encompass a wide spectrum, from articulating simple directions to communicating identity and emotion. People with ASD may struggle at all points along the way. In addition, just because a student has one communication concept mastered, he or she may not have picked up all of the necessary language along the way. In the music therapy realm, music has been used to foster better communication skills for decades (Heflin & Alaimo, 2007). Our challenges within the Prism Project are often twofold. First, we typically need to choose a song that provides many opportunities for students to express their understanding of the music. Second, when the music is chosen, we need to teach the music in a way that provides the performers multiple opportunities to express their understanding of simple music concepts (e.g., musical form). The following examples are designed to shed light on these challenges while offering strategies that are appropriate for each level of communication functioning.

"Rattlin' Bog"

The traditional Irish folk song "Rattlin' Bog" was used to incorporate multiple means of expression into a musical performance for students who struggle with communication. The "Rattlin' Bog" has a form similar to the "Twelve Days of Christmas" with phrases that repeat and the addition of an item/lyric on each repetition, for example, flea, feather, and bird (see Figure 4.1). This works very well with children on the spectrum who have trouble with memory. They can learn just the verse or the verse and any item that they can remember.

This folk song was taught to our green group, which was the most challenged verbally. In rehearsal, we used a series of techniques to assist students with the lyrics. First, we would assign each student a phrase that had a specific keyword. For example, "feather" is one item that is repeated over and over again. When it was time to sing this verse, the instructor would make sure it was obvious that it was that child's turn by making eye contact and sitting next to that particular student. Then the instructor would leave out the word "feather." Some of the more verbal students would fill in the word for the instructor. Others would point to the picture of the feather to demonstrate that they knew when, in the music, the word fit. For some

Figure 4.1. The "Rattlin' Bog."

students in the green group, it was obvious that even though they could not express the lyric, they knew where the lyric fit within the music. The chorus of this folk song is very repetitive. We would include clapping during the chorus, and many of the students knew that during the chorus it was time to clap and would often do this on cue and in time with the music, thus demonstrating an understanding of the form of the piece.

The Prism Project green group[6] performed this in 2011, and each student held a placard of the subject of each verse. This was done in lieu of needing to worry about articulating each word of the verse. The students were able to sing what they could and hold up the sign for the rest. Many of the students could only articulate a phrase or a word, and that was fine. This can be done with any song that repeats in this type of form and works well for students who struggle to communicate.

It is important to point out that most of the parents of the green group reported that they heard this song at home in whatever iteration their child could articulate—often with the correct pitch and in rhythm, with whatever words or utterances they chose to express. It was clear that the green group was hearing this music and adding it to their musical memory. We may assume that because some children with autism cannot articulate music, they are not having a musical experience or adding to the repertoire of music that they hear in their minds. We found the opposite to be true with many of the students in the Prism Project.

"Imagine"

As students develop basic communication skills, they also begin to develop expressive communication skills. At the Prism Project, we attempt to assist with this by applying understandable lyrics and themes to popular songs in performances. In 2013, we used the song "Imagine" (by John Lennon) as a palette and added additional verses created by the students to add meaning for them. When completing this type of change to a song, there may be copyright issues. However, when used for educational purposes with no profit from the performance, typically permission is given.

Thematic materials were centered on everyday challenges the students face. Verses that described bullying, loneliness, making friends, keeping friends, and other subjects were included in the song (Figure 4.2). Students wrote some of the lyrics, and some were written in collaboration with the college student buddies. Ross,[7] one of our performers, programmed his verse into an assistive communication device and played it in time with the beat of the song during the performance over the sound system. This was a very powerful moment for everyone involved.

> **(Ross with his Assisted Communication Device)**
> *Imagine there are no bullies*
> *It isn't hard to do*
> *Nothing to push or shove for*
> *And no reason to*
> **(Trio: Alex, Shaun, and Violet)**
> *Imagine there is no violence*
> *Imagine if you can*
> *No reason for hate or anger*
> *A brotherhood of man*

Figure 4.2. Student lyrics for John Lennon's "Imagine."

COMMUNICATION AND EXPRESSION FOR HIGH-FUNCTIONING STUDENTS WITH AUTISM SPECTRUM DISORDER

Sometimes verbal instructions can be complicated even for students who have high-functioning autism (including Asperger syndrome). However, writing down clear instructions and pairing these directions with either pictures, modeling, or simple verbal instructions is usually more effective than verbal instructions alone (Charlop-Christy & Kelso, 2003). In the Prism Project, we have found that this can also work both ways. Students with high-functioning autism may want to express themselves in a certain way but have limited expressive language skills to do so.

We have found that as students with high-functioning autism become more and more interested in socializing with their peers, this communication challenge becomes a hurdle in allowing them to express themselves to their peers. In the Prism Project, we tend to focus on these constructs with students who have limited verbal skills. However, after many years of working with the students in the Prism Project, we realized that we were ignoring the higher-functioning students and their needs. They also had communication challenges, but in a different way. They tended to be more verbal but lacked the ability to express to others the things they liked and had interests in. For example, the red group in the Prism Project was organized to include preteen and teenaged students who are able to read, write, and communicate very clearly. In addition, most of the students can carry on an extended conversation. However, the more time you spend with students with high-functioning ASD, the more you realize that they are socially awkward and fascinated by extraordinary things that other students their age may or may not find interesting.

Music and adolescent identity has been the focus of much research in music education (North & Hargreaves, 1999; North, Hargreaves, & O' Neill, 2010). The issue of identity can also be excluded from the discussion of communication when working with these exceptional young people. Often we focus on functional language rather than some of the more abstract uses of language. For example, communicating an identity is an important part of being a teenager, especially when forming an identity is a challenge (Campbell, Connell, & Beegle, 2007). Whether it is through music, art, sports, or theater, many teenagers spend a lot of time expressing themselves at this age. However, high-functioning students with autism often are challenged in this area. Because of the characteristics associated with autism, they may not wear the coolest clothes or know about the latest pop group. They may be behind their chronological age in social norms and therefore have difficulty expressing their identity or may be met with unexpected responses from peers.

Many of the students we work with are interested in hip-hop or other forms of popular music, and many of the themes of the hip-hop culture are about self-expression and identity. In the field of music therapy, hip-hop music is used as a means of expressions for adolescents (McFerran, 2010).

The Prism Project directors chose a song by Eminem entitled "Not Afraid" (Figure 4.3). Many of the verses of "Not Afraid" were inappropriate for our kids, but we decided that the chorus (Figure 4.3) was empowering for our students and appropriate for our use. This idea originated from the New Orleans Prism Project: Roux Roux Productions by Jeremy Love, MT-BC. The red group in the Ball State Prism Project explored this idea with their "Not Afraid" performance in 2013 after seeing the earlier performance by the New Orleans Prism Project.

Each student wrote lyrics about themselves in four- to six-line stanzas (Figure 4.4). Each verse started with "My name is . . .," giving them a sounding board to express what *they* saw as their identity. Many of the students talked about the things they liked or what was important about them. This was all done in a high-energy performance with a backup rock band.

"Not Afraid" by Eminem

I'm not afraid (I'm not afraid)

To take a stand (to take a stand)

Everybody (everybody)

Come take my hand (come take my hand)

We'll walk this road together, through the storm

Whatever weather, cold or warm

Then you know that, you're not alone

Holla if you feel like you've been down the same road (same road)

Figure 4.3. Lyrics to the chorus of Eminem's "Not Afraid."

> **(Joel)**
> My name is Joel
> I am really cool
> Challenge me in drawing
> You must be a fool
> Changing the world is my ultimate goal
> Goal . . . **goal** . . . **gggggoal**
> **(Zavier)**
> My name is Zavier
> I like mythology
> I like studying birds (they call that ornithology)
> The Prism Project is what I like to do
> This is my super-cool rap . . . Hollah!!

Figure 4.4. Student lyrics for Eminem's "Not Afraid."

Students did not always rhyme correctly; however, these high-functioning teenagers were able to express their identity through music.

From a music education perspective, we also wanted the students to learn the intricacies of being a part of a popular music group. For example, one of the students played drums for the group in lieu of rapping. In rehearsal, we spent a great deal of time with dynamics. He struggled with when to play quietly (while the students were rapping) and when it was his time to shine while keeping a steading rhythm. The rappers had to work hard to support each other on stage while their group members were rapping. Should they dance? How could they get the crowd involved? All of these questions and techniques were part of the process and authentic to being a part of a popular music group.

Another aspect of identity and communication, particularly among adolescents, is *feeling cool.* Imagine being 13 years old, being in a rap group, and performing for 700 people in a concert hall. The red group accomplished this and never felt cooler—a big boost to their self-confidence, self-efficacy, and, most important, identity. Since then, they have been asked to do actual "gigs" or other performances that have further enhanced their self-esteem.

BEHAVIOR

There are challenges that come with behavior, music, and autism, particularly since behavior is at the fulcrum of the diagnosis of autism. Behavior in children with autism manifests itself in three threads: behaviors related to anxiety, communication, and social behavior.

First, students may experience meltdowns or outbursts based on events that could occur during a music lesson—a new routine, loud noises, stubbornness, or simply not feeling well. These behaviors may occur when an activity requires an increased amount of executive skills (e.g., the ability to focus on and execute simple tasks), especially with fine motor activities or when the activity is too challenging. Students will sometimes attempt to misbehave to get out of doing a task. However, at the Prism Project, we have found that the performers do not improve their skills or experiences if we do not require them to go through the motions of the executive skill to try the musical task. We attempt to weigh all that is going on when deciding the next course of action. Often the special education consultant or the parent will provide us with insight into these behaviors as we seek to find the balance between completing a task and giving the student a break.

When students do have a meltdown, we attempt to keep clear communication channels open with parents, buddies, and other stakeholders. We are trained to keep students from hurting themselves and others and we use positive reinforcement to curb behaviors.[8] The special education consultants also assist with behavior plans and interventions to assist the performers. Often the BSU students learn valuable techniques for their future classrooms or clinical settings.

Social Behavior

Social behavior is a significant challenge for students with autism. We work with students who have challenges with simple social cues such as a teacher calling their name or another student saying hello and then responding appropriately. Higher-functioning students may react awkwardly or inappropriately to these and other social situations or withdraw from their peers altogether.

For example, Tommy (pseudonym) was our oldest performer and had been with the Prism Project for five years. He was 16, going through puberty, and beginning to be interested in girls. The challenge came in his approach to trying to make friends with Mary (pseudonym). He would attempt to hug or kiss her and could not think about anything else during the entire duration of the rehearsals. He would follow her around for the full length of the rehearsal, which, of course, made Mary feel uncomfortable.

There are many reasons this happens for students on the spectrum. First, they often are behind socially from their chronological age. They may have emotions and changes in their maturing bodies that they do not understand. Second, people with autism often struggle with empathy. Tommy could not comprehend how his behavior was affecting Mary. Finally, many students with autism express obsessive-compulsive behaviors and have

Personal Space

I come to Prism Project to hang out with my friends.

I like to hang out with my friend, Mary.

Here are some things I can do with Mary:

Wave "Hi" or "Goodbye."

Talk to Mary. Sit or stand next to her.

I have to respect Mary's personal space.

It is **not** okay to:
- Hug Mary
- Kiss Mary
- Touch Mary

I have other friends at Prism Project. I can sit next to them and talk to them sometimes, too.

Figure 4.5. Social story about personal space.

difficulty with self-regulation. Even if Tommy knew he was causing Mary to feel uncomfortable, he may have had difficulty monitoring or self-regulating his emotions and resultant behavior.

After consulting with our special education consultants (similar to what music teachers might do in this instance), we constructed a social story for Tommy (Figure 4.5) to help him learn about personal space and appropriate behavior with Mary. Social stories are simple narratives that assist people with autism with behavior, anticipating change, or anything that would require advanced conversation. A creative social story can assist with correcting behavior or alleviating anxiety (Gray, 2000).

COGNITION AND STUDENTS WITH AUTISM SPECTRUM DISORDER

Each child is different in the way he or she communicates, behaves, and thinks; however, there are some consistent characteristics that are common for most people on the spectrum. We see these traits with the performers at the Prism Project and attempt to take them into consideration when planning music, theater, and dance performances. The challenges that students with autism have in the area of cognition can affect their ability to learn music (Heaton, Allen, Williams, Cummins, & Happe, 2008). This section will discuss some areas of cognition as they relate to music learning and children with autism and examples are used to help reinforce concepts.

Theory of Mind

The idea of *theory of mind* or *mind-blindness* (Peterson, Wellman, & Liu, 2005) has a direct relationship to music learning and meaning making because of the affective nature of musical expression. People who struggle with mind-blindness typically have difficulty attributing mental states (including emotions) to self and others. For example, a child on the autism spectrum may have trouble understanding why people cry. Some people cry because they are happy and others because they are sad. It all depends on context. Some people with autism can be confused by the act of crying. They may feel that the act of crying should only happen when people are sad. They may also have trouble predicting why someone might want to cry. This is a common challenge for people with ASD.

Empathy is also part of this equation. It can be difficult for a child on the spectrum to predict the likes, dislikes, and basic mental or emotional state of others. For example, when you ask people on the spectrum what a friend might want for his or her birthday, they might choose something *they* want instead. They may have no idea (because of theory of mind) what their friend might want for his or her birthday. Many people with autism exhibit this trait or characteristic. Because of this, students with autism tend to have odd or inappropriate reactions to the mental states of others. For example, a person with autism may laugh at someone who is crying or laugh at other inappropriate times.

Theory of mind and empathy go hand in hand and affect how a student can engage with a group of students for a shared or intended outcome or "shared intentionality" (Cross, Laurence, & Rabinowitch, 2012). Many students with autism excel in a technical or cognitive manner when they learn or perform music. However, these same students have difficulty understanding the emotional content of the music and will not be able to share in the group experience of performing within this emotional context.

In the Prism Project, we have found that the younger and more challenged students need to explore the extremes of the emotional spectrum. For example, in 2013, we used the song "I Love to Laugh" from *Mary Poppins* to explore humor and laughter (Figure 4.6).

The students in the green group were students who had limited verbal skills (some were nonverbal) and had some behavioral challenges. In addition, theory of mind issues were also prevalent within this group. Many of our students had difficulty with facial expressions, figures of speech, slang, innuendo, irony, and eye gaze, which resulted in frequent challenges with socialization. This limited their ability to share in jokes and other fun experiences. Therefore, we started by exploring the appropriate reaction to someone being funny ("Ah, ha, ha, ha"). When someone is funny, we laugh. We considered the kinds of things that make people funny. We taught the students how to respond to a knock, knock joke by adding the "who's there" and ". . . who." During the final performance, we allowed certain students to tell their jokes to the audience. Finally, the choreography required funny hats and glasses. We also explored the facial expressions that go with something being funny by exaggerating them when laughing or telling jokes. This allowed the students to connect the expressions with the laughter and the jokes. All of this was designed to support affective development and theory of mind challenges. More important, it was fun for the performers. It was hoped that the members of the green group were able to experience much of what it means to be funny, how to react appropriately, and how to share in humorous events. These are the kinds of explorations that are needed for students who struggle with decoding emotional content in music and life.

Chorus from *I Love to Laugh* (from Mary Poppins)
Richard M. Sherman and Robert B. Sherman

I love to laugh (Ah, ha, ha, ha)
Loud and long and clear
I love to laugh (Ah, ha, ha, ha)
It's getting worse ev'ry year

The more I laugh (Ah, ha, ha, ha)
The more I fill with glee
And the more the glee
The more I'm a merrier me
It's embarrassing!
The more I'm a merrier me!

Figure 4.6. Lyrics to the chorus of "I Love to Laugh."

Central Coherence Theory

Central coherence theory (CCT) is an often-misunderstood trait displayed by persons with autism. It refers to the tendency of a person to focus on the global aspects of a subject or object instead of the global inferences (Happe, 2005). For example, a student with autism may be interested in Star Wars. She may be able to tell you all of the characters of the film, the gadgets and equipment used, the years the movies were released, the actors, the writers, the composers, and so forth. However, when another student says, "I like Han Solo," she may not be interested. If you learn music from another science fiction movie during music class, she may demand that you teach Stars Wars. If you decide to teach Star Wars, she may not be able to focus on the music. Instead, she might start listing all of the things mentioned previously.

These issues, similar to obsessive-compulsive characteristics, can be difficult to curtail. Metaphorically, CCT is like having a persistent itch that people with autism need to scratch. It is difficult for them, once they start listing all of the things they know, to let go of the subject. It is best to give them an outlet. It is appropriate to slowly try to redirect while giving students an opportunity to get the information out of their heads.

This presents a problem in any classroom, not just the music classroom. In the Prism Project, we use a device called a time timer (http://www.timetimer.com). If a student begins this "drill down" behavior instead of engaging with the class music, theater, or dance activity, we set the timer and say, "Okay, Susie, you have one minute to tell me about Star Wars; then it is back to learning music." We then assign something to do outside of rehearsal such as drawing pictures, listing websites, or making lists about the student's personal topic to show us at the next rehearsal. This allows students to explore the topic without feeling ignored.

Executive Function and Memory

Students with autism also struggle with executive function (Ozonoff, South, & Provencal, 2005). This refers to the use of (or inability to use) functions of the brain such as planning, working memory, and impulse control (Hill & Frith, 2003, p. 285). This challenge can manifest itself in the teaching of executive skills in music such as a position or a drumstick grip or multistep directions such as dance moves or multipart songs.

We have noticed two challenges when assisting students in the Prism Project. First, simply because a student does not complete the task quickly does not mean that he or she cannot eventually complete the task.

For example, we often begin drum circle activities with echoing patterns. Andrew (a Prism performer) would not echo patterns for many weeks into the project. We decided to give him more and more time to process the pattern, requiring ourselves to count to 30 before moving to the next student. When given that time, Andrew would echo the pattern with perfect or almost perfect accuracy.

Many of our college students come from special education programs where hand-over-hand assistance is a well-meaning but impulsive—and often unhelpful—reaction to assist students. We insist that students be allowed time and multiple attempts to complete a task before using hand-over-hand assistance.

Another issue we noticed in the Prism Project was multistep directions, particularly when paired with memory problems. Often students with autism display problems with converting working memory to long-term memory (Hill & Frith, 2003). The best way to help students with these issues (multistep directions and memory) is repetition and pairing modes of instruction (e.g., visual with kinesthetic). For example, a college student buddy may model the verbal instructions given and write out the instructions as well.

Learning Together

The Ball State University Prism Project is now entering its seventh year and has expanded to two other cities in the United States. Over the past five years, the performers of the Prism Project have provided insights into pedagogy, compassion, tolerance, and expression for students on the autism spectrum. We will continue to evolve and learn from each other.

Our involvement with the Prism Project has helped us to realize that the students who participate often spend most of their day realizing and coming to terms with the challenges they face with people who do not think and interact in the same manner as they do. The arts can be a safe place to be an individual and for these learners to build musical and social skills in expressive ways. Most important, they can find things that they *can* do.

NOTES

1. As of 2014, the Prism Project is in its seventh year.
2. Ball State University is located in Muncie, Indiana.
3. More information concerning Applied Behavior Analysis can be found at http://www.abainternational.org.
4. Examples of content for the Prism Project can be found at http://prismproject.iweb.bsu.edu.

5. More information about immersive learning at Ball State University can be found at http://www.bsu.edu/immersive.
6. Participants in the Prism Project are divided into groups that have color names.
7. Participant names and images are used with permission.
8. See Hammel and Hourigan (2013) for examples of concrete positive behavior support systems.

REFERENCES

American Psychiatric Association. (2013). *Diagnostic and statistical manual of mental disorders* (5th ed.). Arlington, VA: American Psychiatric Publishing.

Autism Society of America. About Autism (2015). http://www.autism-society.org

Campbell, P. S., Connell, C., & Beegle, A. (2007). Adolescents' expressed meaning of music in and out of school. *Journal of Research in Music Education, 55*(3), 220–236.

Charlop-Christy, M. H., & Kelso, S. E. (2003). Teaching children with autism conversational speech using cue card/written script program. *Education and Treatment of Children, 26*(2), 108–127.

Charman, T. (2003). Why is joint attention a pivotal skill in autism? *Philosophical Transactions: Biological Sciences, 358*(1430), 315–324.

Cross, I., Laurence, F., & Rabinowitch, T. (2012) Empathy and creativity musical practices: Towards a concept of empathetic creativity. In *Oxford Handbooks Online: The Oxford Handbook of Music Education*. G. McPhearson and G.F. Welch, eds. (Vol. 2).

Gerrity, K. W., Hourigan, R. M., & Horton, P. W. (2013). Conditions that facilitate music learning among students with special needs: A mixed-methods inquiry. *Journal of Research in Music Education, 61*, 144–159.

Gray, C. (2000). *The new social story book*. Arlington, TX: Future Horizons.

Hammel, A. M., & Hourigan, R. M. (2013). *Teaching music to children with autism*. New York, NY: Oxford University Press.

Happe, F. (2005). The weak central coherence account of autism. In F. R. Volkmar, R. Paul, A. Klin, & D. Cohen (Eds.), *Handbook of autism and pervasive developmental disorders* (pp. 640–649). Hoboken, NJ: John Wiley & Sons.

Heaton, P., Allen, R., Williams, K., Cummins, O., & Happe, F. (2008). Social and cognitive deficits curtail musical understanding? Evidence from autism and Down syndrome. *British Journal of Developmental Psychology, 26*, 171–182.

Heflin, J. L., & Alaimo, D. F. (2007). *Students with autism spectrum disorders*. Upper Saddle River, NJ: Prentice Hall.

Hill, E. L., & Frith, U. (2003). Understanding autism: Insights from mind and brain. *Philosophical Transactions: Biological Sciences, 358*(1430), 281–289.

Kientz, M. A., & Dunn, W. (1997). A comparison of the performance of children with and without autism on the sensory profile. *American Journal of Occupational Therapy, 51*, 530–537.

McFerran, K. (2010). *Adolescents, music, and music therapy*. Dexter, MI: Thompson Schore.

North, A. C., & Hargreaves, D. J. (1999). Music and adolescent identity. *Music Education Research, 1*(1), 75–92.

North, A. C., Hargreaves, D. J., & O' Neill, S. A. (2010). The importance of music to adolescents. *British Journal of Education Psychology, 70*, 255–272.

Ozonoff, S., South, M., & Provencal, S. (2005). Executive functions. In F. R. Volkmar, R. Paul, A. Klin, & D. Cohen (Eds.), *Handbook of autism and pervasive developmental disorders* (pp. 606–627). Hoboken, NJ: John Wiley & Sons.

Peterson, C. C., Wellman, H. M., & Liu, D. (2005). Steps in theory of mind development for children with deafness or autism. *Child Development, 76*(2), 502–517.

Prizant, B. M., & Wetherby, A. M. (2005). Critical issues in enhancing communication abilities for persons with autism spectrum disorders. In F. R. Volkmar, R. Paul, A. Klin, & D. Cohen (Eds.), *Handbook of autism and pervasive developmental disorders* (pp. 946–976). Hoboken, NJ: John Wiley & Sons.

Reynolds, P. H. (2004). *Ish.* Cambridge, MA: Candlewick Press.

White, S. W., Bray, B. C., & Ollendick, T. H. (2011). Examining shared and unique aspects of social anxiety disorder and autism spectrum disorder using factor analysis. *Journal of Developmental Disorders, 42,* 874–884.

CHAPTER 5

Assistive Technology to Support Students in Accessing the Music Curriculum

EMILY H. WATTS, KIMBERLY McCORD,
AND DEBORAH VANDERLINDE BLAIR

A dvances in technology have made it possible for students (Bryant & Bryant, 2003), and for most of us, to do ordinary and sometimes extraordinary things with considerably more ease, efficiency, and independence. Educators strive to make learning possible for the widest range of students, with the aim of independence in this pedagogical mix. Devices and specialized equipment to help people with disabilities have existed for some time in other fields such as medicine, communication disorders, and rehabilitation. Particular technologies in schools that are defined as *assistive technology* (AT) are relatively new tools that add to the knowledge base of special education (Blackhurst, 1997; Edyburn, 2000, 2013). Only in recent US legislative history has there been a definition of assistive technology devices, with assistive technology services codified into the 1990 Individuals with Disabilities Education Act (IDEA), thus sending a legal imperative to school districts across the United States. This reauthorization of the special education law also required that if a student had an Individualized Educational Program (IEP), the IEP team must consider whether the student needs assistive technology. The law describes assistive technology as twofold: assistive technology devices and assistive technology services.

ASSISTIVE TECHNOLOGY DEVICES

There is disagreement within the field of education as to what may appropriately be considered assistive technologies. The US Department of Education's

Office of Special Education Programs (OSEP) has stated that there is not a listing of what can and cannot be considered assistive technology. Without clear parameters, this complicates the work of school IEP teams. Following the federal law's definition is a mandated requirement for school IEP teams, even though it is conceptually very broad. The law states that an assistive technology device, by definition, is "any item, piece of equipment, or product system, whether acquired commercially off the shelf, modified, or customized, that is used to increase, maintain, or improve functional capabilities of children with disabilities" (Individuals with Disabilities Education Improvement Act of 2004). In general, digital learning tools would most likely qualify as assistive technology for students with disabilities (Edyburn, 2013). However, there is one exception. It does not include "a medical device that is surgically implanted, or the replacement of such device" (Individuals with Disabilities Education Improvement Act [IDEIA], 2004, Sec. 1401(1)(B)). For example, in development is the Rewalk, a bionic suit that provides support and through sophisticated sensors and tiny computers is able to restore mobility to individuals with significant physical disabilities. This suit is not implanted but worn, so it would be assistive technology. Another device is a jacket that contains a tiny camera that is linked to an implanted device that helps a person with a certain type of vision loss to detect changes in light and dark. This is implanted, so it would not qualify as AT.

Table 5.1 provides examples of AT applications for music activities routinely used in schools. The Skoog is not commonly found in schools but when available is very effective.

Table 5.1 EXAMPLES OF ASSISTIVE TECHNOLOGY DEVICES IN MUSIC EDUCATION SETTINGS

School Setting: Music Education Classrooms	Specific Student with a Disability	Assistive Technology Solution	Educational Outcomes
General music	6-year-old boy with a moderate level of cerebral palsy that affects his fine motor grasping abilities	Egg shaker with Velcro	Allows the student access to and participation in the general education curriculum; fosters student independence in music activities

(continued)

Table 5.1 (CONTINUED)

School Setting: Music Education Classrooms	Specific Student with a Disability	Assistive Technology Solution	Educational Outcomes
Band	13-year-old girl with low vision	Computer software program that magnifies electronic notation provided by her band director 	Allows the student access to and participation in practicing her selected part for the spring concert
Choral music	17-year-old boy with learning disabilities (e.g., severe reading difficulties) in chorus	Lyric sheets printed using a symbol-based software program that allows for icons, photos, or graphics for decoding text 	Allows the student access to and participation in choral activities and concerts
General music	10-year-old boy with Down syndrome	The Skoog, which allows the student to participate with his peers playing recorder but on a device that does not require the degree of fine motor control or memorization of fingerings 	Allows the student access to and participation in general music recorder curriculum

Range of Assistive Technology Devices

AT devices can range from simple items to sophisticated, multicomponent product systems. Applied science, engineering advances, and the digital revolution have resulted in literally thousands of items or devices that progress from low to high technology. According to Blackhurst and Lahm (2000), low-tech devices are considered mostly to be those items that either are inexpensive or have no cost and require little or no training to use. Furthermore, these items are considered easily obtainable. For example, Dycem® is a nonslip material that comes in a roll much like ordinary kitchen plastic wrap (see Figure 5.1). However, when used to stabilize an Orff instrument in music class for a student with a physical disability, Dycem becomes an AT item. Blair[1] used Legos® bricks in her music classroom to create a tactile melodic contour board for a student who was blind.

Medium-tech devices are those that often have some electronic or computerized components, are moderately priced, and require some training on the part of the user. For a student with significant reading difficulties, a text reader (i.e., text-to-speech) software program that reads aloud digital documents would be considered medium tech. Any word files, such as poems, lyrics, or class assignments, would then be accessible to the student who struggles with reading. Today, most text-to-speech software programs have natural-sounding voices that the user can choose along with the capability of converting written text into audio files (e.g., MP3 or WAV for CD players or iPods). Tablet apps could also be considered medium-tech AT devices since they are fairly inexpensive but require some training for the user.

At the upper end of the range of AT devices would be those designated as high tech. These devices are often expensive, possibly have more than one component, are electronically complex, and have a steep learning curve for the user. An example of a high-tech device would be an infrared switch coupled with a reflective sensing material and software that allows the user to control the cursor on the computer screen as he or she moves his or her

(a)    (b)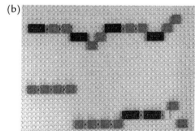

Figure 5.1. Dycem® and Legos® as assistive technology.

head when using music composition software. Most educators and AT specialists would agree that determination of what point along the continuum of low tech to high tech some devices fall is ill-defined. Nonetheless, features of simplicity or complexity certainly should be carefully evaluated periodically when considering whether or not a device matches the student's anticipated needs, activity requirements, and task demands, as well as barriers (Bryant & Bryant, 2003; King-Sears & Evmenova, 2007; Scherer & Craddock, 2002; Zabala, Bowser, & Korsten, 2005). Perhaps most important, the cost of the device cannot be a factor in the decision whether to provide a device or not because federal law mandates the right of students with disabilities to "a free, appropriate public education . . . that is provided at public expense, under public supervision and direction, and without charge" (IDEIA, 2004, Sec. 602(9)(A)).

Assistive Technology Categories

Beyond the designation on a continuum, AT device possibilities have been grouped into a host of types or categories. RehabTool, an information technology company, provides 11 categories of AT tools: communication aids, computer access aids, daily living aids, education and learning aids, environmental aids, ergonomic equipment, hearing and listening aids, prosthetics and orthotics, recreation and leisure aids, seating and positioning aids, and vision and reading aids.

In 2003, RehabTool's categorization of AT devices and equipment was revised to include the additional category of creativity aids for music (Thompson, Watts, Wojcik, & McCord, 2003). The new category of creativity aids was given the following definition: "products that allow participation or promote creative expression through the arts, such as music composition or improvisation, creation of visual arts (e.g., painting, drawing, sculpture), theatre and dance performance" (see Appendix A).

ASSISTIVE TECHNOLOGY SERVICES

Assistive technology encompasses not only devices but also services. Providing an AT device for a qualified student to use is only part of the school district's responsibility. The law, by mandating AT services, places importance on providing "essential supports" for implementing AT (Dell, Newton, & Petroff, 2008, p. 7). Here, too, the US federal law is conceptually broad in its definition of what constitutes a service. An assistive technology service is defined as "any service that directly assists a child with a disability in the selection, acquisition, or use of an assistive technology device" (IDEIA, 2004, Sec. 1401(2)).

Using the same examples of school settings and students with a specific disability as shown in Table 5.1, Table 5.2 shows what AT services might look like.

Table 5.2 EXAMPLES OF ASSISTIVE TECHNOLOGY (AT) SERVICES IN MUSIC EDUCATION SETTINGS

School Setting: Music Education Classrooms	Specific Student with a Disability	Assistive Technology Service	Educational Outcomes
General music	6-year-old boy with a moderate level of cerebral palsy that affects his fine motor grasping abilities	Service is provided when the occupational therapist collaborates with the general music teacher to "fit" or match the appropriate shaker for the student from several choices of shakers.	1. Allows the student access to and participation in the general education curriculum; fosters student independence in music activities. 2. Music educator becomes aware of possible AT solutions. 3. Music educator and occupational therapist may benefit from the collaborative process.
Band	13-year-old girl with low vision	AT specialist or special education educator teaches this student how to use the computer software program that magnifies electronic music notation.	1. Allows the student access to and participation in practicing her selected part for the spring concert. 2. Student gains a new skill in using a software program.
Choral music	17-year-old boy with learning disabilities (e.g., severe reading difficulties) in chorus	AT specialist or special education educator collaborates with choral music educator and produces lyric sheets printed using a symbol-based software program that allows for icons, photos, or graphics for decoding text.	1. Allows the student access to and participation in choral activities and concerts. 2. Choral music educator gains awareness of specialized instructional software. 3. Choral music educator gains individualized, print instructional materials to use with the student.

(continued)

Table 5.2 (CONTINUED)

School Setting: Music Education Classrooms	Specific Student with a Disability	Assistive Technology Service	Educational Outcomes
General music	11-year-old boy with Down syndrome	AT specialist consults with the general music educator on how to physically program the Skoog for recorder sounds and how to program the Skoog hot spots to respond to pitches displayed in the colored recorder notation the teacher displays for all students.	1. Allows the student access to and participation in creative music production while collaborating with typical peers. 2. General music educator gains knowledge and skills in using a specialized musical instrument. 3. General music educator and AT specialist may benefit from the collaborative process.

Range of Assistive Technology Services

AT services under the IDEIA (2004) include an array of possibilities depending on the needs of the student and, consequently, the needs of those intimately involved in the student's use of that AT device. First and foremost, there is a mandate allowing for an evaluation of the student's "needs, attributes, and tasks to be done . . . across multiple environments" (Bryant & Bryant, 2003,6). The law explicitly uses the wording "functional evaluation of the child's customary environment" (IDEIA, 2004, Sec. 602(1)(A)). This may include all those areas and places in which the child functions—the cafeteria, bus loading zone, music room, band room, library, school building hallways, home, community park, and so forth. Beyond the evaluation, the law allows for a host of other services, in particular:

Purchasing, leasing, or otherwise providing for the acquisition of assistive technology devices;

Selecting, designing, fitting, customizing, adapting, applying, maintaining, repairing, or replacing assistive technology devices;

Coordinating and using other therapies, interventions, or services with assistive technology devices, such as those associated with existing education and rehabilitation plans and programs;

Training or technical assistance for such child, or where appropriate the family of such child; and

Training or technical assistance for professionals (including individuals providing education and rehabilitation services), employers, or other individuals providing services to, employ or otherwise substantially involved in the major life functions of such child. (IDEIA, 2004, Sec. 602(1)(A))

Both the coordination of AT services and training or technical assistance, as mandated by law, have particular relevance and utmost importance for general music educators. No longer is it acceptable for students with disabilities to be "sent to music" without the general music educator's knowledge of the AT device's features, how the student should use the device once he or she arrives in the music room, and how the educator can integrate the AT device into music activities or assess criteria for success. Nor is it acceptable for the general music educator to "leave it up to the special education educator or special education aide" who accompanies the student to music class to be the only support person in the setting to know (1) the features of the AT device, (2) when and how the student should use the device, or (3) how to integrate the AT device into music activities.

It is the responsibility of the general music educator who serves a student with disabilities in his or her music class to recognize his or her own need for help and then ask for strategies that encourage learning. That support can take many forms; however, the first and most important step to take in seeking support is to ask to meet with the student's IEP team. Likewise, it is the responsibility of the special educator to support and collaborate with the general music educator. If you teach a student with a disability, you can inquire about student support through legal requirements associated with any one of the following laws: IDEIA (2004), Section 504 of the Rehabilitation Act of 1973, or the Americans with Disabilities Act of 1990. These three federal laws impact students' access to and participation in education programs and, ultimately, training and use of assistive technology devices and services. Each provides protection from discrimination for a student having a disability, with IDEIA having the "greatest impact on school age students" (Dell et al., 2008, p. 284).

Individuals with Disabilities Education Improvement Act's Individualized Education Program

In the United States, every school-age student (i.e., 3 to 21 years of age) with a diagnosed disability must have an IEP developed to meet that student's individual needs. At the time the IEP is being developed, one of the special issues beyond bus transportation or related services (e.g., speech therapy, physical therapy) to be considered is assistive technology devices and services "to maximize children with disabilities' access to and participation in the general education curriculum" (IDEIA, 2004, Sec. 1481(d) (4)(6)). To complicate matters, in this worthy undertaking of decision making on whether or not the student needs assistive technology, there is no definitive, concise legal definition that exists on how to undergo the AT consideration process.

Simply stated, the IDEIA (2004) mandates that IEP teams must "consider assistive technology" but does not mandate how to carry out this process. Since 1990, this has been a substantial problem facing many school districts across our nation. Yet, there have been encouraging developments surrounding AT consideration.

Some IEP teams have settled upon using resources that serve as a framework or model for decision making during the AT consideration process in the absence of any legal guidelines. See the sidebar "Resources on the Process of AT Consideration."

SIDEBAR: RESOURCES ON THE PROCESS OF ASSISTIVE TECHNOLOGY CONSIDERATION

Frameworks or models for considering assistive technology (AT) for students with disabilities in classroom settings are available from a variety of sources. The following represent a few models used by school-based teams:

- The SETT framework is an intuitive, practical tool for guiding Individualized Education Program (IEP) teams when considering four areas: Student, Environment, Tasks, and Tools. Questions that guide the team's decision-making process are outlined in each of the four areas of concern (Zabala, 2005). See http://www.joyzabala.com.
- Education Tech Points for Assistive Technology Planning is a well-documented model that is incorporated within six specific points that mirror each stage of the IEP process. See http://www.educationtechpoints.org
- The Wisconsin Assistive Technology Initiative (WATI) includes two products for use by IEP teams: an AT Consideration Guide and an AT Checklist. See http://www.wati.org.
- AT Coplanner is a model that incorporates four stages of the team process for AT decision making: Orientation, Assessment and Planning, Implementation and Evaluation, and Reporting. See Haines and Sanche (2000).
- The Consortium Model for Children and Youth with Disabilities and Special Health Care Needs addresses the AT consideration process for young children who have an Individualized Family Service

(continued)

Plan. This 10-step framework is comprehensive in that it includes the child and family needs, as well as identifying funding sources. See Long, Huang, Woodbridge, Woolverton, and Minkel (2003).

- The Matching Person and Technology (MPT) model emerged from rehabilitation research with consumers and consists of an assessment process involving interviews described as person-centered and for use in rehabilitation, education, and other settings. See Scherer (1997).

Additional resources are listed as follows:

- Quality Indicators for Assessment of Assistive Technology Needs is in the format of a process planner. See http://www.qiat.org.
- The National Assistive Technology in Education Network (NATE Network), located at the University of Buffalo, has a variety of resources on AT in the IEP, AT laws, AT consideration, and assessment of AT.
- Every US state has an AT access center. Contact the National Office of the Alliance for Technology Access Resource Centers to find your state's resource center at http://www.ataccess.org.
- The PACER Center, which is located in Minneapolis, Minneapolis, has a dedicated, national center to support families and educators in learning about the latest assistive technology. See the Simon Technology Center at http://www.PACER.org.
- The TAM: Technology and Media Division of the Council for Exceptional Children has several books and resources for assistive and instructional technology planning tools. More recently, they have published teacher guidebooks on integrating apps and mobile devices. See http://www.tamcec.org
- Abledata is a searchable database for information on tens of thousands of assistive technology devices/equipment. See http://www.Abledata.com.

The following are several models or frameworks for considering assistive technology: the SETT Framework, Education Tech Points for Assistive Technology Planning, the Wisconsin Assistive Technology Initiative (WAIT), and Matching Person & Technology (MPT). These strategies are tools to guide IEP teams in the decision-making and assessment process. In light of the relative newness of the AT consideration mandate, the majority of AT assessment tools have not been empirically studied with respect to their reliability or validity as assessment measures (Watts, O'Brian, & Wojcik, 2004). Therefore, IEP teams should proceed with caution when choosing a particular framework or model in the absence of any legal guidelines for AT consideration.

With this cautionary notion in mind, IEP teams still have another positive option to support their continued efforts. Research-based quality indicators have been developed for the AT consideration process that may help IEP teams when choosing a framework or model (QIAT Consortium, 2005). The QIAT Consortium is a group of AT consumers, professionals, and policy makers that have as a mission to provide AT resources for implementing AT in school settings. In general, the members of the consortium have agreed that the AT consideration process must be collaborative, based on the IEP and access to curricular and extracurricular activities, and data based; provide for exploration of a range of AT devices and services; and document the process along with corresponding rationales to support the team decisions. The need for "better instruments to measure assistive technology (AT) outcomes" (Watson & Smith, 2012) is critical. Therefore, IEP team members should evaluate features of more than one model or framework with these quality indicators in mind when choosing an AT consideration process to use with students and to document outcomes.

Assistive Music Technology

Many devices, including electronic devices and instruments, can also be classified as assistive technology. For example, students often play Orff instruments as they sit in front of them on the floor. Students in wheelchairs have difficulty accessing these devices if they are located on the floor. If the instruments are placed on commercially available adjustable rolling stands, they can be moved in close to the child in a wheelchair at a height that is appropriate for playing. There are many different types of stands available for holding all sorts of instruments; if the stand makes the instrument accessible to the student with a disability, it is assistive technology.

Electronic instruments such as the Skoog offer alternatives to traditional instruments that are more difficult to play. With sophisticated samples of acoustic instruments, these electronic versions can sound as good as a well-played acoustic instrument. My Breath My Music (http://www. mybreathmymusic.com/en/) makes a device that resembles a wind instrument and is operated by the breath, but head position determines pitch. The Soundbeam (http://www.soundbeam.co.uk/) is an electronic instrument that responds to movement through sensors and plays single notes, chords, or loops of prerecorded music. Movement can be small (e.g., the blink of an eye) or large (e.g., a wheelchair moving across a stage). Drum machines can be programmed to play endless sampled and synthesized sounds by tapping rubber pads. Many drum machines are so sensitive that students with very weak muscle control can easily create loud cymbal crashes with a light tap on a pad. Other students who tend to play with force or those who need a larger surface might have better success with one of the larger drum pads such as the Korg Wavedrum.

Devices such as the Korg Kaossilator operate with a touchpad embedded on the small handheld box. The device is used to compose grooves and record improvisations using the preprogrammed sounds, rhythm loops, and bass lines. There is now an app version of the Kaossilator that works very similarly to the actual device.

Mobile Technology: iPads and Tablets

Mobile technologies have added a new dimension to assistive technologies. The use of iPads in particular allows teachers to provide a wide range of musical engagement that can extend to the child's other classrooms and to the home environment. For students who need to use headphones or who need physical distance from classmates, iPads offer the opportunity to engage in musical activities with peers but possibly in a different part of the room. As competence and confidence with musical ideas and performance increase, students may be able to decrease distance and move closer to classmates.

The highly visual nature of iPads combined with their accessible touch-screen fosters a level of engagement that moves beyond novel to intriguing and exciting. For students who are aware of popular culture, there seems to be an intuitive understanding that this is the technology of their peers, something that makes it cool yet also relevant and authentic in its use. These added benefits allow for a seamless entry into music and musical engagement when one seeks to consider ways that universal design can be accomplished through assistive technologies.

Using iPads in the classroom is not without its challenges due to the plethora of apps that are available. When working with small groups of students—for example, in a self-contained classroom of six to eight students—the teacher may need to consider specific apps for each learner. Once a teacher learns about the curricular and social goals for his or her students, he or she can find a selection of musical apps to support these goals. There are numerous apps that use touch (gesture) and iconic representation to create or improvise music (e.g., Bebot, TocaBand, Soundrop, Pitch Painter, SoundBrush, Wavebot, and SoundGrid).

Blair (2012) found that students quickly transitioned to using iPads and would work for long periods of time with amazingly few outbursts provided that they could self-select which app to use (from the group of apps selected by the music teacher) and could move to a new app when ready. Students, when stressed or in need of a sensory break, were encouraged to move to an app like Bloom to relax or a whiteboard app to write numbers (or whatever may be appropriate) until ready to resume the musical activity. Apps like Seussband fostered some levels of tracking (an IEP goal for some of the students), and students who had mastered a level would begin to improvise or could anticipate the melodies (something not previously accomplished in other musical settings). MagicFingers was very useful for students who were nonverbal. They were motivated to make musical sounds or words to record their visual maps and replay them.

iPads allow learners with exceptionalities to work at their own musical level due to the mobile nature of the technology. Paradoxically, students also seemed motivated to work with or near others and showed an increased level of joint attention. Students would move across the room to see what their peers were doing or would willingly play a musical game with a teacher or paraprofessional. MadPad was a favorite app for several students, and because it required videotaping short sound bites, students needed the assistance of others; thus, increased communication, joint attention, and cooperation resulted.

With the growth of educational apps, assistive technology has expanded exponentially for individuals with disabilities. Devices that previously were very expensive and limited in capabilities can be somewhat duplicated in an app form, which then can be customizable to an individual student. For example, Tap to Talk is a very basic communication device that enables the student to tap icons or words that speak. Another app, Join Me, allows the user to see a Smartboard screen on a tablet computer. This is valuable for students with vision loss who need the flexibility of increasing the size of the Smartboard up close.

Educators can generate visual supports easily using apps such as See. Touch.Learn or Choiceworks by Bee Visual that will allow distracted students, using touch technology, to understand in a concrete, visual form the sequence of music activities for that class session. Many students on the autism spectrum and those with sensory integration disabilities struggle with feeling overwhelmed by the level of sound in a typical music room. Imagine a student with sensory issues playing an instrument like a triangle (an instrument whose volume is difficult to control and that can be irritating to those who are sensitive to the high-pitched, ringing sound). If the triangle is an app the student can play while wearing noise-cancelling headphones and the student can control the volume, he or she can experience the instrument in a way that is more comfortable. Using a wireless Bluetooth speaker placed away from the student but close to typical students allows the student with sensory integration issues to participate with the class. Almost every imaginable instrument, including many instruments unique to certain countries, now are sampled and available on some sort of app. Even Japanese tuned Taiko drums can be played via many apps!

SUMMARY

- The US federal mandate to provide assistive technology devices and services is a legal imperative for school districts and must be considered for every student who has an IEP.
- Definitions of AT devices and services are designated in the Individuals with Disabilities Education Improvement Act of 2004. This chapter gives examples of AT devices and AT services in music education settings.
- In general, AT may range on a continuum from simple (low-tech) items to sophisticated, multicomponent (high-tech) devices. Also, devices can be grouped into a host of categories (see Appendix A).
- Because AT must be considered for every student with an IEP and AT "consideration" is not clearly defined in the law, school teams should follow research-based quality indicators when undergoing the consideration process. Fortunately, there are a number of readily available resources to support AT "consideration."

APPENDIX A

Assistive Technology Categories

Adapted from http://www.rehabtool.com
(Thompson, Watts, McCord, & Wojcik, 2003)

Communication: Speech/Language Aids

- Definition: Products and equipment designed to help persons with speech/language disabilities.
- Examples: Electronic or computerized communication devices with speech synthesizers, note-taking devices, communication boards, DynaVoxT10, Go Talk, BigMAC Communication Device, CheapTalk 8/communicator, Tech-Four, Step-by-Step Communicator.

Communication: Writing and Spelling Aids

- Definition: (a) Products that assist people to physically write using a pen/pencil/chalk/marker, a computer, or a drawing slate; other input devices to make writing production easier, more legible, or larger or to facilitate change from print to cursive. (b) Products that assist people to compose written language (grammar, punctuation, organization) along with the editing or revision process, and in spelling (visual patterning, word sorting, word families, proofreading, rule-based strategies, sound–letter correspondence, base forms, suffixes/prefixes).
- Examples: (a) Lined paper, slant boards, pencil grips, large pencils, grooved fiber writing cards, color-coded lines, Five Finger Typist software, wipe-off markers. (b) Talking word processor, voice recognition software, spellcheckers, word prediction, Dana, Braille text editor, outlining/brainstorming software, Internet encyclopedias and dictionaries, Franklin Homework Helper, Word Maker software.

Computer Access Aids

- Definition: Hardware and software products that enable persons with disabilities to access, interact with, and use computers at home, work, or school.
- Examples: Alternative and adaptive keyboards, expanded keyboards, head-operated pointing devices, eye-gaze pointing devices, voice recognition/voice command software, Intellikeys keyboard, Kinesis keyboard, head pointer, mouthstick, Dragon Naturally Speaking software, Maltron (a one-handed keyboard).

Creativity Aids

- Definition: Products that allow participation or promote creative expression through the arts, such as music composition or improvisation, creation of visual arts (e.g., painting, drawing, sculpture), and theater and dance performance.
- Examples: Music notation and sequencing software, electronic instruments (e.g., Skoog, percussion synthesizer), musical shaker egg with Velcro, adaptive paintbrush holders, computer-based drawing software, touch technology (e.g., iPad).

Daily Living Aids

- Definition: Devices that assist persons with disabilities in daily living activities such as dressing, personal hygiene, bathing, home maintenance, cooking, and eating.
- Examples: Clothing and dressing aids (zipper pull, button aid), eating and cooking aids (large-handled utensils, utensil grips, scoop plates, plate guards), home safety/maintenance aids (alerting devices, easy grips), toileting and bathing aids.

Educational Aids: Math

- Definition: Products that assist people to learn math facts, follow sequential procedures and directions with multiple steps, take measurements, use computational symbols, count money and make change, do written calculations, conceptualize time, and balance a checkbook.
- Examples: Handheld calculators, talking calculators, on-screen calculators, big number buttons and large keypads, textbooks on CD-ROM, abacus, Braille protractor, tactile clock face, number line, math skills game, math software; also see "Reading" category.

Educational Aids: Reading

- Definition: (a) Products that help people in the physical act of reading with assistance in tasks such as visual tracking, focusing, left-to-right orientation, top-to-bottom orientation, page turning, and book holding. (b) Products that assist people in the cognitive act associated with reading readiness/early literacy, decoding (word recognition in terms of sight words, phonics, fluency), understanding meaning (vocabulary, listening and text comprehension), and study skills (dictionary use; references such as charts, maps, glossaries; outlining; note taking).
- Examples: (a) Reading ruler, tactile letters, language flash cards in Braille, reading pen, multimedia books, screen readers, books on tape, variable-speed-control tape recorders, screen magnification or enlargement software, head pointer, highlighters, switch with eBooks, slant board, Dycem, book holder, electronic page turner. (b) Internet-based dictionaries and books, phonics software, multimedia books, screen readers, books on tape, variable-speed-control tape recorders, screen magnification or

enlargement software, personal dictionaries, Inspiration/Kidspiration software, Post-it notes, websites with differentiated reading levels.

Environmental Aids

- Definition: Adaptations that remove or reduce physical barriers for individuals with disabilities; environmental adaptations that involve building construction, engineering, and architecture; also includes environmental controls and switches that can control an entire living environment
- Examples: Environmental Control Units (ECUs) that control various appliances, lights, telephones, and security systems, as well as worksite/school/home design or modification for accessibility such as ramps and specially designed bath areas.

Ergonomic Equipment and Aids

- Definition: Equipment or devices designed to reduce the likelihood of repetitive stress injuries often associated with work-related situations.
- Examples: Adjustable workstations, adapted furniture, modified seating and lighting, arm/wrist supports, and back supports.

Hearing and Listening Aids

- Definition: Products designed to assist people who are deaf and hard of hearing access environmental sounds.
- Examples: Sound Field Amplification FM system, infrared/personal amplification systems, TV amplifiers, visual signaling and alerting systems such as a flashing alarm clock, Telecommunication Devices for the Deaf (TDD) and Teletype Devices (TTY).

Memory and Organization Aids

- Definition: Products that assist people in cognitive skills associated with generating and organizing thoughts (e.g., note taking, gathering facts, categorizing, identifying patterns, sorting necessary and unnecessary information), as well as memory recall (facts, sequence of tasks or events/schedules).

- Examples: Smartphones with note features; Post-it notes; wipe-on/off calendar board; memo pad; To-Do-List, DayRunner, or Franklin Planner; Internet-based services for cell phones, pagers, or email; Inspiration Software.

Mobility, Positioning, and Transportation Aids

- Definition: Products that help people with physical disabilities move around their environments; positioning products that provide greater body stability, maintain upright posture and head/trunk support, and reduce pressure to the skin.
- Examples: Canes, cane accessories, crutches, walkers, walker accessories, adapted and modular seating, adaptive musical instrument mount, cushions and wedges, standing tables, bolster chairs, corner chairs, seat lifts, therapeutic seats, scooters and wheelchairs; also vehicle conversions such as customized cars and vans and adaptive driving controls; wheelchair clip for paddle drum.

Prosthetics and Orthotics

- Definition: Replacement, substitution, or augmentation of missing or malfunctioning body parts with artificial limbs or other orthotic aids.
- Examples: Splints, braces, helmets, artificial limbs.

Recreation and Leisure Aids

- Definition: Products that help persons with disabilities to participate in sports, social, and cultural events.
- Examples: Adapted toys, modified sports equipment, audio description for movies, adaptive controls for video games, adaptive fishing rods, cuffs for grasping paddles or racquets, volley beep ball, seating systems for boats, adapted soprano recorder, guitar barre (for chords).

Vision Aids

- Definition: Products designed to assist people with low vision and blindness access visual information from their environment.

- Examples: Auditory and speech output devices, reading machines, scanning/document reading systems, talking equipment (clocks/watches, calculators, etc.), Braille transcription and translation devices, Braille music transcription software, screen magnifier/enlarger, large-button phones, speaker phones, large-print books, taped/audio books.

NOTE

1. See http://musicalmaps.weebly.com/musical-maps-and-assistive-technology.html

REFERENCES

Blackhurst, A. E. (1997). Perspectives on technology in special education. *Teaching Exceptional Children, 29*(5), 41–48.

Blackhurst, A. E., & Lahm, E. A. (2000). Foundations of technology and exceptionality. In J. Lindsey (Ed.), *Technology and exceptional individuals* (3rd ed., pp. 3–45). Austin, TX: Pro-Ed.

Blair, D. V. (2012). *iPads in music education.* Presentation at eCornucopia 2012: Creativity Through Technology Conference. Rochester, MI: Oakland University, June 9, 2012.

Bryant, D. P., & Bryant, B. (2003). *Assistive technology for people with disabilities.* Boston, MA: Allyn and Bacon.

Dell, A. G., Newton, D. A., & Petroff, J. G. (2008). *Assistive technology in the classroom: Enhancing the school experiences of students with disabilities.* Upper Saddle River, NJ: Pearson.

Edyburn, D. L. (2000). Assistive technology and mild disabilities. *Focus on Exceptional Children, 32*(9), 1–24.

Edyburn, D. L. (2013). Critical issues in advancing the special education technology evidence base. *Exceptional Children, 80*(1), 7–24.

Haines, L., & Sanche, B. (2000). Assessment models and software support for assistive technology teams. *Diagnostique, 25*(4), 291–306.

Individuals with Disabilities Education Improvement Act of 2004, 20 U.S.C. ss 1401, 1481.

King-Sears, M. E., & Evmenova, A. S. (2007). Premises, principles, and processes for integrating TECHnology into instruction. *Teaching Exceptional Children, 40*(1), 6–14.

Long, T., Huang, L., Woodbridge, M., Woolverton, M., & Minkel, J. (2003). Integrating assistive technology into an outcome-driven model of service delivery. *Infants and Young Children, 16*(4), 272–283.

QIAT Consortium. (2005). *Quality Indicators for Assistive Technology Services: Research-based update.* Retrieved from http://www.qiat.org

Scherer, M. J. (1997). *Matching assistive technology and child: A process and series of assessments for selecting and evaluating technologies used by infants & young children.* Webster, NY: Institute for Matching Person & Technology.

Scherer, M. J., & Craddock, G. (2002). Matching person & technology (MPT) assessment process. *Technology and Disability, 14*, 125–131.

Thompson, J. R., Watts, E. H., Wojcik, B. W., & McCord, K. (2003). *The AT matching game.* Unpublished manuscript, Illinois State University at Normal.

Watson, A. H., & Smith, R. O. (2012). Comparison of two school-based assistive technology outcome instruments. *Technology and Disability, 24,* 83–92.

Watts, E. H., O'Brian, M., & Wojcik, B. W. (2004). Four models of assistive technology consideration: How do they compare to recommended educational assessment practices? *Journal of Special Education Technology, 19*(1), 43–56.

Zabala, J. (2005). Ready, SETT, Go! Getting started with the SETT framework. *Closing the Gap, 23*(6), 12–13.

Zabala, J., Bowser, G., & Jorsten, J. (2005). SETT and ReSETT: Concepts for AT implementation. *Closing the Gap, 23* (5), 1–4.

CHAPTER 6

SoundOUT

Examining the Role of Accessible Interactive Music Technologies within Inclusive Music Ensembles in Cork City, Ireland

GRAINNE McHALE

Inclusive practice is increasingly becoming a prominent educational, social, and cultural issue internationally. In Ireland, there is a growing need to develop a more inclusive music education system that accommodates the diversity of needs in music classrooms today. In this chapter, I explore the inclusive principles and context-specific practices of SoundOUT—a community-based organization that provides inclusive music-making and learning opportunities for approximately 400 young people with and without disabilities in Cork City, Ireland. It particularly focuses on SoundOUT's inclusive music ensemble initiative. The inclusive music ensembles integrate a range of accessible interactive music technologies to facilitate active music making and learning for young people with profound physical disabilities within school and community settings. The term *accessible interactive music technology* in this chapter refers to electronic music devices, such as movement sensors, switch technologies, and wind synthesizers, that facilitate active music making for people with limited mobility. Examining the role of accessible interactive music technology in facilitating meaningful music-making and learning opportunities within inclusive settings is a complex issue as there are significant historical, social, political, and cultural factors to be taken into consideration. This topic within music education research is largely unexplored in Ireland.

It deserves more attention, particularly as issues of inclusion and techno-logical advancements are becoming more integral to societal development.

To contextualize the SoundOUT principles and practices, I will first outline recent and significant research and policy developments that have influenced the emergence of inclusive music education practice in Ireland. I then introduce a recent qualitative study that documented the experiences and perceptions of young people with and without profound physical disabilities using a range of accessible interactive music technologies within inclusive settings. These experiences and perceptions aim to provide evidence whether the use of accessible interactive music technology within inclusive settings can enhance access to meaningful music making and learning. The young people participating in this study are involved in two of the SoundOUT inclusive music ensembles in Cork City. One of the ensembles is school based and involves people aged between 14 and 18 years, four who have profound physical disabilities and four who do not. Although this ensemble takes place within a school context, it is a voluntary, extracurricular activity. The second ensemble operates within a community context and involves one 21-year-old with profound physical disabilities and six people between the ages of 18 and 26 years. Adopting an ethnographic approach, I engaged as a participant observer within each ensemble over a period of 24 weeks. I also conducted a range of semiformal interviews and focus groups with ensemble members, ensemble directors, classroom teachers, and family members.

Music educator and researcher Dillon (2006, p. 273) suggests that it is necessary to take three factors into consideration to create and document a music program that facilitates meaningful music making:

1. Attention to the distinctiveness of the context
2. Attention to the modes of creative engagement
3. Examination of whether these clearly lead to personal, social, and cultural meaning for the participants

These three factors have significantly influenced the development of SoundOUT and also how I have approached the data collection for this study. These three factors emerge as themes throughout the chapter; however, I primarily focus on the music-making experiences of SoundOUT ensemble participants. I present these experiences and perceptions regarding the use of accessible interactive music technology within inclusive music ensembles from the perspectives of the participants themselves and their families, music tutors, and classroom teachers. These preliminary findings are organized within these key areas—personal, social, and musical development—as well as the challenges within these ensembles.[1]

This study aims to use these experiences and perceptions to understand the complex relationships among disability, music, technology, and inclusion within the context of the individual, ensemble, family, and wider community. To do this, I suggest an interdisciplinary theoretical framework that is underpinned by a social constructivist perspective. Social constructivism is a sociological theory of knowledge that examines how social phenomena are constructed in social contexts. John Dewey could be considered the philosophical founder of social constructivism through his work on democracy and learning (Dewey, 1910, 1916). Vygotsky (1978) is considered the founder of social constructivism and is one of the most influential theorists within the field. Within a music education context, a social constructivist theory assumes that music students are not given knowledge but construct their own meaning and values from their musical and social interactions with their peers and within their wider social and cultural contexts (Blair & Wiggins, 2010, p. 21). This is a useful perspective to examine the use of accessible interactive music technology within inclusive music settings as the experiences and perceptions of such use are continuously evolving and responding to social interactions, within both the ensemble and the wider community. This framework also draws upon theoretical insights and contexts from the fields of disability studies, inclusive education, sociology of music education, and cultural studies.

INCLUSIVE EDUCATION: AN OVERVIEW OF IRISH AND INTERNATIONAL POLICIES

The educational provision for people with disabilities in Ireland has evolved significantly over the past two decades (Griffin & Shevlin, 2007). Governmental policies and reports have focused on examining the educational provision for students with special educational needs with a view toward moving from segregated education to more inclusive models of education. Such policies and reports have been influenced by international demands for a more equitable and inclusive education system that celebrates and accommodates diversity (R. Rose, Shevlin, Winter, & O'Raw, 2010, p. 359). These policies and reports have resulted in the development of inclusive models for education where students with disabilities are increasingly being included in mainstream education provision.

The most recent policy developments in Ireland have been the Education for Persons with Special Educational Needs Act (EPSEN; 2004) and the Disability Act (2005; Oireachtas, 2004, 2005). These acts advocate for a more inclusive model of education that supports rights for people with disabilities and their parents (Griffin & Shevlin, 2007).[2] There is a disparity between practice and policy for inclusive education in Ireland. Unfortunately, many of the provisions outlined in the EPSEN Act were to be introduced over a five-year period (2005–2010; Oireachtas, 2004). These provisions were not introduced and there is no timetable for renewed implementation. The lack of action on the implementation of these policies is impacting negatively on the educational rights of children with disabilities in Ireland (Logan, 2006). There are limitations to students' access to educational services. Evidence suggests that children with disabilities have been compromised in accessing appropriate participation within inclusive environments due to the lack of provision and support (Kilkelly et al., 2005; Logan, 2006).

Inclusive education has been described as a global agenda (Pijl, Meijer, & Hegarty, 1997). In the European Union, all countries now have legislation promoting inclusive practice within educational settings (R. Rose et al., 2010, p. 3). UNESCO addressed the educational provision for students with special educational needs, along with the issue of inclusion, for the first time during a conference in Spain in 1994, which resulted in the Salamanca Statement (UNESCO, 1994). This conference provided a "platform to affirm the principle of education for all and to discuss the practice of ensuring that children and young people with special educational needs are included in all such initiatives and take their rightful place in a learning society" (Jellison, 2012, p. 65). In 2009, UNESCO developed guidelines on inclusion in education; these guidelines refer to the rights of a diverse group of children, including children with special educational needs, to inclusion in education—encompassing also education in the arts:

> Inclusion is seen as a process addressing and responding to the diversity of needs of all children, youth and adults through increasing participation in learning, cultures and communities, and reducing and eliminating exclusion within and from education. It involves changes and modifications in content, approaches, structures and strategies with a common vision that covers all children of the appropriate age range and a conviction that is the responsibility of the regular system to educate all children. (UNESCO, 2009, pp. 8–9)

These developments have had significant influence on the development of inclusive education policy, research, and practice in Ireland.

Inclusive Music Education

Inclusive music education is a rapidly developing area of music education research internationally. Inclusive music education refers to students with and without disabilities making and learning music together where the experiences are meaningful (Jellison, 2012, p. 66).

In the development of the SoundOUT inclusive music ensembles, I have drawn insights from the guidelines presented by Jellison (2012) for the development of inclusive music programs. The musical lives of children with special educational needs (SENs) can be improved when:

1. A meaningful music curriculum is designed to be flexible and accessible, instructional practices are effective, individual adaptations are only as "specialized" as they need to be, and student progress is assessed.
2. Culturally normative music experiences and participation in socially valued roles and activities with typical children are part of the routine of daily life.
3. Self-determination is fostered in music environments where children feel safe and secure and where they experience autonomy, demonstrate competence, and make decisions about music, music making, and other music activities in their lives.
4. Social interactions with same-age "typical" peers in inclusive music environments are frequent, positive, and reciprocal.
5. The design implementation and evaluation of an individualized music education program involves collaboration and coordinated effort among parents, guardians, professionals, other significant individuals in the child's life, and the child (when appropriate). (p. 67)

Adamek and Darrow (2005) examine effective adaptations and strategies for the inclusion of children with SENs in music education, with the aim of creating a successful and inclusive learning environment for all students. In a recent study, Adamek and Darrow (2012) critically analyzed and compared the perceived benefits and challenges of inclusive music education with those of segregated education. Among the perceived benefits of inclusive music classes was peer interaction, which could result in all students accessing reciprocal positive models for behavior and musical skills. Challenges of inclusive environments included insufficient and inconsistent expertise of general music teachers within inclusive environments. The availability of sufficient time to adapt materials for diverse learners was recognized as a significant challenge in the development of inclusive music classrooms. The perceived benefits of segregated music classes included the availability of resources such as assistive technology and augmented communication devices to adapt materials for a music class. Generally, special music classes have fewer students, enabling students to gain more "one to one" attention from the music educator and to have opportunities to take leadership roles within the music class. The perceived challenges of such segregated learning environments include the lack of social interaction with "typically developing" peers (Adamek & Darrow, 2012, p. 89).

Universal Design for Learning

Universal design for learning is a concept that deeply resonates with inclusive music education research and practice. Universal design is a strategy that promotes flexible teaching strategies that enable universal access to meaningful music learning for various abilities and disabilities within the one classroom (Jellison, 2012, p. 69). D. H. Rose and Meyer (2006, p. ix) have developed an in-depth framework that has three principles of universal design for learning:

1. To provide multiple and flexible methods of presentation that give learners various ways to acquire information and knowledge.
2. To provide multiple, flexible methods of expression and apprenticeship that offer students alternatives for demonstrating what they know.
3. To provide multiple, flexible options for engagement to help learners get interested, be challenged, and stay motivated.

Jellison (2012, p. 70) suggests that when these principles of universal design for learning are applied within inclusive music education settings:

1. Students with and without disabilities are engaged in meaningful music making and learning.
2. There are multiple entry points for students to access and participate in music education activities.
3. Appropriate learning goals are present for all students with and without disabilities.
4. The musical development of all students is assessed.

The application of the principles of universal design within an inclusive music education setting, involving young people with and without SENs, avoids the overspecialization of individual adaptations or exclusion of students with SENs from classroom activities (Jellison, 2012, p. 70). Universal design for learning operates on the premise that all learners with varying abilities and disabilities can be accommodated without exclusion and without compromising academic standards (Bowe, 2000; D. H. Rose & Meyer, 2006).

MUSIC EDUCATION IN CORK CITY, IRELAND

There are significant inequalities within music education provision in Ireland (Grant, 2006). To address issues of exclusion, a range of music education reports in Ireland have advocated for locally provisioned high-quality music education and performance opportunities for young people throughout the country who are marginalized from mainstream music education.[3]

In 2009, a feasibility study was commissioned to examine how a publicly funded system of local music education services could be provided in Ireland. After a series of pilot studies and reports, a collaborative partnership model was deemed "a workable and replicable framework for development of music education services . . . on a wider scale throughout Ireland" (Music Network, independent evaluation, 2009[4]). Upon receiving 7 million euro of philanthropic funding from U2 and the Ireland Funds, Music Generation was established to roll out the recommendations of these reports on a phased basis between 2010 and 2015 throughout Ireland. Music Generation is one of the most significant developments for music education in Ireland over the past decade. The development of local music services involving instrumental and vocal instruction is being facilitated through music education partnerships (MEPs) throughout the country. Music Generation funding is allocated to each MEP on a competitive basis. Cork's MEP received funding in 2011 to target the city's most educationally disadvantaged areas.

Music Generation Cork City supports a model for inclusive music education, involving young people with and without disabilities making and learning music within the same educational setting in Ireland. As a key partner of Music Generation Cork City, SoundOUT is bringing the inclusive agenda to the core of music education development in Cork City. There is a specific emphasis on accessible interactive music technology as a tool for inclusion in music instruction and performance, along with music tutors throughout the city engaging in continuing professional development in the area of inclusive music education. Inclusive music education principles and practices are now being introduced into many other MEPs throughout the country through collaborative and consultative practices with SoundOUT. In 2013, the Department of Education and Skills has committed to ongoing financial support for this inclusive music initiative.

SoundOUT

SoundOUT was established in 2011 to address a gap in the provision of inclusive music-making and performance opportunities for young people in Cork City, Ireland. SoundOUT offers a range of instruction and music ensemble projects within inclusive environments. There are currently 400 young people with and without disabilities engaging in music instruction and ensemble activities provided by SoundOUT throughout Cork City. A core objective of SoundOUT is to provide progressive opportunities for musical and social development of all students. Inclusive music education discourse, where inclusion, adaption, and universal design are paramount, has significantly influenced the inclusive principles and practices of SoundOUT. All music instruction and ensemble activities integrate a range of accessible interactive music technologies where appropriate. This chapter focuses on exploring the experiences and perceptions of using accessible interactive music technology within two diverse inclusive music ensembles.

A range of accessible interactive music technologies including Soundbeam, the Magic Flute, and the iPad is being integrated into all SoundOUT inclusive music ensemble activities. All of these devices enable active music making and performance through limited movement. The matching of each technological device to a student depends on a range of factors including movement patterns, interest, motivation, and musical taste.

Soundbeam

Soundbeam music technology refers to a device that is composed of movement sensors and switch interfaces. It combines sonar technology and MIDI (Musical Instrument Digital Interface) to convert gestures, through movement in air and the pressing of switches, into digitally generated music and sound (http://www.soundbeam.co.uk). Soundbeam was developed in the 1980s to enable contemporary dancers to experience a unique, real-time interaction between movement and sound within live performances. Today, Soundbeam is mainly used to enable people with limited movement to access music making and performance within educational and therapeutic settings (Swingler & Brockhouse, 2009). The development of the movement sensors was inspired by the kinetic approach to musical performance, previously demonstrated by the Thereminox (or often referred to as the Theremin)—an electronic musical instrument that was played without the need for physical touch. Interruption of and movement within these sensors translate information about the distance, speed, and direction into a digital language, otherwise known as MIDI. These MIDI signals facilitate the triggering of digital sounds and samples within a range of digital musical instruments. Soundbeam also encompasses various ranging controls, which enables the invisible beam to be compressed to just a few centimeters and expanded up to six meters, accommodating the movements the performer wishes or is capable of playing (Swingler & Brockhouse, 2009). It can be "tuned" to respond to a range of movements, from the tiniest gestures as small as the blink of an eye to the most sweeping movements, resulting in a broad range of mobility being accommodated. Since its initial development,

Soundbeam has evolved alongside technological advancements, particularly in the area of MIDI controller data, to accommodate the varying needs, interests, and ambitions of its users. Soundbeam 5, the latest version of the Soundbeam system, enables players to trigger notes, chords, and samples in sequence. It also allows players to use effects such as vibrato, pitchbend, chorus, panning, phasing, portamento, and reverb in real time. The system supports ensemble opportunities as it is possible to have four movement sensors and eight switches playing melodies and harmonies simultaneously. The use of Soundbeam technology within contemporary dance practice was highly acclaimed; however, it was soon surpassed by its inclusive potential within educational and therapeutic practices. Most research relating to the use of Soundbeam technology has taken place within therapeutic settings (Ellis, 1997; Magee & Burland, 2008; Swingler & Brockhouse, 2009), as well as within educational settings (McCord & Rogers, 2010).

Soundbeam is the main piece of accessible interactive music technology used within the SoundOUT inclusive music ensemble. It is integrated into each ensemble as a musical instrument alongside other digital and acoustic instruments.

The Magic Flute

The Magic Flute is a wind-controlled MIDI instrument that is designed to provide access to music performance without the use of hands. Placed on a tripod, the Magic Flute can be easily tilted up by the musician's head movements—overcoming the physical challenges of musical performance. The Magic Flute can be used as a stand-alone system or connected to a digital sampler via MIDI connection. The Magic Flute is fully controllable by the player as all the controls are accessible by a "sip/blow" trigger method. Unfortunately, the Magic Flute is only accessible to individuals who are able to blow. Many SoundOUT students with cerebral palsy are not able to access the Magic Flute.

The Magic Flute was designed and produced by Ruud Van Der Wel of My Breath My Music (Netherlands) and Brian Dillon of Click to Go (Ireland). The Magic Flute is used within the SoundOUT secondary school inclusive music ensemble.

iPad Music Applications

iPad technology is used within both the community and the school ensemble as a compositional tool, primarily using the application

Garageband, which is used to record and arrange compositions. In the school ensemble, the iPad is used for recording, composing, and arranging; it is also a music performance tool in its own right. Live triggering of the Garageband sampler, keyboard, strings, and guitar is mainly used. The Garageband application is very flexible as chords, melodies, and sounds are easy to access and adapt to suit the particular song and the specific movement patterns of the player. The application iKaosilisator, a digital version of the kaos pad, is frequently used with the school ensemble. This application uses colors to control a range of sounds and beats. The AirVox application is also used for improvisation activities. This is very effective as the player's hand movements are represented visually and sonically in real time. iPad technology is a very effective performance and learning tool as most students have access to iPads, enabling practice in between weekly ensemble sessions.

Community-Based Ensemble

The SoundOUT community-based ensemble comes together every Tuesday in Togher Community Centre, Cork City. There are seven ensemble members; six of the members are involved in a community-based music education initiative where they are all learning new musical instruments, including drums, keyboards, guitar, and bass. The ensemble members range in age from 18 to 26 years. One member, Kevin, has profound cerebral palsy. Kevin has extremely limited movement and no vocal speech. He uses Soundbeam technology to make music with the ensemble. He mainly communicates with his eyes—he looks up for yes and down for no. He also uses a range of assistive technologies to communicate, for example, Eye Gaze software. Eye Gaze enables him to use his eyes to trigger digital voices on a mobile computer system called Dynavox. Kevin uses this Eye Gaze software to write music lyrics. He also works with his personal assistant to create lyrics if the Eye Gaze software becomes too tiring. Kevin composes his music using the iPad application Garageband. Kevin needs support to use this application as it is not compatible with Eye Gaze. Once the music is composed with Garageband, the specific chords and melodies are digitally input into the Soundbeam system and subsequently triggered by Kevin's minimal movements. Kevin primarily uses the beam to improvise using various scales. He uses three head switches to play chords and short melodies that he has composed. The Magic Flute is somewhat more flexible as it can be controlled independently; however, it is not suitable for Kevin as it is only accessible by "blowing" into it. This is not possible for many students with profound cerebral palsy. Kevin receives individual instruction on using

Soundbeam technology, music theory classes, and composition workshops on a weekly basis before the ensemble meets.

A local music tutor, Gareth, teaches these classes. Gareth also facilitates ensemble activities when necessary; however, the group usually works informally and somewhat independently, similar to a band rehearsal situation. This ensemble has released its own single and is currently working on its new album. Ensemble members regularly perform at various civic events throughout the city, as well as gigs at local nightclubs. The ensemble has played for the Irish president at Aras an Uachtarain and ranked as a "runner up" in the international Soundbeam competition in 2013.

Secondary School Ensemble

Inspired by the success of the community-based ensemble, SoundOUT developed a school-based ensemble that brings four students from a secondary school together with four students from a local special educational needs school. This group meets every Wednesday to create and perform original music. All of the ensemble activities are extracurricular. As with the community ensemble, Soundbeam technology is used within all ensemble activities. The Magic Flute and iPad technology are also included as musical instruments in the ensemble. The iPad technology in the community ensemble is mainly used as a composition tool. In the secondary school ensemble, Soundbeam is played by Jack, a teenager with profound muscular dystrophy. He has vocal speech and limited movement in one hand. Jack uses his hand to improvise in the beam, mainly using a pentatonic scale. Jack also combines iPad technology to play chords using GarageBand in real time. Deirdre, a teenager with spina bifida, uses the Magic Flute. Deirdre is a wheelchair user with some movement in her hands. She also plays keyboard using a color-coordinated system to recognize chords. Conor, a young man with cerebral palsy, started to use iPad technology to play drums; however, he preferred to play the acoustic drumset. This drum kit is adapted to his movement patterns. Sara, a young girl with cerebral palsy, used Soundbeam technology and the Magic Flute for approximately four years and became a very prolific player. However, during these ensemble activities, she typically chose to sing. There are three music tutors facilitating this ensemble. Two of these tutors are comfortable with supporting the young people with disabilities using the interactive music technology in activities. Ensemble activities are structured to place peer learning and collaboration at the core of all ensemble activities. One special needs assistant and one classroom teacher from the special educational needs school attend weekly ensemble gatherings There have been a range of performances in both the mainstream secondary school and the special educational needs school since the ensemble's inception in September 2012.

The community ensemble began on a voluntary basis. Today, both ensembles have secured funding from Music Generation Cork City to continue until 2015 (http://www.musicgenerationcorkcity.com). The Department of Education and Skills in Ireland has committed to ongoing funding for this work beyond 2015.

RESEARCH INQUIRY

A qualitative study that adopts ethnographic research methods was deemed the most appropriate to capture the experiences and perceptions of using accessible interactive music technology within inclusive music ensembles in Cork City. Unique teaching and learning find value within qualitative research methodology as the designs allow or demand extra attention to physical, temporal, historical, social, political, economic, and aesthetic contexts (Bresler & Stake, 2006).

The aim of this study was to examine whether accessible interactive music technology can provide access to meaningful music making within inclusive ensemble settings in Cork City. Research methods include participant observation, video recording, field notes, semiformal interviews, and focus groups with ensemble members, music tutors, classroom teachers, and families. I engaged as a participant observer in both these ensembles as lead tutor for the first 12 weeks of the program. Participant observation is "a field strategy that simultaneously combines document analysis, interviewing of respondents and informants, direct participation and observation and introspection" (Denzin, 1989, pp, 157–158).

After the initial 12 weeks, local music tutors were provided with professional development training on the use of accessible interactive music technology within inclusive music settings to continue the work. The following 12 weeks I continued to attend the weekly ensemble gatherings, again as a participant observer; however, I was no longer the ensemble leader. Informal interviews took place in May 2013 with six secondary school ensemble members (Deirdre, Sara, Conor, Jack, Dawn, and Derek), three community ensemble members (Kevin, David, and Hannah), one family member (Ann, Kevin's mother), one tutor (Gareth), one classroom teacher (Meave), one principal (Tara), and one person-centered planner for a local adult service center for people with physical disabilities in Cork City (Mary). These multiple sources of data were triangulated to validate outcomes (Yin, 2003).

Various challenges emerged during this data collection period. As some of the ensemble members had limited or no speech, it was necessary to integrate alternative and augmented communication systems within semi-formal interviews. I also emailed questions to ensemble members so they could answer at their own pace using the assistive technology with which they were comfortable. These digitally answered questions were later supported by a video interview with ensemble members. This video interview enabled the student with limited speech to also use nonverbal communication to express their experiences and perceptions.

SoundOUT Experiences and Perceptions

The experiences and perceptions of using accessible music technology within inclusive music ensembles are discussed using five themes: personal development, social development, musical development, advocacy, and challenges.

Personal Development

Research respondents referred to the involvement in the inclusive music ensemble as providing opportunities for self-expression and self-empowerment, leading to an increase in confidence both inside and outside of ensemble settings. All participants shared that involvement in the ensemble, through the use of accessible interactive music technology, provided opportunities for identity development as an individual and within the context of the ensemble, family, and wider community.

Deirdre, a participant in the school ensemble, noted that the inclusive music ensemble provided a platform for her to express herself, to make new friends, and to develop more confidence on a personal, social, and musical level. She plays a range of instruments within the ensemble including Soundbeam technology and the Magic Flute, as well as keyboards using a color-coordinated system. She described being involved in the project as "changing my life! It was the best thing ever invented" (Deirdre). An ensemble member from the community-based project shared that "with a bit of support and Soundbeam technology I can do this and I can let people know how I feel" (Kevin). Ann, Kevin's mother, emphasized the importance of the project:

> Kevin now has something to live for. That's the be all and end all. There's just a change in him in the sense that he knows what he wants and he's glad that he's found a way that he can express it . . . through the lyrics and then getting to actually perform his own songs and to be included in a band. This is just brilliant for him. (Ann)

Kevin described his involvement in the inclusive music ensemble as

> the most important thing in my life to date. It has given me an outlet and opened up a new life for me. Before I wrote my first song, I didn't have much excitement in my life; I thought my life would be fairly boring. It was only after I had written a song that I discovered that I could put my feelings into words and perform it using technology. I'm delighted!

The person-centered planner at a local service center for people with physical disabilities stated that Kevin's involvement in the inclusive music ensemble "brought out parts of him that we hadn't been aware of before which was great. It was really positive" (Mary). She went on to describe that the performance made her aware of "how much being involved in this project has enabled people to express themselves" (Mary).

All research participants in both the school and community setting emphasized that involvement in the inclusive music ensembles provided opportunities for identity development. This was expressed through creative music making, which incorporated a range of accessible music technologies and song writing. Kevin wrote a song called "Locked In." It describes his experience and his own self-perception as a young man with severe cerebral palsy living in Cork City. The lyrics provide a powerful reference to the use of accessible music technology as an empowering tool that provides access to inclusive music making, which he believes leads to a "world outside" (i.e., outside the disability services):

I am locked, locked, locked, into a daily life that I can't get out of.
I see a world outside that I want to live in.
But now I see a way out, where I have a chance, to live my life outside.

Ann, his mother, perceives these lyrics to represent how Kevin strives to use music to express his self-identity. "When he is up there [on stage] he is not disabled. Kevin doesn't want to be in that bracket: 'I'm the disabled' person. He wants to break from that. He just wants to be the person who happens to be in a wheelchair rather than the other way around. In his head he doesn't have a disability" (Ann).

The provision of a range of accessible interactive music technology gives more independence for people with profound physical disabilities to access active music making. Through the independent use of the technology, students were empowered to choose when and how to contribute musically to the ensemble. The provision of choice both to access the ensemble and to engage in activities within the ensemble was central to the ensemble's development. All participants, their parents, and the music tutors recognized this as a positive aspect. Many times choice is something that is not readily available in local disability services and within some educational settings in the city—often as a result of limited resources and funding cuts. Kevin's mother highlighted that "it was his choice to go there and do his own thing there. It was his choice and he loved the fact that he was making it himself" (Ann).

A huge sense of pride resulting from these choices emanated from the participants, particularly during the performance phases of the project. The opportunity to perform emerged as significant for all participants. Ann described the pride of her son in relation to his first public performance: "He was so proud. He wanted to surprise me and go 'look what I can do.'" (Ann). Kevin also stated, "I have gained so much confidence in myself from performing and writing lyrics and being included in other bands to perform my music. I feel very proud of myself!" (Kevin). Involvement in the inclusive ensemble was also a catalyst for increased motivation to use assistive technology for academic achievement. Kevin demonstrated a renewed sense of motivation to learn to write more effectively with eye gaze technology. Ann said, "He wants to sort out his reading and literacy so he can put together his lyrics more independently. This has motivated him again" (Ann).

Social Development

The provision of opportunities for social interaction among all students was a priority within both of the SoundOUT ensembles. All of the tutors noticed that there were fewer opportunities for social interaction in the school ensemble than in the community ensemble; possibly, the higher number of students in the school ensemble contributed to this. To accommodate the needs of the school's timetable, the ensemble was more structured compared to the community ensemble. Both the tutors and the classroom teachers felt that time constraints limited social interaction among students. When students were asked about their experiences within the ensemble, they felt that the social aspect of making new friends from other schools was a very significant aspect of the ensemble. The school ensemble meets for one and a half hours on a weekly basis, and the community ensemble comes together for two hours each week including lunch together after rehearsals. This socializing time has been crucial for the community ensemble to bond as a band. When the community ensemble participants were asked about their experiences of working in an inclusive ensemble, there was more of a focus on the musical developments of the ensemble.

Conor, a participant in the secondary school ensemble, stated, "You need Soundbeam or the Magic Flute or something like that to make music if you have no hands and can't speak. You can use your legs or your head to make the sounds you want. You can still be in a band then. It's cool" (Conor). Mary, the person-centered planner from the local disability service, described the use of accessible interactive music technology as "outstanding. People like Kevin would never have been involved in something like this without the technology. It's brilliant to include people who have always been at the edge. So it's hugely important" (Mary).

As the ensemble developed, communication among band members evolved significantly. Initially, some of the ensemble members were insecure about communicating with the young people who were nonverbal. As time progressed and the group created music together, attitudes changed. David said, "I see Kevin differently now. I was a bit shocked at first because I didn't expect him to be so disabled but now I see him differently. He's someone I can hang out with. Sure—he's one of us" (David).

The classroom teacher in the special educational needs school suggested that social inclusion is a priority over musical development. The majority of the children involved in the school program are significantly marginalized from society in general as they attend a segregated school and have difficulties expressing themselves on a daily basis. "It's giving the students an opportunity to express themselves. At the end of the day whether they succeed in playing an instrument is not the important thing, it's that they tried and they enjoyed it, so that's the paramount" (Maeve). Ann, Kevin's mother, felt the social interaction outside of ensemble activities was just as important as the musical interactions. She felt that engagement with the inclusive music ensemble on a weekly basis over a sustained period of time was essential to enable participants to engage meaningfully with each other. "It takes awhile for the lads to become comfortable with each other" (Ann).

Throughout the 24 weeks, both ensembles had opportunities to perform publically. This enabled significant social interactions within the wider musical community of Cork City. Each ensemble made musical contributions to mainstream music events and festivals throughout the year. All research participants recognized this opportunity to contribute to the vibrant musical life in Cork City as a very positive aspect of being involved in the inclusive music ensemble.

Musical Development

Where possible, an informal, person-centered approach with an emphasis on collaboration was adopted throughout this project. Students often were involved in leading ensemble activities. While "cover versions" of popular songs formed the basis of some music learning, it was felt that there was more value in creating new music. A parent noted that the participants' choice of music that was being facilitated enabled a more flexible approach to the provision of inclusive practice. "I think the type of music you were doing was important as well. He wasn't just sitting at the drum and watching others. It was something he liked" (Ann).

All the tutors felt a team facilitation approach was essential to providing meaningful music-making opportunities for the inclusive music ensemble. This approach enabled one facilitator to work with the technology and others to facilitate ensemble activities. There was also a level of support and opportunity for collaborative peer learning among the tutors within a group teaching environment. The practices of SoundOUT tutors resonate deeply with the core principles of community music, where themes of empowerment, inclusion, informality, diversity, and facilitation are prioritized over teaching methods (Higgins, 2008).

Within the ensemble activities in the school setting, all tutors used Soundbeam 2 (a stand-alone version), Desktop Soundbeam (digital version connected to a PC), and Soundbeam 5, the latest version of the Soundbeam system. Soundbeam 5 is a stand-alone system that has the ability to record samples and backing tracks. All of the research participants noted that it is significantly more user friendly than Soundbeam 2 and Desktop Soundbeam. Throughout this inclusive music project, the classroom teachers and tutors felt more comfortable using Soundbeam 5 within workshop situations. "I think as an early intervention tool, Soundbeam 2 or Soundbeam 5 is far more inclusive and you can take it out quickly, you can set it up quickly and there is little fear that it's going to crash or start becoming very temperamental, unlike Desktop Soundbeam" (Maeve). The tutors in the school setting preferred Desktop Soundbeam for performance purposes as it had the ability to connect to high-quality digital sounds using the sampler Reason, as well as connecting to visual software. However, Soundbeam 5 was deemed more useful for rehearsal situations.

Desktop Soundbeam was used within the community ensemble by Kevin. Both Kevin and Gareth stated that the system was not flexible enough to fully engage with some of the more creative ensemble activities. There is an option to input a series of notes to play in the beam in advance of ensemble activities; however, both Gareth and Kevin felt that the system wasn't accessible enough to enable Kevin to independently change keys and scales when he needed to. Kevin relied on Gareth to do this, which was too time consuming, particularly during improvisation activities. Gareth suggested that this limitation impeded Kevin's musical development. He noted that in the band situation, often the group starts "jamming" and it is difficult to change the necessary information on the Soundbeam to keep up with key changes during improvisation activities. Gareth highlighted that this lack of artistic control over the instrument in comparison to other ensemble members limited Kevin's musical development particularly within the areas of improvisation and creative music making in ensemble settings.

When discussing the use of accessible interactive music technology as a tool for active music making and learning, the responses were very positive. The students who used the technology themselves discussed the delights of engaging in the music activities that were now accessible because of the technology:

> I think the Soundbeam is brilliant. You can do different beats and learn how to trigger them in the right place. Its good way that I can get everyone involved. I can now be involved. It's hard enough though. . . . You have to know when to come in and out. Everybody is happy when we're playing though. . . . I love playing the beam and the iPad too. I move my hand up and down in one beam and make sax sounds using that scale and then I do different beats with the other and then I can use the guitar too on the Garageband and do chords with it all. It's good . . . hard, but really good. (Jack)

Deirdre described her experience of using the Magic Flute as

> brilliant. . . . You don't use your hands with it, you just use your mouth to move it up and down to play the notes of the tunes. My hands are not really great at moving small things. . . . I'm finding it very hard. The Magic Flute is good for me. It's better than the flute that you play sideways. It's better because I can play the Magic Flute. I really love playing it, but all I need now is more practice on it. (Deirdre)

There is a very strong sense of musical development combined with ambition for more musical development among the research respondents.

The students with and without disabilities who did not use the technology had positive things to say about its use within the ensemble, both from an inclusive and from a musical perspective. All participants made reference to the perceived level of difficulty it takes to play the instrument. It was first believed that the level of difficultly it took to play accessible interactive music technology was minimal, unlike "real" instruments. "Ya, Soundbeam is very easy. You just have to move your hand up and down. It's different to the guitar. You have to learn how to play that" (Sara). At the early stages of development, some of the typical ensemble members felt the technology was used solely as an inclusive tool rather than as a musical instrument that contributes as much as any other instrument in the band. These perceptions evolved once the musical skills necessary to play accessible interactive music technology within an ensemble situation were understood and acknowledged.

Swingler and Brockhouse (2009) address the issue of musical development using Soundbeam technology in "Getting Better All the Time: Using Music Technology for Learners with Special Needs." Central to their article is the question: Can interactive music technology—with an emphasis on accessibility [Soundbeam]—provide a genuine long-term musical learning trajectory in the same way that "real" instruments do? Accessible interactive music technology such as iPads, Soundbeams, and the Magic Flute offers instant access for all abilities. Instant accessibility, however, can often give the impression that there is no room for musical development. All of the technologies described in this chapter facilitate opportunities for the musical development of players. Swingler and Brockhouse suggest that "the entry point [to music making and learning with Soundbeam technology] may be simple and accessible but the software is sufficiently refined to allow for a developing musical intelligence which can be as sophisticated as the user wants it to be" (p. 2). They refer to Csíkszentmihályi's (1997) notion of "flow" when examining the issues of accessibility and development within the context of using Soundbeam music technology in educational settings. This notion suggests that there needs to be a balance between ability and challenge, because if an activity is too easy, there is a danger of it becoming boring. However, if an activity is too difficult, it can be somewhat demotivating (Swingler & Brockhouse, 2009).

Advocacy

Advocacy for social development is a theme that emerged particularly within the community-based ensemble. "I wanna give the world somebody to think about" (Kevin). This is a quote from a song that Kevin wrote. The promotion of the use of accessible interactive music technology within active music making and performance was central to some of the participants' goals. Kevin, the first SoundOUT Soundbeam player,

> wants to be an inspiration for somebody else down the line. He wants to show them that there's a life there, there's something else to look forward to because when he was down there [at school] he had nothing. He didn't think there was something like this he could look forward to but because he's found music now he has a life whereas if he hadn't found music in his mind he wouldn't have had much of a life. (Ann)

Kevin's involvement in the community ensemble has inspired a cultural change within the local school and community centers: a range of inclusive music ensembles are now continuously being developed.

Kevin describes his ambitions for the removal of barriers to music making and performance in musical lyrics:

Unlock these doors;
Smash down these walls;
Break down these fences;
And let me be free.

He has become a symbol of inclusivity and the promise of future possibilities within the musical culture of Cork City. The prominence of the inclusive music ensembles and the subsequent respect for the quality of music created within the wider community were seen to "give people a little bit of promise and is making changes within the city . . . . It's had a hugely positive impact on the centre really. I don't think the service users have ever seen each other get involved in bigger stuff outside of here. Kevin has had an opportunity to get involved and be recognised as a person with a talent rather than a person with a disability" (Mary). Maeve, the classroom teacher in the special needs school, stated that the secondary school inclusive music ensemble "exceeded expectations" (Maeve). Exceeding expectations extended to parents and sometimes the participants themselves. "I think through the writing Kevin is able to express himself more. Through the music he is coming up with things that I didn't even dream he was thinking about but I should have known that he would be thinking about those things. We didn't ever think any of this could be a possibility because of the physical disability" (Ann). These changes in attitude have been influenced by the young people in the inclusive ensembles advocating through music making and performance for a more inclusive model of music education and society in general.

Challenges

Issues surrounding sustainability are one of the main recurring themes noted by the research participants including parents, tutors, and family members from both ensembles. Much of the participants' engagement in music projects to date has been on a short-term basis and presented as access programs. Unfortunately, there are few opportunities for young people with profound physical disabilities to access music programs in mainstream settings in Cork City. There are also a limited number of music tutors able to use accessible interactive music technology within their practice. "Yeah, he wants to learn more but it's been hard to find the right course that can accommodate his needs. It's been very hard. Kevin would be more comfortable in mainstream if that was possible but it doesn't seem to be possible anywhere else apart from the SoundOUT project" (Ann).

The main barrier for progressive opportunities in musical development has been the lack of resources and expertise in existing music schools. There were also attitudinal barriers, both from the music schools and from the students themselves and their families. A core vision of SoundOUT is that accessible interactive music technology will become normalized within music practice to ensure universal accessibility and progression opportunities for persons of all abilities in the city. These ensembles have been developed with limited funds and the vision of individuals. They have brought together musicians and educators who are committed to social justice and equality within the music classroom. This community of inclusive music practice aims to bring the ethos of inclusive music education from the margins to the core of music education development and practice in Ireland. This is urgent to avoid further exclusion of young people with disabilities from active music making and learning in Ireland, particularly during this turbulent economic climate where the education system is stretched and resources are limited.

To address this issue of sustainability, the provision of efficient and continuous professional development on the use of accessible interactive music technology is crucial for tutors, students, and classroom teachers. One classroom teacher describes her experiences of using Soundbeam technology within a school context as extremely challenging and time consuming: "So I go into school early, I come home late but I'm still not there with it. You need hours and if it's something that you haven't used consistently over and over, I do feel that you forget it very, very quickly" (Maeve). Ongoing support for classroom teachers from SoundOUT music tutors has been beneficial for the school-based support of the inclusive music ensemble.

The teacher in the special needs school shared that the lack of time to facilitate ongoing communication and collaboration with music tutors and special needs assistants was extremely challenging. It was felt that this process was essential to the effective use of the accessible interactive music technology with the young people with disabilities to provide meaningful music-making and learning opportunities. This communication and coordination often occurred during individual tutors' personal time.

Performance was represented as a significant and positive aspect of the SoundOUT inclusive music ensembles. The presence of young people with physical disabilities in the live music scene in Cork City highlighted the lack of accessible music venues and performance spaces in the city. Most venues in Cork City are not wheelchair accessible. Some venues had wheelchair access but did not have wheelchair access to performance areas. Physical access to performances spaces was an unforeseen challenge in this project.

This is something that all the participants noticed and commented on when discussing their experiences.

Progression opportunities for young people with physical disabilities using accessible interactive music technology are limited in Ireland. People with disabilities are significantly underrepresented in music education research both nationally and internationally (Jellison, 2000). Children with disabilities demonstrate just as wide a range of musical abilities as their able-bodied peers. It is clear that children across the spectrum of ability/disability can display innate musicianship given appropriate support. As part of the significant Sounds of Intent research initiative, Ockelford (2008) examined issues of attainment and progress within music education practice involving children and young people with profound disabilities in the United Kingdom. His study revealed that progress and attainment were often perceived as overlapping. All students, regardless of whether or not they have special educational needs, are motivated by progress. Music learning and development is not an inappropriate goal for young people with disabilities; however, the provision of appropriate progression routes is insufficient (Swingler & Brockhouse, 2009). There is ongoing research in the United Kingdom exploring accessible and equitable routes for progression and music development in music education. The Associated Board of the Royal Schools of Music, in collaboration with music consultant David Ashworth, the Soundbeam Project, and the Drake Music Project, is currently establishing a research initiative examining the idea of a set of graded examinations in the use of electronic technology, like Soundbeam technology, for live performance. Issues surrounding curriculum, assessment, and resources are emerging and are currently being discussed via an online debate (go to https://sites.google.com/site/davidashworthorguk/.

There has been considerable technological advancement over the past three decades that has significant implications for inclusivity within music education practice. The recently developed Soundbeam 5 is significantly more accessible than previous versions for students to use independently; however, it is not universally accessible for students with profound physical disabilities. This has been a consistent issue that has emerged from the interviews with research participants. Kevin emphasized his love of active music; however, he recognized its limitations in terms of full independence. He advocates for more technological developments within this area. "I look forward to every music session and performance and I hope to work the Soundbeam or something like it independently in the future. To date the Soundbeam has been the only way for me to access and play an instrument" (Kevin). This frustration is also reflected in the secondary school ensemble. A classroom teacher from the special education needs school felt "at present, the Soundbeam is not digitally interfacing. It doesn't interface with eye gaze. It doesn't interface with camera mouse—all things that our students need to work independently" (Maeve). She continues to advocate for more digitally interactive methods that adhere to the principles of universal design. "I think the next generation is going to be far more inclusive, it's going to enable everybody regardless of their physical disability to be able to meaningfully engage with music" (Maeve).

REFLECTIONS

This chapter has presented the experiences and perceptions of young people with and without disabilities using accessible interactive music technology within two inclusive ensembles in Cork City. These experiences and perceptions resonate with recent research within the field of sociology of music education. Wright (2010) suggests that inclusion is one of the main issues facing music educators of the twenty-first century (p. 251). There are differing levels of engagement with educational processes and contexts, where the capacity to gain benefits from education is not evenly distributed throughout society (Wright, 2010, p. 251). Wright supports a more unified vision for the goals and purposes of music education to stem from a sociological perspective while focusing on issues of inclusion and collaboration. She suggests that this paradigm shift would "level the playing field" for children and young people of less advantaged social groups entering music education, including children with disabilities (Wright, 2010). Bernstein (1996) advocates that "education is central to the knowledge base of society, groups and individuals. Yet education also, like health, is a public institution, central to the production and reproduction of distributive injustices" (p. xix). He advocates that for education, including music education, to become truly democratic, all students need to receive the three educational rights of enhancement, participation, and inclusion. Enhancement refers to the experience of pushing the boundaries—boundaries that exist between past and future possibilities. Participation and inclusion refer to students having the right to be engaged socially, intellectually, culturally, and personally. The experiences and perceptions of using accessible interactive music technology within inclusive music ensembles in Cork City reflect such enhancement and engagement.

These preliminary findings also reflect research within the area of inclusive education and the emerging field of inclusive music education. Adamek and Darrow's (2012) examination of the perceived benefits and challenges of inclusive music programs resonate with the experiences and perceptions presented in this chapter. These preliminary findings suggest there are significant personal, social, educational, and artistic benefits of using accessible interactive music technology to engage in active and meaningful music making within inclusive settings. However, there are also significant challenges including sustainability, training of musicians, universal accessibility of technology to accommodate students with profound physical disabilities, and provision of progression routes beyond access programs. The concept of universal design for learning has emerged as a benchmark for inclusive music education. SoundOUT strives, where possible, to embed universal design for learning principles within all music-making and learning activities. The aim is to provide appropriate and universally designed progression routes for inclusive music education for all young people in Cork City. SoundOUT is committed to the view that every student has the right to a sustained and sequential education. Twenty-first-century music education, in the words of educational philosopher Maxine Greene, should "break with the 'cotton wool' of habit, and of mere routine . . . to seek alternative ways of being" (Greene, 1988, p. 5).

Websites

http://www.soundout.ie
http://www.soundbeamproject.co.uk
http://www.mybreathmymusic.com
http://www.click2go.ie
http://www.musicgenerationcorkcity.ie

NOTES

1. This study emerged from a larger study (McHale, 2014) that involves the examination of five inclusive music ensembles. These ensembles consisted of 40 ensemble members, approximately 7 members in each ensemble—18 students with disabilities and 22 students without disabilities. There are also approximately 12 research participants including family members, tutors, and teachers who have contributed to this study to contextualize the experiences and perceptions of using accessible interactive music technology within inclusive music settings.
2. See also Griffin and Shevlin (2007) for a more in-depth view of the policy development of inclusive education in Ireland.
3. See also PIANO report (PIANO Review Group, 1996), MEND report (Heneghan, 2001), A National System of Local Music Education Services (Music Network, 2003), and The Use of Music as a Tool for Social Inclusion (Minguella, 2009).
4. See http://www.musicgeneration.ie.

REFERENCES

Adamek, M. S., & Darrow, A. A. (2005). *Music in special education*. Silver Spring, MD: American Music Therapy Association.

Adamek, M. S., & Darrow, A. A. (2012). Preparing for the future: Music students with special education needs in school and community life. In G. McPherson & G. Welch (Eds.), *The Oxford handbook of music education* (Vol. 2, pp. 81–97). New York, NY: Oxford University Press.

Bernstein, B. (1996). *Pedagogy, symbolic control, and identity: Theory, research, critique*. London, England: Taylor and Francis.

Blair, D., & Wiggins, J. (2010). Teaching for musical understanding: A constructivist approach. In J. Ballantyne & B. L. Bartlett (Eds.), *Navigating music and sound education* (pp. 16–30). Newcastle, UK: Cambridge Scholars Publishing.

Bowe, F. G. (2000). *Universal design in education: Teaching nontraditional students*. Westport, CT: Bergen & Garvey.

Bresler, L., & Stake, R. (2006). Qualitative research methodology in music education. In R. Colwell (Ed.), *MENC handbook of research methodologies* (pp. 270–312). Oxford University Press in cooperation with MENC: National Association for Music Education.

Csíkszentmihályi, M. (1997). *Finding flow: The psychology of engagement in everyday life*. New York: Harper Collins Publishers.

Denzin, N. (1989). *The research act: A theoretical introduction to sociological methods* (3rd ed.). Englewood Cliffs, NY: Prentice-Hall.

Dewey, J. (1910). *How we think*. Boston, MA: D. C. Heath & Co.

Dewey, J. (1916). *Democracy and education*. New York: McMillan.

Dillon, S. (2006). Assessing the positive influence of music activities in community development programs. *Music Education Research*, 8(2), 267–280.

Ellis, P. (1997). The music of sound: A new approach for children with severe and profound and multiple learning difficulties. *British Journal of Music Education*, 14(2), 173–186.

Grant, E. (2006). *A community music approach to social inclusion in music education in Ireland*. Unpublished doctoral dissertation, Department of Education, University College, Cork, Ireland.

Greene, M. (1988). *The dialectic of freedom*. New York, NY: Teachers College Press.

Griffin, S., & Shevlin, M. (2007). *Responding to special educational needs: An Irish perspective*. Dublin: Gill & MacMillan.

Heneghan, Frank. (2001). MEND Report: a review of music education in Ireland, incorporating the final report of the Music Education National Debate DIT: Dublin.

Higgins, L. (2008). The creative music workshop: Event, facilitation, gift. *International Journal of Music Education*, 26, 326–377.

Jellison, J. A. (2000). A content analysis of music research with disabled children and youth (1975-1999). In M. S. Adamek, P. A., Codding, A. A. Darrow, A. P. Gervin, & K. E. Gfeller (Eds.), *Effectiveness of music therapy procedures: Documentation of research and clinical practice* (pp. 199–264). Silver Spring, MD: American Music Therapy Association.

Jellison, J. A. (2012). Inclusive music classrooms and programmes. In G. McPherson & G. Welch (Eds.), *The Oxford handbook of music education* (Vol. 2, pp. 65–80). New York: Oxford University Press.

Kilkelly, U., Kilpatrick, R., Moore, L., Scraton, P., Davey, C., Dwyer, C., Lundy, L. (2005). *Children's rights in Northern Ireland*. Belfast: Northern Ireland Commissioner for Children and Young People.

Logan, A. (2006). The role of the special needs assistant supporting pupils with special educational needs in Irish mainstream primary schools. *Support for Learning*, 21(2), 92–99.

Magee, W. L., & Burland, K. (2008). An exploratory study of the use of electronic music technologies in clinical music therapy. *Nordic Journal of Music Therapy, 17*(2), 124–141.

Minguella, M. (2009). The use of music as a tool for social inclusion, Cork City Council.

McCord, K. A., & Rogers, L. (2010). Students with disabilities making music. *Orff Echo, 42*(4), 29–31.

McHale, G. (2015). *Lines of Flight—Inclusive Music Bands, Digital Musical Instruments and Meaningful Engagement.* Unpublished doctoral dissertation, University College Cork, Ireland.

Music Network. (2003). A National System of Local Music Education Services: report of a feasibility study, Department of Arts Sport and Tourism: Dublin.

Ockelford, A. (2008). *Music for children and young people with complex needs.* New York: Oxford University Press.

OIREACHTAS. (2004). *Education for Persons with Special Educational Needs (EPSEN) Act.* Dublin: The Stationary Office.

Oireachtas. (2005). *Disability Act.* Dublin: The Stationary Office.

PIANO Review Group. (1996). Report on the Provision and Institutional Arrangements Now for Orchestras and Ensembles, Department of Arts, Culture and the Gaeltacht; Dublin

Pijl, S., Meijer, C., & Hegarty, S. (1997). *Inclusive education: A global agenda.* London:Routledge.

Rose, D. H., & Meyer, A. (Eds.). (2006). *A practical reader in universal design for learning.* Cambridge, MA: Harvard University Press.

Rose, R., Shevlin, M., Winter, E., & O'Raw, P. (2010). Special and inclusive education in the Republic of Ireland: Reviewing the literature from 2000-2009. *European Journal of Special Needs Education, 25*(4), 359–373.

Swingler, T., & Brockhouse, J. (2009). Getting better all the time: Using music technology for learners with special needs. *Australian Journal of Music Education, 2,* 49–57.

UNESCO. (1994). *The Salamanca Statement and Framework for Action,* Paris: United Nations Educational, Scientific and Cultural Organization.

UNESCO. (2009). *Policy guidelines on inclusion in education.* Paris: Author. Retrieved from http://unesdoc.unesco.org/images/0017/001778/177849e.pdf

Vygotsky, L. S. (1978). *Mind in society: The development of higher psychological processes.* Cambridge, MA: Harvard University Press.

Wright, R. (2010). *Sociology and music education.* Aldershot, England: Ashgate Press.

Yin, R. (2003). *Case study research, design and methods* (3rd ed.). Newbury Park, CA: Sage Publications.

CHAPTER 7

Music Activities for Children with Disabilities

An Example from Taiwan

LIZA LEE

Music in the soul can be heard by the universe.

Lao Tzu, Chinese philosopher

Children with a profound degree of cognitive, sensory, or physical impairment may have strong responses to music and sound (McPhail, 2003). However, Ockelford observes, "music education for children and young people with complex needs is still a pedagogical infant" (2008, p. 3). The field of special education in Taiwan has changed greatly over the past few decades. With this change, the responsibilities of music educators and therapists have also changed. Music professionals in the schools must keep abreast of approaches, materials, and technology to meet the needs of children with disabilities.

My studies in the field of music education and music therapy have led me to see music as an innovative tool for building learning connections for the development of all children, especially those with disabilities. Through a number of recent studies[1] and my own teaching as an early childhood educator in Taiwan, I have seen positive effects for developmentally challenged children who are given the opportunity to interact and experiment with musical instruments, both simple and complex. Children with disabilities are in need of effective learning activities to help enhance their development. Any educational activity that can supplement existing methods used in educational and social development can be beneficial. With this in mind, I have created and implemented a music-based curriculum that uses music activities, tactile materials, and technology to create an engaging learning environment for children.

Figure 7.1 depicts my framework for developing a holistic strategy for children that describes the process of including all children in music experiences. There are two crucial levels of professional abilities for teachers as they seek to implement an efficient music curriculum for children. The first level of competence includes advanced music and technology skills. The second level of ability consists of professional music educational knowledge and hands-on experiences in early childhood, special education, and technology applications. After becoming a qualified music educator in Taiwan, one is qualified to implement a music curriculum for children with and without disabilities. The final goal in a holistic approach to educating children with disabilities is to integrate language, cognition, physical

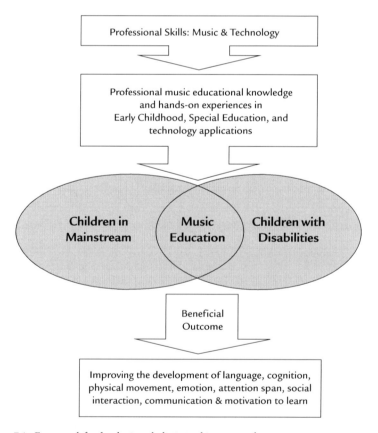

Figure 7.1. Framework for developing a holistic teaching approach.

movement, emotion, improved attention span, social interaction, communication, and motivation to learn.

As a music educator in Taiwan for 20 years, I have explored learning opportunities for all children, especially for those with disabilities. I have come to understand that music is an engaging medium for communication and development for children with and without disabilities. Therefore, the purpose of this chapter is to share a Taiwanese perspective for developing a holistic method of integration of music education for children with disabilities in the Taiwanese school system. Using music as a medium for communication and engagement rather than just a subject to be learned, this chapter addresses the importance of musical activities for children with disabilities. When children with disabilities have the opportunity to participate in music activities and experiences, they get not only the benefit of a richer learning environment but also the advantage of developing behavior and social skills.

THE BENEFITS OF MUSIC ACTIVITIES FOR CHILDREN WITH DISABILITIES

It is important to note individual differences among children, especially when teaching children with disabilities. Prior to teaching, setting up targeted goals and objectives is very important for designing effective music experiences. Based on the positive outcomes from my research, the following areas are some of the skills that music supports in the education and social development of children with disabilities.

Concentration and increased attention span. Music activities, especially learning a musical instrument or listening to a story with added music, will help children to develop concentration over extended periods of time. In particular, joint attention is an essential skill that children with autism need to develop. Joint attention means to focus on and look at what is important. For example, when teaching reading, teachers may track words on a visual of some kind or share a storybook with children. Joint attention is difficult for many children with autism, but if it is not developed, the child will likely be delayed in important literacy skills (Hammel & Hourigan, 2013; Mundy & Neal, 2001; Mundy & Newell, 2007; Pennington, 2002; Sigman & Ruskin, 1999). Developing concentration musically may transfer to other critical areas of learning outside of the classroom.

Physical movement: gross and fine motor skills. Learning to play an instrument enhances fine motor coordination. Playing instruments such as drums or wind instruments not only teaches children musical rhythm and memorization but also increases fine motor skills due to the variety of grips and hand positions to produce a sound on a musical instrument. In addition, I have observed that learning to play musical instruments also improves hand-eye coordination (Lee, 2010a, 2011e, 2011f, 2012a).

Social interaction. In a group setting, playing music can promote social skills, such as turn taking and following directions. This is also a way to increase joint attention. Playing musical instruments with others can also build a sense of communication for children with poor social skills who are not connected through language. Being able to express themselves through singing and playing instruments may be easier for some children than verbal communication (Lee, 2010a, 2010f, 2011d, 2012a).

Self-confidence. Music provides a medium through which children may learn to express themselves. It leads children to develop a more effective link between their perceptions of the world and their ability to communicate with others. When a child learns music, many behavioral and cultural ways of being have the potential to be cultivated, including creativity, self-expression, self-discipline, self-esteem, self-confidence, self-efficacy, self-discovery, cooperation, time management, appreciation of other cultures, and increased interest in school. Moreover, children who practice self-expression and creativity often become better communicators later in life (Lee, 2010a, 2011d, 2012a).

EXCEPTIONAL CURRICULUM FRAMEWORK

Provided in this section is a list and description of the types of activities that elicited positive responses from the children with disabilities whom I have observed or with whom I have interacted in teaching or research settings.

Singing activities enrich and support cognition and language development. Since for most children singing is as natural as talking, children learn to sing just as they learn to talk, by imitating other people. Singing activities support a child's need to socialize, play, and improve speech and language skills. Improvements in speech and language skills include vocalization, verbalization, articulation, language expression and reception, rhythm, and breath control.

Action songs, such as songs designed to aid in transitions, are a good way to practice social skills that include song lyrics that provide instructions for what children should do during transitions. The rhythm and beat of the song supports timing and structure for movement. Social development requires awareness of self and others. Children's songs like "Head and Shoulders" include basic body parts that can improve children's cognitive development. Motor movement in Chinese songs like "Come and Come" and "Move Your Finger Up" can increase awareness of a child's body.

Singing activities that integrate call and response also help motivate children to communicate and connect within small groups or with a partner. This supports development and understanding of cause and effect, how to initiate interactions, and how to indicate "yes" or "no" through gestures such as nodding or shaking the head. Songs that use lyrics linked with memorable melodies can facilitate and motivate children to learn these skills.

Playing instruments improves gross and fine motor skills that contribute to coordination, balance, range of motion, and strength and may contribute to developing social skills including participation and cooperation. Instruments such as the ocean drum provide a useful way for sensory defensive children to connect touch and hearing. Playing the ocean drum is a pleasant experience and can be soothing to sensory defensive children.

Movement activities facilitate the development of gross motor skills including mobility, agility, balance, and coordination. Moving to music with contrasting elements such as high and low, slow and fast, loud and quiet, stop and go, and long and short helps children to better understand these concepts by experiencing them through music. Playing games with sound, singing, chanting, and movement or dancing helps children with disabilities to practice specific language skills and to develop cognitive and social development. Music and rhythm games can help children learn and retain information and skills.

Listening to music often puts children at ease. For children with disabilities, listening to music can be an effective tool for language development and communication, expression of feelings, and development of a sense of rhythm. Children on the autism spectrum often lack the social skills for play; listening with others is a good starting place for learning to engage with peers and enabling participation in other social situations.
Musical storytelling is an ideal tool for helping children in either a regular classroom or a special needs classroom to develop and enhance attention span. Through work with young children in Taiwan, I have developed an approach that can be used by early childhood educators, music teachers, and parents.

The goal of this approach is to demonstrate musical storytelling techniques, curriculum development, and creation of instructor materials to promote young children's learning motivation and enhance their attention span. Figure 7.2 represents an example of a curriculum framework for musical storytelling that I developed to be used with preschool children with autism.

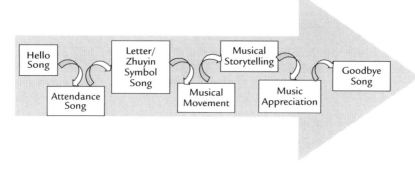

Figure 7.2. The full procedure of the musical storytelling curriculum framework.

I have used this curriculum framework in my research and teaching for 11 years in Taiwan. Children with severe disabilities at this age level benefit from repetition and structure. Repeating the same routine and using the same sequence help children with autism become more secure with what will occur in music classes. The content of the curriculum framework includes the following activities:

> *Hello song:* My teaching goals are to develop children's awareness of classroom rituals, improve social development, and enhance cognition.
>
> *Attendance song/call and response:* Teaching goals are to develop children's self-awareness, social interaction with peers and adults, physical movement using gross and fine motor skills, cognitive development, and language ability.
>
> *Letter song/Zhuyin symbol song:* Teaching goals are to develop language ability and sing and recognize the letters of the English alphabet and Zhuyin[2] (phonetic notation) of Chinese pronunciation.
>
> *Musical movement/games:* Teaching goals are to develop physical movement and musical intelligence.
>
> *Musical storytelling:* Teaching goals are to motivate and engage children, stimulate visual and aural cognition, and increase attention span.
>
> *Musical skills:* Teaching goals are to identify musical elements, develop vocabulary, and use movement.
>
> *Relaxation time:* The teaching goal is to have children relax from the activities. This helps calm children who easily become overly stimulated during music.
>
> *Goodbye song:* Teaching goals are to develop awareness of class rituals, enhance social development, and review the targeted objectives.

MUSIC ACTIVITIES INCORPORATING
TECHNOLOGY FOR CHILDREN WITH DISABILITIES

Using technology in the practice and research of music therapy provides strategies and techniques that can be applied to music education. This assists in the training and development of new tools for educators and therapists (Crowe & Rio, 2004). Music activities that incorporate technology offer an excellent way to reach children with disabilities through multiple learning modes (Lee, 2012a).

Soundbeam Technology

The Soundbeam[3] is a new electronic device that can be used effectively in both special and music education and therapy. At the International Society for Music Education conference in 2006, I learned of the Soundbeam from a conference presenter, Professor Phil Ellis, who is a pioneer in the field of sound therapy. After learning the technology with Professor Ellis at the University of Sunderland in the United Kingdom, I set up a dedicated Soundbeam room at my university and implemented a pilot study (Lee, 2009) using the Soundbeam to enhance typical children's creativity. The study showed positive results for young children; therefore, I continued to expand the participant group and applied this technology to children with various types of disabilities.

An Introduction to Soundbeam

Soundbeam is a device that converts physical movement into sound. Using ultrasonic sensors, the Soundbeam system detects the speed, gate, and distance of even the smallest movements that can be made with anything from a fingertip to the entire body. These ultrasonic signals are converted by the Soundbeam controller into MIDI (Musical Instrument Digital Interface) information that can then be processed by a sound module, keyboard, or sampler (Soundbeam Project, 2003).

Soundbeam provides a medium through which the most profoundly physically or cognitively disabled individuals can become expressive and communicative using music and sound (Ellis, 2007, 2008). Its success rests upon two factors: (1) the sensitivity of the beam, which means that even the most unreachable or immobilized individuals can "play" independently, and (2) electronic technology that makes available a huge palette of possible soundworlds, releasing the player from the traditional limitations of percussion-based activity (Soundbeam Project, 2003).

Soundbeam for Young Children with Disabilities

Soundbeam has had dramatic effects in the field of disability and special education. It is a musical instrument that, when played by children with disabilities through use of movement in space, can be accommodated to recognize movement as small as a blinking eye to larger movements such as dancing (McPhail, 2003).

Research shows that sound therapy combines the power of new technologies with an aesthetic response to sound. This noninterventionist approach can encourage users' interaction and development of their communicative skills (Ellis, 1995). Through sound therapy sessions, a child with autism made progress in many areas of development, including movement control, attention span, eye contact, vocalization, social interaction, and positive emotions (Ellis & Van Leeuwen, 2000). My own study found the effectiveness of using Soundbeam technology on developing creativity in four typical young children (Lee, 2009).

A complex musical instrument, the Soundbeam can be played with multiple switches and beams positioned at different heights according to the size and movement range of the child. Switches are flat, brightly colored pads that accommodate the child's hand or foot. The switches and sensor beams are programmed to respond by playing certain sounds or rhythms. The sensor beam responds to pitch by playing higher pitches the closer the individual moves to the sensor. Pitches can be programmed to include scales or chord tones. With the newer model of Soundbeam, the user can record sampled sounds that can be activated through either the sensor beam or the switches.

Additional kinesthetic stimulation can be achieved by using a vibrating beanbag-type chair that produces adjustable vibrations linked to the sounds the child makes through movement. Lights can also be added to provide a visual stimulus that is also connected to the sound produced by the child. The child who responds to a multisensory environment becomes highly motivated to interact with the Soundbeam and attached devices.

Here, I summarize four of my key studies using Soundbeam technology that demonstrate its effectiveness.

Research Study I: Assessing the Effectiveness of Applying Soundbeam Technology on Enhancing an Autistic Child's Disruptive Behaviors and Development (Lee, 2010f)

The purpose of this study was to investigate the effectiveness of applying Soundbeam technology to improve the disruptive behavior and other areas of development of a child with autism. The specific purposes were (1) to assess the effectiveness of applying Soundbeam technology on countering the participant's disruptive behavior and (2) to investigate the effectiveness of applying Soundbeam technology to improve the participant's other areas of development.

The research methodology of the study was a qualitative approach. The therapeutic procedures included the establishment of goals, observational assessment, and successive evaluation. A variety of teaching techniques and styles were used to adjust the participant's learning situation. The duration was 22 weeks with 30-minute instructional sessions twice a week.

The participant was a 4-year-old boy who had received a clinical diagnosis of autism with profound and multiple learning disabilities; he was selected by purposive sampling to participate in the study. Prior to the study, the participant had no spoken language, serious disruptive behavior, limited cognitive development, and a short attention span.

The results, also confirmed by the participant's parents, showed the positive efficacy of using Soundbeam technology to enhance the participant's disruptive behavior and other areas of development, such as cognition, language, increased attention span, and controlling negative behavior. The changes in the student's disruptive behaviors and other areas of development are shown in Table 7.1.

Table 7.1 CHANGES IN THE PARTICIPANT'S DEVELOPMENT

Stage / Development	Stage I Accommodation Stage (Week 1 to 4)	Stage II Vocalization Stage (Week 5 to 7)	Stage III Shifting Stage (Week 8 to 13)	Stage IV Stable Stage (Week 14 to 22)
Disruptive behavior	Serious disruptive behavioral problems, such as biting, hitting, kicking, slapping, and scratching people and hurting himself	Improved slightly	Improved more	Behaviors of violence and other problems were decreased obviously
Cognitive development	Poor	Could do a few correct responses	Understood directions more	Responded to few directions without help
Language competence	Mute most of the time	Making few vowel sounds and rhythmic and melodic sounds sometimes	Mainly making vowel sounds and humming with rhythmic melodies within one octave	Making vowel sounds and melodic phrase
Attention span	Could not focus on anything	Lasted few seconds	Lasted from 10 seconds to 7 minutes	Lasted from 10 seconds to 10 minutes
Emotions	Negative emotions all the time	Negative emotions decreased	Started showing his positive emotions	More positive emotions

Additional vibration equipment could be used to send sound through vibrating seats or cushions. It would be a good choice of media to help the participant gain a sense of knowing that through his movements, he is making the changes he hears.

Different sound effects, settings, and sensor positions might create different results. For example, when some individuals heard minor pitch sequences, they became emotional and cried. With no specific guidelines for using Soundbeam in these settings, it is imperative for teachers and researchers to observe the child and provide adaptations based on his or her reactions.

In this study, the child with autism demonstrated dramatic positive changes in behavior and to a lesser degree in other areas of development. It suggests to me that the Soundbeam may serve an effective avenue for enhancing development for children with autism.

Research Study II: A case study on integrating Soundbeam technology and music activities to enhance a special needs child's development of motor skills and attention span (Lee, 2011f)

The purpose of this study was to (1) integrate Soundbeam technology and music activities to assist a young child with Williams syndrome with the development of motor skills and (2) integrate Soundbeam technology and music activities to increase attention span for a young child with Williams syndrome.

The methodology of the study was both quantitative analysis and qualitative reports. The former was based on assessment scales used in the pretest and posttest by a physical therapist and observation forms by four observers. The latter included interviews with parents, observation reports from four observers, and the researcher's teaching log. This was a 20-week study, with half-hour sessions twice per week (40 sessions). Observations during all sessions were recorded on videotape.

The participant was a 4-year-old girl with physical disabilities who had received a clinical diagnosis of Williams syndrome. The child was enrolled in a regular private kindergarten in Taichung, Taiwan, and was selected by purposive sampling to participate in the study.

Throughout 10 weeks of research teaching, the participant's gross motor skills progressed, including running with stability at greater speeds and changing direction. The child was also able to hop on one foot, to roll a ball while sitting on the floor, and to catch the ball from three meters. Therefore, the activities during the research had a positive effect on the participant's gross motor skills. By the end of the study, the participant's attention span had increased. Her scores on increased attention span began at 1.125 and progressed to the end of the study to 3.75.

Through the sensor, the Soundbeam and its related equipment transformed the participant's movements into sounds and images. The participant demonstrated greater motivation for using physical movement. Therefore, throughout the research sessions, the participant's gross motor skills for running, jumping, and hopping were more stable and her fine motor skills for catching, throwing, pushing, and pulling were also positively improved. The Soundbeam technology and music activities created a positive effect on improving the young child's attention span. When adding images to sound games, the participant's attention increased. Other music activities also played a crucial role for the participant's learning, including substituting different movement directions from the "Hello Song" and the use of musical storytelling.

Research Study III: Exploring the efficiency of music therapy in enhancing the attention span of young special needs children (Lee, 2007)

The purpose of this study is to examine the use of music activities in helping to improve attention span and language ability in this critical group. Research questions were (1) Can young children with autism enhance their attention span through music activities? (2) Can young children with autism be motivated to make sounds through the use of musical instruments? (3) Can young children with autism be motivated to say one word through the use of musical instruments? (4) Can young children with autism be motivated to engage in simple conversation through the use of musical instruments?

The methodology of the study was a multiple-baseline-across-individuals design model. All observations of participants undertaken during baseline and intervention phases were recorded on videotape. Both qualitative and quantitative methods were used to obtain the results. Three 4- to 5- year-old children enrolled in a private kindergarten in Taichung, Taiwan, were selected by purposive sampling to take part in the experiment. These children all had been clinically diagnosed with autism.

The duration of this study was 20 weeks with 40-minute sessions once per week of specific, study-focused music education lessons. The initial four weeks of the study were dedicated to baseline observation. In assessing the participants' initial behavior, the number of observations for each child varied according to the research design. During this period, participants were observed in their regular school-day group activities. The baseline observations ended for each case when the observers were in agreement about the specific nature of each participant's behavioral and developmental challenges.

Prior to the start of the formal curriculum that served as the intervention, one free-play musical instrument session was held where each student was given the opportunity to choose, unprompted, musical instruments that he or she found attractive (Table 7.2). Their preferences were then used during activities and throughout the program. Mandarin Chinese was used for curriculum, materials, and all target sounds and words.

Table 7.2 PARTICIPANTS' PREFERENCES FOR MUSICAL INSTRUMENTS

Participant	Participant's Preferred Instruments
4-year-old, female, autism along with developmental delay	Rattles and hand-bell A
4.2-year-old, male, autism along with developmental delay	Bells
5-year-old, male, autism along with developmental delay	Different kinds of drums

Experimental Phase 1: The main goal of this stage was to attract children's learning attention by playing different instruments. Curriculum design is shown in Table 7.3.

Table 7.3 CURRICULUM DESIGN OF EXPERIMENTAL PHASE 1

Musical Activities	Instruments Used	Target Objectives
Hello song	Guitar	By hearing the sound of a guitar and becoming familiar with the song, children will develop the concept that music class is starting and focus attention on the instructor.
Attendance song	Participant's preferred instruments	By playing children's preferred instruments, they will pay attention to the activity.
Musical storytelling	Sound effect instruments	By playing different sound effect instruments, children will be more attentive in the class.
Relaxation time	Recorded music by researcher	By listening to the recorded music, children will calm down after the class activities.
Goodbye song	Guitar	Develop children's concept that music class is ending.

Experimental Phase 2: The main goal of this stage was to promote children's language ability, specifically in making sounds. Curriculum design is shown in Table 7.4.

Table 7.4 CURRICULUM DESIGN OF EXPERIMENTAL PHASE 2

Musical Activities	Instruments Used	Target Objectives
Hello song	Guitar	Children will be able to do the sound echo part of the song.
Attendance song	Participant's preferred instruments	By playing children's preferred instruments, they will be able to echo sounds of instruments.
Sound games	String instrument: Nan-Hu Blown instruments: recorder, slide-whistle, etc.	By playing the Nan-Hu, children will imitate and make nonsense sounds and different sounds. By playing the blown instruments, children can form more correct lip shapes.
Relaxation time	Singing soft sound song accompanied by guitar	By listening to the song, children will be able calm down after the class activities.
Goodbye song	Guitar	Develop children's concept that the music class is coming to an end.

Experimental Phase 3: The main goal of this stage was to promote children's language ability in speaking one word. Curriculum design is shown in Table 7.5.

Table 7.5 CURRICULUM DESIGN OF PHASE 3

Musical Activities	Instruments Used	Target Objectives
Hello song	Guitar	Children will be able to echo one word.
Attendance song	Participant's preferred instruments	By playing children's preferred instruments, they will be able to echo one sound related to the sound of the instruments.
Sound games	String instrument: Nan-Hu	By playing the Nan-Hu, children can make nonsense sounds and imitate the instrument's sound.
Relaxation time	Singing lullaby accompanied by guitar	By listening to the lullaby, children will calm down after the class activities.
Goodbye song	Guitar	Children will be able to sing one word.

Experimental Phase 4: The main goal of this stage was to promote children's language ability and be able to have a simple conversation. Curriculum design is shown in Table 7.6.

Table 7.6 CURRICULUM DESIGN OF PHASE 4

Musical Activities	Instruments Used	Target Objectives
Hello song	Guitar	Children will be able to sing a simple greeting sentence.
Attendance song	Participant's preferred instruments	Children respond to prompts by saying "Here I am" and playing their preferred instruments.
Singing activities, movement, and musical storytelling	Pitched and unpitched instruments, that is, sound effect instruments, castanets, bells, xylophone	By participating in different activities, children will be able to imitate and learn simple sentences.
Relaxation time	Listening to recorded soft music	By listening to the recorded music, children will calm down after the class activities.
Goodbye song	Guitar	Children will learn a simple greeting sentence, such as "See you next time, goodbye," etc.

The assessment instruments included a pretest and posttest conducted by a medical doctor, semistructured observation forms to gather data on attention span and language ability from three observers, and interview reports from the teachers and the parents. All intervention sessions were recorded on video and these were viewed and scored by three observers.

The pretest and posttest were conducted by a pediatric physician at a local hospital. Three observers who were trained graduate students conducted the observation session. The three participants' parents and teachers participated in interviews. At the end of the study, three social reliability assessment reports were completed by a parent, a teacher, and the school's principal.

According to the report forms from interviews with the parents and teachers at the beginning and at the end, the results showed that all participants made positive progress. Attention span was increased through music activities. Participants were motivated to make sounds through the use of musical instruments. They were also motivated to verbalize one word and engage in simple verbal conversation through the use of musical instruments. The results of this research provide support for the efficacy of music activities in increasing attention span and improving the language ability of children with autism. Further, the study was able to show that a positive learning environment helped the participants to be more comfortable participating.

The findings of the study also showed that (1) storytelling accompanied by sound effects is a useful tool for enhancing attention span in children with autism; (2) blowing musical instruments or whistles can be helpful for lip-rounding skills, as well as for supporting the production of certain phonemes; and (3) sound effect instruments, such as rain sticks, ocean drums, thunder tubes, and bird whistles, motivated and attracted the children's attention.

Research Study IV: Investigating the Impact of Music Activities Incorporating Soundbeam Technology on Children with Multiple Disabilities (Lee, 2015)

The purpose of this study was to investigate the impact of music activities incorporating Soundbeam technology on improving the development of children with multiple disabilities. Four 2- to 6-year-old children with multiple disabilities enrolled at an early intervention center in central Taiwan were selected by purposive sampling to participate. The duration of the study was 16 weeks with 50-minute instructional sessions once per week.

A mixed-method study, a quantitative analysis to measure validity based on assessment scales was used in the pretest and posttest administered by the classroom teacher. Three trained observers also collected qualitative data from observation forms and interviews with the parents and classroom teachers.

The participants were children who had received a clinical diagnosis of visual loss and multiple disabilities. Three of the children had severe cerebral palsy and one child had autism. They were enrolled in a public early intervention center in Taichung, Taiwan, and were selected by purposive sampling to participate in the study.

This was a 16-week study with weekly 50-minute sessions of specific, study-focused music activities that included parental involvement. Prior to the beginning of the study, four observations were used to assess the participants' strengths and challenges. All observations of the participants undertaken during all sessions were recorded on videotape.

The goal of the first stage was aimed at improving the participants' positive behaviors using music activities in a group setting. The goal of the second stage was to continue positive behaviors while enhancing their cognitive development.

Curriculum Design and Assessment

The curriculum included a hello song, attendance song, musical movement, music appreciation, musical storytelling, relaxation time, and a goodbye song.

The assessment instruments included the children's information from a medical doctor and the early intervention center, semistructured observation forms to gather data on the development of emotional responses and communication skills from the parents and three trained graduate student observers, interview reports from the teacher at the early intervention center and the parents at home, and teaching logs from the researcher.

All intervention sessions were recorded on video and these were viewed and scored by three trained observers. At the end of the study, four parents and three observers completed seven social reliability assessment reports.

The results of the study were that (1) through the music activities incorporating Soundbeam technology, the participants' positive behavior progressed, and (2) music activities incorporating Soundbeam technology had positive effects on the communication skills for the children with multiple disabilities.

The study also demonstrated that a safe and nonthreatening environment can be invaluable in a group therapeutic setting for children with multiple disabilities. Children with multiple disabilities are often unable to participate in music classes that use traditional learning methods. Using the Soundbeam, all children are able to participate by creating, performing, and/or responding.

Using switches with the Soundbeam creates additional opportunities for children with multiple disabilities, such as those with cerebral palsy and visual loss. By using even limited movement, children with multiple disabilities are able to receive immediate feedback from their movement using switches and sensors when they make a connection between the sound they hear and their movement.

ASSESSMENT RESOURCES FOR TEACHERS AND RESEARCHERS

Ongoing assessment is essential throughout teaching or during research-based teaching interventions. This includes assessment prior to beginning a study with young children with severe disabilities. Then, prior to teaching, teachers and researchers must make informed lesson plans that are developmentally appropriate for the child's needs. During teaching, educators must continually observe the children's responses. After teaching, an assessment of the learning outcomes must be made to make adjustments for more effective instruction. The teacher resources provided outline some areas of assessment used to support the teaching and learning process (see Appendix A).

Assistive technology devices such as Soundbeam and multisensory environments have been designed to help children participate more actively and more completely in the educational and developmental process. Children who are directly involved in instructional activities develop independence and become more active learners. The studies noted here have demonstrated that music activities with technology and multisensory environments provide positive outcomes for young children with disabilities. The following describe some of the benefits of using technologies and multisensory environments:

1. Opportunities to experience an ideal and fun way for children who need more exposure or practice in a motivating setting
2. Opportunities to experience dramatic effects for all participants to soothe their moods and calm their minds
3. Opportunities for an environment through which even profoundly physically disabled or learning-impaired individuals can become expressive and communicative using music and sound
4. Student motivation to receive musical feedback from whatever movement children may have

APPENDIX A

Teacher Resources for Initial and Summative Assessments

Part I: Child's Information Chart	
Name	Male or Female
Date of Assessment	
Primary Diagnosis	
Secondary Diagnosis	
Presenting Characteristics	
Medications	
Adaptive Devices	
Positioning Considerations	
Other therapies	
Availability of family and other support	
Current health status	
Infection control procedures	
Religious preference	
Cultural considerations	

Part II: Cognitive Functioning

Attention span/concentration

_____ Attending to tasks for 10 seconds at a time

_____ Attending to tasks for 20 seconds at a time

_____ Attending to tasks for 30 seconds at a time

_____ Attending to tasks for 60 seconds at a time

Participation

_____ Engaging in musical activity session for 10 minutes

_____ Engaging in musical activity session for 15 minutes

_____ Engaging in musical activity session for 30 minutes

_____ Engaging in musical activity session for 50 minutes

Ability to follow directions

_____ Performing tasks with manipulation (putting through)

_____ Performing tasks with light physical prompts

_____ Performing tasks with repeated and simplified directions

_____ Performing one-step tasks with simplified directions

_____ Performing tasks with two- to three-step verbal directions

Decision making

_____ Making decisions when structure is provided with limited options

_____ Making decisions with structure and unlimited options

_____ Making decisions independently

Other comments:

Part III: Fine, Gross, and Sensorimotor Behaviors

Tactile sensitivity

Describe head support

Visually focuses on source of musical stimulus for 2–3 seconds when stimulus is presented:

_____ Directly in front of client

_____ 45 degrees to the right of client

_____ 45 degrees to the left of client

_____ 90 degrees to the right of client

_____ 90 degrees to the left of client

Visually tracks source of musical stimulus as it is:

_____ Moving from in front of client to 45 degrees right of client

_____ Moving from in front of client to 45 degrees left of client

_____ Moving from in front of client to 90 degrees right of client

_____ Moving from in front of client to 90 degrees left of client

Visually locates source of musical stimulus presented:

_____ Above client   _____ Below client

_____ Behind client   _____ Anywhere in room

Visually orients to source of musical stimulus:

_____ Reaching toward and touching stimulus

_____ Grasping stimulus object

_____ Shaking object to produce sound for 2–3 seconds or two deliberate to
     and from motions

Shakes instrument for:

_____ 10 seconds with right _____ left _____ hand

_____ 20 seconds with right _____ left _____ hand

_____ 30 seconds with right _____ left _____ hand

_____ 60 seconds with right _____ left _____ hand

If physically disabled, accomplishes the above items with the use of adaptation (specify):

Grasps mallet using palmar prehension and beats drum:

_____ At least 2 times with right _____ left _____ hand

_____ At least 4 times with right _____ left _____ hand

_____ At least 10 seconds with right _____ left _____ hand

_____ At least 20 seconds with right _____ left _____ hand

_____ At least 30 seconds with right _____ left _____ hand

_____ At least 60 seconds with right _____ left _____ hand

If physically disabled, accomplishes the above items with the use of adaptation (specify):

Using two mallets, plays drum:

_____ In parallel motion

_____ In alternating motion

Using one mallet, plays drum by crossing midline:

_____ Right to left

_____ Left to right

Child can:

_____ Transfer an instrument from one hand to the other

_____ Clap hands

_____ Hit sticks together

_____ Use pincer grasp to play xylophone

_____ Walk at consistent speed

_____ Stomp feet to specific tempi

_____ March to specific tempo

_____ Use body movements to imitate animals or other imaginary
     activities

Other comments:

Part IV: Social Validity

To support the validity of the study, a feedback form should be used by parents, school faculty, and/or observers. In this example, all respondents would score various aspects of the study on a "5 to 1" Likert scale.

Feedback Questions	Strongly Agreed (5)	Agreed (4)	No Comment (3)	Disagreed (2)	Strongly Disagreed (1)
Part I					
The research teaching has a crucial meaning for children with disabilities.					
Goals					
The research goals fit with the needs of children with disabilities.					
Music activities have positive effects on children with disabilities.					
Music activities are the same, not dangerous learning methods, and good for children with disabilities.					
You accept the use of music activities to teach children with disabilities.					
Total of the percentage	%	%	%	%	%

Feedback Questions	Progressed a lot (5)	Progressed (4)	No Progress (3)	Regressed (2)	Regressed a lot (1)
Part II					
Motor Skills and Attention Span					
After taking the class, the participant's gross motors have:					
After taking the class, the participant's fine motor skills have:					
After taking the class, the participant's attention span has:					
After taking the class, the participant's attention span while listening (including speaking with people, listening to stories and music) has:					
After taking the class, the participant's participation in group and class activities has:					
Total of the percentage:	%	%	%	%	%

Other comments:

NOTES

1. See Lee (2010a–i, 2011a–f, 2012a–g).
2. Zhuyin is a phonetic notation system for transcribing spoken Chinese, especially Mandarin. Taiwanese have a different approach to Chinese pronunciation. In China, people use the Pinyin system. In Taiwan, people use the Zhuyin system.
3. See http://www.soundbeam.co.uk/.

REFERENCES

Crowe, B. J., & Rio, R. (2004). Implications of technology in music therapy practice and research for music therapy education: A review of literature. *Journal of Music Therapy*, 41(4), 282–320.

Ellis, P. (1995). Incidental music: A case study in the development of sound therapy. *British Journal of Music Education*, 12, 59–70.

Ellis, P. (2007). *The development of interactive multisensory environments for expression, 1992–2007*. Keynote presentation at the Luxembourg Society for Music Therapy. Luxembourg.

Ellis, P. (2008). *Sound therapy*. Paper presented at the International Conference for the 2007-2008 Academic Year: The Application of Technology for Early Childhood Education and Special Education. Taiwan: Chaoyang University of Technology.

Ellis, P., & Van Leeuwen, L. (2000). *Living sound: Human interaction and children with autism*. Paper presented at the ISME Commission on Music in Special Education, Music Therapy and Music Medicine, Regina, Canada.

Hammel, A. M., & Hourigan, R. M. (2013). *Teaching music to students with autism*. New York: Oxford University Press.

Lee, L. (2007). Exploring the efficiency of music therapy in enhancing the attention span of young special needs children. *Journal of College of Humanities and Social Sciences*, 5(1), 211–240.

Lee, L. (2009). An action study on developing young children's creativity and physical movement through modern technology. *Journal of College of Humanities and Social Sciences*, 7(2), 1–40.

Lee, L. (2010a). *Music therapy for young children*. Taiwan: Hsin Shue Ling Publication.

Lee, L. (2010b). Assessing the effectiveness of applying Soundbeam technology on enhancing an autistic child's disruptive behaviors and development. In L. Lee (Ed.), *Proceeding of the 18th international seminar of the Commission on Music in Special Education, Music Therapy, and Music Medicine* (pp. 10–23). International Society for Music Education. China: Beijing.

Lee, L. (2010c). Music therapy enhances attention span and promotes language ability in young special needs children. In L. Schraer-Joiner & K. McCord (Eds.), *Proceeding of the ISME commission seminar on Music in Special Education, Music Therapy, and Music Medicine* (pp. 34–45). International Society for Music Education.

Lee, L. (2010d). The use of musical instruments and supplemental materials to enhance spoken language acquisition by children with autism: A case study. In L. Schraer-Joiner & K. McCord (Eds.), *Proceeding of the ISME commission seminar on Music in Special Education, Music Therapy, and Music Medicine* (pp. 83–94). International Society for Music Education.

Lee, L. (2010e). An empirical study on teaching a foreign language through music to preschoolers at an inclusive class in Taiwan. In W. Sims (Ed.), *Proceeding of the 29th International Society for Music Education World Conference* (pp. 120–123).

Lee, L. (2010f). Assessing the effectiveness of applying Soundbeam technology on enhancing an autistic child's disruptive behaviors and development. In L. Schraer-Joiner & K. McCord (Eds.), *Proceeding of the ISME commission seminar on Music in Special Education, Music Therapy, and Music Medicine* (pp. 8–22). International Society for Music Education. .

Lee, L. (2010g). Music therapy enhances attention span and promotes language ability in young special needs children. In L. Schraer-Joiner & K. McCord (Eds.), *Proceeding of the ISME commission seminar on Music in Special Education, Music Therapy, and Music Medicine* (pp. 34–45). International Society for Music Education.

Lee, L. (2010h). The use of musical instruments and supplemental materials to enhance spoken language acquisition by children with autism: A case study. In L. Schraer-Joiner & K. McCord (Eds.), *Proceeding of the ISME Commission Seminar on Music in Special Education, Music Therapy, and Music Medicine* (pp. 83–94). International Society for Music Education.

Lee, L. (2010i). An empirical study on teaching a foreign language through music to preschoolers at an inclusive class in Taiwan. W. Sims (Ed.), *Proceeding of the 29th International Society for Music Education World Conference* (pp. 120–123).

Lee, L. (2011a). *Soundbeam 5—Chinese instruction manual.* Taiwan: Zhong Zhen Company.

Lee, L. (2011b). *Soundbeam 5: Curriculum.* Taiwan: Rong Zen Company.

Lee, L. (2011c). *Soundbeam 5—Research reports.* Taiwan: Zhong Zhen Company.

Lee, L. (2011d). Music, a natural connection for young learners' development. In K. Kumpulainen & A. Toom (Eds.), *The proceedings of the 21st annual conference of the European Teacher Education Network (ETEN)* (pp. 16–22). ETEN and the University of Helsinki, Finland.

Lee, L. (2011e). A study of the use of technology of sounds and physical movement with visually impaired children. *Journal of College of Humanities and Social Sciences, 9*(2), 87–108.

Lee, L. (2011f). A case study on integrating Soundbeam technology and music activities to enhance a special needs child's development of motor skills and attention span. *Journal of College of Humanities and Social Sciences, 9*(1), 87–108.

Lee, L. (2012a). *Theory & practice of music educational therapy for young children with disabilities: A report of the industry-university collaboration research at Taichung Early Intervention Center (theory).* Taiwan: Taiwan Fund for Children and Families.

Lee, L. (2012b). *Theory & practice of music educational therapy for young children with disabilities: A report of the industry-university collaboration research at Taichung Early Intervention Center (research report I).* Taiwan: Taiwan Fund for Children and Families.

Lee, L. (2012c). *Theory & practice of music educational therapy for young children with disabilities: A report of the industry-university collaboration research at Taichung Early Intervention Center (research report II).* Taiwan: Taiwan Fund for Children and Families.

Lee, L. (2012d). *Theory & practice of music educational therapy for young children with disabilities: A report of the industry-university collaboration research at Taichung Early Intervention Center (research report III).* Taiwan: Taiwan Fund for Children and Families.

Lee, L. (2012e). *Theory & practice of music educational therapy for young children with disabilities: A report of the industry-university collaboration research at Taichung Early Intervention Center (research report IV).* Taiwan: Taiwan Fund for Children and Families.

Lee, L. (2012f). Music, a wonderful window for young children's learning. *The Learning Teacher Magazine, 3*(2), 6–7.

Lee, L. (2015). Investigating the impact of music activities incorporating Soundbeam Technology on children with multiple disabilities. *Journal of the European Teacher Education Network, 10,* 1–12.

Lee, L., & Liu, H. (2012). Evaluating the effectiveness of music activities on emotions and communication for a child with autism in a multi-sensory environment. In L. E. Schraer-Joiner

(Ed.), *Proceedings of the 18th International Seminar of the Commission on Music in Special Education, Music Therapy, and Music Medicine*. Nedlands, WA: International Society for Music Education.

McPhail, P. (2003). *Soundbeam in special education: Movement into music*. UK: Soundabout.

Mundy, P., & Neal, A. (2001). Neural plasticity, joint attention, and a transactional social-orienting model of autism. *International Review of Research in Mental Retardation: Autism*, 23, 138–168.

Mundy, P., & Newell, L. (2007). Attention, joint attention, and social cognition. *Current Directions in Psychological Science*, 16(5), 269–274. doi:10.1111/j.1467-8721.2007.00518.x

Ockelford, A. (2008). *Music for children and young people with complex needs*. New York, NY: Oxford University Press.

Pennington, B. (2002). *The development of psychopathology: Nature and nurture*. New York, NY: Guilford Press.

Sigman, M., & Ruskin, E. (1999). Continuity and change in the social competence of children with autism, Down syndrome, and developmental delays. *Monographs of the Society in Research in Child Development*, 64, 1–114.

Soundbeam Project. (2003). Soundbeam 2®. Retrieved from http://www.soundbeam.co.uk/

CHAPTER 8

Behavioral Issues in the Music Classroom

Promoting the Successful
Engagement of All Students

ALICE ANN DARROW
AND MARY ADAMEK

There is no doubt that students who consistently disrupt class instruction are some of the most difficult to include in the music classroom. Such students present significant challenges to their teachers and to their peers alike. They generally require an inordinate amount of the teacher's time and they interfere with the learning of their peers. Behavioral disruptions in the music classroom can be particularly discouraging to the beginning teacher, thus leading to disillusionment and early departure from the profession. Students with extreme misbehaviors can often challenge even the most seasoned and gifted teacher.

Music educators strive to enrich the lives of all their students through active engagement in music. When some students become disruptive, disengaged, or unmotivated, they no longer are active learners. These students require instructional strategies that will engage them or interventions that will decrease or extinguish their problem behaviors. Students may engage in minor misconduct that is easily remedied with surface behavior techniques, or students may exhibit severe misbehaviors that require major behavioral interventions. The best teaching approach is to prevent problem behaviors before they occur, although not all problem behaviors can be prevented.

There are many reasons for students' problem behaviors, and some—such as violence in the home—are often out of the control of the teacher. In addition, schools are more diverse than ever before, and while this diversity is positive and can provide an enriching environment for all concerned, it can also create difficulties for music educators, who typically teach large numbers of students, all with varying cognitive, physical, and psychosocial abilities. Music educators generally work with students from throughout the school, and while music is a highly desirable activity for most, the sheer number of students who enter the music room can make classroom management difficult. Nevertheless, music educators often find that successfully teaching students who present special challenges can be rewarding and, ultimately, one of the most gratifying experiences of their career.

TO LABEL OR NOT TO LABEL?

No one wants to be defined by his or her disability. Defining individuals by their disabilities, as if the disability makes up the entirety of the person, fails to recognize the humanness of individuals that goes well beyond their disabilities. A disability is not the most important descriptor of any individual (Adamek & Darrow, 2010). Nevertheless, there are useful aspects to labeling students' disabilities in the educational context. Labels are sometimes a prerequisite to acquiring the necessary accommodations for a student or to receiving federal funding for the programs and schools he or she attends. Labels also provide a way for professionals to communicate about a group of students and their specific needs (Darrow, 2013).

Labeling is a process of creating descriptors to identify persons who differ from the norm. *Normal* is a broad relative term. Everyone is different in some way from everyone else. The type and extent of the difference, however, are the real issue in determining descriptive labels for students with disabilities, particularly those who have emotional or behavioral disabilities. Behavior is a social construct, and there is no clear consensus on what constitutes abnormal or aberrant behavior. All students exhibit behaviors at one time or another that might be considered inappropriate. There are, however, three criteria that must be met for a student's behavior to be considered a disability (Heward, 2012):

1. *Chronicity:* The behavior must be exhibited over a period of time.
2. *Severity:* The behavior must be extreme and outside the bounds of typical behavior.
3. *Pervasiveness:* The behavior must be present across school settings and adversely affect school performance.

With these criteria in mind, the authors will use the term *emotional and behavioral disabilities* to identify the group of students addressed in this chapter.

PREVALENCE OF EMOTIONAL AND BEHAVIORAL DISABILITIES

Some studies indicate that 3% to 6% of youth exhibit persistent behavioral problems in school (Blanchard, Gurka, & Blackman, 2006; Kauffman & Landrum, 2009). Approximately 1% of the total US school-aged population receives services for diagnosed emotional and behavioral disabilities (see Table 8.1). This is approximately 6% of all students receiving special education services under the Individuals with Disabilities Education Act (IDEA). In addition to these identified students, those who have been diagnosed with attention deficit hyperactivity disorder (ADHD; which is categorized under "other health impairment") and autism have diagnoses

Table 8.1 STUDENTS WITH DISABILITIES SERVED UNDER IDEA IN 2011, AGES 3–21

IDEA Disability Category	Number of Students Receiving Special Education Services Under IDEA (2011 Data)	Percentage of Students Receiving Special Education Services Served Under IDEA
Specific learning disability	2,363,890	36
Speech/language impairment	1,413,289	22
Other health impairment[a]	**754,527**	**12**
Intellectual disability	443,054	7
Autism[b]	**458,208**	7
Developmental delay (before age 9)	393,138	6
Emotional disturbance	**374,552**	**6**
Multiple disabilities	132,986	2
Hearing impairment	78,545	1
Orthopedic impairment	61,763	1
Visual impairment	29,047	1
Traumatic brain injury	25,969	<1
Deaf/blind	1,583	<1

Note. IDEA = Individuals with Disabilities Education Act. From Data Accountability Center, 2011, http://www.ideadata.org.
[a] Category includes students with attention deficit hyperactivity disorder.
[b] 2007 data shows autism at 4%; increase of 3% in 4 years.

that are specifically related to atypical or inappropriate behavior. Students who have difficulty learning, communicating, and interacting with others due to other disabilities (i.e., intellectual disabilities, learning disabilities, deaf/hard of hearing) may also demonstrate problem behaviors in the classroom. In the United States, these disabilities are listed in the IDEA as disability categories under which students are eligible for special education services.

DEFINING EMOTIONAL AND BEHAVIORAL DISABILITIES

Defining emotional and behavioral disabilities is difficult for a number of reasons. Teachers' expectations for students' behavior vary, as do their tolerance for certain behaviors. In addition, school administrators responsible for maintaining discipline often determine whether behaviors are considered typical or aberrant. Professionals also define emotional and behavioral disabilities differently. This incongruence is based on differences in the theoretical model used, differences in interpreting and measuring behavior, and variations in terms of what is acceptable and unacceptable behavior related to cultural and societal norms. The US federal definition is even subjective and open to interpretation. The definition of emotional disturbance adopted by the US Department of Education and included in PL 94-142 and IDEA 2004 is as follows:

(i) Emotional disturbance means a condition exhibiting one or more of the following characteristics over a long period of time and to a marked degree that adversely affects educational performance:
   (a) an inability to learn which cannot be explained by intellectual, sensory, or health factors;
   (b) an inability to build or maintain satisfactory interpersonal relationships with peers and teachers;
   (c) inappropriate types of behaviors or feelings under normal circumstances;
   (d) a general pervasive mood of unhappiness or depression;
   (e) a tendency to develop physical symptoms or fears associated with personal or school problems.

(ii) Emotional disturbance includes schizophrenia. The term does not apply to children who are socially maladjusted, unless it is determined that they have an emotional disturbance. (IDEA, 2004, p. 46756)

Many of the terms used in this definition are vague. What is "inappropriate behavior"? What constitutes "unhappiness"?

The *Diagnostic and Statistic Manual of Mental Disorders*, fifth edition (DSM-V; American Psychiatric Association [APA], 2013), identifies a variety of behavioral disabilities including oppositional defiant disorder, intermittent explosive disorder, and conduct disorder in a category titled "disruptive, impulse-control, and conduct disorders." ADHD and autism are both listed in the section titled "neurodevelopmental disorders." While the DSM-V lists criteria for diagnosing the disabilities (APA, 2013), teachers may be as equally concerned with the manifestation of the behaviors in their classroom as they are with the specific disability diagnosis. However, teachers may want to be aware of some characteristic behaviors when informed of a student's diagnosis. Table 8.2 lists the basic diagnostic features noted in the DSM-V (APA, 2013).

Table 8.2 DIAGNOSTIC AND STATISTICAL MANUAL OF MENTAL DISORDERS (DSM) DIAGNOSIS AND BEHAVIORS

DSM Diagnosis	Diagnostic Features	Possible School Behaviors
Attention deficit hyperactivity disorder (ADHD)	Pattern of inattention and/or hyperactivity-impulsivity	Inattention: makes careless mistakes; difficulty sustaining attention to task; avoids school work; loses items, disorganized; forgetful Hyperactivity-impulsive: fidgety; interrupts others; difficulty waiting for turn; frequent movement/out of seat; unable to engage in quiet play
Autism spectrum disorder	Difficulty with social communication and social interaction	Difficulty expressing self or understanding intent of others, leading to frustration, misunderstandings with teachers and peers, and possible behavioral outbursts
	Restricted patterns of behavior or unusual behaviors	May have difficulty with transitions, flexibility, and changing focus in school setting, creating anxiety and negative behaviors
Oppositional defiant disorder	Pattern of irritable or angry mood, with argumentative or defiant behavior	Argumentative, loses temper easily, defies authority figures, deliberately annoys others
Conduct disorder	Persistent pattern of behavior where the rights of others or age-appropriate social norms are violated	Bullying, threatening others, fighting, destruction of property, theft, lying

School psychologists generally consider four dimensions of a behavior when defining behavioral or emotional disabilities: (1) the frequency of the behavior, (2) the intensity of the behavior, (3) the duration of the behavior, and (4) the age appropriateness of the behavior (Gargiulo, 2012). All teachers know of times when students talk out in class, leave their seats at inappropriate times, or have emotional outbursts. These behaviors may be problematic at times but not have the frequency, intensity, or duration to necessitate a formal behavioral intervention. To determine the need for short- or long-term intervention, problem behaviors must be defined objectively and in measurable terms. To do so, the four dimensions of a behavior need to be considered (frequency, intensity, duration, and age appropriateness). It could be that simple time away to diffuse a behavior is all that is required; however, if a student has serious emotional or behavioral issues, a more in-depth approach may be required.

RISK FACTORS AND CAUSES ASSOCIATED WITH EMOTIONAL AND BEHAVIORAL DISABILITIES

Many biological, environmental, and psychosocial risk factors are associated with emotional and behavioral disabilities in children. Biological risk factors are associated with genetic influences or biological insults from injury, infection, toxins, or poor nutrition. Family stress or discord, neglect or abuse, poverty, and parents' poor mental health are psychosocial risk factors that can negatively affect a child's behavioral outcomes in school (Gargiulo, 2012). In addition to these risk factors, students may have difficulty in classrooms where teachers have inconsistent or ineffective behavior management skills, inappropriate expectations for students, or nonfunctional or irrelevant curriculum and instruction. Some emotional and behavioral disabilities are idiopathic and no risk factor or cause can be determined.

Why Music?

Music is a highly desirable activity that can be motivating and engaging even for students with the most severe disabilities. Music is flexible and adaptable and appeals to students of all ages. Preferred music and musical experiences can be used as reinforcement in a behavior management plan to aid in the development of students' positive behaviors. Additionally, some music behaviors, such as singing, are incompatible with inappropriate behaviors, such as talking out in class; consequently, engagement in these music behaviors may strengthen students' positive behaviors and decrease their negative behaviors. Music has been used successfully to promote positive behaviors in a variety of placements for students with emotional or behavioral disabilities (Epstein, Pratto, & Skipper, 1990; Rio & Tenney, 2002; Silverman, 2003). Despite music's appeal and ability to prompt prosocial behaviors, music educators have indicated that students with behavioral disabilities are the most difficult to teach in the music classroom (Darrow, 1999).

PREVENTING PROBLEM BEHAVIORS

Some teachers do not see students with behavioral disabilities as having a legitimate disability, and consequently, they expect them to control their behaviors when they enter the classroom. These students, like many students with disabilities, require assistance to manage their disability and to help them become educated and sociable adults. There are many ways to support students with emotional and behavioral disabilities. One way is to prevent their problem behaviors before they occur. Too often teachers think of managing behaviors after they occur. By determining the rewards for appropriate behaviors and the consequences for inappropriate behaviors a priori, teachers can avoid many of the disruptive behaviors that occur in the classroom. Classroom management should be seen as a total process that affects all students by creating an environment conducive for learning.

By utilizing effective teaching techniques, teachers can create an environment that supports students' positive behaviors. Using an appropriate curriculum and careful pacing help to keep students engaged. A positive and motivated teacher can also serve as a model for the kind of attitude students need to learn. Even setting up the physical environment with thoughtful planning can help prevent off-task or problem behaviors. All students will have better experiences in music class when positive behaviors are increased and negative behaviors are kept to a minimum. In the following paragraphs are some specific areas to consider when setting up or reviewing the process of behavior management (Adamek & Darrow, 2010).

Positive teacher attitude with high expectations for students. Teachers who have a positive attitude and confidence in their teaching can contribute to students' feelings of security in class. It is also important to have high expectations for students of all ability levels and to make sure that all students are challenged at appropriate levels of difficulty.

Clear expectations, known by all students. Teacher effectiveness can be influenced by developing and maintaining classroom rules and procedures (Marzano, 2003). However, all students must know the rules to follow them. Often teachers will utilize student input to develop classroom rules, thus giving students ownership in the process and end result. Rules may be broad, such as "respect others" or "follow directions," although specificity is recommended by some experts, such as "use instruments carefully" or "stay in assigned area" (Madsen & Madsen, 2000). Students also need to be reminded when they are following the rules (doing the right thing) and when they are not following the rules (inappropriate behaviors). Following through on the rules and frequent reinforcement when students are observed following classroom rules help to promote a positive classroom structure.

Appropriate and motivating curriculum and classroom activities. Students are motivated to engage in music experiences when they see them as valuable to their lives, interesting, and at the appropriate level of challenge for their abilities. Teachers can help students understand how the music pertains to their lives, as well as why the music is important to the broader culture. Boredom, lack of interest, and frustration can often lead to behavior problems. Fortunately, we can engage students in music with many levels of complexity. It is up to the teacher to be flexible and to adapt with more complexity or less complexity depending on the changing needs of individual students.

Pacing and clear directions. Appropriate pacing is important as it helps students stay engaged, interested, and successful. Pacing that is too slow can create boredom, and pacing that is too fast can create feelings of frustration. Both situations can lead to student disengagement. Often it takes a creative teacher to master appropriate pacing in a class with students of varying abilities. Students might work together in collaborative learning groups, with students at all levels in each group, providing opportunities for leadership, peer mentoring, and additional time for review and practice.

Structure in teaching and in the environment. Teachers typically have a clear idea of the desired outcome for their music classes. An important skill for all teachers is to be able to create a series of logical steps—building on previous knowledge and abilities—to help the students successfully reach the intended goals. This well-structured approach is in contrast to a class where information is presented in unrelated or random experiences for the students, making it difficult for them to build on previous skills. A structured environment is essential to create a visual sense of order for students and to decrease opportunities for off-task behaviors. Distracting objects abound in a music classroom, so a thoughtful look by the teacher of what the students experience in class can provide ideas for creating a more structured and less distracting environment.

Positive teacher responses. Teachers must also be sure to let students know when they are behaving appropriately, following directions, and meeting the teacher's expectations. Too often teachers ignore when students are doing what they are asked to do. When teachers stop and give attention to students whose behavioral expectations are being met, they encourage student engagement and often prompt the positive behaviors of other students.

Tolerating selected behaviors. At times, teachers may need to ignore certain behaviors that may seem troublesome or only slightly disruptive. One must consider the student's level of functioning, developmental stage, and abilities when attempting to modify behaviors. Some instances where teachers may need to tolerate behaviors rather than impose consequences include when a student is learning a new skill (learner's leeway), when the behaviors are due to a disability, and when the behaviors are typical for the development of the student (Long & Newman, 1980; Shea & Bauer, 2012). Teachers may need to provide additional support and differentiated instruction, as well as redirection, to help students succeed.

While teachers can prevent some behavioral issues by creating a positive learning environment, not all behavior problems can be prevented, even with the most careful planning and effective teaching techniques. Classroom management is a total process that involves a wide array of strategies and interventions. Some behavioral interventions are instituted school-wide and are used with all students; others are specific to an academic program, such as music; and still others are used by individual teachers. All teachers need to determine what interventions and strategies work for them and their students. Doing so ensures that students will be poised for successful experiences in the music classroom.

SCHOOL-WIDE INTERVENTIONS TO PROMOTE POSITIVE BEHAVIORS

Good classroom management is critical to teaching all students, though particularly so to reach students who find it difficult to comply with teachers' expectations and classroom rules. Even teachers with good classroom management frequently need to employ interventions for students with emotional and behavioral disabilities. A positive approach is recommended as the first course of action (Zirpoli, 2012). There are a number of interventions that are commonly recommended by behavior specialists and professionals in the field of special education. The first three interventions discussed next are also required as a part of IDEA (2004).

Functional Behavioral Analysis

The purpose of a functional behavioral analysis is to determine the function of problem behaviors, to identify positive strategies, and to substitute behaviors that can serve the same function as the problem behaviors. By identifying significant, pupil-specific social, affective, cognitive, and/or environmental factors associated with the occurrence of problem behaviors or the nonoccurrence of the desired behaviors, behavioral interventions can better address the causes of students' misbehaviors. Brady and Halle (1997) identified three components of a functional behavior assessment:

1. Interviews with the student, parents, teachers, and classmates about the occurrence of the behavior and surrounding circumstances
2. Observations of the student when the behavior occurs, noting antecedents and consequences to the behavior, as well as what occurs during the behavior
3. Manipulation of specific variables (called analog probe) such as setting, activity, or participants to gain a better understanding of when and why the behavior occurs

The first two components are generally considered functional assessments, and the third is considered functional analysis. Of the two assessments, the more reliable method is to directly observe students' behaviors in their natural environment and to analyze the behaviors' antecedents (environmental events that immediately precede the problem behaviors) and consequences (environmental events that immediately follow the problem behaviors).

Three important outcomes are achieved through functional assessments (Hardman, Drew, & Egan, 2008):

1. A concrete definition of the problem behavior
2. One or more predictions regarding when, where, and under what conditions the problem behavior will occur
3. Identification of the function the problem behavior serves, such as to get attention, to avoid work, or to control others

Information gathered from a functional behavioral assessment is used to determine what initiates, sustains, or ends a behavior, and with that information, a behavior intervention plan (BIP) is developed. This plan should include positive behavioral support strategies designed to teach appropriate replacement behaviors (Hallahan, Kauffman, & Pullen, 2009).

Positive Behavioral Supports

The purpose of positive behavioral support (PBS) is to create a supportive and successful environment for all students, though particularly for those with emotional and behavioral disabilities. It refers to a range of preventive and positive interventions designed to eliminate challenging behaviors and to replace them with behaviors that are conducive to academic and social success. PBS is also a comprehensive research-based approach intended to address all aspects of a problem behavior. It involves a proactive, collaborative, assessment-based process to develop effective, positive individualized interventions for individuals with challenging behaviors (Koegel, Koegel, & Dunlap, 1996; Shepherd, 2010). Lewis and Sugai (1999) identified six components of a PBS program:

1. A statement of purpose
2. A clearly stated list of behaviors that students are expected to exhibit
3. Procedures for teaching expected behaviors
4. Procedures and incentives for reinforcing expected behaviors
5. Procedures and consequences for discouraging inappropriate behaviors
6. Procedures for maintaining records and assessing the effectiveness of the procedures

In addition to these components, PBS utilizes a three-tier system of increasing support. Primary supports are provided to 80% to 85% of the student body. These supports are generally implemented in environments such as the cafeteria, hallways, or recess. Secondary supports are provided to 10% to 15% of the study body, and tertiary supports to those in the 5% to 10% who present the most challenging behaviors.

Along with reducing problem behaviors, the PBS approach is structured to address quality-of-life issues and plans for the student's future. It is an approach that merges values regarding the rights of people with disabilities with practical application of how learning and behavioral change occur. The principal goal of PBS is to improve the daily lives of students and their support providers in home, school, and community settings (Hallahan et al., 2009; Turnbull, Turnbull, & Wehmeyer, 2010). PBS is supported by recent mandates, including the 1997 amendments to the IDEA, which call for the use of functional behavioral assessment and positive supports and strategies (IDEA, 2004).

Response to Intervention

Response to intervention (RTI) has been used to identify students with learning disabilities, but it has also been used to identify students who present problem behaviors that interfere with learning (Fairbanks, Sugai, Guardino, & Lathrop, 2007; Gresham, 2005). It is a process that provides research-based interventions that address a student's specific problem behaviors. Like the PBS approach, it utilizes a three-tier model with primary, secondary, and tertiary interventions. Primary or universal interventions are school-wide behavioral interventions used with all students. Secondary interventions are specialized interventions used with specific students or classrooms. Tertiary interventions are comprehensive, individualized, extensive interventions used for students who are not responding to the primary or secondary interventions (Shepherd, 2010). Music educators generally implement the interventions at the primary or secondary levels; behavior specialists are often consulted to design and implement interventions at the tertiary level.

The RTI process uses data to examine the student's behavior over time and to make appropriate educational and behavioral decisions based on those data. In the RTI process, one or more research-validated interventions are used to address a student's problem behaviors. The student's behaviors are monitored frequently to determine if the interventions are effective, as evidenced by a reduction in the student's problem behaviors. If collected data indicate the student is not demonstrating adequate progress despite multiple implemented research-based interventions, alternative placements are considered.

Applied Behavioral Analysis

Applied behavioral analysis (ABA) is a process of systematically applying the methods of science (description, quantification, and analysis) to improve behaviors of social significance and to demonstrate that the interventions employed are responsible for the improvement in behavior (Baer, Wolf, & Risley, 1987; Madsen & Madsen, 2000; Sulzer-Azaroff & Mayer, 1991). Behaviors are identified that need to be extinguished, as well as those that are to be taught and reinforced. ABA focuses on clearly defining the problem behavior within the context of the environment, reliably measuring and objectively evaluating the target behavior, arranging the environment and providing consequences for decreasing undesirable behaviors, and teaching desirable behaviors through reinforcement-based opportunities for response (Hunt & Marshall, 2005).

In ABA, problem behaviors are defined objectively. Imprecise terms such as *aggression* or *disruptive* are redefined in terms of behaviors that are observable and measurable, so their frequency, duration, or other measurable properties can be recorded (Sulzer-Azaroff & Mayer, 1991). For example, a child's "disruptive behavior" might be defined as "yelling out, leaving seat, or hitting other students." The goal of "developing classroom discipline" might be defined as "requesting permission to leave seat, raising hand before speaking, completing work assignments in the allotted time."

Individualized interventions are an essential component of programs based on ABA methodologies (Shepherd, 2010). This process includes the following components (Alberto & Troutman, 1999; Cooper, Heron, & Heward, 1987; Sulzer-Azaroff & Mayer, 1991):

- Selection of interfering behavior or behavioral skill deficit
- Identification of goals and objectives
- Establishment of a method of measuring target behaviors
- Evaluation of the current levels of performance (baseline)
- Design and implementation of the interventions that teach new skills and/or reduce interfering behaviors
- Continuous measurement of target behaviors to determine the effectiveness of the intervention; and
- Ongoing evaluation of the effectiveness of the intervention, with modifications made as necessary to maintain and/or increase both the effectiveness and the efficiency of the intervention

Behavioral-based approaches have been found to be effective with a broad range of problem behaviors in music education (Standley, 1996).

Self-Monitoring Strategies

Students with emotional and behavioral disabilities often have little understanding or awareness of their own behavior and its effect on those around them. The implementation of self-monitoring strategies is an attempt to remedy this deficit. Such interventions teach students to recognize and to track their own problem behaviors. Self-monitoring strategies are most effective with students who are motivated to improve their behaviors due to contingent external reinforcers or the threat of negative consequences. Self-monitoring strategies are reported to be among the most useful and effective strategies for students with behavioral problems (Mitchum, Young, West, & Benyo, 2001; Todd, Horner, & Sugai, 1999). In addition, some researchers have found that self-monitoring strategies foster independent functioning and require fewer prompts from others (Koegel, Koegel, Harrower, & Carter, 1999). There are five steps involved in planning a self-monitoring intervention (Loftin, Gibb, & Skiba, 2005, p. 12):

1. Identify the problem behavior.
2. Select/design a self-monitoring system.

3. Choose reinforcers and how the student will earn them.
4. Teach the student to use the self-monitoring system.
5. Fade the role of the adult in the intervention.

Cognitive-Behavioral Interventions

Although generally more successful with adults, cognitive-behavioral interventions are used with students who are highly verbal and who have high cognitive functioning. Cognitive-behavioral interventions involve a body of methods and strategies to alter behaviors through actively engaging students in understanding and taking control of their thoughts, feelings, and behaviors (Mayer, Van Acker, Lochman, & Gresham, 2009). Cognitive-behavioral interventions go beyond the purely behavioral approach, which is employed solely to manage behaviors. Like traditional counseling, cognitive-behavioral interventions address students' thought processes along with their behaviors. Behaviors that are most responsive to cognitive-behavioral interventions are typically internalizing behaviors, such as withdrawing from others, excessive fantasizing or crying, feigning illness, and conveying frequent feelings of sadness, fear, or depression. School counselors generally initiate cognitive-behavioral interventions rather than music educators, who may not have the training required to provide counseling-type interventions.

TEACHING PRACTICES THAT SERVE TO IMPROVE BEHAVIOR AND PREVENT PROBLEM BEHAVIORS

Teaching Problem-Solving Skills. At some time, all students will face social dilemmas. Students with behavioral disabilities face social dilemmas daily. In such situations, students must make choices about their behavior. Exhibiting positive behaviors involves determining what is right and wrong for a given situation, making a choice to do what is right, and having the confidence to do it. For students to assume responsibility and control for their behaviors, they will need to develop a skill set that includes problem solving. Knowing how and when to implement problem-solving strategies is important to developing prosocial behaviors. Music educators can teach problem-solving skills in the classroom by asking students to identify their problem behavior, generate various possible solutions, and predict the outcome of each solution.

Promoting Self-Determination. Promoting self-determination has been recognized as best practice in the education of adolescents with disabilities since the early 1990s, when the IDEA mandated increased student involvement in transition planning; however, it has been only during the past decade or so that self-determination theory has been applied systematically to specific disabilities. In addition to transition planning, self-determination is important to students' development of prosocial behaviors. Self-determination is not a fixed trait or characteristic of an individual, but one that is situational and changes according to the individual's ability to adapt his or her behaviors to various situations. Students with emotional and behavioral disabilities face many challenges as they progress through school. These students may encounter difficulties related to social acceptance and peer pressure. Self-determination is enhanced through the support and advocacy of educators and family members who encourage students to make wise choices about their behaviors (Malian & Nevin, 2002). Music educators who design the curriculum to foster creativity, flexibility, and self-esteem will do much to promote self-determination in students with emotional and behavioral disabilities.

Applying UDL in the Music Classroom. Application of universal design for learning to the music classroom involves the provision of (1) multiple means of representation (options for perceiving and comprehending information), (2) multiple means of action and expression (options for learners to navigate a learning environment and to express what they know), and (3) multiple means of engagement (options to capture learners' interest and to motivate). Consequently, students with emotional and behavioral disabilities benefit from options for accessing information, demonstrating knowledge, and engaging in the learning process. Many students with behavioral challenges are resistant to doing what is expected and react well to having choices or options in how they will respond in class. In addition, such students are frequently unmotivated to learn (Pierangelo & Giulini, 2008). Using multiple means of engagement—options to capture learners' interest—increases the likelihood that students with emotional and behavioral disabilities will find learning appealing. If the principles of universal design for learning are applied appropriately, options for learning are available to all students, not just to those with disabilities, eliminating the stigmatization of students who are subject to behavioral interventions.

THE USE OF MUSIC TO MODIFY STUDENTS' PROBLEM BEHAVIORS

Music is a highly desirable activity for even the most challenging student. As a result of its desirability, music is particularly powerful as a subject matter, and as a tool in managing challenging behaviors. Adamek and Darrow

(2010, pp. 150–153) have detailed a number of ways in which music can be used in teaching students with emotional and behavioral disabilities.

Using Music as a Competing Behavior

There are many musical behaviors that are incompatible with undesirable behaviors. For example, a student cannot play a guitar while striking another student or play the piano while walking around the room. A student cannot sing while swearing or shouting out in class. Musical behaviors should be selected that compete with the problem behaviors a student might exhibit. Most students would choose to play the drums rather than to throw objects or to engage in any number of other inappropriate behaviors.

Using Music as a Contingency

Music has been used contingently for many years to effectively modify challenging behaviors. Using music as a contingency has been done to modify inappropriate bus behaviors (McCarty, McElfresh, Rice, & Wilson, 1978), verbal behaviors to parents (Madsen & Madsen, 1968), and disruptive classroom behaviors (Montello & Coons, 1998; West et al., 1995). Savan (1999) found that even the contingent use of classical background music resulted in the reduction of students' aggressive behaviors. Periods of preferred listening are often an effective reward for students with behavioral disabilities to initiate or maintain appropriate classroom behaviors such as:

- staying in their seat;
- completing work assignments;
- being punctual;
- raising their hand to speak; or
- participating in class activities.

Using Music Learning to Modify Inappropriate Behavior

Learning music, such as a new instrument, requires many behavioral prerequisites: sitting still, holding an instrument, manipulating the instrument, and reading music. The process of music learning increases the likelihood that students with behavioral disabilities will engage in these adaptive behaviors, and that the musical product itself will motivate continued engagement (Gardstrom, 1987; Kivland, 1986). For students with emotional and behavioral disabilities, the positive sense of self that comes from learning a musical skill does much to enhance their confidence and, consequently, their willingness to socialize appropriately with others. While learning music, students can participate in various musical organizations that allow for rewarding social contacts with their peers. An additional benefit of participation in musical organizations is that they often require regular school attendance and satisfactory grades and conduct reports. In addition, the development of performance skills can do much to enhance students' self-esteem.

Using Music to Modulate Mood

Depression is a frequent secondary condition of students with behavioral disabilities (Heward, 2012). According to researchers, one of the benefits of music for individuals with depression is its ability to induce or to alter mood states (Keneally, 1998; Mornhinweg, 1992; Silverman, 2003). Music has also been found to alter the behaviors and cognitive thought processes of depressed individuals (Williams & Dorow, 1983). Although music can be used to modify a student's affect or to elicit socially appropriate behaviors, it may also encourage inappropriate behaviors in certain situations (Durand & Mapstone, 1998). Furthermore, students with varying diagnoses such as attention deficit disorder (ADD) and ADHD have been shown to react differently to background music: some students may find that background music focuses their attention, while others are distracted by it (Pratt, Abel, & Skidmore, 1995). Musical preferences of the students must be considered in addition to the sedative or stimulative characteristics of the music itself. Listening to preferred music, regardless of style (heavy metal, rap), has been shown to induce positive changes in mood. Thus, adolescents who prefer heavy metal music may experience an increase in positive affect upon listening to their preferred style of music. Although heavy metal music and rap are often blamed for encouraging aggressive and violent behaviors in teenagers, some researchers do not support this premise (Took & Weiss, 1994); others (Dimsdale & Friedman, 1998) suggest that adolescents who experience strong negative emotions to music are at an increased risk of participating in risk-taking behaviors. Research shows that, contrary to popular belief, adolescent listeners do not pay close attention to lyrics and are therefore not significantly influenced by them (Wanamaker & Reznikoff, 1989).

Using Music to Modulate Physical and Cognitive Activity

Sedative or stimulative music can be used effectively to modulate students' physical activity (Harris, Bradley, & Titus, 1992; Skaggs, 1997). Students will often remain in their seats to listen to their preferred music. Music that sedates hyperactive or inappropriate behavior may be a quick, efficient, and noninvasive way to manage difficult behavior (Saperston, 1989). Although stimulative music such as rap and heavy metal may stimulate muscle activity, preferences for these kinds of music do not predict behavior problems (Epstein et al., 1990).

Children with attention deficits require interventions to modify not only their physical behaviors but also their cognitive behaviors, such as attending to and focusing on a task. Miller (2007) found that music combined with neurofeedback significantly improved the executive functioning and attention scores of children with ADHD. Executive functions require the completion of tasks and attention to detail. While not a practical classroom intervention, music combined with neurofeedback holds promise for students with ADHD, a growing population of students who experience problems in learning and in managing their behaviors.

Using Lyric Analysis with Students Who Have Emotional and Behavioral Disabilities

Students with behavioral disabilities often choose inappropriate ways to express their emotions. Music can provide these students with an alternative means of communication and an opportunity to express their emotions through song writing or lyric analysis. Students' preferred music can provide a structure and means for discussing issues such as substance abuse, suicide, and coping with stress (Mark, 1987; Pelletier, 2004; Trzcinski, 1992). Lyric analysis relies on the text component of music. The music educator or the adolescent student can select appropriate song lyrics to use as the impetus for discussion.

CONCLUSIONS

There is no doubt that students with emotional and behavioral disabilities present significant challenges to their teachers and peers. They typically exhibit unacceptable patterns of behavior, are nonconforming to the norms of the classroom, and often make the learning environment unproductive for themselves and other students. Nevertheless, students with emotional and behavioral disabilities are deserving of the same educational assistance as students with physical, cognitive, or sensory disabilities. Effective classroom management—which involves clear communication, behavioral and academic expectations, and a mutually respectful and cooperative relationship between teacher and student—is one of the most productive ways teachers can assist students with emotional and behavioral disabilities. Fortunately for music educators, music is also a powerful tool in managing the behaviors of these students and in helping them to develop the social skills they need to succeed in school. The advantage music educators have in reaching students who have emotional and behavioral disabilities is that music creates an environment that is inherently inviting and engaging. Music offers even the most reluctant students a nonthreatening and creative medium to explore their emotions and to develop the self-discipline they will need in their adult lives (Duerksen & Darrow, 1991).

Some of the personal attributes music educators will need to succeed with students who have emotional and behavioral disabilities are patience, perseverance, equanimity, and the ability to see potential in all students. Heward (2012) also stressed the importance of maintaining differential acceptance and an empathic relationship. Differential acceptance refers to the ability to not respond in kind to a student who exhibits extreme behaviors, but to accept the student—though not the behaviors. Having an empathic relationship refers to the ability to understand the nonverbal cues that indicate a student's emotional needs. Teaching students with emotional and behavioral disabilities also requires effective planning, organization, and flexibility, attributes that make educators more successful with all students. Consequently, working successfully with students who have emotional and behavioral disabilities can be one of the most gratifying experiences music educators will have in their professional lives. There is great joy and reward in positively impacting the lives of students who struggle in school and helping them to become educated, productive, and musical adults.

REFERENCES

Adamek, M. S., & Darrow, A. A. (2010). *Music in special education* (2nd ed.). Silver Spring, MD: American Music Therapy Association.

Alberto, P. A., & Troutman, A. C. (1999). *Applied behavior analysis* (5th ed.). Columbus, OH: Merrill.

American Psychiatric Association. (2013). *Diagnostic and statistical manual of mental disorders* (5th ed.). Arlington, VA: American Psychiatric Publishing.

Baer, D., Wolf, M., & Risley, R. (1987). Some still-current dimensions of applied behavior analysis. *Journal of Applied Behavior Analysis, 20,* 313–327.

Blanchard, L., Gurka, M., & Blackman, J. (2006). Emotional, developmental, and behavioral health of American children and their families: A report from the 2003 National Survey of Children's Health. *Pediatrics, 117,* 1202–1212.

Brady, N. C., & Halle, J. W. (1997). Functional analysis of communicative behaviors. *Focus on Autism and Other Developmental Disabilities, 12,* 95–104.

Cooper, J. O., Heron, T. E., & Heward, W. L. (1987). *Applied behavior analysis.* Columbus, OH: Merrill.

Darrow, A. A. (1999). Music educators' perceptions regarding the inclusion of students with severe disabilities in music classrooms. *Journal of Music Therapy, 36*, 254–273.

Darrow, A. (2013). What's in a name? Referring to students with disabilities. *Orff Echo, 45*(3), 11–14.

Dimsdale, J., & Friedman, L. (1998). Adolescent emotional response to music and its relationship to risk-taking behaviors. *Journal of Adolescent Health, 23*(1), 1–2.

Duerksen, G. L., & Darrow, A. A. (1991). Music class for the at-risk: A music therapist's perspective. *Music Educators Journal, 78*(3), 46–49.

Durand, V. M., & Mapstone, E. (1998). Influence of "mood-inducing" music on challenging behavior. *American Journal on Mental Retardation, 102*, 367–378.

Epstein, J. S., Pratto, D. J., & Skipper, J. K., Jr. (1990). Teenagers, behavioral problems and preferences for heavy metal and rap music: A case study of a southern middle school. *Deviant Behavior, 11*, 381–394.

Fairbanks, S., Sugai, G., Guardino, D., & Lathrop, M. (2007). Response to intervention: Examining classroom behavior support in second grade. *Exceptional Children, 73*, 288–310.

Gardstrom, S. C. (1987). Positive peer culture: A working definition for the music therapist. *Music Therapy Perspectives, 4*, 19–23.

Gargiulo, R. M. (2012). *Special education in contemporary society.* Thousand Oaks, CA: Sage.

Gresham, R. M. (2005). Response to intervention: An alternative means of identifying students as emotionally disturbed. *Education and Treatment of Children, 28*, 328–344.

Hallahan, D. P., Kauffman, J. M., & Pullen, P. C. (2009). *Exceptional learners: An introduction to special education* (11th ed.). Boston, MA: Allyn & Bacon.

Hardman, M. L., Drew, C. L., & Egan, M. W. (2008). *Human exceptionality: School, community, and family* (9th ed.). Boston, MA: Houghton Mifflin Company.

Harris, C. S., Bradley, R. J., & Titus, S. K. (1992). A comparison of the effects of hard rock and easy listening on the frequency of observed inappropriate behaviors: Control of environmental antecedents in a large public area. *Journal of Music Therapy, 29*, 6–17.

Heward, W. L. (2012). *Exceptional children: An introduction to special education* (10th ed.). Upper Saddle River, NJ: Pearson Educational.

Hunt, N., & Marshall, K. (2005). *Exceptional children and youth: An introduction to special education.* Boston, MA: Houghton Mifflin.

Individuals with Disabilities Education Improvement Act of 2004. Retrieved from http://idea.ed.gov/download/statute.html

Kauffman, J., & Landrum, T. (2009). *Characteristics of emotional and behavioral disorders of children and youth* (9th ed.) Upper Saddle River, NJ: Pearson Education.

Keneally, P. (1998). Validation of a music mood induction procedure: Some preliminary findings. *Cognition and Emotion, 2*, 11–18.

Kivland, M. J. (1986). The use of music to increase self-esteem in a conduct disordered adolescent. *Journal of Music Therapy, 23*, 25–29.

Koegel, L. K., Koegel, R. L., & Dunlap, G. (Eds.). (1996). *Positive behavioral support: Including people with difficult behavior in the community.* Baltimore, MD: Paul H. Brookes.

Koegel, L. K., Koegel, R. L., Harrower, J. K., & Carter, C. M. (1999). Pivotal response intervention I: Overview of approach. *Journal of Association for Persons with Severe Handicaps, 24*(3), 174–185.

Lewis, T. J., & Sugai, G. (1999). Effective behavior support: A systems approach to proactive schoolwide management. *Focus on Exceptional Children, 31*(6), 1–24.

Loftin, R. L., Gibb, A. C., & Skiba, R. (2005). Using self-monitoring strategies to address behavior and academic issues. *Impact: Feature Issue on Fostering Success in School and Beyond for Students with Emotional/Behavioral Disorders, 18*(2), 12–13.

Long, N. J., & Newman, R. (1980). Managing surface behaviors of children in schools. In N. J. Long, W. Morse, & R. Newman (Eds.), *Conflict in the classroom: The education of emotionally disturbed children* (4th ed.). Belmont, CA: Wadsworth.

Madsen, C. K., & Madsen, C. H., Jr. (1968). Music as a behavior modification technique with a juvenile delinquent. *Journal of Music Therapy, 5*, 72–76.

Madsen, C. H., & Madsen, C. K. (2000). *Teaching discipline: A positive approach for educational development* (4th ed.). Raleigh, NC: Contemporary.

Malian, I., & Nevin, A. (2002). A review of self-determination literature: Implications for practitioners. *Remedial and Special Education, 23*(2), 68–74.

Mark, A. (1987). Adolescents discuss themselves and drugs through music. *Journal of Substance Abuse Treatment, 3*, 243–249.

Marzano, R. J. (2003). *Classroom management that works: Research-based strategies for teachers.* Alexandria, VA: Association for Supervision and Curriculum Development.

Mayer, M. J., Van Acker, R., Lochman, J. E., & Gresham, F. M. (2009). *Cognitive-behavioral interventions for emotional and behavioral disorders.* New York, NY: Guilford Press.

McCarty, B. C., McElfresh, C. T., Rice, S. V., & Wilson, S. J. (1978). The effect of contingent background music on inappropriate bus behavior. *Journal of Music Therapy, 15*, 150–156.

Miller, E. B. (2007). *Getting from psy-phy (psychophysiology) to medical policy via music and neurofeedback for ADHD children.* Unpublished dissertation, Bryn Mawr College, Graduate College of Social Work and Social Research, Bryn Mawr, PA.

Mitchum, K. J., Young, K. R., West, R. P., & Benyo, J. (2001). CSPASM: A classwide peer assisted self-management program for general education classrooms. *Education and Treatment of Children, 24*, 111–140.

Montello, L., & Coons, E. E. (1998). Effects of active versus passive group music therapy on preadolescents with emotional, learning, and behavioral disorders. *Journal of Music Therapy, 35*, 49–67.

Mornhinweg, G. C. (1992). Effects of music preference and selection on stress reducing. *Journal of Holistic Nursing, 10*, 101–109.

Pelletier, C. L. (2004). The effect of music on decreasing arousal due to stress: A meta-analysis. *Journal of Music Therapy, 41*, 192–214.

Pierangelo, R., & Giuliani, G. (2008). *The educator's step-by-step guide to classroom management for students with emotional and behavioral disorders.* Thousand Oaks, CA: Corwin Press.

Pratt, R. R., Abel, H. H., & Skidmore, J. (1995). The effects of neurofeedback training with background music on EEG patterns of ADD and ADHD children. *International Journal of Arts Medicine, 4*, 24–31.

Rio, R. E., & Tenney, K. S. (2002). Music therapy for juvenile offenders in residential treatment. *Music Therapy Perspectives, 20*, 89–97.

Saperston, B. M. (1989). Music-based individualized relaxation training (MBIRT): A stress-reduction approach for the behaviorally disturbed mentally retarded. *Music Therapy Perspectives, 6*, 26–33.

Savan, A. (1999). The effect of background music on learning. *Psychology of Music, 27*, 138–146.

Shea, T. M., & Bauer, A. M. (2012). *Behavior management: A practical approach for educators* (10th ed.). Boston, MA: Pearson.

Shepherd, T. L. (2010). *Working with students with emotional and behavior disorders.* Upper Saddle River, NJ: Merrill.

Silverman, M. J. (2003). The influence of music on the symptoms of psychosis: A meta-analysis. *Journal of Music Therapy, 40*, 27–40.

Skaggs, R. (1997). Music-centered creative arts in a sex offender treatment program for male juveniles. *Music Therapy Perspectives, 15*, 73–78.

Standley, J. M. (1996). A meta-analysis on the effects of music as reinforcement for education/therapy objectives. *Journal of Research in Music Education, 44*, 105–133.

Sulzer-Azaroff, B., & Mayer, R. (1991). *Behavior analysis for lasting change.* Fort Worth, TX: Holt, Reinhart & Winston.

Todd, A. W., Horner, R. H., & Sugai, G. (1999). Effects of self-monitoring and self-recruited praise on problem behavior, academic engagement, and work completion in a typical classroom. *Journal of Positive Behavior Interventions, 1*, 66–76.

Took, K. J., & Weiss, D. S. (1994). The relationship between heavy metal and rap music and adolescent turmoil: Real or artifact? *Adolescence, 29*, 613–621.

Trzcinski, J. (1992). Heavy metal kids: Are they dancing with the devil? *Child and Youth Care Forum, 21*(1), 7–22.

Turnbull, A., Turnbull, R., & Wehmeyer, M. (2010). *Exceptional lives: Special education in today's schools* (6th ed.). Upper Saddle River, NJ: Merrill.

Wanamaker, C. E., & Reznikoff, M. (1989). Effects of aggressive and nonaggressive rock songs on projective and structured tests. *Journal of Psychology, 123*, 561–570.

West, R. P., Young, K. R., Callahan, K., Fister, S., Kemp, K., Freston, J., & Lovitt, T. C. (1995). The musical clocklight: Encouraging positive classroom behavior. *Teaching Exceptional Children, 27*(2), 46–51.

Williams, C., & Dorow, L. G. (1983). Changes in complaints and noncomplaints of a chronically depressed psychiatric patient as a function of an interrupted music/verbal feedback package. *Journal of Music Therapy, 20*, 143–155.

Zirpoli, T. J. (2012) *Behavior management: Positive applications for teachers* (6th ed.). Boston, MA: Pearson.

CHAPTER 9

Specified Learning Disabilities and Music Education

KIMBERLY McCORD

James plays trumpet in the sixth-grade band. He began playing trumpet in the fourth grade and loves it. Many of the teachers complain about him because he can be short-tempered and impulsive, but his biggest struggles are reading and getting assignments done.

We are working in our band method books and playing a short tune that includes written solos. I like to use this exercise to determine if students can count and play dotted quarter notes followed by eighth notes. When it is James's turn, he plays his solo exactly as the previous student played hers. The problem is her solo was written differently than James's solo. We stop and I ask James to look at his music and try it again. When it was his turn he wasn't looking at his music and made a mistake. He was looking at the music of the girl next to him. James replies, "I don't need to look at the music. I just know how it goes."

My first impulse is to respond with a sarcastic comment I have heard other music teachers use: "The music isn't written on Lauren's head; it is written in your book!" but I realize that it now makes sense to me why he writes the names of his notes in his book and sometimes forgets his book but brings his trumpet to band. He struggles with reading music. James is learning music by ear and watching Lauren's fingers to know which notes to play. That is how he figures out "how the music goes."

I talk to his special education teacher and she says he has a learning disability that impacts his ability to read and also struggles with being organized. I share the incident in band class and she confirms that he probably has trouble reading music too. She helps me to understand that he needs extra time to process and will likely never be fluent enough to sight-read music, even short, simple exercises. When he is under pressure, it is more difficult for him to concentrate and do well.

I feel awful. For months I have been making him erase the note names in his band book and forcing him to read without names written under the notes. He received a B on his quarter grade because he doesn't try hard enough to read music and he frequently forgets his band book.

I am also frustrated with the special education teacher. Why didn't she tell me I needed to adapt instruction for James? I didn't even know students could have learning disabilities that impacted them in music. As a music teacher, I never know which students have disabilities in my classroom. I actually don't want to know because I want everyone to meet the same high expectations, but I wonder if by expecting everyone to learn the same, have I created a classroom that excludes students who struggle with reading music?

Students like James are in every music class and many ensembles. Some are clever about hiding their disabilities. They are sometimes gifted in music or other subjects or skills (twice exceptional). They often improvise well, some can play several instruments, or they come to class able to play popular songs that they figure out by ear. Some amaze the other students with their abilities yet struggle with remembering how to play F sharp. They are the students who chronically forget their pencils or who struggle with a steady beat; they are the students who are least understood and often the students who quit music out of frustration (McCord, 1997).

TEACHING STUDENTS WITH LEARNING DISABILITIES IN THE UNITED STATES

Historically, educators have been most concerned with children who struggled with reading. Research that identified reading disabilities emerged first in Germany in 1884 when an ophthalmologist, Berlin, first identified dyslexia. He connected six cases of adults with dyslexia who struggled with reading despite having normal language abilities (Anderson & Meier-Hedde, 2001). In the United States, by 1918, all states had passed laws requiring children to attend school. Consequently, educators began to be more involved and interested in finding ways to assess and remediate children with reading challenges.

Later, physicians studied soldiers with brain injuries from World War I and began to identify head wounds with specific problems in speech, reading, and writing. Remedial programs for helping these soldiers began to emerge. However, it was not until Fernald developed a remedial reading program for students with reading and writing challenges in 1921 that included multisensory approaches to teaching (aural, visual, kinesthetic, and tactile) that actual research began to occur in educational settings focused on ways to help children with reading and writing challenges (Fernald & Keller, 1921).

Goldstein (1936, 1939) studied adults with brain injuries and identified behaviors that included hyperactivity, figure–background confusion, and what was later termed obsessive-compulsive disorder. In addition to these studies, researchers began to study children and adults with intellectual disabilities. Cruickshank was a leader in differentiating between individuals with intellectual disabilities and individuals with specific learning challenges. He was particularly interested in perceptual-motor abilities and discovered a difference between individuals with intellectual disabilities and those with difficulty in arithmetic (Cruickshank, Bentzen, Ratzeburg, & Tannhauser, 1961).

The term *learning disability* (LD) was first defined in Kirk's 1962 publication:

> A retardation, disorder, or delayed development in one or more of the processes of speech, language, reading, writing, arithmetic, or other school subject resulting from psychological handicap caused by a possible cerebral dysfunction and/or emotional or behavioral disturbances. It is not the result of mental retardation, sensory deprivation, or cultural and instructional factors. (p. 263)

As a result of Kirk's research, a group of parents in 1963 founded the Association for Children with LD (ACLD), now renamed the LD Association.

Bateman (1965) was the first researcher to identify that learning disabilities were related to an achievement–aptitude discrepancy. The US federal government sponsored two task forces to investigate learning disabilities during the late 1960s. One task force was composed of medical researchers and the other was a group of educators. The task forces could not agree on a single definition until 1968 when a new committee chaired by Kirk developed this definition adopted by the US Office of Education:

> Children with special (specific) LD exhibit a disorder in one or more of the basic psychological processes involved in understanding or in using spoken or written language. These may be manifested in disorders of listening, thinking, talking, reading, writing, spelling, or arithmetic. They include conditions which have been referred to as perceptual handicaps, brain injury, minimal brain dysfunction, dyslexia, developmental aphasia, etc. They do not include learning problems that are due primarily to visual, hearing or motor handicaps, to mental retardation, emotional disturbance, or to environmental disadvantage. (US Office of Education, 1968, p. 34)

During the 1960s and 1970s, learning disability research included visual and visual-motor auditory comprehension, but despite the passage of Public Law 91-230, learning disabilities were still not considered a disability with supported federal assistance and protection under the Education of the Handicapped Act previously passed in 1966. Inclusion of individuals with specific learning disabilities finally occurred in the United States with the passage of the Education for All Handicapped Children Act in 1975. The US Department of Education used language in documents that identified LD as a severe discrepancy between achievement and intellectual ability when diagnosing children.

Researchers and the government still struggled with a definition that all were satisfied with and essentially retained a similar statement to Kirk's original 1962 definition when the Individuals with Disabilities Education Act (IDEA) was reauthorized in 1997. By the twenty-first century, educators looked for a better way of identifying children with specified learning disabilities. The discrepancy formula required at least a year of testing and meetings to finally enable educators to identify and help children who were not succeeding in the classroom. In 2002, an alternative approach to identifying children with learning disabilities emerged with response to intervention (RTI), which provided intervention and support as soon as a child is identified as struggling in reading, writing, or math. RTI disregards the discrepancy approach and offers alternatives to identification and diagnosis of learning disabilities (Gresham, 2002). The following year, Vaughn and Fuchs (2003) classified RTI as a more effective method for early intervention for children with learning disabilities Their approach advocated for using an at-risk rather than a deficit model that helped to identify children earlier and aided in eliminating bias with a stronger focus on student outcome. In the United States, RTI is the currently agreed upon system for identifying and providing support for children with specified learning disabilities.

WHAT ARE LEARNING DISABILITIES?

Learning disabilities are the most common disability, also referred to as a high-incidence disability. Currently, the National Center for Health Statistics (2010) estimates that 2.4 million or 41% of children in the United States receiving special education services are diagnosed with one or more specific learning disabilities. What are learning disabilities and how do they impact music learning?

Dyslexia

Specific reading disability (SRD) is commonly known as dyslexia. Students with dyslexia are identified as poor readers. Phonological awareness requires that the child perceive individual sounds in words, segment words into smaller phonemes, maintain strings of sounds or letters in short-term memory, and retrieve these sounds from memory. When children struggle with using phonemes, their reading is very slow and inaccurate, and they often lose their place, causing poor comprehension. The currently accepted definition of specific reading disability is as follows:

> Dyslexia is a specific learning disability that is neurobiological in origin. It is character-ized by difficulties with accurate and/or fluent word recognition and by poor spelling and decoding abilities. These difficulties typically result from a deficit in the phonologi-cal component of language that is often unexpected in relation to other cognitive abili-ties and the provision of effective classroom instruction. Secondary consequences may include problems in reading comprehension and reduced reading experience that can impede growth of vocabulary. (Lyon, Shaywitz, & Shaywitz, 2003)

In addition, nonlinguistic deficits such as difficulty with concentration, poor short-term memory, and challenges with organization may also be present (Helland & Asbjornsen, 2000; Reid & Green, 2007). Dyslexia var-ies in different languages due to unique linguistic features and cognitive demands of the language (Besson, Schon, Moreno, Santos, & Magne, 2007; Chung, Ho, Chan, Tsang, & Lee, 2010; Lam, 2010). This is due to the dif-ferences in alphabetic and character-based languages.

Music and Dyslexia

Atterbury (1985) first noticed children with learning disabilities experi-encing difficulty with rhythm patterns when performing previously heard patterns in musical examples. Since her landmark research, others have identified similar difficulties with rhythm and meter but also issues with pitch and reading notation. In addition, there have been a large number of studies that have identified links between music and language.

Children with dyslexia struggle with hearing and perceiving speech rhythm and timing; this also impacts perception of musical rhythm. Goswami (2011) identified difficulties in children perceiving amplitude rise time to be one cause of developmental learning difficulty. Rise time refers to the amount of time a pitch takes to reach maximum intensity. Different instruments respond faster and slower, and musicians learn how to compensate for rise time by adjusting the speed of air, bow, pressure from a mallet, and so forth. Children with dyslexia have significant difficulty in their ability to gauge rise time as compared with typical peers.

Phonological awareness is the ability to recognize and reflect on the structure of language. It involves identifying and using parts of oral language, including words and syllables. Children unable to distinguish that syllables and words are composed of phonemes and that boundaries within spoken sentences exist struggle to read fluently with poor comprehension. Ziegler, Pech-Georgel, George, and Foxton (2012) discovered a link between impaired pitch processing and abnormal phonological development in children with dyslexia. Auditory perception of rise time is related to perception of musical meter structure and connects to the development of phonological and literacy growth in children. A primary sensory impairment in developmental dyslexia occurs in tracking the lower-frequency modulations in the speech envelope (Huss, Verney, Fosker, Mead, & Goswami, 2010).

Goswani (2013) explains, "Beat structure in music depends partly on some notes having greater accentuation than others, a bit like strong and weak (stressed and unstressed) syllables" (p. 108). This was discovered through a test for musical beat perception; the children with dyslexia were significantly worse in hearing strong and weak beats than their typical age-matched peers (Huss et al., 2011). In this similar study by Huss et al., which was expanded to reading-level-matched controls, summarized that "individual differences in perceiving patterns of beat distribution, in both language and music, are intimately connected with reading development and dyslexia" (p. 1373).

The ability to perceive and follow rhythmic patterns or entrainment in children and adults with dyslexia is another area in which Goswani and others have focused their research in recent years. "Children and adults with dyslexia were much more erratic than controls in tapping in time with a metronome at 2 Hz" (Goswani, 2013, p.108).

Goswani (2013) has developed a "temporal sampling" framework to highlight why poor rhythmic entrainment, poor perception of acoustic rhythm, and poor perception of rise time are all associated with developmental dyslexia and with prosodic and sublexical phonological difficulties. She advocates for remediation using music for improving phonology in dyslexic individuals. Rhythm is more pronounced in music than in language, and focusing on musical rhythm that links to meter and beat will strengthen beat structure in language and improve rhythmic entrainment (Bhide, Power, & Goswami, 2013). In addition, Goswani (2012, 2013) encourages educators and therapists to coordinate rhythmic movement in time with speech and music to strengthen rhythmic entrainment.

A multisensory approach to teaching children with specified learning disabilities has long been at the top of recommendations to music teachers (Atterbury, 1990; Hammel, 2013; Heikkila & Knight, 2012; McCord, 2004; Overy, 2003; Pratt, 2008; Register, Darrow, Standley, & Swedberg, 2007; Westcombe, 2002). For example, Heikkila and Knight (2012) encourage music teachers to assist students who have difficulty identifying high and low pitches by projecting notation on a screen and having the students follow the pitch contour with their hands as they sing. Using a combination of aural, visual, and kinesthetic/tactile approaches to learning a musical concept supports learning.

Besson et al. (2007) found that children with dyslexia had difficulty in discriminating strong pitch changes as compared to typical children and that pitch processing in music and speech can be improved through music experiences and practice. This might indicate problems with tuning and balance when playing or singing with others.

Reading Music

Perhaps the earliest documented research and strategies for improving music reading was introduced through the work of Margaret Hubicki, who developed the Colour-Staff system of music notation in 1970 specifically for learners with dyslexia. Researchers in special and music education recognized that some children with dyslexia struggled with reading black text on white paper and discovered that printing text on colored paper or using colored overlays relieved some of the fatigue caused by reading most typically printed text (Solis, 2010–1012). Hubicki (2001) expanded on the idea by relating each pitch to a color. Hubuki writes, "One of the Colour-Staff's basic aims is to fix the symbols in the learner's imagination" (p. 86). Although the colors aid the musician in reading, it can be adapted to grayscale for persons with color-blindness. Square pieces are used to represent pitches on the staff and are actually placed on the staff. These have the pitch name written on them. The Colour-Staff can also be adapted to represent a violin fingerboard and other instruments. Images can be substituted for colors if preferred. The goal is to help the musician learn to associate visual stimulus with pitch and the way it is represented in notation so it becomes easier to read and remember. Hubicki eventually transitioned students from color to black and white and then to traditional musical notation as they became more confident notation readers.

For musicians with dyslexia, reading notation can be challenging, but reading notation and words in choral settings creates added frustration. Songs in an unfamiliar foreign language add another layer of difficulty for learners to fluently process everything in the music (Bryson, 2013). Supporting notation with recordings that can be listened to outside of rehearsal helps to create a multisensory path toward more efficiently learning the music. Bryson uses recordings that begin with just the vocal line and eventually add sequences with accompaniment and additional choral parts as needed.

Music Supporting Reading and Writing Skills

There are many studies that support the use of music for acquisition of reading and writing skills (Chandrasekaran & Kraus, 2010; Corrigall & Trainor, 2011; Forgeard et al., 2008; Goswami, 2012; Overy, 2003; Przybylski et al., 2013; Register et al., 2007; Strait & Kraus, 2011). However, Cogo-Moreira et al. (2012) conducted a search of databases and found no randomized controlled trials testing music education for the improvement of reading skills in children with dyslexia. They determined that there is no evidence to base a judgment about the effectiveness of music education for the improvement of reading skills in children and adolescents with dyslexia.

Overy (2000, 2003) identified abnormal neural processing difficulties in individuals with dyslexia and correlated music training, particularly rhythmic training, as a possible intervention to improve temporal processing ability in children with dyslexia.

Hornickel and Kraus (2013) studied brain function in children with dyslexia and found that dyslexics have weak auditory processing skills. This occurs particularly when words are spoken too quickly. They surmise that musical training aids in building stronger processing networks in individuals with dyslexia. Rhythm sensitivity was found to be a precursor skill to oral language acquisition, and the ability to perceive and manipulate time intervals in sound streams may link performance in both rhythm and phonological skills (Moritz, Yampolsky, Papadelis, Thomson, & Wolf, 2013). Chandrasekaran and Kraus (2010) discovered that individuals with musical training do better with distinguishing conversations from background noise. This is a particular challenge for many with dyslexia.

Dyscalculia

Dyscalculia, arithmetical learning disability, or specific mathematics disability occurs in about 3% to 6% of the population who are impaired enough to be considered disabled. There is very little research related to the impact of dyscalculia and music, although those with dyscalculia often report great difficulty with reading music notation according to a forum post in http://www.dyscalculiaforum.com (2012).

"The intuitive understanding of numbers and related concepts such as how numbers grow and diminish with calculation may be viewed as having a parallel to the initial reading skill of phonemic awareness, which includes the earliest awareness of how words are made up of discrete sounds" (Lewis, Shapiro, & Church, 2013, pp. 408–409). In addition, persons with dyscalculia misuse signs, forget to carry, misplace digits, or have trouble approaching problems from left to right (Shalev, 2004). Many children with dyscalculia also have dyslexia. According to Geary (1993), there are three subtypes of mathematical disability: procedural, semantic memory, and visuospatial.

Children who have difficulty understanding the concepts underlying procedural use also often experience sequencing multiple steps in a complex procedure. When considering music notation reading, it is probable that musicians with this subtype of dyscalculia may have difficulty remembering the order of accidentals in a key signature, names of lines and spaces in the staff, tempo markings, and dynamic markings. Semantic memory impacts retrieval of facts and influences the ability to remember errors in problem solving. Although this is pure speculation, it is possible that the musician who forgets to play an accidental multiple times may have a semantic memory dyscalculia subtype learning disability. Visuospatial subtypes experience difficulty in spatially representing numerical and other forms of mathematical information and relationships and also sometimes misinterpret or misunderstand spatially represented information. This is likely the subtype of individuals that struggle the most with music reading. Music notation is visual and relies on spatial relationships both vertically and horizontally. Duration of notes comes to mind first. Sixteenth notes appear closer together on the staff than do half notes and might be interpreted as "fast" notes and half notes as "slow" notes. Pianists reading chords that are written out with vertical stacked notes might see mostly "line notes" and play as many line notes that 5 or 10 fingers can manage.

Poole (2001) recalls common problems with reading music:

> Rather than try to memorize written notation I try to remember visual patterns that my fingers can then play. My piano teacher would never accept that I needed time to think in silence about what I was about to play. If I played a wrong note I needed to pause before attempting to correct it—I needed the time to work out where in fact my fingers ought to have gone. (p. 55)

Others writing on the online dyscalculia forum relate trouble with reading music but not struggling to play an instrument by ear: "The musical notes look like a bunch of random symbols on a paper and they confuse me. . . . I actually play by ear; in other words, I memorize what I hear until I get it correct. Some might consider it tedious but it's the only way I can play an instrument." Others admit that music notation is just a sort of guide: "I see music notes as letters rather than symbols." Another admits, "I lose my place in music. I learned everything by ear and faked it in elementary school band, but got busted in high school and gave up playing an instrument" (Dyscalculia Forum, Retrieved September 3, 2013).

McCord (2004) observed a child using a computer software program closing her eyes and listening to her composed music. She was shutting out the visual notation of music to eliminate the confusion she experienced by trying to read music. Students with specified learning disabilities often watch the hands and fingers of their peers when playing in instrumental ensembles rather than reading music notation. Students who write the letter names of notes underneath notation in method books might also be trying to shut out the overload of deciphering music notation and instead substitute their own self-compensating strategies for learning to read music.

Dysgraphia

Dysgraphia, or specific writing disability, is seen in children with typical motor development but with handwriting problems. Handwriting for the individual with dysgraphia is an orthographic learning disability characterized by frequent spelling errors. Visual memory is required to spell accurately, and children with dysgraphia experience difficulty in recalling spelling of words or trouble with finding written words to express ideas. Orthographic processing delays impact the child's ability to write at an age-appropriate speed because the time it takes to process how to visually represent words takes longer than typical children need to write. In most current special education literature, specific writing disability is now termed dyslexia. There are no published studies on music and dysgraphia, but these students likely would have difficulty writing music or writing notes within a space or on a line.

Dyspraxia

Dyspraxia, or developmental coordination disorder, is often referred to as clumsy child syndrome. Children with dyspraxia have trouble planning and completing fine motor tasks that require single steps or multiple steps. Buttoning clothes and tying shoes involve performing multiple small steps and can be difficult for the child with dyspraxia. Imagine children with dyspraxia putting together a wind instrument; the process is likely to be highly frustrating for them. Others have trouble coordinating muscle movements involved in speech, and some have problems estimating space, including difficulty moving objects from one place to another. Some children have trouble distinguishing their left from right hand.

Dyspraxia is appearing less and less in the special education literature, perhaps because the symptoms can be addressed as dyslexia or speech disabilities. There are no published studies of dyspraxia and music, although children with dyspraxia are certain to struggle with playing instruments that require muscle coordination and embouchure control.

COMMON CHARACTERISTICS ACROSS ALL SPECIFIED LEARNING DISABILITIES

Processing information is the one characteristic across all types of learning disabilities that is most problematic. There are three avenues involved in brain processing: input, internal, and output. If music notation appears blurry or if the notes seem to jump around the page, then input is the process that likely bothers the person with a learning disability. If the child seems to take a long time to identify the name of a musical symbol, internal brain processing is slow. When the child reverses letters or is a messy writer, then output is indicated. This helps teachers to understand that there can be multiple ways to circumvent the learning disability. When musicians close their eyes or look away from music notation, it might be that they are making self-adaptations to help themselves process the music more efficiently.

Because processing is slow, it is important to give wait time for students to respond. Wait time needs to be silent without other students calling out the answer. Ideally, all students will wait patiently for the student with a learning disability to respond. When the person with a learning disability experiences anxiety or stress, it makes it more difficult to process efficiently. A common problem that occurs while processing is distractions. The student literally loses his or her place and has to start over. For example, the teacher asks, "What is the fingering for F sharp?" The student has to retrieve the fingering from memory and might first think about the familiar F natural fingering, but he or she knows something different has to be done to make it an F sharp. At this point in his or her processing, someone in the room drops a mouthpiece cap and it bangs on the floor. The student's thinking process is interrupted and he or she loses his or her place and has to work through the process again to come up with the answer. Occasionally the student becomes so lost in his or her thinking that he or she needs to ask the teacher what the question was again.

Allowing extra time is essential for the student with a learning disability. This can look different depending on the task, but consider this task that might occur in a music education setting: a student is learning the alto part of a choral piece in the ninth-grade chorus. The teacher could provide a recording of only the alto part before the piece is introduced in the choir rehearsal. The student is then able to learn in his or her most comfortable learning style. That student might elect to learn the alto part completely by ear and not use the music notation at all. The student could also listen to the music and follow the words with his or her finger, eventually also making some connection to the music notation. The student might look at an adapted score with all other parts left off except the alto part, shown with colored highlights appearing in each space of the treble clef. Color overlays might be used, or the music can be printed on colored paper or with enlarged notation or some combination of these. For example, "Good King Wenceslas" is shown in Figure 9.1 with only the alto voice line.

Seeing just the alto part requires less processing than asking the musician to read from the full choral score (Figure 9.2).

Figure 9.1. Alto voice line isolated from choral score.

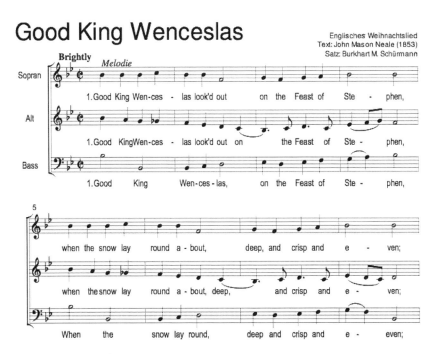

Figure 9.2. Full choral score.

With adapted parts created in some types of notation software, students can also have access to electronic recordings of their part to hear it at slower tempos. Another option is to take the teacher-created audio recording and, using the free software from Amazing Slow Downer (http://amazing-slow-downer.en.softonic.com), create audio files at different tempos. The software will slow down tempos without changing the pitch of the recording. Students can also use the program to adapt tempos themselves.

Another example of allowing extra time in a music setting at the elementary level might look like this:

The class is learning an Orff piece that has a bass xylophone part with a syncopated pattern. The teacher pairs students onto each instrument and assigns students number one or two. The teacher knows the student with the learning disability needs additional processing time to learn the part, so to allow the student with LD to experience the part first through body percussion, the teacher assigns him number two in the pairing.

The students who are number one play the part first, and then the song is performed again with the number two students playing the instruments. This allows the students who are number two to watch their peers play the part first. The teacher has a routine for students who are not playing to continue using with body percussion while their instrument partner plays. This is a multisensory approach to learning the part. While the number two students watch their peers play the part, they are continuing with body percussion and are also hearing what the part sounds like. This enables aural, visual, and kinesthetic learning to occur at the same time.

Music teachers need to be aware of setting students up for success by allowing for adaptations such as the ones illustrated previously. It is likely that typical students in the class or ensemble benefit from some of the same adaptations as well. All of this should be worked out privately with the student first. The student needs to decide if the adaptation works best for him or her or if something else works better. The student also might decide that he or she would rather try to learn the same way the other students are learning, and the teacher should then support the student in pursuing that avenue. *Self-determination* is an important skill that students with disabilities need to learn.

Ryan and Deci (2000) define self-determination as "an outlook that involves a combination of attitudes and abilities that lead people to set goals for themselves, to take the initiative to reach those goals, and to realize those goals" (p. 76). Parents and teachers often step in and help students instead of letting them struggle and learn from their mistakes. Students with a sense of self-determination are able to advocate for their own learning by letting teachers know which approach works best for them. For example, the elementary music teacher removes bars from an Orff instrument so the typical students can focus only on the bars that are used for their particular part. However, a student with vision loss cannot see the bars and misses them while trying to play the part. He raises his hand and says, "Is it all right if I put these bars together so I can play them better?" This is self-determination.

Psychologist Martin Seligman (1975) first identified a behavior he later termed *learned helplessness* as a result of studying dogs being given electric shocks while unable to escape. The animals began to behave as if they were helpless to change the situation, similar to the way people with depression experience some situations. People with depression will easily give up, a behavior also observed in people with disabilities, especially people with learning disabilities. "Persistence is a byproduct of success, and if success is repeatedly out of reach of the student, he or she learns not to try" (p. 23). "Students exhibit *learned helplessness* when there is not a good match between learning objectives and student attributes; therefore, one single set of standardized objectives cannot be expected to meet the unique learning abilities of individual students in inclusive classrooms" (Stainback et al., 1997). Self-determination is a positive skill that enables people with disabilities to cope in the real world. It prevents learned helplessness and enables the child to become more successful in music and in life.

Children with learning disabilities do not like being confronted by the unknown; it is strategic to establish routines and develop trust as soon as possible to help them relax and do their best in learning. Avoid asking students with learning disabilities to read or play by themselves in front of peers without asking them first. If teachers want them to do this, it is best to let them know several days before so they have time to prepare.

Many people with learning disabilities talk about the amount of concentration and effort it takes to process difficult content. For some it creates fatigue and can eventually make the task or activity something the student tries to avoid. This is quite prevalent among children with reading disabilities; they grow to dislike reading because it is so exhausting. Teachers can help by recognizing when a student becomes frustrated or gives up easily and then adapt or require fewer problems or tasks connected to an assignment or assessment than typical students. It also helps to provide a distraction-free place to work on assignments and tests without requiring completion within a certain time.

Use of repetition with added multisensory supports is immensely helpful and is often appreciated by typical students. Teachers should sequence information and activities so students do not become overwhelmed by having to hold too much material in their memory.

Many students with learning disabilities also struggle with short-term memory problems. It is difficult for them to hold material in their short-term memory without losing it. Through many repetitions, a student can transfer new material to long-term memory and remember content better.

Teachers can help by anticipating that students might have trouble and forget some of the many bits of information taught. For example, students in the string orchestra might all have a sheet of paper fastened to their music stand or kept with their music that shows not only fingerings but also other musical terms. This then gives students a way to look things up without them having to ask in front of peers and risk embarrassment.

Conductors can help students who have trouble quickly processing music notation or who get easily lost by calling out rehearsal numbers as the ensemble plays or sings music. If these students know that eventually the teacher will call out a rehearsal number, they can look ahead and be ready to join back in.

Hammel (2013) advises teachers to consider using what she calls the "Big Four." The Big Four are used to assist students in reading music and include color, size, modality, and pacing. Color has been discussed and may include overlays, printing on colored paper, or highlighting music in color. Size can be used to make music larger and bolder, which is easier to read. Hammel gradually adds more information after beginning with a blank score. With the earlier choral example of "Good King Wenceslas," the teacher can sequence learning by beginning with only the notation of the alto part, perhaps even removing the time and key signatures, title, and so forth. In the following week, if the student is mastering the pitch, duration, and words, then the removed items can be added. Then the teacher can add the slurs and possibly in the next lesson or rehearsal add the full score. The printed music can be supplemented with recordings that gradually add these items in as well.

Modality has been discussed earlier in this chapter as multisensory learning. Hammel advocates for teaching music in at least three ways using visual, aural, and kinesthetic learning modes. She records lessons or rehearsals and allows students to review the recordings at home. In addition, Hammel suggests that teachers allow students to respond in their strongest learning mode when being assessed—for example, students with writing difficulties can verbally answer questions.

This brings up an area of concern as many students with learning disabilities struggle with auditions. If processing music notation is identified as a difficulty, why do we continue to make students with disabilities sight-read in auditions? Auditions are stressful, and musicians with learning disabilities are already going to struggle in that sort of environment, but if music reading is difficult, they will likely not compare well with other musicians.

Audition judges and teachers should ask themselves if sight-reading flu-ently is really a necessary skill for students to demonstrate. If it is, then they should recognize that students with learning disabilities will likely do poorly in an audition requiring sight-reading.

Finally, Hammel (2013) defines pacing as allowing for individual needs regarding one's speed of introduction and subsequent material. She pro-vides a valuable list of steps that students with organizational challenges can use to learn a new piece. A checklist that helps organize practice rou-tines will help to ensure that the musician is provided guidance and support for learning music away from the teacher.

Heikkila and Knight (2012) advise teachers to help students with tracking music by projecting music on a screen and pointing to music as it advances or pointing to sheet music in individual lessons. Some chil-dren with dyslexia struggle with tracking words on a page, and occasion-ally this problem occurs with reading music. The musician literally looks at notes for too long and is not able to look ahead and is delayed in read-ing music. Special educators often use devices that cover up sentences except for the word the child should be looking at and then move a little window ahead to help train the child to read ahead. This can be applied to music. Many musicians will still choose learning aurally as the best solution for them.

The musician with the visuospatial subtype of dyscalculia may be observed struggling with traditional fingering charts when learning instru-ments. Most fingering charts are created as if the instrument were reversed and laid on a table. Students will often try to hold the instrument up to the chart in an effort to make sense of how the chart works, or they might play fingerings wrong due to difficulty understanding how the fingerings relate to the way they experience the instrument. The student looks at the instrument from the angle it is played. A guitar being played and fingered looks different from the fingering charts; a flute is angled off to one side, and when the student looks at the instrument while it is up to the mouth, he or she sees the fingers differently from how the traditional flute finger-ing chart looks. McCord, Gruben, and Rathgeber (2014) have developed adapted fingering charts (see Figures 9.3, 9.4, and 9.5). Figure 9.3 shows an example of how a chart can be adapted to help students who have trouble understanding traditional recorder fingering charts (McCord et al., 2014). To create a tactile version, the teacher can add puff paint to the holes that are covered; that way, the student can see and feel the fingering and then transfer it directly to the instrument.

Photographs add additional realism. A guitar chord is shown through both a photograph and a fingering that appears as if the guitar is being viewed from the playing position (see Figure 9.4).

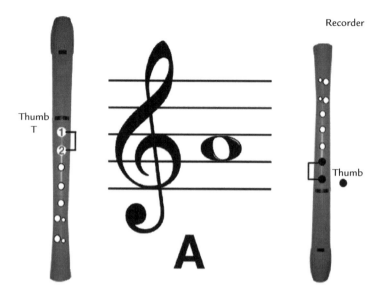

Figure 9.3. Traditional and adapted fingering on recorder.

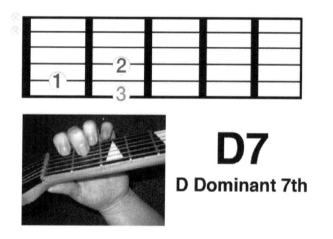

Figure 9.4. Adapted guitar chord fingering.

Students who write the names of the notes in their method books are practicing self-determination and adapting for their own learning needs. Creating examples of this (Figure 9.5) might help students who have not yet figured out how to do this for themselves.

Teachers should consider rise time if they are involved in the choice of instruments with the student and his or her family. When selecting instruments that will primarily be used in ensembles with other people, rise time can impact the student's ability to accurately play durations. Music marked

Hot Cross Buns

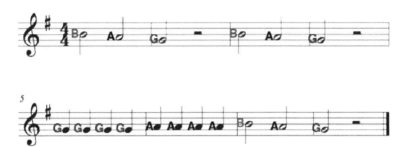

Figure 9.5. Adapted color-coded notation.

with staccato and legato markings might be difficult for students with learning disabilities to accurately understand and perform.

Music teachers frequently clap or click sticks together to make a loud and steady beat when ensembles slow down or speed up the tempo. If the student is dyslexic, research discussed earlier in this chapter indicates that he or she may always experience delays in keeping a steady beat or processing musical meters. It is essential that percussionists are competent in keeping a steady beat. The student with difficulty maintaining a steady beat will not only become frustrated in him- or herself but also probably be a frustration to his or her fellow musicians and conductor.

IN SUMMARY

There is a need for further research, especially among students with dyscalculia, dysgraphia, and dyspraxia. Little is understood about whether this disability impacts music learning and, if so, how to assist the student in learning. There is also a need for practitioners to try adaptations and talk to young musicians about strategies that help them to succeed in music despite their challenges. In the meantime, the "Big Four" are helpful for all learners. Teachers who allow for flexibility in their teaching using the principles of universal design for learning (Rose & Meyer, 2002) will find it much easier to include all students in the classroom and ensemble (McCord et al., 2014). Learning music by ear is a viable expression of musicianship and can be embraced as a valuable tool used by all students and teachers.

Returning to James—what happened to him and did he continue with his trumpet playing? His story includes good and bad news. He became frustrated in the high school band. The pace of the rehearsals was difficult for him to keep up with, although he did successfully participate in the high school jazz band and was the star jazz soloist. His teacher made an exception to a rule that students can only participate in jazz band if they are members of the concert band. This flexibility enabled James to continue playing the instrument he loved and to find success in one of the few areas in school where he could really shine. There are so many gifted musicians like James who love music and who benefit from developing their musicianship and engagement with peers. With flexibility and patience, they can all find a way to make music with others.

REFERENCES

Anderson, P. L., & Meier-Hedde, R. (2001). Early case reports of dyslexia in the United States and Europe. *Journal of Learning Disabilities, 34,* 9–21.

Atterbury, B. W. (1985). Musical differences in learning-disabled and normal-achieving readers, aged seven, eight and nine. *Psychology of Music, 13*(2), 114–123.

Atterbury, B. W. (1990). *Mainstreaming exceptional learners in music.* Englewood Cliffs, NJ: Prentice Hall.

Bateman, B. (1965). An educational view of diagnostic approach to learning disorders. In J. Hellmuth (Ed.), *Learning disorders.* Seattle, WA: Special Child Publications.

Besson, M., Schon, D., Moreno, S., Santos, A., & Magne, C. (2007). Influence of musical expertise and musical training on pitch processing in music and language. *Restorative Neurology and Neuroscience, 25,* 399–410.

Bhide, A., Power, A., & Goswami, U. (2013). A rhythmic musical intervention for poor readers: A comparison of efficacy with a letter-based intervention. *Mind, Brain and Education, 7*(2), 113–123.

Bryson, K. J. (2013). Teaching a student with dyslexia. *Journal of Singing, 69*(4), 429–435.

Chandrasekaran, B., & Kraus, N. (2010). Music, noise-exclusion, and learning. *Music Perception, 27*(4), 297–306.

Chung, K. K. H., Ho, C. S. H., Chan, D. W., Tsang, S. M., & Lee, S. H. (2010). Cognitive profiles of Chinese adolescents with dyslexia. *Dyslexia, 16,* 2–23.

Cogo-Moreira, H., Andriolo, R. B., Yazigi, L., Ploubidis, G. B., Brandao de Vila, C. R., & Mari, J. J. (2012). Music education for improving reading skills in children and adolescents with dyslexia. *Cochrane Database of Systematic Reviews, 8.*

Corrigall, K. A., & Trainor, L. J. (2011). Associations between length of music training and reading skills in children. *Music Perception, 29*(2), 147–155.

Cruickshank, W. M., Bentzen, F. A., Ratzeburg, F. H., & Tannhauser, M. T. (1961). *A teaching method of brain-injured and hyperactive children.* Syracuse, NY: Syracuse University Press.

Dyscalculia Forum. (2012). http://www.dyscalculiaforum.com (2012). Retrieved September 3, 2013.

Fernald, G. M., & Keller, H. (1921). The effect of kinesthetic factors in the development of word recognition in the case of non-readers. *Journal of Educational Research, 4,* 355–377.

Forgeard, M., Schlaug, G., Norton, A., Rosam, C., Iyengar, U., & Winner, E. (2008). The relation between music and phonological processing in normal-reading children and children with dyslexia. *Music Perception, 25*(4), 383–390.

Geary, D. C. (1993). Mathematical disabilities: Cognitive, neuropsychological, and genetic components. *Psychological Bulletin, 114*, 345–362.

Goldstein, K. (1936). The modification of behavior consequent to cerebral lesions. *Psychiatric Quarterly, 10*, 586–610.

Goldstein, K. (1939). *The organism*. New York, NY: American Book.

Goswami, U. (2011). A temporal sampling framework for developmental dyslexia. *Trends in Cognitive Sciences, 15*, 3–10.

Goswami, U. (2012). Entraining the brain: Applications to language research and links to musical entrainment. *Empirical Musicology Review, 7*(1–2), 57–63.

Goswami. U. (2013). Dyslexia-in tune but out of time. *The Psychologist*. 26. 106-109.

Gresham, F. M. (2002). *Identification of learning disabilities: Research to practice. The LEA series on special education and disability*. Mahwah, NJ: Lawrence Erlbaum Associates Publishers.

Hammel, A. (2013). *Constructive curricula for students with exceptionalities: Creating positive learning environments*. Paper presented at Intersections: Arts and Special Education Conference, The Kennedy Center, Washington, DC, August 10, 2013.

Heikkila, E., & Knight, A. (2012). Inclusive music teaching strategies for elementary-age children with developmental dyslexia. *Music Educators Journal, 99*(1), 54–59.

Helland, T. A., & Asbjornsen, A. (2000). Executive functions in dyslexia. *Child Neuropsychology, 6*(1), 37–48.

Hornickel, J., & Krause, N. (2013). Unstable representation of sound: A biological marker of dyslexia. *Journal of Neuroscience, 33*(8), 3500–3504.

Hubicki, M. (2001). A multisensory approach to the teaching of musical notation. In T. R. Miles & J. Westcombe (Eds.), *Music and dyslexia: Opening new doors* (pp. 85–100). London, England: Whurr Publishers.

Huss, M., Verney, J. P., Fosker, T., Mead, N., & Goswami, U. (2010). Music, rhythm, rise time perception and developmental dyslexia: Perception of musical meter predicts reading and phonology. *Cortex, 47*(6), 674–689.

Kirk, S. A. (1962). *Educating exceptional children*. Boston, MA: Houghton Mifflin.

Lam, C. C. C. (2010). *Developmental dyslexia: Neurobiological perspectives*. Hong Kong, China: The Hong Kong Institute of Education.

Lewis, M. E. B., Shapiro, B. K., & Church, R. P. (2013). *Specific learning disabilities*. In M. L. Batshaw, N. J. Roizen, & G. R. Lotrecchiano (Eds.), *Children with disabilities* (7th ed.). Baltimore, MD: Brookes Publishing Company.

Lyon, G. R., Shaywitz, S. E., & Shaywitz, B. A. (2003). A definition of dyslexia. *Annals of Dyslexia, 53*, 1–14.

McCord, K. A. (1997). Adapting music technology for students with learning disabilities. In *Proceedings of the Fourth International Technological Directions in Music Education Conference*, San Antonio, TX, February.

McCord, K. A. (2004). Moving beyond "That's all I can do": Encouraging musical creativity in children with learning disabilities. *Bulletin of the Council for Research in Music Education, Winter*(159), 23–32.

McCord, K. A., Gruben, A., & Rathgeber, J. (2014). *Accessing music: Using UDL to enhance student learning in the general music classroom*. Van Nuys, CA: Alfred Publishing.

Moritz, C., Yampolsky, S., Papadelis, G., Thomson, J., & Wolf, M. (2013). Links between early rhythm skills, musical training, and phonological awareness. *Reading and Writing, 26*(5), 739–769.

National Center for Health Statistics. (2010). *The condition of education: Number and percentage distribution of 3- to 21-year-olds served under the Individuals with Disabilities Education Act (IDEA), Part B, and number served as a percentage of total public school enrollment, by type of disability: Selected school years, 1980-81through 2009–10*. Retrieved from http://www.cdc.gov/nchs/index.htm

Overy, K. (2000). Dyslexia, temporal processing and music: The potential of music as an early learning aid for dyslexic children. *Psychology of Music, 28*, 218–229.

Overy, K. (2003). Dyslexia and music: From timing deficits to musical intervention. The neurosciences and music. 999(1), Retrieved from the *Annals of the New York Academy of Sciences* website: http://www3.interscience.wiley.com.libproxy.lib.ilstu.edu/cgi-bin/fulltext/118876638/HTMLSTART doi:10:1196/annals.1284.060

Poole, H. (2001). My music and my dyscalculia. In T. R. Miles & J. Westcombe (Eds.), *Music and dyslexia: Opening new doors* (pp. 53–56). London, England: Whurr.

Pratt, C. M. (2008). In and around the classroom. In T. R. Miles, J. Westcombe, & D. Ditchfield (Eds.), *Music and dyslexia: A positive approach* (pp. 19–25). West Sussex, England: Wiley.

Przybylski, L., Bedoin, N., Krifi-Papoz, S., Herbillon, V., Roch, D., Kotz, S., & Tillmann, B. (2013). Rhythmic auditory stimulation influences syntactic processing in children with developmental language disorders. *Neuropsychology, 27*(1), 121–131.

Register, D., Darrow, A. A., Standley, J., & Swedberg, O. (2007). The use of music to enhance reading skills of second grade students and students with reading disabilities. *Journal of Music Therapy, 44*(1), 23–27.

Reid, G., & Green, S. (2007). *100 ideas for supporting pupils with dyslexia.* London, England: Continuum.

Rose, D. H., & Meyer, A. (2002). *Teaching every student in the digital age, universal design for learning.* Alexandria, VA: ASCD.

Ryan, R. M., & Deci, E. L. (2000). Self-determination theory and the facilitation of intrinsic motivation, social development, and well-being. *American Psychologist, 55*(1), 68–78.

Seligman, M. (1975). *Helplessness: On depression, development and death.* San Francisco, CA: W. H. Freeman.

Shalev, R. S. (2004). Developmental dyscalculia. *Journal of Child Neurology, 19*, 765–771.

Solis, M. (2010–2012). *The effects of colored paper on musical notation reading on music students with dyslexia.* Masters thesis. Texas Tech University. Retrieved from https://repositories.tdl.org/ttu-ir/bitstream/handle/2346/ETD-TTU-2010-12-1100/SOLIS-THESIS.pdf?sequence=2

Stainback, S., Stainback, W., Stefanich, G., & Alper, S. (1997). Learning in inclusive classrooms; what about curriculums? In S. Stainback & W. Stainback (Eds.) *Inclusion: A guide for educators.* Baltimore, MD: Brookes Publishing.

Strait, D., & Kraus, N. (2011). Playing music for a smarter ear: Cognitive, perceptual and neurobiological evidence. *Music Perception, 29*(2), 133–146.

U.S. Office of Education. (1968). *First annual report of National Advisory Committee on Handicapped Children.* Washington, DC: U.S. Department of Health, Education, and Welfare.

Vaughn, S., & Fuchs, L. S. (2003). Redefining learning disabilities as inadequate response to instruction: The promise and potential problems. *Learning Disabilities & Practice, 18*, 137–146.

Westcombe, J. (2002). How dyslexia can affect musicians. In T. R. Miles & J. Westcombe (Eds.), *Music and dyslexia: Opening new doors* (pp. 9–18). London, England: Whurr.

Ziegler, J. C., Pech-Georgel, C., George, F., & Foxton, J. M. (2012). Global and local pitch perception in children with developmental dyslexia. *Brain and Language, 120*(3), 265–270.

CHAPTER 10

Including Students with Disabilities in Instrumental Ensembles

CHRISTINE M. LAPKA

Social learning as presented by Bandura and Walters (1963) suggests that a model is essential to the learning process. The following scenes present models of music learning and teaching within a range of contexts for children of differing abilities and the ways that teachers included these students in performance ensembles. Their stories provide possible ways to enable students to have authentic roles in instrumental ensembles.

By all accounts, Mark[1] was an unlikely candidate for beginning band. He used a walker, had asthma, and could not hold an instrument. However, in an effort to include Mark, his junior high band director, Ms. Richards, completed a brief assessment. She quickly ruled out woodwinds because of physical limitations. Percussion might work, but the drumsticks were not a good match. She looked at what Mark could do. He was able to sit in a chair and produce a buzzing sound on a trombone. Then she formed a plan; she often allowed beginning tuba players to use a special stand called the Tuba Tamer to hold the tuba.[2] She went to the practice room and rolled a tuba in front of a surprised Mark. He was able to make a sound and they mutually decided on tuba as his band instrument.

However, the story does not end there. It took Mark several months to produce a sound in rehearsal. The beginning band and the entire band program at his school allowed students to progress at their own pace. Some met the requirements for the top group in one year, while others might continue in the intermediate group. If needed, students might remain in the beginning band. Ms. Richards anticipated that Mark would quit trying, but that was not part of this young man's background. Mark has two parents who did not accept "no" for an answer. At birth, the doctors told the parents to have low expectations. That just would not do. Mark's parents made sure their son was receiving the best medical care for cerebral palsy with various physical therapies. At one point, it took him nearly two hours to get dressed for school, but with persistence, he improved.

Mark's support system was an important part of his success but, again, not the entire story. Mark himself had a great deal to do with his persistence. He wanted to join band because he saw the band perform at his elementary school. To him the band sounded great and worked together as an amazing team. Mark was hooked. The next step involved getting his parents to take him to "meet the instrument" night. They were apprehensive but supported their son in other endeavors like Boy Scouts, so why not band? Their advocacy served Mark throughout school and was important in his persistence with learning to play the tuba.

With the support of his parents, his love of music, and the patience of his teacher, who allowed students to progress at their own pace, Mark began to make sounds and then music in band. In fact, Mark developed so much that he made the eighth chair in the all-state junior high band. Because of his success with the all-state band, Mark realized that tuba could be more than "his thing" at school; tuba could be a career. From his start as a struggling sixth-grade tuba player, Mark persevered to complete a bachelor's degree in tuba performance (Lapka, 2011, 2013b).

Tim was a student with hearing loss. The hours he spent alone in the practice room were familiar to him because he was already isolated from conversations. Being alone was fine, so practicing alone was more of the same. Therefore, he felt that music was a good fit. Sometimes Tim encountered teachers who did not want him to be a part of groups: "You can play on your own, but you cannot play with others." However, Tim changed their minds when he taught them what he needed from them as teachers to function in an ensemble. He asked the teachers to demonstrate, to provide him with reading materials about music or the pieces they were playing, and to understand that sight and sightlines were important, and sometimes he would need to use touch to figure out what was going on. They discovered that he could describe the feeling of his tone when it was clear or fuzzy. His teachers realized that learning from Tim was an important part of teaching Tim. Other members of the orchestra began to figure out what helped and began to make adjustments. Violin bows provided visual cues for starting and stopping, and students began to take on the responsibility of protecting his necessary sight lines. If Tim needed to see the violins and the conductor, other students took care to be in the right spot. Tim was an important contributor to his own inclusion in orchestra (adapted from Fulford, Ginsborg, & Goldbart, 2011).

* * *

Jenny was excited to start band with her fourth-grade classmates. She was fortunate that her elementary music teacher, Ms. Smith, was also the beginning band director. This music teacher was well aware of the diagnoses listed in Jenny's Individual Education Plan: autism spectrum, apraxia, and low muscle tone. When signing up for band, the parents asked if a tutor would be beneficial and Ms. Smith arranged to teach Jenny privately after school. Before Jenny began trumpet, Ms. Smith consulted with the speech pathologist to find out more about the motor planning issues of apraxia, a disorder in which the brain has trouble moving the articulators needed to make sounds. Ms. Smith specifically asked how they addressed consonant sounds in speech and transferred the same strategies to tonguing when playing the trumpet.

To deal with muscle tone, Ms. Smith received ideas from the physical therapist. Together they decided to give Jenny extra physical space so she could move without hitting other students or their instruments. To support better posture, Jenny sat in a smaller-sized chair. One of Jenny's classmates had trouble sitting still in his chair and the physical therapist suggested a fidget seat. While the fidget seat helped the other student, Jenny did not need the accommodation. However, the ideas from the physical therapist helped to make band a better place for all students.

It truly took a team to get Jenny through band. Much of the information about reading and eye tracking came from the classroom teacher. The classroom teacher reported that Jenny had trouble reading words; they subsequently discovered issues with music reading. Similar to the cover-ups used in reading language, Ms. Smith devised a plan to cover part of the page with sticky notes. She told Jenny to "take a piece of pizza instead of the whole pie." Jenny read music better when she could see one phrase at a time. To make reading letter names easier and to keep the page free from the clutter of writing in the note names, they highlighted each note with a specific color selected by the student. For example, "E" was purple. Eventually, Jenny color-coded the letter names on her own.

When Jenny was in seventh-grade band, Ms. Smith started to ask, "What are you having trouble with?" Jenny was beginning to independently identify personal challenges. On one occasion, she reported having trouble determining if a note was on a line or in a space. Ms. Smith enlarged the music and traced the lines of the music staff with a yellow highlighter. With the visual contrast of individually highlighted staff lines, Jenny no longer needed to color-code the letters and she could quickly enough play in time with the ensemble.

With the help of her band director, classroom teacher, speech therapist, and physical therapist, Jenny was able to participate in band for five years. Jenny did not pursue band in high school. However, the team believed that in addition to a music education, participating in band helped to improve her upper body strength and reading (personal communication with teacher, August 15, 2013).

INCLUSION IN INSTRUMENTAL MUSIC ENSEMBLES

Teachers make accommodations to lessons and teaching strategies, modify the difficulty of the curriculum, communicate/collaborate, and use the principles of universal design to support all learners. Suggestions of how to accommodate and modify the curriculum are noted to follow in a summary of a research study by Scott, Vitale, and Masten (1998), who synthesized studies from 1982 to 1996 regarding classroom teacher perceptions and instructional adaptations in general education classes.

1. Modifying instruction: typical: concrete classroom demonstrations, monitoring classroom understanding; substantial: adjusting the pace to individual learners, giving immediate individual feedback, using multiple modalities
2. Modifying assignments: typical: providing models; substantial: breaking tasks into small steps, shortening assignments, lowering difficulty level
3. Teaching learning skills: typical: study skills, note-taking techniques; substantial: learning strategies, test-taking skills
4. Altering instructional materials: substantial: using alternative materials, taping textbooks, using supplementary aids
5. Altering curriculum: substantial: lowering difficulty of course content
6. Varying instructional grouping: substantial: using peer tutoring, using cooperative groups
7. Enhancing behavior: typical: praise, offering encouragement; substantial: using behavioral contracts, using token economies, frequent parental contact
8. Facilitating progress monitoring: typical: reading tests orally; giving extended test-taking time; giving frequent, short quizzes; providing study guides; substantial: retaking tests, obtaining direct daily measures of academic progress, modifying grading criteria (p. 107)

These strategies include ways to accommodate learners by changing what teachers do, by changing how students respond, or by changing the materials they use in the room (strategies 1, 2, 3, 4, and 8). The researchers also describe when it is necessary to modify the curriculum (strategies 2, 4, and 5) and ways to motivate students (strategies 6, 7, and 8).

More recently, the Center for Applied Special Technologies (CAST) has recognized the importance of accommodating students, modifying the curriculum, and motivating students and offers suggestions for all students (CAST, 2011). Based on the research of cognitive neuroscience and related fields, CAST developed universal design for learning (UDL). In short, the framework and guidelines included in UDL are methods that will work for the population as a whole. There is a clear connection between the principles of UDL and the practice of accommodating learning or modifying the curriculum. Principle III of UDL, "Provide Multiple Means of Engagement," outlines ways to motivate students (CAST, 2011). It is important to note that the method works for students with disabilities and students without disabilities so that when students with disabilities join the ensemble, the supports are already in place (Hall, Meyer, & Rose, 2012).

In addition, researchers in inclusive education widely accept communication and collaboration as necessary components of inclusive classrooms (Friend & Bursuck, 2011; Friend & Cook, 2010; Hammel & Hourigan, 2011). In Jenny's scene, teachers and therapists worked together to find solutions. It would be difficult to find an individual teacher who understood all of the information from all of the professional fields (physical therapy, speech therapy, music, reading). It is essential that teachers seek and share information.

The following sections will describe accommodation, modification, communication, collaboration, and motivation as key strategies in inclusive education. These constructs provide a solid foundation for music teachers to build inclusive music communities in their ensemble classrooms.

UNDERSTANDING ACCOMMODATION AND CURRICULUM MODIFICATION

Music teachers routinely make accommodations and curriculum modifications to enable students with various abilities to participate in music. The UDL framework (Principles I and II) offers guidelines for teachers as they seek to make appropriate accommodations and modifications.

Accommodations change the method of delivery or the way students engage in music (CAST, 2011). Principle I exhorts the teacher to present information and content in different ways. Teachers could provide multiple examples and nonexamples to emphasize critical features. Principle II allows students to express what they know in different forms (CAST, 2011). Some students might be able to play traditional instruments, like the saxophone, while others might use an iPad application to make music. Accommodations do not change the level of difficulty; they help the student access the curriculum.

On the other hand, modifications to the curriculum change the level of difficulty. UDL's Principle III discusses how learners vary in their skills and abilities (CAST, 2011). The guidelines suggest "differentiating the degree of difficulty or complexity" for completing core activities. The modification does not have to change the nature of the entire ensemble. The change can be

Figure 10.1. Simplified musical notation.

one of the many choices made when thinking about what individuals do to contribute to the musical whole. A simple modification occurs when a director selects which part someone plays. In the percussion section, a student can play triangle instead of snare drum. Conductors often place brass players capable of playing in high registers on part I, while struggling musicians who may have a limited range play part II. A more complex modification would be to alter the written music. If a student is struggling with a physical limitation, he or she might have difficulty playing 16th notes on the trumpet. The teacher can highlight the notes to play or rewrite the part to have the students perform fewer notes in what I call the skeleton (see Figure 10.1).

Suggestions for Accommodations in Performance Ensembles

Directors accommodate students by finding ways to strengthen each learner's musicianship. Sometimes the accommodation can be as simple as selecting an appropriate private teacher or giving the student more time to complete a task. These simple accommodations might work, but then again they may not be specific enough for the needs of the student (Brownell, Smith, Crockett, & Griffin, 2012). After the accommodation is made, directors should monitor the plan for its effectiveness.

Students with different physical concerns may benefit from a wide range of devices. Prosthetics are a perfect example of individualization. For example, Canadian violinist Adrian Anantawan was the subject of a documentary by ZAP Production called "Adrian Anantawan: The Story Behind the Notes." Born without a right hand, he completed a degree from the Curtis Institute, has established himself as a performer, and is a supporter of arts for those with disabilities (Adrian Anantawan Biography, n.d.). Anantawan plans to attend the Harvard Graduate School of Education to "research the role of adaptive instruments within a UDL curriculum" (Adrian Anantawan Upcoming Events, n.d.).

There are several prosthetic companies and researchers who are developing custom devices for musicians, and some offer ways to cover the costs. In the United States, Shriner's Hospitals for Children will pay the costs not covered by insurance until the student reaches age 18 (UPI, 2011). During that time, the technicians will alter or create new prosthetic limbs as the student grows. The group will also create specific orthotics for holding or playing instruments. Local companies and organizations do similar work and can be found through online research.

Some students develop alternative playing techniques. Guitarist George Dennehy began playing cello in middle school (Dennehy, 2007). He was fortunate to take private lessons from a teacher who could envision how someone born without arms could play cello with his or her feet. A special cello stand held his instrument horizontal to the floor, and his teacher created exercises that gave him increased dexterity with his feet and toes. As a high school student, Dennehy developed his own way to comfortably play the guitar. Similar to the way he plays the cello, Dennehy lays the guitar flat and uses his left foot to hold the pick and strum, while his right foot presses the strings (Dennehy, 2011).

Devices can help people play instruments. There are low-technology options like the Chord Buddy or E-Z Chord that act like chord capos on the guitar. Some teachers use popsicle sticks to create tools to play chords on the piano. Lukas Bratcher, a euphonium player, uses a special electronic attachment because he is unable to push the pistons of his instrument fast enough (Edutopia, 2005). With the help of Robin Amend's instrument repair shop, an attachment was created. Amend was predisposed to think about disabilities because his grandfather was a Vaudeville musician with one arm. The grandfather assisted other musicians with missing limbs. With Amend's family background and the help of a mechanical engineer, Andrew Coleman, a joystick-controlled solenoid mechanism was developed to depress the piston valves on a euphonium. Amend seeks to inspire other instrument repair shops to be innovative (Riddle, 2008). Like Amend, there are technicians who make mechanical changes to instruments that enable people to play woodwind instruments with one hand using toggle keys (Haar, 2006) or assist short or missing fingers with added extensions to keys (Flute Lab, 2013).

Typical students, too, can find assistance with a variety of instrument holders, neck straps, and instrument stands. Many school programs own several marching drum stands so that harnesses are not required during practice or when playing in the stands during sporting events. As mentioned in the opening scene, Mark used a tuba stand. Many able tuba players use small stools to make instrument playing more ergonomic. With the emphasis on comfort and injury-free playing, manufacturers are making instrument support systems and accommodations for players of all abilities. Some examples include:

ErgoBrass Instrument Support System for Brass: http://www.ergobrass.com/cor/eng/eng_cor_etusivu.html
Tuba Essentials: http://www.adjustabletubastand.com/

Swan Neck Flute: http://www.flutelab.com/swan.html
Vertical Flue Headjoint: http://www.flutelab.com/vertical.html
Fiddle Ezy Violin Support Strap: http://www.merrylandsmusic.com.
au/Merrylandsmusic/Fiddle-Ezy.htm
Vandoren Universal Saxophone neckstrap: http://www.vandoren.fr/
PDF%20accesoires/Accessoires%20en.pdf
BG France woodwind accessories: http://www.bgfranckbichon.com/

After teachers meet with students and determine their needs, they might first search to find a manufacturer that already produces the necessary support. If one is not available, a next step is to find an interested instrument technician to create a specific accommodation. Teachers must then establish an attitude of celebrating diversity to help foster an understanding that all human beings are musical and capable of participating in an ensemble regardless of how one might hold his or her instrument.

Accommodations can be much simpler. One might enlarge the music for students with low vision or with reading disabilities like dyslexia. Color-coding specific pitches, using icons to help with rhythm, and using technology for listening are strategies for people with dyslexia in music education (Bryson, 2013; Miles, Westcombe, & Ditchfield, 2008; Oglethorpe, 2002). Breaking down large performance requirements into smaller parts and enlisting peer tutors are common practices in performing ensembles (Friend & Bursuck, 2011; Hammel & Hourigan, 2011). It is routine to rehearse a specific section of a piece rather than an entire work. In addition, if the curriculum requires students to play all of the major and minor scales, the teacher can add one major and relative minor scale each week. The strategy aligns with UDL Principle III.8, "Encourage division of long-term goals into short-term objectives." Peer tutors (or section leaders) need ideas and individual strategies to reach struggling students. However, in these cases, teachers should continue to develop new strategies for breaking down tasks in music, while also being aware that peer tutors may need assistance on how to best support their classmates.

Teachers can use Marzano's (2009, p. 1) six steps to building vocabulary:

1. Provide a description, explanation, or example of the new term.
2. Ask students to restate the description, explanation, or example in their own words.
3. Ask students to construct a picture, pictograph, or symbolic representation of the term.
4. Engage students periodically in activities that help them add to their knowledge of the terms in their vocabulary notebooks.
5. Periodically ask students to discuss the terms with one another.

6. Involve students periodically in games that enable them to play with the terms.

While conductors engage students in explanations, definitions, and activities (performance) involving musical vocabulary, teachers can make use of notebooks or portfolios in ensemble rehearsals. Wolfman (n.d.) describes the use of notebooks with his high school orchestra. Students keep the notebooks on their stand during rehearsal and are asked to write a wide range of items in the notebook: concert reviews, dictation, critiques of their own playing, ideas for improvement, or a journal of their own musical activities. "Through this process, students become responsible for their own musical progress and the teacher continually guides them in their musical journey" (p. 2). The steps for building vocabulary originated in special education, but like many other accommodations, they are universal in scope.

Music teachers should understand that every student is unique and will require different techniques. UDL recommends that teachers allow students to be unique—that they encourage independence while offering support. For example, students who are blind might learn to play pieces by listening to audio files provided by the teacher. Later, students can learn how to scan music and turn it into a sound file.

In addition, students need time to figure things out. Braille music might help some students, while learning by ear might be best for other students. One of my former students, Leslie Hamric, was able to earn a college music degree with Braille music. She used Dancing Dots (http://www.dancing-dots.com) to learn Braille music in high school. As a college student, she could turn notation into Braille on her own with software from Dancing Dots and a Braille embosser (Lapka, 2013a).

Students will benefit from mentors who have disabilities. If a beginner is not sighted, advise him or her to enlist the help of the National Federation of the Blind (NFB; https://nfb.org/about-the-nfb) and NFB message boards. Students learn to rely on their own abilities and find natural supports in the ensemble. Natural supports might be practicing after school with a friend or using a smartphone to record their part for at-home practice. Small group practice sessions and cooperative learning benefit all students. Working together as peers requires the students to think deeply about what they are doing.

As students will not always have a teacher when they graduate, learning to determine when they need assistance and who can provide that assistance is important. Students should be empowered to state their needs. Teachers need to guide students toward the right type of assistance. If students are capable of the task, they should not ask for help. The teacher putting an instrument together when the student can do the task could be a hindrance in the future. As mentioned earlier, it is important to encourage independence. Music teachers should assess the situation to see if the student is asking for necessary help. It could be that when teachers provide unnecessary assistance, students learn to take advantage of the system. Student identification of environmental supports and independence and then matching the support to their needs are aspects of self-determination, an educational outcome (Wehmeyer, Agran, & Hughes, 1998). Teachers should be actively involved in supporting self-determination in all students. In this area, students learn to be their own advocates. When young musicians learn how to govern their own supports, they have a way to be involved in lifelong music making.

In performance, using technology and reading Braille were ways for Leslie to be empowered. As musicians mature, they will need tools to enable them to continue to make music. In the adult world, they should understand how to ask for these tools outside of the school setting. Self-determination will help enable students to become contributing agents in their own lives. Until they become their own agents, teachers will need to continually evaluate and find appropriate accommodations.[3]

Suggestions for Modifying the Curriculum in Performance Ensembles

Band and orchestra directors are accustomed to altering the difficulty level of their band literature and curriculum. "This year, my band is advanced and we are ready to play 'Variations on a Korean Folk Song' by John Barnes Chance," or "My band struggled when we attempted to sight-read the piece, so we need a different selection." However, intellectual disabilities can require teachers to do more than change the piece or to use previously described accommodations. This time the students need a modified curriculum.

Students with intellectual disabilities might need supports to comprehend or read notation. When reading is the problem, teachers adapt the written notation to something more intuitive (see Figure 10.2) or allow the students to learn their parts through imitation. Figure 10.2.shows timpani notation created in PowerPoint. Blue squares represent the tonic, F, while the yellow triangle is a code for dominant, C. The blue squares or same-sized triangles represent a one-beat note on tonic F. The broken shapes represent two sounds sharing the beat (two 8th notes). The longer triangle lasts for two beats. If needed, the colored shapes can be placed on the drums to help the student remember which drum corresponds with the color. The figure is only one example of the many ways teachers can alter what

 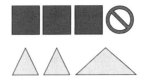

Figure 10.2. Adapted notation (provided by Brett Hartigan).

students read. Because the example shows a change so far from traditional notation, it appears in the modifications section. However, some might see the alteration as an accommodation (similar to Braille, highlighting notes, or enlarging the print). Whatever category, changing what students read can improve their accuracy.

Most students will be able to read music. However, students with certain disabilities will require alternatives for visual information. As a step toward the goal of reading music, students with reading problems (learning disabilities, visual disabilities) need to hear their part while they look at/feel the notation. Sometimes, they might play music by ear first. After producing a good tone and becoming fluent, students may learn what the notation looks like or feels like in Braille. It is likely that some students will only be fluent when they imitate the sound produced by their neighbors or when they listen to a MIDI (Musical Instrument Digital Interface) file converted from Finale. In this scenario, students are not unaware of the notes on the page. They can identify the symbols but need auditory support to perform with a sense of simultaneity with the rest of the ensemble.

Young musicians with severe disabilities may not be able to play at the same degree of difficulty as their peers. In this case, think about what students can do and the importance of success. Before the euphonium player, Lukas, was fitted with the toggle switch, he only played the open notes—tones produced without depressing the valves. Lukas followed the music and patiently waited for the open notes. While the method of playing a few notes is not often used in band, it does work for handbell playing and did work for Lukas until the toggle switch mechanism was attached to the euphonium.

In addition to handbell choirs, general music teachers and music therapists have been using the "play your note" strategy for some time. It is common to have children play the chords on guitar, keyboard, or xylophone. The students are assigned a note or chord and they wait for a cue from the teacher or they follow a written chord symbol or color card to know when to play their chord/note. As a group, all the parts are covered. Individually, they play one specific fragment. Teachers have altered the goals for these students by looking at what the students are capable of performing. Instead of making the student play the specific part, teachers make a part that fits the level of the student. In the case of Lukas, the modified curriculum was a necessary step that other students did not need, but it gave him a place to begin.

When the student's musical task is daunting, educators can help by breaking down the task into more manageable sections. Teachers simplify the music and simultaneously keep players challenged. It might take time to write new parts, but the effort is necessary. Perhaps the students can learn how to highlight the notes they will play in a passage (see Figure 10.1). Adapting their own music will be useful in their musical life outside of school.

In addition to altering the parts, students might play different types of instruments, like the electronic instruments of GarageBand and other iPad applications. Sometimes the electronic sounds can cover/replace instruments that might be difficult to purchase on limited budgets. Whether it is a change in the printed part or a different type of instrument, a creative teacher will be able to find something the student can play (Glass, Blair, & Ganley, 2012).

To set low expectations is a disservice to students of all abilities. Teachers need to set reasonable expectations and realize that some of their students are novices and some may have had more prior musical experiences (private lessons, etc.). Being a novice does not mean that they are not capable of contributing to the group. For example, if playing an instrument is a goal for a band class, then allowing students to listen to the group instead of playing does not enable them to reach the goal. Orchestra and band members play instruments. Music educators should not be asked to alter the goals of the ensemble to the point that the activity cannot be recognized as band. UDL is quite clear in the application of guidelines. If a guideline changes the original goal of the lesson (i.e., playing an instrument), then the guideline (i.e., listening) is not appropriate (Lapinski, Gravel, & Rose, 2012). For students who want to learn how to listen, the school curriculum should offer different types of courses for listening. Schools should offer a full range of courses that will be of interest to different individuals: choir, composing, listening to jazz, and so forth. Once a variety of course offerings are in place and a student with a physical limitation decides that band is the most desirable way to be involved in music, then his or her teachers need to find a way for that student to meet his or her goal (Lapka, 2013c).

Setting reasonable expectations is important. UDL 8.2 states, "Vary demands and resources to optimize challenge." This supports Vygotsky's (1978) theory of teaching within a child's zone of proximal development (CAST, 2011). Vygotsky asserts that with the right assistance or scaffolds, students can accomplish new tasks. Eventually, the student will be able to complete the task independently. As teachers learn what their instrumentalists can do, they can work to keep them appropriately challenged.

To keep all musicians challenged, advanced players might additionally need an alternate curriculum. For the gifted player, suggest solo literature, encourage auditions for community and honors groups, and encourage participation in individual performance festivals. Struggling students will benefit by performing selected portions of a piece. Some creative rehearsal planning is in order: the group rehearsal may begin with the assigned section. When the large ensemble has met the performance goal, the student might continue to work on his or her assigned section in a practice room. The student does not need to sit in rehearsal while the group practices pieces or sections beyond his or her personal assignment.

Curriculum modifications are appropriate to match the ability levels of each student. Teachers should take care not to bore or frustrate the student and keep the musical and pedagogical goals consistent with the original intent. All students are capable of participating as productive members of the ensemble.

Reverse Inclusion Ensembles

Schools with a large number of students with severe intellectual or behavioral disabilities might offer reverse inclusion ensembles. The goals and subsequent class activities of the ensemble fit the needs of the students with disabilities (i.e., strum a guitar that is tuned to a particular chord, strum the chord at the correct time). Other students join the class as peer models or mentors. The typical students provide musical and social support for the students with disabilities. Peer mentors learn about diversity and students with severe disabilities socialize and learn to be musicians (Zeroski, 2012).

Reverse inclusion instrumental ensembles can be acoustic or electronic. Special Orchestra (Linhart, 2003) uses a mix of electronic keyboards and acoustic instruments tuned to the C chord with simple barred chords to create dominant and subdominant chords. For example, the guitarists use an instrument tuned to the C chord. To create the F chord, they barre the instrument with several fingers across the fifth fret and the G barre at the seventh fret. Musicians could also use *slide bars* or *bottlenecks*. If needed, the guitars, xylophones, and electronic keyboards could be fitted with colored indicator lights that direct students when to change chords. Electronic ensembles often use iPads with various applications like Bloom or GarageBand (Abdulezer, 2011). The applications allow for visual and auditory feedback while technique is a simple touch on the screen.

Some iPad ensembles are in schools for students with disabilities where there is not convenient access to students who are typical (Abdulezer, 2011; Baker, 2012). Because the school does not have students who are typical, their ensembles are considered segregated. Partnering with another school would provide opportunities to include typical models for socialization and peer learning.

The High Five Choir in Chicago offers a model for reverse instrumental ensembles. Peer mentors are educated before the start of school and receive community service credit for participating in the group. The mentors become friends and musical supports (Vaughn 2008). Parents, educators, students with disabilities, and students who are typical alike have shared that being in the choir is a transformative experience (Malone, 2010).

Without reverse inclusion ensembles, some students with disabilities might not have a music education or an inclusive education, as they are not able to participate in other ensembles. Participation is difficult because they might need extreme medical support or excessive scaffolds, or because the curriculum they need is too far outside of the scope of a band or orchestra. When needed, reverse inclusion may be the right choice (Zeroski, 2013).

COMMUNICATION AND COLLABORATION

Collaboration is key when including students with disabilities in classes. Collaboration, as described by Friend and Cook (2010), is much more than working together. It requires true communication; both parties must provide ideas and listen. Teachers work together best when they (1) share information, (2) work toward a common goal, (3) value working together, (4) contribute equally, and (5) share responsibility for the decisions as the student progresses (Friend & Cook, 2010).

Members of the special education staff and related therapists can offer information about how the child reads, moves, or speaks. Jenny's teacher (in the scenario described previously) was an excellent example of collaboration. Professionals can share how the child functions in different classes—the student may have trouble with print and prefer to learn by listening (Friend & Cook, 2010). Perhaps the speech therapist advises that a student might have trouble forming a brass embouchure and wonders if another instrument would be appropriate. Together the two professionals (with the parent and child) make a better decision about an instrument choice than they might make separately.

Collaborating with other professionals is important when students work with specialists like audiologists, physical therapists, music therapists, or other special areas. The most competent teachers cannot be experts in every exceptionality; as research and technology change rapidly, teachers need to continually collaborate with other experts (Friend & Cook, 2010). Music teachers may be able to arm themselves with knowledge about hearing loss or dyslexia but should seek out experts to provide student-specific and current information.

Conversely, other teachers will rely on music teachers' knowledge of performing ensembles. Music directors must share their knowledge to ensure the curriculum is recognizable. Especially when subject-specific information is needed, it is important that all teachers add their piece to the puzzle. Sometimes the collaborative process takes several exchanges of information before teachers may decide upon a direction. It is important for collaborators to communicate effectively to reach a shared final goal (Friend & Cook, 2010).

Co-teaching

During collaboration, educators may determine to use co-teaching as a way to share instruction for the ensemble that has a large number of students with disabilities. Friend and Cook (2010) offer six types of co-teaching approaches: (1) one teach, one observe; (2) one teach, one assist; (3) station teaching; (4) parallel teaching; (5) alternative teaching, and (6) teaming. Perhaps the special education teacher will observe to collect data (one teach, one observe) or sit beside a student to prompt (one teach, one assist). Breaking into stations (separating winds, strings, percussion, or brass into separate rehearsals) is a commonly used method in instrumental ensembles. Parallel and alternative models also require breaking the large group into smaller units or sections. However, finding co-teachers who have the necessary musical understanding and skill set can prove to be a challenge. For multigroup approaches, co-teachers can be other music specialists, or schools might employ private teachers to lead sections. The last approach, teaming, has two teachers leading the class together. In music, one might model by playing the example while the other prompts the class to use content language to describe the musical example. Co-teaching might be an important tool to include students.

Working with Parents

Parents play an important role in collaboration (Friend & Bursuck, 2011). Family members who have experience playing an instrument could offer at-home support; having this information when a student selects an instrument is important. In addition, parents know a great deal about the medical issues and abilities of the student. Implementing their knowledge can save valuable time for the ensemble directors, who typically have large numbers of students in their classes.

Teachers may be hesitant to discuss goals because they are afraid of the answer—they might assume that parents expect their child to exceed and play first chair. Most parents do not expect their child to play at the level of their peers, but they want their child to have a typical school music experience and belong to a group. Knowing this, teachers can modify the curriculum (if needed) and find meaningful ways for the student to contribute to the group.

Collaborative relationships have a dynamic influence on student learning (Bransford, Brown, & Cocking, 2000). Teachers need to share their knowledge of curriculum, accommodations, and best educational practices. They should be careful not to overlook the unique perspective of the parents.

INTRINSIC MOTIVATION

Intrinsic motivation is part of all learning, including music learning in performance settings. Principle III of UDL includes the following guides for motivation: Guideline 7: provide options for recruiting interest; Guideline 8: provide options for sustaining effort and persistence; and Guideline 9: provide options for self-regulation.

Assessment

UDL offers many ideas to challenge, excite, and interest students. It is important to show the relationship between the guidelines and common components of the performance curriculum. For example, students can listen to the rehearsal and provide ideas about what to work on in the next rehearsal and perhaps ways to improve the group's playing of a particular selection. However, they may need to learn how to assess their own playing before they are ready to assess the ensemble.

Discussion regarding student practicing or lack of practice skills is widespread in instrumental circles. Teachers may have used rewards or bribes; however, in the following points, UDL suggests using goals, objectives, and mastery-oriented feedback to get better results (CAST, 2011).

Checkpoint 8.1 Heighten salience of goals and objectives
Checkpoint 8.2 Vary demands and resources to optimize challenge

To achieve these outcomes, detailed rubrics can be used to grade playing assessments. Rubrics serve to make the expectations of the assignment more overt (CAST, 2011).

Standard judging sheets (Figure 10.3) do not have enough information to motivate or encourage students and lack specific goals for the student.

Skillful teachers write performance rubrics that help students reach specific goals. The trombone performance rubric shown in Figure 10.4 includes includes a quality line across the top as a way to score the playing exam. Musical goals appear on the left side with feedback in adjoining boxes (Lapka, 2012).

Young musicians will benefit when provided with the rubric in advance of the playing exam. The rubric information—discussed with the teacher and classmates—will serve to guide their practice. Since students may

Category	Excellent	Good	Poor	Comments
Dynamics	3	2	1	
Legato	3	2	1	

Figure 10.3. Rubric #1—Standard judging sheet.

Category	3 points	2 points	1 point	Other Comments
Dynamics	Performs dynamics; brings them to life off of the page! Performance has interest because of dynamics.	Performs most of the dynamics. Some loud/quiet sections need more contrast. Make the music more interesting with dynamics.	Make sure you look at the dynamics and perform them so others can perceive the written markings. Make the music more interesting with dynamics.	
Legato	Plays smooth and connected legato. Uses correct syllable. Slide movement creates natural slurs.	Most legato sections are smooth. Check the placement of your tongue and use a softer syllable like "d." Review natural slurs.	All legato notes need to be more connected. Check the placement of your tongue and use the syllable, "d." Natural slurs and practicing lip slurs will help improve this area.	

Figure 10.4. Rubric #2—Trombone performance rubric.

not know how to make "excellent dynamics," writing down what you, the expert, are looking for is necessary. Learners cannot meet the goal if they do not know what the goal is. All students benefit when they use rubrics, a tool to show goals and sustain effort and persistence (CAST, 2011).

Other strategies include modeling some examples and allowing students to use the tool to assess the teacher's modeled performance. Students might take turns assessing each other as a part of group rehearsal—one person can play while the other uses the rubric to assess the performance. Knowing the criteria in advance will improve performance (McTighe & O'Connor, 2005). It is important to focus on objectives during practice; students are not experts yet and need appropriate guidance.

Universal design additionally encourages teachers to allow student autonomy by directing their own education. Students may be more motivated to reach rubric objectives when they have a role in creating the rubric (CAST, 2011). Self-direction engages students (Pink, 2010). Older students will benefit from writing performance expectations. To write the expectations, musicians will have to think deeply about performance practice. Describing good technique encourages good practice habits, as teachers want students to practice smart.

The use of rubrics can lead to more engaged students in the rehearsal. As teachers encourage students to assess their individual playing, they can begin to expect better ideas from young musicians about ensemble performance. The end goal is to transfer previously learned skills to subsequent rehearsals.

Guiding Practice

Rubrics may provide focus for group practice, but some students need more help with independent practice. The part of the brain that is responsible for executive functions does not reach maturity until late adolescence or adulthood (Rose, Gravel, & Domings, 2012). These functions help students organize their practice time. However, instrumental music programs expect students to practice outside of rehearsal. Creating a practice routine is not new, but recent findings show the importance of guiding practice for beginners who are still developing their executive functions (Rose et al., 2012). Instead of giving students a page of stickers or gold stars to manipulate their actions (Kohn, 1993), teachers should use music to reinforce practice. Music is an effective positive motivator (Standley, 1996). The following routine uses repertoire as a way to motivate students to begin their practice. Once they begin playing, students select from a list of activities. The plan rewards students with favorite selections (Standley, 1996), individual selection, and autonomy (CAST, 2011, p. 73).

1. Start by playing your solo (selected by the student, a favorite piece).

Select two of the following:

2. Record the piece and share it with a friend/parent (perhaps via social media).
3. Play the scale for the piece and create melodies using that scale.
4. Look through your music and select sections that were marked in rehearsal as "needing work."
5. Record the section and listen for improvement (compare with yesterday's practice session) or use assessment software to provide feedback. (Finale has an assessment feature.)
6. Complete assigned exercises. For example, brass players work on long tones and lip slurs: Is your tone full or open? Are your slurs smooth or faster?
7. Play along with the recording/accompaniment of the feature song of the week.

In addition, the teacher must foster ways for students to understand why music is important (CAST, 2011). UDL Principle III.7.2 states that information and activities that are relevant and valuable to student interests or goals will engage the students in learning. People join band and orchestra for a variety of reasons; teachers should not assume that their students are making valuable or relevant connections. To help students make these connections, share events that will happen in band as they advance or ask them to provide examples of what they can do with music in the community. Encourage them to select solo literature that motivates practice. Sometimes you might not like the piece, but if they spend time playing, they win. Find out what they want to do with music and make the connections between this ensemble and their goals.

As teachers use UDL, they will find techniques and guidelines to assist a diverse population.[4] As teachers begin to learn more about UDL, they may identify strategies currently in use in their classrooms. When new ideas are required, the guidelines, supported by research, will assist teachers as they find new ways to motivate a wide range of learners.

BENEFITS OF INCLUSIVE EDUCATION

Everyone has the right to learn in music. With collaboration among a student's support team and caring perseverance, children with exceptionalities can have rich musical experiences in performing ensembles. Inclusive classrooms do more than teach music; they promote diversity

(Villa & Thousand, 2005). When students spend time together and the teacher models a proinclusive attitude, everyone learns a valuable life lesson: we are more alike than we are different. Perhaps these natural supports will continue in ensembles beyond high school with community members who continue to accept diversity in both musical and nonmusical event situations.

Music teachers can play an important role in desegregation. George Dennehy believes that he would not be playing guitar today without the eight years that he spent in orchestra. Sometimes he was frustrated or thought about quitting; now he is thankful for the background he received in school orchestra. There were also times when he really wanted to have arms because of the way others looked at him, but he now has an optimistic outlook (Dennehy, 2013). Because teachers included students like Dennehy, people with disabilities are less segregated. With improved teaching practices, we will see many more success stories.

NOTES

1. Pseudonyms used for all participants.
2. Wenger Corporation: http://www.wengercorp.com.
3. For more information see the CAST website: http://www.udlcenter.org/aboutudl/udlguidelines.
4. For more information regarding Principle III, see http://www.udlcenter.org/aboutudl/udlguidelines/principle3.

REFERENCES

Abdulezer, S. (2011). Hands on music: An iPad band for students with disabilities. Retrieved from http://vimeo.com/27061399

Adrian Anantawan biography. (n.d.). Retrieved from http://www.adriananantawan.com/biography.php

Adrian Anantawan upcoming events. (n.d.). Retrieved from http://www.adriananantawan.com

Baker, M. (2012). iPad band of autistic students post song on iTunes. Retrieved from http://www.foxnews.com/tech/2012/10/25/ipad-band-autistic-students-original-song-goes-on-itunes/

Bandura, A., & Walters, R. H. (1963). *Social learning and personality development.* New York, NY: Holt, Rinehart and Winston.

Bransford, J. D., Brown, A. L., & Cocking, R. R. (Eds.). (2000). *How people learn: Brain, mind, experience, and school.* Washington, DC: National Academy Press.

Brownell, M. T., Smith, S. J., Crockett, J. B., & Griffin, C. C. (2012). *Inclusive instruction: Evidence-based practices for teaching students with disabilities.* New York, NY: Guilford Press.

Bryson, K. J. (2013). Teaching a student with dyslexia. *Journal of Singing, 69*(4), 429–435.

Center for Applied Special Technologies (CAST). (2011). *Universal design for learning guide-lines version 2.0.* Wakefield, MA: Author. Retrieved from http://www.udlcenter.org/aboutudl/udlguidelines

Dennehy, G. (2007). Miracle music. Retrieved from http://www.youtube.com/watch?v=YV8BUp5xp6U

Dennehy, G. (2011). George Dennehy—The interview & live at Musikfest with Goo Goo Dolls. Retrieved from http://www.youtube.com/watch?v=v4eehjVoeAY

Dennehy, G. (2013). Virginia currents: George Dennehy-My life story. Retrieved from http://ideastations.org/video/virginia-currents-george-dennehy/william-king-museum-2013-02-05

Edutopia. (2005). Assistive technology makes a difference for Lukas Bratcher. Retrieved from http://www.edutopia.org/assistive-technology-lukas-bratcher-video

Flute Lab. (2013). Flute key modifications. Retrieved from http://flutelab.com/flutelab.com/adaptive-wind-wind-instruments/

Friend, M., & Bursuck, W. D. (2011). *Including students with special needs: A practical guide for classroom teachers* (6th ed.). Boston, MA: Pearson.

Friend, M., & Cook, L. (2010). *Interactions: Collaboration skills for school professionals* (6th ed.). Columbus, OH: Merrill.

Fulford, R., Ginsborg, J., & Goldbart, J. (2011). Learning not to listen: The experiences of musi-cians with hearing impairments. *Music Education Research, 13*(4), 447–464. doi:10.1080/14613808.2011.632086

Glass, D., Blair, K., & Ganley, P. (2012). Universal design for learning and the arts option. In T. E. Hall, A. Meyer, & D. H. Rose (Eds.), *Universal design for learning in the class-room: Practical applications* (pp. 106–118). New York, NY: Guilford Press.

Haar, P. (2006). Playing the saxophone with one hand. *Saxophone Journal, 30*(3), 18–24.

Hall, T. E., Myer, A., & Rose, D. H. (2012). An introduction to universal design for learn-ing: Questions and answers. In T. E. Hall, A. Meyer, & D. H. Rose (Eds.), *Universal design for learning in the classroom: Practical applications* (pp. 1–8). New York, NY: Guilford Press.

Hammel, A. M., & Hourigan, R. M. (2011). *Teaching music to students with special needs: A label-free approach.* New York, NY: Oxford.

Kohn, A. (1993). *Punished by rewards: The trouble with gold stars, incentive plans, A's, praise, and other bribes.* Boston, MA: Houghton Mifflin.

Lapinski, S., Gravel, J. W., & Rose, D. H. (2012). Tools for practice: The universal design for learning guidelines. In T. E. Hall, A. Meyer, & D. H. Rose (Eds.), *Universal design for learning in the classroom: Practical applications* (pp. 9–24). New York, NY: Guilford Press.

Lapka, C. M. (2011). A desire to push past the comfort zone. *Illinois Music Educator, 72*(2), 100.

Lapka, C. M. (2012). Changed by design: The starting artist. *Illinois Music Educator, 72*(1), 80–81.

Lapka, C. M. (2013a). Change in a life without sight. *Illinois Music Educator, 73*(3), 86–87.

Lapka, C. M. (2013b). *Case study of a tuba player with cerebral palsy.* Unpublished manuscript.

Lapka, C. M. (2013c). Five strategies for teaching students with disabilities in band/orchestra. *Illinois Music Educator, 74*(1), 72–73.

Linhart, G. (2003). *Special Orchestra method & song book: Written for all providers, friends and teachers: Musical background not needed.* Gair Linhart and Special Orchestra. Retrieved from http://www.specialorchestra.org/bookdown.htm

Malone, T. (2010, December 21). Choir emphasizes teens' ability to sing. *Chicago Tribune.* Retrieved from http://articles.chicagotribune.com/2010-12-21/news/ct-met-school-disability-choir-20101221_1_special-education-teacher-music-students

Marzano, R. J. (2009). *The art and science of teaching/six steps to better vocabulary instruction.* Alexandria, VA: Association for Supervision and Curriculum Development. Retrieved from

http://www.ascd.org/publications/educational-leadership/sept09/vol67/num01/
Six-Steps-to-Better-Vocabulary-Instruction.aspx

McTighe, J., & O'Connor, K. (2005). *Seven practices for effective learning.* Alexandria, VA: Association for Supervision and Curriculum Development. Retrieved from http://www.ascd.org/publications/educational-leadership/nov05/vol63/num03/
Seven-Practices-for-Effective-Learning.aspx

Miles, T. R., Westcombe, J., & Ditchfield, D. (Ed.). (2008). *Music and dyslexia: A positive approach.* West Sussex, England: John Wiley & Sons.

Oglethorpe, S. (2002). *Instrumental music for dyslexics: A teaching handbook.* West Sussex, England: John Wiley & Sons.

Pink, D. (2010). Drive: The surprising truth about what motivates us. Retrieved from http://comment.rsablogs.org.uk/2010/04/08/rsa-animate-drive/

Riddle, J. (2008, Fall). Wired for music. *Whitworth Today.* Retrieved from http://www.amend-musiccenter.com/PublicationWiredForMusic.aspx

Rose, D. H., Gravel, J. W., & Domings, Y. (2012). Universal design for learning "unplugged": Applications in low-tech settings. In T. E. Hall, A. Meyer, & D. H. Rose (Eds.), *Universal design for learning in the classroom: Practical applications* (pp. 9–24). New York, NY: Guilford Press.

Scott, B. J., Vitale, R., & Masten, W. G. (1998). Implementing instructional adaptations for students with disabilities in inclusive classrooms: A literature review. *Remedial and Special Education, 19*(2), 106–119.

Standley, J. M. (1996). A meta-analysis on the effects of music as reinforcement for education/therapy objectives. *Journal of Research in Music Education, 44*(2), 105–133.

UPI. (2011, July 24). Shriners Hospitals to start charging. Retrieved from http://www.upi.com/Health_News/2011/07/24/Shriners-Hospitals-to-start-charging/UPI-41131311521938/#ixzz2dDz4jHb4

Vaughan, Susan. (2008, February). *New Trier High School High Five Choir.* Clinic performance presented at the Illinois Music Education Association All-State Convention, Peoria, IL.

Villa, R., & Thousand, J. (2005). The rationales for creating and maintaining inclusive schools. In R. Villa & J. Thousand (Eds.), *Creating an inclusive school* (pp. 41–56). Alexandria, VA: Association for Supervision and Curriculum Development.

Vygotsky, L. (1978). *Mind in society: The development of higher psychological processes.* Cambridge, MA: Harvard University Press.

Wehmeyer, M. L., Agran, M., & Hughes, C. (Eds.). (1998). *Teaching self-determination to students with disabilities; Basic skills for successful transition.* Baltimore, MD: Paul H. Brookes.

Wolfman, G. (n.d.). The changing instrumental rehearsal. Retrieved from http://ws.conn-selmer.com/archives/keynotesmagazine/article/?uid=178

Zeroski, M. (2012). *Teaching students with severe cognitive and emotional disabilities using reverse inclusion and the arts.* Master's thesis, California State University, San Marcos, College of Education. Retrieved from http://csusm-dspace.calstate.edu/bitstream/handle/10211.8/236/ZeroskiMichael_Summer2012.pdf?sequence=3

CHAPTER 11

Music for Children
with Hearing Loss

ALAN GERTNER AND LYN SCHRAER-JOINER

Individuals with hearing loss are denied complete access to environ-mental sounds, including salient speech information. Adults and children with severe and profound hearing losses are significantly limited in sound perception. Even mild to moderate hearing losses have consider-able negative consequences for children because of their developmentally reduced vocabulary, constraints related to limited language experience, lack of comprehensive daily working schema, incomplete auditory sys-tem development, and overall immature linguistic analyzing framework (Delage & Tuller, 2007). The impact of auditory deprivation can be last-ing: "Considerable evidence exists that early auditory experience shapes function and the lack of auditory experience can have detrimental effects. These detrimental effects are more dramatic and may show less response to intervention when precipitated during early development" (Sinninger, Doyle, & Moore, 1999, p. 1). Negative effects of hearing loss extend beyond language development. According to Nicholas and Geers (2006, p. 287):

> Children who are deprived of sufficient amounts and/or quality of language input in their earliest years are at risk for poor outcomes in both language and academic endeavors later in childhood. . . . Poor language skills . . . early in life are associ-ated with concurrent socio-emotional and behavioral problems and have been associated with later deficits in language development, reading, lower verbal intelli-gence, poorer social-emotional development and self-esteem, and some psychiatric diagnoses.

HEARING LOSS INTERVENTION

Intervention for hearing loss is thus critical: "A good program of early intervention, including effective parent training and early use of hearing aids to exploit auditory potential, can help children who are deaf or hard of hearing to generate spontaneous spoken language more comparable to that used by their normal hearing peers in both type and level of utterance" (McConnell & Liff, 1975, p. 77). As Carol Flexer (2013) states, "Hearing is a first-order event for the development of spoken communication and literacy skills. Anytime the word 'hearing' is used, think 'auditory brain development'! Acoustic accessibility of *intelligible* speech is essential for brain growth."

Comprehensive educational and therapeutic intervention for children with hearing loss is thus vital, and music education should be central to this endeavor. According to E. Thayer Gaston (1968), we cannot consider music without man or man without music. Music is a form of human behavior, unique and powerful in its influence (Gaston, 1968, p. 32). Similarly, Barton (2010) emphasizes that music is a pervasive part of our culture, sustaining us from birth to death. Numerous studies have revealed that individuals who are deaf or hard of hearing and involved in music training have benefited in areas such as cognitive, linguistic, and social development; improved memory acuity; and music perception (Chen et al., 2010; Galvin, Fu, & Nogaki, 2007; Wong, Skoe, Russo, Dees, & Kraus, 2007). For example, Ford's (1988) investigation on the effects of school musical experiences and age on the ability of children with hearing loss to discriminate pitch at 250 and 500 Hertz revealed that children with hearing losses do perceive the complex tones of music. Moreover, Darrow (1985) found that music combined with speech therapy can aid in the development of good listening habits, auditory skills, auditory figure–background discrimination, sequential memory, and rhythm of speech. Similarly, Silvestre and Valero (2005) found that music education can have positive effects on the development of the suprasegmental elements of language, voice quality, and the structuring of simple sentences. Still other findings include those of Schraer-Joiner and Chen-Hafteck (2009), who found that participants in their study demonstrated independence during music activities and exhibited an interest in skill mastery as evidenced by their desire to show their teachers and teachers' aides what they could do (p. 796). Such findings challenge the notion of musicality as musical experience, enjoyment, and expression vary for the individual regardless of background or ability.

The Hearing Mechanism

Facilitating music education for children with hearing loss requires an understanding of the nature of hearing loss, consideration of the technology used by children with hearing loss, and appreciation of adaptations to music lessons that will benefit hearing-impaired children. The hearing mechanism is divided into four parts: the outer ear, the middle ear, the inner ear, and the central auditory processing system. The outer ear consists of the auricle, the physical ear that we see on the side of the head and the ear canal ending at the tympanic membrane (TM). The purpose of the outer ear is threefold: to funnel sound to the TM, to recess the middle ear for protection, and to enhance high-frequency speech sounds for improved speech perception. This latter aspect is referred to as the "external ear effects." The middle ear is a small cavity that is medial to the TM and houses the three smallest bones of the body (the malleus, incus, and stapes). They function to transfer sound vibrations from the TM across the middle ear space to the inner ear. Other middle ear structures include muscles, tendons, blood vessels, and the Eustachian tube, which equalizes air pressure between the middle ear and the outside barometric pressure. The inner ear is composed of the vestibular (balance) system and the hearing system, located in a portion of the inner ear called the cochlea. Within the cochlea is the end organ of hearing, the organ of Corti. The organ of Corti houses thousands of hair cells that have stereocilia projecting out of them. These stereocilia are very small bundles of tiny hairlike extensions whose movement triggers a neurochemical process that results in an action potential, an electrical signal that travels along the eighth cranial nerve to the brainstem. The sound signal then traverses the central auditory pathways from the brainstem to the cortical auditory centers that decode and integrate the acoustic message into a meaningful percept. This process of the auditory signal ascending the central auditory pathways to the auditory brain centers is referred to as auditory processing and has been defined by the American Speech-Language-Hearing Association (ASHA) task force on central auditory processing as follows:

> Broadly stated, (Central) Auditory Processing [(C)AP] refers to the efficiency and effectiveness by which the central nervous system (CNS) utilizes auditory information. Narrowly defined, (C)AP refers to the perceptual processing of auditory information in the CNS and the neurobiologic activity that underlies that processing and gives rise to electrophysiologic auditory potentials. (ASHA, 2005)

Hearing Losses

Hearing loss is defined by its degree, type, and configuration. Degree of hearing loss refers to magnitude of loss. Hearing loss is measured in "decibels hearing level" (dB HL). The average best hearing of a group of normal-hearing people is referred to as 0 dB HL (Gelfand, 2009, p. 113). Some people have exceptional hearing and may hear at −5 or even −10 dB HL at certain frequencies. Others hear slightly below the statistical normal, perhaps hearing at 5 or 10 dB HL. Increased decibel levels signify worsening hearing acuity. Degree of hearing loss is typically categorized by a range of decibel levels as follows. The normal hearing level for children is considered 15 dB HL or better at all tested frequencies; mild hearing loss falls in the range of 16 dB HL through 39 dB HL; moderate hearing loss is in the range of 40 dB HL through 69 dB HL; severe hearing loss ranges from 70 dB HL through 89 dB HL; and hearing levels of 90 dB HL or worse are in the profound range of hearing loss.

Type of hearing loss relates to the anatomic locus of hearing damage. Two parts of the peripheral hearing system, conductive and sensorineural, are designed to transmit sound signals to the central nervous system. The outer and middle ears conduct the signal via vibratory and mechanical action down the ear canal to the TM and across the bones of the middle ear. Hearing losses that result from damage to this conductive part are referred to as conductive hearing losses. By blocking or preventing sound from reaching the inner ear, all sound frequencies are diminished in a somewhat uniform pattern. Causes of conductive hearing losses include wax buildup, foreign bodies in the ear canal, external otitis (infection of the outer ear canal), perforations of the TM, fluid collection in the middle ear (frequently secondary to allergies or colds), and otitis media (middle ear infections). These conditions are often treatable with surgery or medication. Their effects can, however, fluctuate over time, causing children to have normal hearing on one day with mild to moderate hearing losses on another day.

Sensorineural hearing loss (SNHL) results primarily from inner ear stereocilia damage (the sensory element), but there are specific conditions that can affect the transmission of the hearing signal from the stereocilia to and along the eighth cranial nerve (the neural element). Inner ear damage results typically from destruction of cochlea stereocilia. If the stereocilia are damaged, they cannot bend and shear with sound stimulation, and thus the neural signal is prevented from being generated. The effect may be disruption to isolated frequency regions of hearing, or there can be nearly total damage to much of the inner ear stereocilia. The cochlea is laid out much like a piano keyboard, but with higher frequencies along the basal end and lower frequencies toward the apical end. A piano keyboard analogy, depicting specific regions of stereocilia damage, might have piano keys from two octaves above middle C (C_6) broken or missing. An analogy of complete stereocilia loss would have the entire keyboard broken or missing. In the former situation, a child with SNHL would have better hearing in some frequency regions, in this case regions below C_6, but poor hearing in the regions above C_6. Audiologists refer to this type of loss as a high-frequency hearing loss; lower-frequency (bass) sounds may be perceptible, but higher-frequency (treble) sounds may not. In the latter example of complete keyboard destruction, few if any sounds would be available to the child.

Conditions that prevent cochlear-generated neural signals from being transferred to and along the eighth cranial nerve to the brain result in neural hearing deficits. As described by Sharma, Cardon, Henion, and Roland (2011):

> Unlike more traditional forms of SNHL which result mainly from abnormalities in cochlear (outer) hair cells (OHC), in ANSD [auditory neuropathy spectrum disorder], the outer hair cells appear to be functioning in many or most cases. Starr and colleagues (1996) proposed that the site of lesion in ANSD could be the cochlear receptors or inner hair cells (IHC), the synapse between the IHC and the VIII nerve, or the VIII nerve itself (e.g. demyelination). (p. 98)

The severity of ANSD varies significantly, ranging from mild impairments in speech perception to that of near-complete inability to understand speech. Traditional hearing aid amplification has limited benefit to children with ANSD due to the lack of signal transmission to the brain. Cochlear implants have been shown to be effective in many children with ANSD, providing the eighth nerve is present.

Configuration of hearing loss refers to the hearing loss pattern presented on an audiogram (a graph that portrays the degree and shape of a person's hearing levels). The following patterns of hearing loss are depicted on the audiograms in Figure 11.1. Fairly equal hearing loss across all frequencies is referred to as a "flat" configuration. A hearing loss that worsens toward the higher frequencies (on the right side of the audiogram) is referred to as a falling or sloping hearing loss; rising or reversed slopes affect lower frequencies. U-shaped hearing losses (previously referred to as "cookie-bite" patterns) impact middle pitches, and inverted V patterns (tent shaped) result in better mid pitches.

Understanding the degree, type, and configuration of a child's hearing loss gives the music teacher an appreciation for what the child cannot hear and, importantly, what the child can hear. In addition to recognizing the child's limitations, the teacher will be able to identify and target the child's residual hearing strengths and abilities.

Children who have hearing loss also experience individual differences that they bring to the learning environment. Those who experience

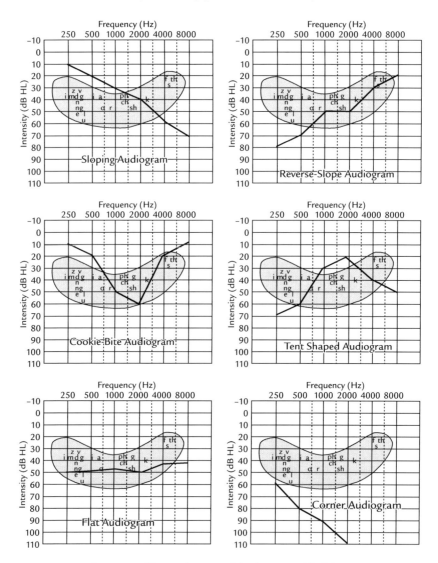

Figure 11.1. Configurations of hearing loss: Top left: sloping; middle left: U shaped; bottom left: flat. Top right: rising; middle right: inverted V; bottom right: corner audiogram.
Retrieved from http://hubpages.com/hub/The-Best-Hearing-Loss-Simulations-Understanding-Audiograms-and-the-Impact-of-the-Speech-Banana

prelingual hearing loss are very different from those who experience postlingual hearing loss. Prelingual hearing loss ". . . refers to hearing loss present at birth or prior to the development of speech and language" (Schow & Nerbonne, 2013, p. 8). Children with prelingual hearing loss do not have the opportunity to experience sound in the typical fashion, and thus their auditory growth and development is considerably impacted. Postlingual hearing loss ". . . means that loss occurs after about age 5; its overall effects are therefore usually less serious. Even though language may be less affected, speech and education will be affected substantially" (Schow & Nerbonne, 2013, p. 8). Sounds develop meaning for children with post-lingual hearing loss. Their language has begun to develop; they have considerable experience with environmental sounds and often with music. Hearing loss significantly impacts these children because their vocabulary development is immature, abstract reasoning has not emerged, and they do not have equal access to sound in the classroom or other environments that have competing background noise.

PRACTICAL APPLICATIONS: CONSIDERING THE CLASSROOM ENVIRONMENT

An important consideration when working with children who have hearing loss is room acoustics. Room size, shape, and properties (whether highly reflective or highly damped), as well as background noise levels, influence the acoustic environment. A classroom's size, shape, and properties combined with the child's position in the room impact how sound will be perceived by the child—the larger the room is, the farther the child may be from the sound source. The inverse square law states that ". . . sound intensity is inversely proportional to the square of the distance from the sound source" (Emanuel & Letowski, 2009, p. 100). This definition explains why it is imperative that children in learning environments, especially hearing-impaired children, remain in close proximity to the teacher or sound speaker. If the sound source is five feet from a child, the sound is 2.2 times quieter than when emanating from the source. In a large classroom, if the child is sitting 20 feet from the sound source, sound reduces by nearly 4.5 times. Therefore, strategic placement is important to maximize a child's reception to sound stimulation: "the critical distance in most rooms is 6 to 8 feet" (Crandell & Smaldino, 2002, p. 611). Reverberation is another extremely important aspect of room acoustics. Haughton (2002) defines reverberation as "the persistence of sound due to multiple echoes" (p. 342), while Crandell and Smaldino (2002) define it as "the prolongation or persistence of sound within an enclosure because of sound waves reflecting off hard surfaces (bare walls, ceilings, windows, floor)" (p. 609). The measurement of reverberation is accomplished by computing the reverberation time (RT). RT is defined as "the time that would be required for the sound pressure level in the enclosure to decrease by 60 decibels, after the source has been stopped" (Haughton, 2002, p. 343). Classrooms with RTs of over one second are considered poor learning environments (Berg, Blair, & Benson, 1996; Crandell & Smaldino, 2000;

Schow & Nerbonne, 2013), and rooms with even mild reverberation have a negative impact on children with hearing loss (Schow & Nerbonne, 2013). "Reverberation time . . . should be less than about .7 seconds" (C. Johnson, 2012, p. 233). Reverberation interferes with speech perception and sound appreciation because reverberant sound masks the following direct sound stimulation. Crandell and Smaldino (2002) note, "To explain, reverberant speech energy reaches the listener some time after the direct sounds, over-lapping subsequently presented speech sounds. This results in a 'smearing' or masking of the directly transmitted speech signal" (p. 609). Figures 11.2 and 11.3 illustrate the concept of reverberation.

Background noise, another significant barrier to crucial sound percep-tion, is any acoustic signal that competes with the main sound signal, or as described by C. Johnson (2012), "noise is any unwanted sound" (p. 232). The primary sources of classroom noise are HVAC systems, outside noises entering through windows, hallway noises, students talking in the room, and student movement (feet scraping on the floor, papers shuffling, etc.). As noise increases, it interferes by masking the desired sound signal. The index of severity of noise interference is the "signal to noise ratio (S/N),

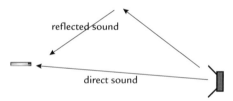

Figure 11.2. Example of reverberation with one sound source and one reflective surface. Reflected sound requires a longer time to reach the target; thus, it begins to mask subsequent direct sounds.
Retrieved from http://www.diracdelta.co.uk/science/source/r/e/reflected%20sound/source.html#.UeLhqW1aSHg

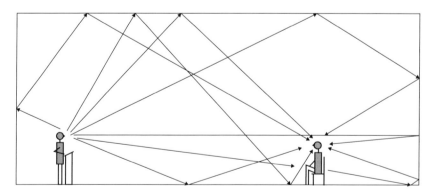

Figure 11.3. More reflected surfaces, as in a classroom, cause greater interference. Imagine this occurring not only with multiple reflective surfaces but also with multiple sound sources!
Retrieved from http://hearinghealthmatters.org/waynesworld/2012/ambient-noise-effect-on-hearing-a-primer/

defined as the relative level of the signal, in decibels (dB), in relation to that of the background noise" (C. Johnson, 2012, p. 232). The S/N for optimum performance for children should be at least +15 dB (Crandell & Smaldino, 2002). Unfortunately, in the United States, classroom S/N is often 0 dB, meaning that the background noise is equal to (as loud as) the teacher's voice.

The combination of S/N and RT can have deleterious effects on all children's classroom performance but is especially degrading to children with hearing impairment. In typical populations, an RT of 0.4 second and an S/N of +12 dB results in word recognition scores of 83%. At the same 0.4 RT but with an S/N of 0 dB, word recognition scores fall to 48%. When the RT increases to 1.2 seconds, an S/N of +12 dB results in word recognition scores of 69%. And with an RT of 1.2 seconds and S/N of 0 dB, word recognition scores fall to 30%. With hearing-impaired children, the same RT and S/N levels result in scores of 69%, 29%, 50%, and 15%, respectively.

Rooms that are large and/or have vaulted ceilings, hard walls, windows, and hard floors have detrimental acoustic environments. If classrooms are noisy due to poor student management, students' performance significantly deteriorates. Locating smaller rooms or using baffling or other acoustic barriers, carpeted floors, and drapery or other sound-damping material is clearly more advantageous for children's learning and performance, and is especially important for children with hearing loss.

HEARING AIDS, COCHLEAR IMPLANTS, AND FM SYSTEMS

Sound enhancement systems are often used to assist children with hearing loss. These systems may be divided into three basic types: hearing aids, cochlear implants, and FM listening systems. The purpose of hearing aids and cochlear implants is to restore as much sound audibility as possible. FM systems function more to improve intelligibility; specifically, "the ability to discriminate the word-sound distinctions of individual phonemes or speech sounds is defined as intelligibility. The ability simply to detect the presence of speech is defined as audibility," (Flexer, 1999, p. 5). Amplification in and of itself does not ensure clear and appropriate hearing. There are a host of factors that influence speech perception: intrinsic higher-level cognitive processes including the listener's attention, motivation, and experience, as well as extrinsic factors including the speaker's rate of speech, production variations, lighting, and room acoustics.

Hearing Aids

Although they provide enormous assistance to a person with hearing loss, "hearing aids offer little speech-perception benefit in noisy or reverberant environments. . . . This result should not be surprising because traditional amplification technology by itself does little to improve the SNR [signal-to-noise ratio] of the listening environment," (Crandell & Smaldino, 2002, p. 612). Hearing aids clearly improve audibility, but as mentioned earlier, audibility predominantly affects detection. If speech or music is not heard, it cannot be understood or appreciated; thus, increasing audibility does improve perception of the auditory environment. However, once heard, perception requires intelligibility. The latter is dependent on capturing the meaning and intent of the speech or music signal. There are newer hearing aid technologies geared toward improving intelligibility. Moreover, newer digital hearing aids take advantage of advanced technology including frequency response modifications, directional microphones, beam-forming microphones, digital noise reduction, and adaptive signal processing. A discussion of these advances is beyond the scope of this chapter (Katz, Medwetsky, Burkard, & Hood, 2009; Schaub, 2008). Children who use hearing aids may not, however, decode and perceive sound events as accurately as some may assume.

Cochlear Implants

Cochlear implants are surgically implanted electronic devices that bypass the inner ear's natural transduction system, the stereocilia shearing movement that converts sound to neuroelectric energy for transmission of sound signals to the brain. Implants, like hearing aids, increase audibility. When implanted in infants and young children, they restore peripheral hearing to normal, laying the foundation for typical speech and language development and music perception. Critical learning periods for language acquisition have been discussed: "Successful language acquisition must take place during a critical window of opportunity in childhood" (Pinker, 1994, p. 26). According to C. Johnson (2012), "Parents should be advised that children's level of achievement is inversely proportional to the age at implantation" (p. 297). Specifically, higher levels of performance are obtained by those children implanted early, particularly before age 2 and not after age 4 to avoid irreversible permanent performance losses (p. 297). The critical learning period for speech and language is known. "The first years of life represent a critical period for the development of auditory perceptual and spoken language abilities. . . . Historically, children with congenital hearing loss have missed out on the rich speech acoustic signal necessary for that critical period of development" (Schow & Nerbonne, 2013 p. 218). Thus, it is imperative that children with prelingual hearing loss be amplified with hearing aids or cochlear implants.

Children with severe and profound hearing loss who receive cochlear implants before age 2 are likely to function normally with regard to speech, language, and music by age 5. Those who receive amplification later (certainly after 5 years of age) will not have the same speech language abilities or music perception. This dichotomy is a direct result of a lack of auditory stimulation that precludes the auditory brain from taking advantage of plasticity. In a child's early years, his or her brain organizes and wires itself based on input; "the central nervous system (CNS) is plastic, that is, capable of cortical reorganization by experience, for some time prior to stabilization of neural function" (Chermak & Musiek, 2007, p. 5). Auditory experience shapes the human brain to recognize environmental sounds, develop and organize a person's native speech sound inventory, and grow language. Without auditory input, the auditory brain does not unfold as it would, which severely limits its growth, development, and organization. When children born with hearing loss are stimulated early (within the first two years of life) with hearing aids or cochlear implants, rich auditory experience takes place and cortical auditory brain centers blossom. Children who do not receive adequate sound input rarely develop appropriate auditory/linguistic systems. "Children with severe to profound hearing loss who do not receive a cochlear implant do not generally develop speech and language normally, because they are not exposed to the sounds of language in daily living" (Schow & Nerbonne, 2012, pp. 11–12).

Cochlear implants have both external and, because they are surgically implanted, internal components. Major external parts include a microphone, speech processor, and magnetic transducer. The microphone captures environmental sounds that are digitized and analyzed by the processor. Specific processing algorithms are developed and coded by each manufacturer. Once processed, electrical signals ascend to the transducer and are transmitted through the skin to internal parts of the implant. Internal parts include the transducer-stimulator and electrode array. The transducer-stimulator accepts the electrical signal that has been conducted from the external transducer, processes it, and transmits it to the electrode array. Fed during surgery through the cochlea, the electrode array is composed of multiple electrodes. Each electrode stimulates a different region of the auditory nerve.

There is often mention about "channels" of cochlear implants. Incoming sound can be divided into discrete frequency regions. A single-channel cochlear implant does not separate sounds into frequency regions but processes the entire signal as one. A two-channel system divides sound signals into low-frequency ranges and high-frequency ranges. The more channels there are, the greater (and narrower/more discretely) the sound signals are divided. Theoretically, modern cochlear implants with more channels, more stimulating electrodes, and advanced programming should improve intelligibility and audibility; however, as discussed, if the critical period of auditory/language development has passed, regardless of the cochlear implant or hearing aid, performance will not be maximized.

There are significant differences between speech and music sound signals that affect sound perception with hearing aids and cochlear implants. Speech has a fairly uniform spectral image, whereas music has an extremely variable spectral composition. When listening to speech, a person develops a spectral "target" that is more easily adapted to and predicted. Music does not provide the same target option. Speech sounds are composed of low-frequency vowels and high-frequency consonants, with vowels providing intensity and consonants distinguishing meaning. Music uses highly variable instruments without the same organized sound region separation. Hearing aids and cochlear implants are also typically designed to amplify the more limited spectral range of speech. Speech sound intensities cover a relatively small range typically limited to a maximum of about 80 dB, whereas music has a more dynamic intensity range that often reaches up to 120 dB. Speech sounds also have a more reduced "crest" factor. Crest refers to the difference in a sound wave's average intensity level and its peaks. Speech has a crest factor of about 12 dB, whereas music has a crest factor of 18 to 20 dB. The dynamics of music often cause hearing aids and cochlear implants to "cut out" or "smear" some sounds that extend to the upper loudness range because of their speech-oriented designs. Because of hearing aid and cochlear implant designs related to acoustic differences between speech and music, music teachers are encouraged to adapt their lessons by decreasing music loudness and attending to room reverberation and background noise conditions.

FM Systems

Due to the degradation of the sound signal with distance (the inverse square law), background noise, and reverberation, the use of a personal FM system does enhance speech intelligibility. An FM system is composed of a teacher-worn microphone/transmitter and a student-worn receiver (both are wirelessly connected to each other). The teacher's voice signal is picked up by the microphone and transmitted to the student's receiver on a radio signal (much as a radio signal is sent from the station to your house or car

FM radio receiver). The real benefit of personal FM systems is that desired sound signals are transmitted directly to the student's ears. Effects of distance, background noise, and reverberation are negated, thus presenting the most ideal signal. Acoustically, the teacher has just walked across the room, bent down to the child's ear, and spoken directly to him or her. Of real interest is that hearing aids and cochlear implants are designed to be compatible with student-worn FM receivers. Coupling an FM receiver directly to the student's amplification system merges the benefits of FM technology with maximum amplification flexibility of the student's personal hearing device. Coupling is accomplished through the use of a direct audio input (DAI) available on virtually all personal hearing devices. FM systems typically provide three listening settings: FM, M, and B. In the FM position, the teacher's microphone is input to the child's receiver. FM amplifies the teacher's voice, essentially bringing it directly to the child's ears, and is ideal for instructional purposes. The M setting turns off the teacher's input and provides access for classroom environmental sound; it permits class discussions. The B setting enables the child to perceive both the teacher's voice and classroom sound. Depending on the activity, the child's FM should be configured to maximize reception, and music teachers should be willing to adjust (or have the child adjust) his or her FM listening setting.

Auditory Training

From an audiologist's perspective, the purpose of auditory training is to achieve maximum communication potential by developing the auditory sensory channel to its fullest (Schow & Nerbonne, 2012, p. 137). Several methods of auditory training have been discussed in the audiologic literature, including analytic, synthetic, pragmatic, and eclectic methods (Blamey & Alcantara, 1994; Sanders, 1972). Analytic and synthetic methods may be addressed as *bottom-up* versus *top-down* approaches. *Bottom-up auditory therapy* focuses on discrete segmental training with the goal being to train the auditory system in detecting and discriminating various speech sound elements. Individual vowels and consonants are presented in isolation and the child is drilled on detecting and discriminating each speech sound element. Examples include exercises emphasizing same–different discrimination of vowel or consonant phonemes in syllables (e.g., /bi-ba/) or words (e.g., /kɪp-kɪt/) (Schow & Nerbonne, 2012, p. 145). The *top-down* principle is a cognitive holistic approach. The child is instructed in using higher-level cognitive cues to assist in identification and comprehension of verbal messages. Speech sounds may be imbedded during therapy but used in the context of whole words, phrases, and sentences. "Training synthetically involves the use of meaningful stimuli. . . . This might involve practicing sentence perception based on prior information about context . . . or having a clinician name a topic and present related words or phrases that the individual must repeat back" (Schow & Nerbonne, 2012, p. 145).

Music as a Stimulus to Train Listening

Music teachers can focus on the premise that the overall goal of auditory training is to teach the child with hearing loss to listen. Of most importance is that they learn to interpret sounds and their meanings utilizing all of the auditory information available to them to open and develop all possibilities for communication (Darrow, 1985, p. 35). Music offers a medium through which listening can be practiced (p. 35). Music can also provide incentive, making even the most tedious auditory training activities more interesting and enjoyable. Music is also naturally motivating to children and can therefore both inspire and excite the child who is deaf or hard of hearing. This is important as the child will not naturally attend to sound-related activities (Darrow, 1990). For example, by singing, a child with hearing loss can develop breath control and flow that will help him or her to focus on vocal pitch and rhythm. Socialization is a natural outgrowth of music activities and has the potential to encourage the communication of ideas, including the musical elements perceived, between the child who is deaf or hard of hearing and his or her peers, teachers, and parents (Darrow, 1990). For example, in their study involving children with cochlear implants, Schraer-Joiner and Chen-Hafteck (2009) observed that the participants interacted socially with their teachers and teachers' aides during music activities and gradually interacted with their peers as lessons progressed. Participants also expressed empathy for their peers both verbally and non-verbally (p. 795).

Music can be motivational in promoting communication, both expressive and receptive language. According to Darrow (1985), the perception interpretation and performance of sound serves as the basis for both speech and music (p. 34). Both involve the ability to distinguish between different sounds, as well as the characteristics of those sounds such as pitch, duration, intensity, and timbre. When referring to music, terms such as *intonation, tempo, accent,* and *rhythm* are used. Terms utilized when referring to speech are *inflection, rate, stress,* and the "*temporal organization*" of speech sounds or rhythm (p. 34). These elements are referred to as the "prosodic features of speech" and convey distinctive information to the listener. Music activity can also help to reinforce vocabulary and serve as a memory aid. Music activity can provide a child with early opportunities for self-expression and creativity, a very powerful tool particularly for a child who is just learning to communicate.

Music as a training activity also provides a foundational framework that promotes brain growth, critical and creative thinking, and auditory-linguistic skills (Parbery-Clark, Skoe, Lam, & Kraus, 2009; Parbery-Clark, Tierney, Strait, & Kraus, 2012; Strait & Kraus, 2011). The linguistic and cognitive benefits of music are valuable for all children, but for children with hearing loss, in particular, music provides noteworthy benefits for listening and auditory skill training (Gfeller, 1990; Olzewski, Gfeller, Froman, Stordahl, & Tomblin, 2005; Rall, Montoya, Partridge, & Ramirez, 2008). Musical experience shapes and benefits listening attention, recognition of speech in the presence of background noise, memory, and may protect the aging brain (Kraus, Strait, & Parbery-Clark, 2011; Parbery-Clark, Anderson, Hittner, & Kraus, 2012; Parbery-Clark, Tierney, et al., 2012; Strait, Parbery-Clark, O'Connell, & Kraus, 2013). Music also lends itself well to both the bottom-up and top-down processes used in auditory training. Thus, music, in addition to enriching life, can serve as an integral piece of a habilitation/rehabilitation program for children who are deaf or hard of hearing.

The auditory system detects, discriminates, and identifies three primary elements: frequency, intensity, and time (duration). When these essential components of sound have been decoded and analyzed, the cortical auditory/language centers comprehend their meaning. Auditory training will improve a person's ability to extract these sound features. The history of auditory training details physicians in the sixth century using ". . . large ringing bells in an attempt to stimulate a hearing response" (Chermak & Musiek, 2007, pp. 78–79). More traditional auditory therapies progress from gross environmental sound detection to finer nonspeech and speech sound discrimination. Auditory therapy typically follows a hierarchy of auditory skill development that includes detection, discrimination, identification, and comprehension of sound signals (Erber, 1982, pp. 92–94).

Music should be considered a primary stimulus for auditory training, not only because research has identified the benefits of musical experience, but also because history details that one of the first attempts at formal auditory training (circa 1800) involved the use of music as a primary stimulus: "Itard attempted to train speech-sound perception directly. . . . He used a shaping procedure to progress, through varied musical instruments . . . to vocal sounds" (Lamberts & Miller, 1979, p. 207). Chermak and Musiek (2007) explain potential benefits of auditory therapy approaches using music (p. 329). Specifically, "music offers many advantages as a vehicle for auditory training" (p. 329). Music is an enjoyable activity that taxes timing skills, and the act of singing emphasizes the sound patterns of speech

(Overy, 2003). Recent reports demonstrate that musical training alters auditory cortical representations. Trainor, Shahin, and Roberts (2003) measured the enhancement of the P2 auditory-evoked potential in adult nonmusicians following auditory training. Gaab et al. (2005) concluded that musical training may enhance the brain's efficiency in distinguishing split-second differences between rapidly changing sounds, and thereby improve temporal processing, Music education classes also offer the opportunity to perform real auditory training: "... group music lessons, as well as more individualized passive and active music listening, may improve timing (i.e., temporal) deficits in children with dyslexia" (Chermak & Musiek, 2007, p. 329).

Music clearly makes use of the auditory elements of frequency, intensity, and time. Perceiving pitch and harmony requires frequency analysis. Realizing spectral composition also requires frequency discrimination. Timbre recognition requires frequency analysis, whereas the dynamics of music is the expression of intensity variation. Rhythm and melody perception both require solid timing abilities.

Knowing the hearing history, auditory experience, and competence of a child with hearing loss gives the music teacher the understanding necessary to accommodate a child's listening and musical needs. Music teachers who understand the impact of hearing loss and the unique needs of children who are deaf or hard of hearing, including their history and auditory experiences, will be able to develop appropriate accommodations and interventions for them.

ACCESSIBILITY FOR ALL CHILDREN

Music teacher Karl Wilson Gehrkens, in 1922, coined the phrase "Music for Every Child—Every Child for Music." This expression later became the official slogan for the Music Educators National Conference (Peard, 2012). If approached and planned properly, the music classroom, in keeping with Gehrkens's philosophy, can provide wonderful experiences for all children. For children who are deaf or hard of hearing, a music education can aid in the further development of perceptual skills, socialization, and musical understanding.

Preparation for Listening Lessons

According to Darrow (1990), a classroom is truly integrated only if the teacher makes an effort to include students with special needs instead of just accommodating them (p. 36). When planning a listening lesson for a classroom that includes a child with hearing loss, the music teacher must therefore take into consideration the child's hearing loss (degree and type), age of onset, and the type of device used (cochlear implant, hearing aid, sound-enhancing system, bone-anchored hearing aid). This should also include reports regarding the child's performance with the device, as well as the child's primary mode of communication. This information is critical for the student's comfort and necessary if teachers are to prepare adequately. For example, students with mild to severe hearing loss can listen to recorded activities or even live performances as long as any hearing devices are adjusted to an appropriate level of loudness. Limiting the loudness levels that devices can transmit to hearing-impaired children may impact the quieter sounds perceived. In the long run, however, students will be insulated from having a loud and therefore painful listening experience.

Additional considerations will also need to be made on behalf of the student with a cochlear implant. For example, listening lessons will often include an assortment of compositions, some that may or may not feature lyrics, and all varying in terms of types and numbers of instruments featured. Compositions for large ensembles such as orchestras or bands may be more difficult for the student to perceive as such pieces extend beyond the receptive capacity of modern cochlear implant systems. This is because the activated electrodes, located along the electrode array inserted into the cochlea, are related to a specific frequency field. When too many frequencies are produced by one electrode, sound clusters result, making the perception of music with the implant difficult. Ultimately, music consisting of single instruments or chamber music may provide optimum listening opportunities for the student with a cochlear implant. Once this preliminary information is gathered, the music teacher can develop lessons that are inclusive, appropriate, interesting, and engaging. Moreover, the teacher can help the student with hearing loss to prepare in advance of the listening lesson.

Instructional Approaches

M. S. Johnson (2009) states that music is not just experienced auditorily but visually, kinesthetically, and haptically as well (p. 17). Thus, musical concepts should be presented from many perspectives, especially as children who are deaf or hard of hearing will rely heavily on their residual hearing, as well as on visual and tactile cues in the classroom. Implementing a multisensory approach will ensure that all children are able to participate and succeed. Listening lessons can be enhanced if the lesson includes a live or video-recorded performance. This is because so much of the music can be conveyed by the gestures and expressions of performers and the conductor. This is also true for vocal performances from which expressive information about the music and its context can be attained via speech reading, facial expression, and body movement (M. S. Johnson, 2009, p. 17). Darrow and Gfeller (1991) affirm that almost any aural concept can be visually reinforced. Additional materials that are visual in nature and that might support the listening lesson include photos, listening maps or charts, and movement that may be coordinated with various music elements such as rhythm, melodic direction, or tempo. Tactile reinforcement for a listening lesson can include positioning the students close to surfaces that will promote vibration. For example, the stereo speaker can be placed on the wooden or tiled floor, and the students can sit either on the floor on in their chairs with their shoes off so that they can feel the vibrations (Shehan-Campbell & Scott-Kassner, 2009). Kinesthetic reinforcement for the enhancement of music listening lessons can include having the students conduct while listening. Students can also use rhythm sticks to keep a steady beat or be encouraged to express themselves through free or creative movement. The latter would be best implemented after the students are familiar with the piece. The methods and materials of Orff, Kodaly, Dalcroze, and Weikert are often recommended because they represent a variety of musical elements visually, kinesthetically, and haptically.

Still other instructional approaches might include the musical "heads up," a preteaching homework assignment for the child with mild to severe hearing loss designed to help him or her become familiar with listening examples in advance of upcoming music classes. Preparation for listening lessons involving a multimovement work might include support materials such as a simplified score of the piece featuring the main melody or theme, and a listening map. A recording featuring a distinguishable melody or theme should also be considered as this will provide guidance for the child and his or her parents as they listen at home together. The latter is an important consideration as the child will feel more comfortable in class while listening to the original composition if he or she is able to identify the melody studied previously. Depending on the lesson, such materials can be sent home one to two weeks prior to the class.

Teachers might also consider a comprehensive whole-part-whole approach. In this instance, the "whole" or initial introduction might include an overall review of the composition, its background including the year in which it was written, the composer, and familiarity to the students (i.e., whether the piece has been used in a commercial or has served as the basis for current music). A few short representative samples of the work to be studied should also be presented. The "heads up" will also help to guide the child with hearing loss through these larger listening examples that are introduced in the music class. The "part" in this instance might include a more detailed study of individual elements such as the rhythmic structure of the piece, melodic structure and contour, and expressive qualities such as the dynamics, tempo, and timbre. The return of the "whole" should involve listening to the sections of the piece studied with particular emphasis on the individual elements studied (Schraer-Joiner & Prause-Weber, 2009).

SAMPLE LISTENING LESSONS

Listening lessons featuring John Williams's "Hedwig's Theme" from *Harry Potter and the Sorcerer's Stone* and Gustav Holst's "Mars, the Bringer of War" from *The Planets* are introduced in this section. Lessons are multisensory in nature and align with the goals and objectives of Erber's levels of auditory development. Where appropriate, recommendations for cross-curricular connections are made. As these listening lessons emphasize larger compositions, the musical heads-up will be particularly important for the student who is deaf or hard of hearing and using devices such as the cochlear implant or hearing aid. Moreover, prior to those lessons featuring larger compositions, these students should also be reminded that it may be necessary for them to adjust the volume control on their cochlear implant and/or hearing aid devices. This can be done as a quiet reminder at the beginning of class. Such a preventative measure will ensure the student's comfort level during the activity (Schraer-Joiner & Prause-Weber, 2009).

Erber's (1982) listening sequence is composed of the levels of *detection, discrimination, identification,* and *comprehension.* Detection is the most basic level of sound perception and is defined as the awareness of the presence or absence of sound. Detection serves as the foundation for the remaining levels. Discrimination, the second level of auditory development, is defined as the ability to determine if two sounds are the same or different. The listener must first be aware of the presence of the two sounds to be able to differentiate between them. The third level is identification, which requires that the listener identify or label the sound perceived. This specific task requires the listener to apply his or her detection and discrimination skills. The final level is comprehension. This is the highest and most complicated of all of the levels of auditory development because the listener is required to integrate all that he or she has learned in previous levels. By doing so, the listener has the foundation necessary to understand the meaning of the sound or the message.

Harry Potter and the Sorcerer's (Philosopher's) Stone

The popularity of the Harry Potter books and movies in the Deaf culture makes the musical themes from this series of movies potentially motivating (Czubek & Greenwald, 2005; Doug, Jones, & Luckner, 2011). The main theme or leitmotif for the movie series is "Hedwig's Theme," part of the *Harry Potter Symphonic Suite* by John Williams's that was first featured in the first film, *Harry Potter and the Sorcerer's (Philosopher's) Stone* (2001). This leitmotif is the most recognizable theme from the movie series and therefore may be a good place to start when introducing a listening lesson. Depending on the class, this lesson may take two class periods.

Lesson 1

In preparation for "Hedwig's Theme," the music teacher should consider preassessing the child with a cochlear implant, in particular, to determine his to her comfort level with the *celesta,* the featured instrument. This particular keyboard instrument has a written range of C3 to C7 and it sounds one octave higher than written. A *musical audiogram,* an aural perception activity, can be administered to provide the music teacher with information pertaining to those tones and dynamic ranges most comfortable for the child (Prause, 2003; Schraer-Joiner & Prause-Weber, 2009). To administer a musical audiogram, the music teacher should select one melodic phrase from a children's songbook. The melody selected should preferably be one that is familiar to the student. Then, the student should be informed that the song will be presented on the piano in different ways (i.e., in different registers and at different dynamic levels) and that he or she is to indicate the example that sounds the best or the most "comfortable" for them. In this instance, the teacher will also want to be sure to play examples in the upper registers of the piano. If the music teacher determines that the instrument does have an impact on the child's comfort level, the musical heads-up materials prepared for "Hedwig's Theme" can reflect the results of the musical audiogram in terms of the instruments used and the ranges in which related music examples are written and performed.

The first lesson featuring "Hedwig's Theme" can begin with a discussion about the composer John Williams (b. 1932) and his contribution to numerous film scores, the author of the Harry Potter books J. K. Rowling (b. 1965), and then the Harry Potter story. The discussion should end with Hedwig, Harry's Snowy Owl. The opening statement of "Hedwig's Theme" (mm 1–33) should then be played, after which students can discuss the primary instrument (celesta) that depicts the owl. A brief discussion of the instrument should follow. If an alternative instrument is required for the child with hearing loss, then this version of "Hedwig's Theme" should also be presented to the class. The next time the leitmotif is presented, the students should be encouraged to move like Hedwig. This is referred to as activation and participation, which, according to Shehan-Campbell and Scott-Kassner (2009), is a "wonderful way to build a work into children's internal repertoire" (p. 196). A PowerPoint presentation might be introduced that includes pictures of author J. K. Rowling, composer John Williams, the instruments the students will be listening to, and characters from the movie, as well as the questions for discussion, such as:

1. How does the music convey Hedwig in flight?
2. What does this music convey about Hogwarts and the other magical places Hedwig has experienced, such as platform 9 & ¾, Gringot's Bank, and Diagon Alley, as well as the Hogwart's Express?
3. What else might the music convey (e.g., mystery, excitement)?

Erber's hierarchy can be applied to "Hedwig's Theme" to help facilitate listening goals and objectives. For example, short sections of the opening statement of "Hedwig's Theme" can be used to introduce the level of detection. Before the activity, movements representing Hedwig can be determined as students' indication of when they perceive the melody line. Their movement should cease when the music stops. As mentioned previously, alternative versions of the leitmotif presented particularly for the child with hearing loss should also be included in this and subsequent levels.

For the level of discrimination, the teacher can present students with two different rhythm or pitch patterns that comprise "Hedwig's Theme," as shown in Figures 11.4a and 11.4b. After the patterns are presented, students should be invited to compare and contrast the patterns and then discuss their findings as a class. Students should also be encouraged to create their own patterns for the exercise. Tactile reinforcement for this level might include having students with hearing loss touch or sit next to a vibration-transmitting source during listening examples. Kinesthetic reinforcement for this activity might include body rhythms as these can be implemented to symbolize rhythmic structure. For instance, standing up straight with legs together and hands held firmly to the sides of the body can represent a single quarter note, while hands placed on bent knees with legs spread apart may represent two eighth notes (Schraer-Joiner & Prause-Weber, 2009). Pitch and melodic contour can also be illustrated using the body and will be discussed in Lesson 2.

Rhythm

Pitch

Figure 11.4. (**a**) Sample rhythm discrimination exercise for "Hedwig's Theme." (**b**) Sample pitch discrimination exercise for "Hedwig's Theme."

Lesson 2

In addition to a review of the concepts introduced in Lesson 1, the final two levels of Erber's hierarchy (i.e., identification and comprehension) should be introduced. For the level of identification, the music teacher should play "Hedwig's Theme" (with the celesta and modified instruments as per the musical audiogram) and encourage the students to identify the rhythmic or melodic patterns they studied in the previous level. They should also be encouraged to listen for melodic direction and to discuss how the direction of the melody might inform the listener of how Hedwig is flying. Students can also add their ideas about where Hedwig is going. This should then be followed by an analysis of the score, whereby the students have the chance to view the melody line and discuss its contour in relation to their ideas about Hedwig's flight. After this analysis, movements can be added the next time the students listen to "Hedwig's Theme." For example, arm movements in an upward or downward direction can represent the melodic direction of Hedwig's flight. If students have limited mobility, they can be given alternate movements such as raising their arms or hands to indicate high pitches, extending them outward for middle pitches, and lowering them down to their sides for lower pitches. These movements can be enhanced by the use of colorful scarves. As students become more comfortable with the listening activity, which is typically longer than the detection and discrimination examples, students may also describe the dynamic level and tempos they perceive. For example, what do the tempo or dynamics of the music also tell us about Hedwig's flight? This analysis can continue in the fourth and final level, comprehension.

To initiate the level of comprehension, the music teacher might first reintroduce the entire opening statement of "Hedwig's Theme" and have the students listen to determine if the whole leitmotif is the same throughout or if it is made up of one or two different sections. This opening statement lends itself well to this detailed study of form. Once they have identified the two sections, then AB form can be discussed. When the students listen again, they can add two different movements used in previous levels to reinforce the A and B sections. Next, the students should listen to the fully orchestrated version of "Hedwig's Theme," during which the students will begin to focus on and identify more than one element in the theme and discuss their understanding of those elements and the role they play in illustrating Hedwig. Afterward, the music teacher can return to the questions initially discussed during the lesson introduction to see if the students have additional suggestions regarding the ways the music conveys Hedwig in flight, the magical places he has experienced, and the magical mood of the composition.

Lesson 3

Flight is a major part of Harry's world. Therefore, a final project for this listening lesson might include a sound composition in AB format that the students can create to convey their own portrayal of a journey by Hedwig, whether it is to deliver a letter to Sirius Black or a gift from Mrs. Weasley. This particular sound composition might include a drawing that represents the sounds for their composition featuring instrument sounds for the A section and voice or body percussion sounds for the B section. Group members should be prepared to discuss their drawing, as well as their feelings and interpretations of Hedwig's journey and the corresponding timbres they have employed. The student groups should also perform their compositions for the rest of the class. Later lessons can center on some of the other winged creatures of Harry's world. For example, comparisons can be made between "Hedwig's Theme" and the beginning of Buckbeaks's flight (*Harry Potter and the Prisoner of Azkeban*) that opens first with timpani and then is followed by flourishing strings. The theme for Fawkes the Phoenix (*Harry Potter and the Chamber of Secrets*) can also be incorporated into later comparisons.

Holst's *The Planets Op. 32*

The Planets, a suite of seven movements composed by Gustav Holst (1874–1934) between 1914 and 1916, can offer wonderful opportunities for an integrative unit featuring science, math, history, and mythology, as well as music. See Figure 11.5 for a sample curriculum or mind map.

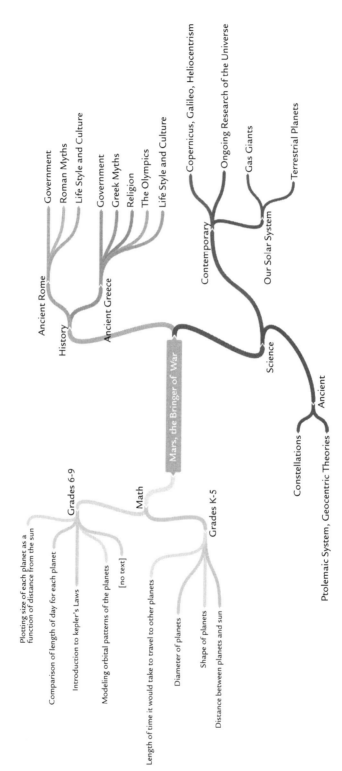

Figure 11.5. Curriculum or mind mapping for Holst's "Mars, the Bringer of War."

Holst intended to portray the mythological traits of the known planets and ordered each planet-named movement according to their distance from Earth (NAXOS, 2013, Gustav Holst, para. 4). Holst actually composed the first movement, "Mars, the Bringer of War," just before the start of World War I, while the remaining movements were written during the war (NAXOS, 2013, Gustav Holst, para. 4). Interestingly, audience members at the inaugural performance of the work in 1918 assumed "Mars" was a depiction of World War I, though Holst claims otherwise (Greene, 1995, p. 19; Libbey & Libbey, 1999, p. 92). The first movement, "Mars, the Bringer of War," will be central to the listening lessons included herein.

Lesson 1

For the child who is deaf or hard of hearing, "Mars, the Bringer of War" is rich with many tangible musical elements that can be perceivable with all of the senses. A musical heads-up of two weeks would help the child with hearing loss to prepare for the class listening lesson and might include a recording that isolates the four musical ideas and a listening map. The anticipatory set will also play a critical role in setting the stage for this listening lesson. Students should first be provided with an overview of the life and interests of Gustav Holst, including his great interest in astrology. Those composers who influenced Holst during this time period, Stravinsky and Schoenberg in particular, should also be mentioned (Holst Foundation, 2007, para. 3). References to *The Planets* in popular culture should also be presented, such as its uses in movies (e.g., *The Gladiator(2000)*, *The Right Stuff*, 1983), video games (e.g., *Super Mario Galaxy*), and rock music (e.g., heavy metal, progressive rock, and electronica; Chew et al., 2010, pp. 117, 190). Finally, the four musical ideas of "Mars," a prominent rhythmic ostinato and three musical themes, should first be introduced within the context of the movement with supportive visuals such as a listening map to help the students identify them as they follow along. Then, the ideas should be isolated so that the students can study the rhythmic and melodic components of each.

"Mars," written in 5/4, opens with a driving rhythmic ostinato in the timpani, harp, and strings that permeates and connects most of the movement. This ostinato, as shown in Figure 11.6, is composed of a triplet, two quarter notes, two eighth notes, followed by another quarter note and played in the note G in both unison and octave. The first musical theme is illustrated in Figure 11.7 and is introduced in the winds and brass. This theme, presented in triads, first appears in measure three and consists of an ascending P5 followed by a descending half step (semitone). The second theme, as shown in Figure 11.8, is presented in the low brass (i.e., trombones and tubas) and begins in measure 43. This theme is composed of a series of dotted quarter notes and eighth notes that descend and ascend in half and whole steps. The third theme is presented in Figure 11.9 and begins with a tenor tuba solo in measure 68 (labeled as "a") and is quickly followed by a soli trumpet flourish in measure 70 (labeled as "b") composed of a dotted 8th and 16th figure, two triplets, and a half note. The dynamics for the movement reach quadruple forte.

A PowerPoint presentation can be used in conjunction with the introduction of the aforementioned musical ideas. The visual presentation might also include a listening map, pictures of the instruments to which the students will be listening, and various pictures of Mars the planet and Mars the mythological figure. Guiding questions for the lesson should also be presented:

1. How effectively does this movement depict Mars the warrior?
2. What musical characteristics help to do this (driving rhythm, dynamics, tempo)?

Figure 11.6. Rhythmic ostinato from Holst's "Mars, the Bringer of War."

Figure 11.7. First musical theme from Holst's "Mars, the Bringer of War."

Figure 11.8. Second musical theme from Holst's "Mars, the Bringer of War."

Figure 11.9. Third musical theme from Holst's "Mars, the Bringer of War."

3. How does the time signature of this movement (5/4) compare with other time signatures we have studied (2/4, 3/4, 4/4)?

Lesson 1 will also serve to draw connections to the other concept areas in the integrative unit. The lesson would also emphasize Erber's (1982) levels of detection and discrimination. To address the level of *detection*, the opening rhythmic ostinato should first be introduced. In fact, as many of the musical themes presented in "Mars" are composed of very small intervals, music teachers may find it best to initially stress the rhythm patterns composing these themes, particularly for the child with hearing loss. After the initial study of the rhythmic ostinato, the students should be instructed to move freely throughout the room when they perceive the ostinato and to stop moving when the ostinato ceases.

For the level of *discrimination*, the students should be presented with two cards, one labeled with the word *same*, the other labeled with the word *different*. The teacher should then present students with two different rhythm or pitch patterns that compose the four main musical ideas presented in "Mars." Examples are included in Figures 11.10a and 11.10b. After the patterns are presented, students should be instructed to raise the *same* or *different* card based on their analysis of the pattern. The students should then be encouraged to share their analysis of the patterns with the class regarding the similarities and differences they perceived between the patterns. Students should also be encouraged to contribute their own patterns to the exercise. Movements such as body rhythms can also be implemented during this level to further reinforce the various patterns presented.

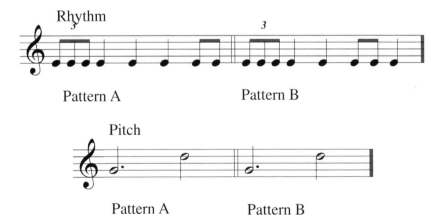

Figure 11.10. (a) Sample rhythm discrimination exercise for Holst's "Mars, the Bringer of War." (b) Sample pitch discrimination exercise for Holst's "Mars, the Bringer of War."

Lesson 2

The second lesson should begin with a review of the concepts introduced in Lesson 1. This is very important as it will determine the students' readiness for the final two levels (i.e., identification and comprehension) of Erber's (1982) hierarchy. To address the level of *identification*, the music teacher should review the main musical themes from the movement and have the students listen for the rhythm and melodic patterns emphasized in the previous level. The students should also be encouraged to listen, individually at first, for other musical elements that present themselves within the movement (e.g., dynamics, tempos, as well as identification of timbres, specifically the entrances and exits of some of the key instruments—percussion, low and high brass). Movements for the level of identification might include marching around the room to "Mars" and using rhythm sticks to play the rhythmic ostinato as the students listen to the entire movement.

As with "Hedwig's Theme," this analysis can continue in the level of comprehension, during which the students will begin to focus on and identify more than one element within "Mars" (i.e., rhythms, melodic contour, dynamics, and tempo) and discuss their understanding of those elements and the role they play in conveying Mars as warrior and planet. Students can also create movements that represent each of the musical ideas presented in "Mars." As they listen to the original composition, the students should perform the designated movement as each theme is presented. After their in-depth study of the movement, the music teacher can return the questions initially discussed during the lesson introduction to see if the students have additional suggestions or ideas.

Lesson 3

In addition to a review of activities associated with Erber's level of *comprehension*, the final culminating activity for this listening lesson should involve the creation of a rhythm composition. The purpose of this composition will be to create a rhythmic theme for Pluto that was not discovered until 1930, well after the completion of *The Planets*. The Pluto theme should be written in 5/4 time and consist of eight measures. The students, in groups of two, should also decide on instrumentation for their composition. They should also be prepared to perform for their peers and to describe how their theme conveys Pluto as a planet and/or god. Future lessons may also include a study of other movements composing Holst's *The Planets*. For example, students might compare the robust "Mars, the Bringer of War" to slow and tranquil movement two, "Venus, the Bringer of Peace."

PROMOTING A LIFETIME OF MUSIC APPRECIATION

Music is accessible to all children if they are given a chance to experience it in ways most perceivable by them. Reducing competing noise and guarding against reverberant environments may transform a diminished acoustic experience into a pleasant listening event. Decreasing the intensity of a recording or reducing the loudness setting on an amplification device may enrich a child's experience and encourage him or her to pursue additional musical encounters. The listening lessons included herein emphasize multiple modalities to ensure that the individual child's needs are met.

The notion of introducing music listening to a child with hearing loss confounds many educators. Misconceptions associated with hearing loss are prevalent, for example, that communication, hearing, and listening for enjoyment are unattainable. The material presented in this chapter challenges such notions but also seeks to reinforce the reality that hearing loss will impact each person differently. Such unique needs of the child with hearing loss require specific instructional modifications. Once incorporated, appropriate adaptations will ensure a successful lesson and foster lifelong music appreciation.

REFERENCES

American Speech-Language-Hearing Association (ASHA). (2005). *(Central) auditory processing disorders—the role of the audiologist* [Position Statement]. Retrieved from http://www.asha.org/policy

Barton, C. (2010). *Music, spoken language, and children with hearing loss: Definitions and development.* Retrieved from http://www.speechpathology.com

Chen, J. K., Chuang, A. Y., McMahon, C., Hsieh, J. C., Tung, T. H., & Li, L. P. (2010). Music training improves pitch perception in prelingually deafened children with cochlear implants. *Pediatrics, 125*(4), 793–800.

Chermak, G., & Musiek, F. (2007). *Handbook of (central) auditory processing disorders: Comprehensive intervention* (Vol. II). San Diego, CA: Plural Publishing.

Chew, L., DeReiter, D., Doheny, C., Gilbert, C., Greenwood, K. F., Huff, T., Spiegelberg, S. (2010). *The daily book of classical music: 365 readings that teach, inspire & entertain.* New York, NY: Walter Foster.

Czubek, T., & Greenwald, J. (2005). Understanding Harry Potter: Parallels to the deaf world. *Oxford Journals: Journal of Deaf Studies and Deaf Education, 10*(4), 442–450.

Doug, W., Jones, D., & Luckner, J. (2011). Promoting literacy development with students who are deaf, hard-of-hearing, and hearing. *Teaching Exceptional Children, 37*(5), 55–62.

Emanuel, D., & Letowski, T. (2009). *Hearing science.* Baltimore, MD: Lippincott Williams & Wilkins.

Flexer, C. (2013).). *Classroom Acoustic Accessibility Using FM and Sound Technologies: A Brain-Based Perspective* PowerPoint presentation at the New Jersey Speech Language Hearing Association Annual Convention, Long Branch, New Jersey, April 25, 2013.

Galvin, J. J., Fu, Q. J., & Nogaki, G. (2007). Melodic contour identification by cochlear implant listeners. *Ear and Hearing, 28*, 302–319.

Gelfand, S. A. (2009). *Essentials of audiology*. New York, NY: Thieme Medical Publishers.

Holst Foundation. (2007). *Compositions: The Planets Op. 32*. Retrieved from http://www.gustavholst.info/compositions/listing.php?work=18

Johnson, C. (2012). *Introduction to audiologic rehabilitation: A contemporary issues approach*. Upper Saddle River, NJ: Pearson Education.

Johnson, M. S. (2009). *Composing music more accessible to the hearing-impaired*. Unpublished doctoral dissertation, University of North Carolina at Greensboro, Greensboro, NC.

Katz, J., Medwetsky, L., Burkard, R., & Hood, L. (2009). *Handbook of clinical audiology*. Philadelphia, PA: Lippincott Williams & Wilkins.

Kraus, N., Strait, D., & Parbery-Clark, A. (2011). Cognitive factors shape brain networks for auditory skills: Spotlight on auditory working memory. *Annals of the New York Academy of Science, 1252*, 100–107.

NAXOS. (2013). Gustav Holst. Retrieved from http://www.naxos.com/person/Gustav_Holst_24507/24507.htm

Nicholas, J., & Geers, A. (2006). Effects of early auditory experience on spoken language of deaf children at 3 years of age. *Ear and Hearing, 27*, 286–298.

Parbery-Clark, A., Anderson, S., Hittner, E., & Kraus, N. (2012). Musical experience offsets age-related delays in neural timing. *Neurobiology of Aging, 33*, 1483.e1-1483.e4.

Parbery-Clark, A., Skoe, E., Lam, C., & Kraus, N. (2009). Musician enhancement for speech in noise. *Ear and Hearing, 30*, 653–661.

Parbery-Clark, A., Tierney, A., Strait, D., & Kraus, N. (2012). Musicians have fine-tuned neural distinction of speech syllables. *Neuroscience, 219*, 111–119.

Peard, K. M. (2012). *The case for instrumental music education: The academic, physical, and social benefits for students*. Paper 23, Honors thesis, Honors College at the University of Maine, Orono, ME. Retrieved from http://digitalcommons.library.umaine.edu/honors/23

Rall, E., Montoya, L., Partridge, L., & Ramirez, R. (2008). *Interdisciplinary management of childhood hearing loss: CATIPIHLER*. Paper presented at the ASHA Convention, Chicago, Ill.

Schaub, A. (2008). *Digital hearing aids*. New York, NY: Thieme Medical Publishers.

Schow, R., & Nerbonne, M. (2013). *Introduction to audiologic rehabilitation* (6th ed.). Upper Saddle River, NJ: Pearson Education.

Schraer-Joiner, L., & Chen-Hafteck, L. (2009). The responses of preschoolers with cochlear implants to musical activities: A multiple case study. *Early Childhood Development and Care, 179*(6), 785–798.

Schraer-Joiner, L., & Prause-Weber, M. (2009). Strategies for working with children with cochlear implants. *Music Educators Journal, 96*, 48–55.

Sharma, A., Cardon, G., Henion, K., & Roland, P. (2011). Cortical maturation and behavioral outcomes in children with auditory neuropathy spectrum disorder. *International Journal of Audiology, 50*, 98–106.

Shehan-Campbell, P., & Scott-Kassner, C. (2009). *Music in childhood: From preschool through the elementary grades*. New York, NY: Schirmer Books.

Silvestre, N., & Valero, J. (2005). Oral language acquisition by deaf pupils in primary education: Impact of musical education. *European Journal of Special Needs Education, 20*(2), 195–213.

Strait, D., & Kraus, N. (2011). Musical training shapes functional brain networks for selective auditory attention and speech in noise. *Frontiers in Psychology, 2*, 1–10.

Strait, D., Parbery-Clark, A., O'Connell, S., & Kraus, N. (2013). Biological impact of preschool music classes on processing speech in noise. *Developmental Neuroscience, 6*, 51-60. Retrieved from http://www.soc.northwestern.edu/brainvolts/projects/music/index.php

Wong, P. C., Skoe, E., Russo, N. M., Dees, T., & Kraus, N. (2007). Musical experience shapes human brainstem encoding of linguistic pitch patterns. *Nature Neuroscience, 10,* 420–422.

Seminal Works

Berg, F., Blair, J., & Benson, P. (1996), Classroom acoustics: The problem, impact, and solution. *Language, Speech, and Hearing Services in Schools, 27,* 16–20.

Blamey, P., & Alcantara, J. (1994). Research in auditory training. In J. Gagne & N. Tye-Murray (Eds.), Research in audiologic rehabilitation [Monograph]. *Journal of the Academy of Rehabilitative Audiology, 27,* 161–192.

Crandell, C., & Smaldino, J. (2002). Room acoustics and auditory rehabilitation. In J. Katz (Ed.), *Handbook of clinical audiology* (pp. 607–630). Philadelphia, PA: Lippincott Williams & Wilkins.

Darrow, A. A. (1985). Music for the deaf. *Music Educators Journal, 71*(6), 33–35.

Darrow, A. A. (1990). The role of hearing in understanding music. *Music Educators Journal, 77*(4), 24–27.

Darrow, A. A., & Gfeller, K. (1991). A study of public school music programs mainstreaming hearing impaired students. *Journal of Music Therapy, 28,* 23–39.

Delage, H., & Tuller, L. (2007). Language development and mild-to-moderate hearing loss: Does language normalize with age? *Journal of Speech, Language, and Hearing Research, 50,* 1300–1313. DOI:10.1044/1092-4388(2007/091)

Erber, N. (1982). *Auditory training.* Washington, DC: Alexander Graham Bell Association for the Deaf.

Flexer, C. (1999). *Facilitating hearing and listening in young children.* San Diego, CA: Singular Publishing Group.

Ford, T. A. (1988). The effect of musical experiences and age on ability of deaf children to discriminate pitch. *Journal of Music Therapy, 25*(1), 2–16.

Gaab, N., Tallal, P., Kim, H., Lakshminarayanan, K., Archie, J. J., Gary H. G., & Gabrieli, J. (2005). Neural correlates of rapid spectrotemporal processing in musicians and non-musicians. *Annals of New York Academy of Sciences, 1060,* 82–88.

Gaston, E. T. (1968). *Music in therapy.* New York, NY: MacMillan Publishing Co.

Gfeller, K. (1990). A cognitive-linguistic approach to language development for the preschool child with hearing impairment: Implications for music therapy practice. *Music Therapy Perspectives, 8,* 47.

Greene, R. (1995). *Holst: The Planets.* Cambridge, MA: Cambridge University Press.

Haughton, P. (2002). *Acoustics for audiologists.* San Diego, CA: Academic Press.

Lamberts, F., & Miller, T. (1979). Itard and language pedagogy: A community for teachers of children with special needs. *Language, Speech, and Hearing Services in Schools, 10,* 203–211.

Libbey, T., & Libbey, T. (1999). *The NPR guide to building a classical CD Collection.* New York, NY: Workman Publishing Company.

McConnell, F., & Liff, S. (1975). Symposium on sensorineural hearing loss in children: Early detection and intervention. The rationale for early identification and intervention. *Otolaryngology Clinics of North America, 8,* 77–87.

Olzewski, C., Gfeller, K., Froman, R., Stordahl, J., & Tomblin, B. (2005). Familiar melody recognition by children and adults using cochlear implants and normal hearing children. *Cochlear Implants International, 6,* 123–140.

Overy, K. (2003). Dyslexia and music: From timing deficits to musical intervention. *Annals of the New York Academy of Sciences, 999,* 497–505.

Pinker, S. (1994). *The language instinct.* New York, NY: Harper Collins Publishers.

Prause, M. (2003). Annaeherung an ein musikerleben mit cochlear implant, schnecke. Zeitschrift der deutschen [Approach to a musical experience with cochlear implant]. *Cochlear Implant Gesellschaft, 41*(14), 18–19.

Sanders, D. (1972). *Aural rehabilitation.* Englewood Cliffs, NJ: Prentice-Hall.

Sinniger, Y., Doyle, K. J., & Moore, J. (1999). The case for early identification of hearing loss in children. *Pediatric Clinics of North America, 46,* 1–14.

Trainor, L., Shahin, A., & Roberts, L. (2003). Effects of musical training on auditory cortex in children. *Annals of the New York Academy of Sciences, 999,* 506–513.

CHAPTER 12

Reading Acquisition Frameworks for Music and Language

Layering Elements of Literacy
for Students with Exceptionalities

ELAINE BERNSTORF

This chapter considers a framework of literacy development focused on reading acquisition within music pedagogy contexts for children with exceptionalities (Bernstorf, 2013b). In meeting the continuum of learner needs, we must explore not only traditional or proven methods of music education but also how such methods intersect with the needs of exceptional learners on both ends of the learning continuum. Ultimately, music educators must understand that music literacy development involves many points of access for individual learners in inclusive music learning environments. A conceptual framework of music acquisition may aid our discussion.

Every music educator's goal is to maximize music reading ability for all children; however, the reality of readers and nonreaders still exists, in both music and language reading. Many classroom management problems may be attributed to frustrations experienced by students who are not able to read (Lavoie, 1989). Many students access neither musical notation nor language reading material as it is presented in the music class. Even when proven music methods such as Dalcroze, Orff, Kodály, Music Learning Theory (Gordon), Suzuki, and Comprehensive Musicianship are presented by excellent teachers who are well versed with the method, we may still find less-than-optimum learning for many students. Many music educators empathize with the frustrations felt by nonreaders in music classes in the same manner that classroom teachers and reading specialists experience the frustration that their students may exhibit when unable to decode or comprehend written language symbols.

Research by Hall (2013) demonstrated the importance of language arts reading skills in preservice music education programs, especially for elementary music classrooms. Forty-two programs across the nation responded to her survey with overall favorable attitudes toward reading integration, as 71% indicated that preservice music teachers should be "knowledgeable about reading content" (Hall, 2013, p. 8). But her survey also demonstrated that this responsibility is usually left to the colleges of education (92%), with her speculation that the instructors of such courses would have "little to no music knowledge and understanding" (p. 8). Therefore, she concluded, "Students would receive very strong reading content knowledge but little understanding in regard to transferability of reading content into music content" (p. 8). Despite several decades of multidisciplinary research on relationships between music and language, there is still much to be learned (Atterbury, 1985; Hansen, Bernstorf, & Stuber, 2004; Hansen, et al., 2014; McMullen & Saffran, 2002; Patel, 2008; Rautenberg, 2015).

How might reading be addressed in the content area of music, and what is a possible relationship between music reading and language reading? Can they both be fostered in inclusive school music programs? This chapter suggests a multitiered approach to building music and language literacy connections for all learners using the following:

- Reading acquisition frameworks as they parallel and intersect with music literacy acquisition, including definitions of important reading skills that relate to music decoding and comprehension
- A suggested music literacy acquisition framework appropriate for inclusion settings, which fosters both reading and music literacy
- Differentiation for students with exceptionalities using response to intervention and fully guided instruction as adaptations in planning, materials, activities, and assessments

READING WITHIN MUSIC LITERACY

Music education covers a broad spectrum of activities that includes music knowledge, skills, and even positive or negative dispositions. As music educators, we want our students to access music, make music, enjoy music, revere music, and even *use* music. The use of music is one of the primary points of intersection between the fields of music education, special music education, and music therapy. We all want our students to use music. But what does that mean, and what does that have to do with music literacy?

Reading teachers teach language reading. Music teachers teach music reading. Both music and reading teachers have a common goal—they want their students to become skilled readers. Both music and reading teachers want their students to learn how to read so they can use reading skills to do other things—to comprehend something, to make decisions, to guide thoughts and actions, to experience something inside that has meaning without action. Silent reading is a primary goal for reading teachers; reading teachers monitor the silent reader, looking for a smile, a nod, a frown—behaviors that signify what is happening inside the mind. The term *reading* is used to represent the simultaneous tasks of decoding symbols (text) and comprehending the message conveyed by the symbols (text). Literate musicians use this same format—look at a score, decode it, and comprehend the distinctive features of sound that the notation represents to hear the music holistically in their heads.

Reading in the Music Environment: Understanding Reading Acquisition Frameworks

A primary tenant of education is to teach decoding skills, thereby aiding a learner's comprehension of various subjects. It is assumed that if students learn to decode words, they will use reading in their lives. The assumption is that decoding leads to comprehension. In a like manner, we could assume that if students learn to decode music well enough to sing or play notes and rhythms (especially if they do so accurately), they will become musicians and continue to engage with music. Neither assumption holds true. Students may be able to decode text fluently but not understand the meaning. In the same way, students may be able to "sound out" or play musical pitches and rhythms but not fully demonstrate comprehensive musicianship or become lifelong musicians.

When we consider students with disabilities, it may be helpful to think in reverse. Students with exceptionalities often seek musical stimulation—this is one of the primary uses of music in therapeutic behavior modification. A love of music may motivate some students to learn to read, both music and language. What we are coming to learn about the actual steps of reading acquisition can and should be to applied foster music literacy for learners with exceptionalities. In this time of educational inclusion, these are questions that pique the interest of musicians, educators, and researchers. A recent study in Germany (Degé & Schwarzer, 2011) showed that musical training could improve the decoding skills of normally developing German-speaking primary school children. For students with reading disabilities (dyslexia), the interest in music and reading has also been important. Music educators have pondered this topic for many years (Atterbury, 1985; Register, Darrow, Standley, & Swedberg, 2007; Törmänen, 2010), yet we still have only bits and pieces of information with few frameworks for understanding the relationship between music and language acquisition (Fedorenko, Patel, Cassanto, Winawer, & Gibson, 2009; Patel, 2003; Patel, 2008).

Parallel Processes or Integrated Processes?

Researchers continue to explore whether music and language are separate (modular) cognitive domains, integrated systems, or parallel processes. Hansen et al. (2004) theorized that these complex processes share many intersections (p. xi) but that both language and music literacy are overlapping continuums. McMullen and Saffran (2004) argue for separation of the processes in adults but almost identical processes for music and language perception in infants. Patel (2003, 2008) and his colleagues (Fedorenko et al., 2009) used a graphic representation with intersections and overlaps to describe the relationship but did not describe identical processes.

Research on infant development (McMullen & Saffran, 2004; Patel, 2008) suggests that infants can process the sounds of language and music beyond their capabilities of knowing/understanding the content that those sounds represent. More recently, Finnish researchers (Burger, Saarikallio, Luck, Thompson, & Toiviainen, 2013) have explored the relationships between emotions in music and music-induced movements. While they concluded that there are "relationships between the emotional content of music and music-induced, quasi-spontaneous movement" (p. 530), they also conceded that "it could be argued that our participants moved rather according to musical features than according to the emotional content" (p. 531). Those of us who work with nonverbal students who have disabilities wrestle with these questions of perception regarding understanding versus emotional impact on a daily basis. It is for these students that music education can be so rich, whether for perceptual development, cognitive development, or both. Such are the overlaps between musical artistry, education, and therapy.

Those of us who have completed advanced studies or degrees in music realize that we now experience music in a completely different way than we did when we were learning to read music. Fluent music notation readers have shifted the act of decoding to an "associative process" rather than a "cognitive process" (Lavoie, 1989). This means that they are able to do more than one thing at a time (associative processes) so that they decode automatically while they are processing (comprehending) the information they have decoded. A musician's fluency in reading and understanding musical scores often determines his or her success in getting jobs, keeping jobs, and enjoying long-term musical work.

READING FRAMEWORKS

Reading comprehension is based on a framework of supporting skills with a primary emphasis on decoding. Since publications by the National Reading Panel on *Teaching Children to Read* (2000), there has been intense interest in reading research internationally. The importance of decoding and comprehension as primary pillars seems universal among the models. Hansen et al. (2004, 2014) applied these findings to music education in their text *The Music and Literacy Connection.* Since that time, numerous framework models and curriculums have been designed around varying bodies of research in reading. Each state department of education, many individual researchers, many literacy organizations, and numerous publishers of literacy materials have developed reading frameworks. These frameworks outline components of reading acquisition and suggest teacher actions designed to help students gain literacy skills. Models are readily available and too numerous to list in this chapter. One framework model that has stood the test of time is that created by Sebastian Wren[1] (2000). Wren's framework stated that the development of two primary abilities is of critical importance for reading acquisition. These skills are *language comprehension* and *decoding.* Language comprehension includes the following building blocks: background knowledge (individual experience with language), phonology (the ability to discriminate characteristics of sound), syntax (grammar), and semantics (vocabulary). Decoding skills include subunits such as phonemic awareness (smallest units of sound for language), knowledge about the alphabetic principle (that certain written symbols can stand for certain spoken sounds), concepts about print (people use print to convey messages), and knowledge about letters (orthographic awareness—the symbols used in a child's cultural alphabet; Bernstorf & Kordonowy, 2013).

Decoding and comprehension are integral to the many models of reading that have been published in the last two decades beginning with the National Reading Panel's work and during the advent of No Child Left Behind legislation. How do decoding and comprehension appear in music learning contexts? Gardner (1983) described people with musical intelligence as those who have "know-that" and "know-how" in the area of music.

In an effort to visualize these comparisons, the following descriptions of music comprehension (know-that) and music decoding (know-how) are offered, as well as the music foundational skills (pillars) needed for each:

- Music comprehension (know-that)
  - o Background knowledge of music
  - o Phonology—ability to discriminate characteristics of musical sound
  - o Syntax—culturally acceptable patterns of musical sound (grammar)
  - o Semantics—vocabulary used to describe music sounds; common musical themes
- Music decoding (know-how)
  - o Phonemic awareness—sound symbol association for musical sounds in a global sense
  - o Concepts about graphic notation (in this case music notation)
    - Alphabetic principle—becomes notation principle; the idea that musical symbols can group to form musical messages
    - Letter knowledge—notation characteristics; the shape and placement of individual symbols convey discrete information about a sound's time and pitch (or lack thereof)

Figure 12.1 (Bernstorf, 2013b) provides a visual framework to facilitate conversation about music perception (decoding) and music comprehension (musicology) with fellow music educators. As each student develops along the hierarchy, the goal should be to gain balance between the two sides of the framework that support music literacy. Music literacy is more than simple reproduction of musical tones as an automatic response to music symbols. This is the same distinction that reading specialists make between reading fluency (quick decoding) and reading comprehension (reading with understanding). True comprehensive musicianship must represent music literacy in the broadest sense, with the addition of performance skills as represented in the conceptual framework for music education (see Figure 12.1). The framework is designed to guide teachers as they make curriculum and activity decisions. The goal is to develop maximum music literacy and performance skills in the quest to foster comprehensive musicianship for all learners.

As students grasp the various subunits of music, they decode language about music at the same time they are learning to reproduce musical sounds both from hearing music and from seeing visual representations of those sounds (notation). Over time, learners may develop both musical knowledge (musicology) and music decoding skills (sight-reading—"reading music"). The ultimate goal is to integrate knowledge ("know-that") and skills ("know-how") into a continuum of abilities—in our case "comprehensive

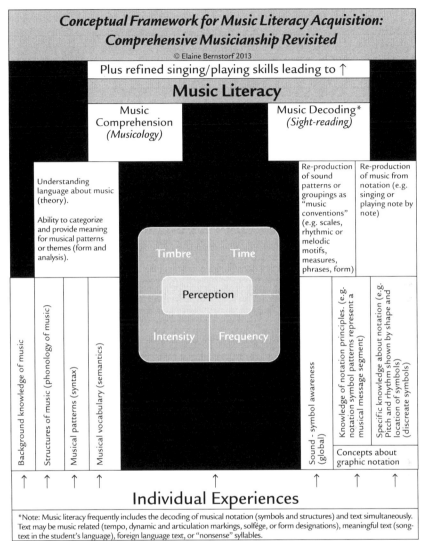

Figure 12.1. Conceptual framework for music literacy acquisition.

musicianship," where a musician decodes music notation and performs that notation (sings or plays) with demonstrated understanding. In language literacy acquisition, the learner ultimately demonstrates reading comprehension. Reading comprehension is the ability to translate text into speech at the same time that one understands that spoken language (even if the spoken language is silent [e.g., silent reading for learning]). Wren (2000) made the point that "all struggling readers have difficulty with either language comprehension or decoding or both" (p. 52). The same may be said for musicians.

Struggling music readers have difficulty with either the concepts of musical structure or decoding music notation, or both. Some musicians have a strong understanding of musical structure and the ability to reproduce music aurally but cannot decode music notation. Other students can decode notation (sight-read) but do not seem to grasp the "musicality" of the tones they are reproducing. Rather, they seem to mechanically match the symbols on the page to some physical action (playing or singing tones). It is the combination of the two skill sets (decoding and understanding) that develops strong independent musicianship. Truly independent musicians are those with the ability to decode fluently; categorize, recognize, and practice important patterns; hone specific physical skills; and perform at high levels in front of others. In other words, to behave as comprehensive musicians is in the truest sense to have "music intelligence" (Gardner, 1983). When we add the additional cognitive and physical loads of doing multiple musical tasks in absolute synchrony with others in real time, we understand why many musicians demonstrate amazing intellect and academic achievement. We also begin to see why students who struggle with synchronized music tasks (keeping the beat) may later be the same students who demonstrate reading difficulties (Wolff, 2002). We need to work with both skill sets.

Sadly, in many school music programs, students develop the decoding side of the framework (fluent performance) with little regard for the knowledge (musicology) aspects, while others develop some knowledge base (music appreciation) with little honing of decoding skills (reading and playing music). Still others become rote imitators of sounds with neither decoding skills nor musicological understandings; all of this "uniformed doing" (Blair, 2009, p. 42) occurs in the name of performances for ratings or to entertain parents and the community. (Many of us have seen the toddler who is trained to recite a story or poem but who has no understanding of the meaning nor the ability to read what has been recited.)

LISTENING, VIEWING, AND SPEAKING SKILLS

Music educators have realized the importance of viewing, listening, and speaking for many years. "The basic skills of listening, viewing, and speaking are central to literacy but are not the same as decoding or comprehension skills. Literacy learning can be integrated across the curriculum through activities that develop good listening, viewing, and speaking skills" (Hansen et al., 2004, p. 111). Music educators will be able to more fully address the exceptional pedagogy of all students (typical learners, lower functioning, and high achieving) when they understand reading development (both decoding and comprehension) within the context of listening and speaking.

I suggest that many students with exceptional pedagogy needs may indeed thrive with more global listening, viewing, and speaking tasks; they even may be able to categorize what they hear and view and understand language and music boundaries such as word or phrase structures (McMullen & Saffran, 2004, p. 303). However, these same students may struggle with the distinctive features related to symbol decoding and symbol comprehension (the reading side of the equation). Internationally, various Common Core Standards may be designed for all learners, but good teachers will need to create multiple tiers of support to address individual student differences in perceptual and expressive abilities. Teachers need to reconsider their instructional input designs and the expressive student outputs to be assessed. Instead of single musical performance goals designed for all students, music teachers provide multiple layers of input with alternate student response options to demonstrate a specific outcome.

Response to Intervention

Under the reauthorization of the Individuals with Disabilities Education Act (IDEA) in 2004, response to intervention (RTI) became important for both researchers and teachers. While many models of intervention existed, RTI research suggested several common approaches to assist students with learning needs (Bernstorf and Brenzikofer, 2013). One was the use of multiple tiers of intervention in service delivery, another was the use of a problem-solving approach, and another was the use of data collection and assessment to inform decisions related to the tiered service delivery approach (National Association of State Directors of Special Education, 2006).

The idea behind RTI is that standards-based instruction should be our initial focus and that it should meet the needs of almost all students (Tier 1, approximately 80%). RTI then suggests two levels of differentiation that may be needed for some students. Tier 2 focuses on "at risk" students (approximately 15% of students). These students need adjustments to the instruction and may need additional time or some additional instruction (preteaching, repetition, or review). Despite adapted and additional instruction, some students still may not succeed. These students (Tier 3, approximately 5%) will need very specific or intense interventions, including an altered curriculum, to meet their major learning or behavior needs. Tier 3 students may need related services offered through special education programs under IDEA. All of these are designed around the regular classroom model. While the model primarily addresses the needs of students who have learning difficulties (those on the "lower end" of the learning continuum), teachers should remember that students who are gifted and talented also may be "at risk" in educational settings.

Music educators understand that not all students learn in the same way. Some students demonstrate greater conceptual understanding of music, while others have specific strengths in particular music skills (singing, playing, dancing, sight-reading, improvising, or composing). As teachers, we are aware of our individual strengths as musicians. Some of us are performers; others are musicologists, conductors, or teachers. We have learned that we have strengths and weaknesses but that to be comprehensive musicians, we are generally Tier 1 learners in most things, but Tier 2 or 3 in some areas. People with perfect pitch would actually be Tier 3 musicians in the area of pitch. Their great ability to encode absolute pitch also may require adaptations for instruction. This is also true for young students or nonverbal students who may become frustrated but do not have language to describe their perceptions.[2]

As music educators, we are keenly aware of the need to adjust and adapt our instruction to maximize accuracy. We may aim for 100% accuracy for pitch and rhythm as our students sing, play instruments, and dance, yet we understand that skill-based learning is dependent on many factors. As we individualize, we develop *differentiated instruction* techniques (Reis et al., 1998, p. 74). The best music teachers, whether private or large group instructors, routinely customize instruction techniques for individual students, but teachers may not have thought of it as differentiated instruction, or of their programs as a multitiered system of support. Without naming the principle as such, we also employ "response to intervention" techniques. An example of a common (yet controversial) RTI for instrumental string instruction is the addition of tapes to help students who need additional visual-tactile feedback as they are learning the spatial relationships of absolute pitches on a stringed instrument. As music educators, we develop interventions automatically. The simple act of "marking music" is a classic example of how we "intervene" to assist music learning for others and ourselves. Such are basic adjustments that we take for granted, but adjustments are extremely important in helping each of our students attain success. When we find something that works for one student, we try it with others who have similar difficulties. Music educators use response to intervention in its most natural form. Our greatest advantage is that while we have state standards, we also have some absolute standards in the elements of sound (pitch and rhythmic accuracy). This is the reason we may become focused on skills and performance over knowledge in our quests for music literacy. The outcomes are clearly being met or not as students sing and play their instruments.

And this may be why many students who have difficulty choose to leave our programs. We may even encourage our "nonfluent" readers and players to drop out. Language arts teachers don't have that option. Music educators may want to reconsider their stance if they find themselves hoping that less successful students will leave the music program.

Multitiered System of Supports (MTSS)

Music educators routinely use the RTI principle to create differentiated instruction (Tomlinson, 1999). While many music educators may believe this in principle, their actions sometimes reflect the idea that the responsibility for learning lies primarily on the student. In other words, "they just need to just practice more." Research in special education has shown that this is not necessarily the case. In fact, it is impossible to practice something one does not understand how to do; such knowledge seldom comes without some kind of direct or guided instruction. But where does a teacher begin?

Music teachers traditionally begin where students respond or demonstrate "readiness." The point of student engagement or ability is not always at the same level as stated in a grade-level curriculum guide or grade-level sequence. This is the reason that the 1994 Music Standards were organized around "beginner, intermediate, proficient, and advanced" categories. While grade levels were included, those who designed the standards strongly reinforced that the standards were *guidelines* and that students who did not have general music in their elementary schools might be "beginners" when they did begin to have instruction no matter what their chronological age or grade. The "readiness" principle has always been in effect for private music teachers, where older beginners and even adult beginners are not uncommon.

Researchers implore parents to foster early exposure to music for infants and toddlers; yet, the reality is that most students have far less parental guidance to music than to language text. Music education involves both conceptual understanding and skill development. Children who have had extensive musical experiences in their environment may actually need multitiered system of supports (MTSS) opportunities to work at a higher level than their peers. As music educators, we have often recommended "private lessons" for these students, or we have organized solo or chamber music experiences for more advanced students. At times, younger students with strong backgrounds (e.g., Suzuki players) have been invited to play in ensembles with older grade levels. Students labeled as "gifted" have been afforded such opportunities readily, but given RTI and MTSS, music teachers should be able to advocate for even more students to participate in this manner. Such is the nature of differentiated instruction. But how do we differentiate *within* traditional grade-level groupings?

Differentiation: Areas to Consider

Tomlinson and her colleagues have proposed that differentiated instruction occurs when teachers modify the curriculum, their teaching methods, their resources, the learning activities, or the resulting products of instruction to meet the needs of small groups of students or individual students so that all children experience their maximum learning (Tomlinson & Allen, 2000, Tomlinson & Imbeau, 2010). These authors suggested a grid of differentiation based on student needs. Their matrix (Tomlinson & Imbeau, 2010, p. 18) provides a helpful model for differentiation by addressing potential changes in instruction based on the needs of the student. They suggested three ways to consider student needs: readiness, interest, and learning profile. They also suggested areas within the teacher's instruction where adaptations could be made: content, process, product, and affect. Their suggestions provide a simple format to consider potential areas for differentiated instruction in music classes. Informed by the work of Tomlinson and Imbeau (2010, p. 18), Figure 12.2 describes possible options for this type of differentiation (Bernstorf, 2013a). The three columns consider the needs of typical learners, those who struggle, and those who need more challenges in the music setting.

Where to Start

A key to successful use of differentiation is for the teacher to be well grounded in the standards-based curriculum. Only then can differentiated instruction function effectively for all students. The goal is to begin by maintaining the regular curriculum through activities that would be appropriate for all students. However, when students need modifications (Tier 2), the goal is that the modifications be suitable for a group of students who have similar needs. The idea behind this type of differentiation is not to have individual private instruction for every student, nor is it a practice to have students who have more severe needs become the "audience" for more capable music students. The goal is that all students can and will participate, but with some adaptations. Given the realities of inclusive group music, most of the suggestions in Table 12.1 are designed to use the same musical

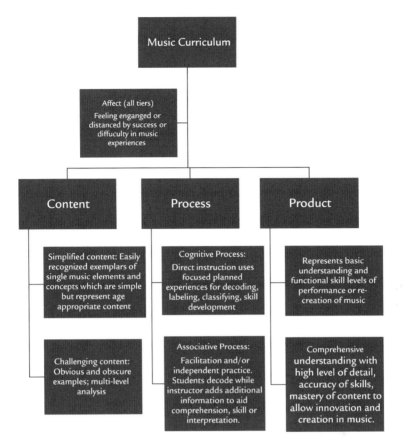

Figure 12.2. Differentiation framework for music instruction.
Reprinted from Bernstorf (2013a), influenced by Tomlinson & Imbeau (2010).

content, but to allow for students to have varied activities that meet their learning needs.[3] Therefore, Table 12.1 is primarily aimed at adjustments in process and product rather than content. However, it is important to remember that content is not just music. Content includes a continuum of music and language input that varies by specificity, vocabulary, and examples. Truly artful teachers are those who are able to choose and use musical content that meets the needs of all students. That is one of the joys of music as a nonverbal medium. Music examples should provide at least one thing that every student can access perceptually, intellectually, and emotionally. Other nonverbal mediums in the arts (dance, mime, and visual art) also provide great options for learners of all levels (see Table 12.1).

Notice that the suggested activities are *conceptually based*. The suggested activities reflect outcomes that have varying levels complexity and specificity.

Table 12.1 ANCHOR STANDARD FOR SPEAKING AND LISTENING:
SAMPLE MUSIC ADAPTATIONS

Anchor Standard for Speaking and Listening	Sample Typical Music Activity	Adaptation for Lower-Level Learners	Adaptation for High Achievers
Prepare for and participate effectively in a range of conversations and collaborations with diverse partners, building on others' ideas and expressing their own clearly and persuasively.	All types of rehearsal activities, especially those using sectionals, chamber ensembles, or part work. Group work of all types (especially group improvisation or composition using a criteria).	Sing/play alone and with others using imitation, call-response, or union; Bourduns or simple ostinatos. Manipulate icons to show understanding of musical structures. Collaborate through expressive movement (nonverbal) to interpret a variety of musical styles.	Work with others for score analysis, improvisation, composing, evaluation, and, of course, performing. Part work of all types; independent or with a peer; assist others with something you already know. NOTE: tutoring should not be a primary role for high achievers—they need their own adaptations, not to become "paras" due to lack of adequate support.
Integrate and evaluate information presented in diverse media and formats, including visually, quantitatively, and orally	Score analysis of all types, using icons, graphing, and contour drawing. All types of aural dictation. Read from scores, tablature, or lead sheets. Any music activities where students follow a conductor, mark scores, discuss musical structures (from the score or aural examples, or to evaluate musical performances).	Arrange pictures to show musical structure or to demonstrate the story of the text. Examples: Choosing, pointing to, or arranging visual graphics of what they hear. Use representations of any musical element, for example, icons or graphics that represent dynamics, timbre (replicas and photos of actual instruments, voice types—man, woman, whisper, etc.), form (patterns, phrases, sections), icons, or physical manipulatives showing melodic or rhythmic patterns.	Virtually all ethnographic experiences with music will fulfill this anchor standard. Take musical dictation such as short folk songs, jazz riffs, or pop music charts from a recording. Read and perform using lead sheets. Experience or invent a visual graphic notation system. Experience ancient and twentieth-century graphic notation styles. Use bar or line graphs to analyze a piece of music. Translate between systems (#s, solfége, absolute pitches). Transpose music in various ways.

Table 12.1 (CONTINUED)

Anchor Standard for Speaking and Listening	Sample Typical Music Activity	Adaptation for Lower-Level Learners	Adaptation for High Achievers
Evaluate a speaker's point of view, reasoning, and use of evidence and rhetoric	All performance evaluations. All music and other art critiques. Evaluations of musical accuracy. Read, write, and discuss music and other art categories. Create a group evaluation rubric.	This one will be more difficult; however, many students with disabilities will easily compare two different performances of the same music and describe similarities and differences, as well as their preferences. Use an adapted rubric that has icons or emoticons Use a para or peer reader to assist.	Evaluate the works of various musical artists, composers, conductors, critics, etc. Consider their support or criticism of specific musical examples. Learn and use empathic critique techniques. Create own evaluation rubrics.
Present information, findings, and supportive evidence such that listeners can follow the line of reasoning and the organization, development, and style are appropriate to task, purpose, and audience.	Draw or use graphic organizers of all types (including staff notation) to demonstrate understanding of musical examples. Design listening maps for different groups of people. Use music to prompt short technical writings describing what is heard.	Use already-prepared graphic organizers or manipulatives to show ability to hear, compare (same–different), or classify examples of musical elements, form, etc. Smartboards, picture exchange communication, and assistive technology may be needed.	Research and write critiques, program notes, or biographies with representative score examples. Develop listening anthologies for varied audiences to represent musical styles, genres, composers, and time periods.
Make strategic use of digital media and visual displays of data to express information and enhance understanding of presentations	All types of musical notation and composition software programs are appropriate. Also audio-visual sound production activities to create "found sound" or layered compositions (such as Orff activities).	Use simple computer programs and apps for the iPad to foster music expression. Use icons and graphic scores to create sound stories (such as Boardmaker and Morton Subotnik's music-making software and apps).	Use digital notation programs and sound production programs to compose for a variety of purposes. Help students use MIDI (Musical Instrument Digital Interface) interfaces to expand their music-making options.

(continued)

Table 12.1 (CONTINUED)

Anchor Standard for Speaking and Listening	Sample Typical Music Activity	Adaptation for Lower-Level Learners	Adaptation for High Achievers
Adapt speech to a variety of contexts and communicative tasks, demonstrating command of formal English when indicated or appropriate	Respond, perform, or create using speech or music to communicate and demonstrate their command of musical terms including foreign language terms for dynamics, tempos, articulation, and timbre markings. Use varied pitch and number systems (solfége, counting systems).	Speak orally or use adaptive communication devices to demonstrate understanding of musical elements. Gazing at the correct answer or pointing on a communicate grid is still a communicative task. Include similar answers but where one is more correct because of vocabulary or grammar used. Speech pathologist may be quite helpful if a student needs these adjustments as it may also meet speech goals.	Describe, sing, play, improvise, or compose for a variety of purposes. Advanced students could do detailed analysis of music as prompts for technical writing. Other options include having a student critic write for a school newspaper or send letters to the editor commenting on recent musical performances in the community.

Note. From Bernstorf (2013a). Suggested resources: Bartel (2012); Bernstorf (2013a); NCCAS (2013); Tomlinson and Imbeau (2010).

Empathic critique is the search to discover what has happened in the work. Since much of what happens in any creative endeavor is intuitive, capricious, and unintended, we naturally expect the unexpected and unintended to make significant contributions and make new insights possible. The empathic critique finds ways to allow the creator of the work to discover what has been noticed by others. The maker gets credit for the potential value of his or her own unintended outcomes (mistakes). The maker is made to feel empowered by self-awareness. The artist constructs new knowledge based on discoveries brought to light based on considerate questioning. The art studio class becomes a community of learning (Bartel, 2012).

Take Time to Ask Other Professionals for Suggestions

In practices like RTI, all professionals are encouraged to work as facilitators for every student. Music teachers routinely work with all learners in the school. Music teachers also serve as resources for teachers, other professionals, and community members who have questions related to music. It is important that music teachers understand that they also have the right to ask for assistance in meeting student learning needs, especially related to literacy in music settings. Research continues to highlight the role of music in early childhood language learning and emergent literacy (Jäncke,

2012; The College Board, 2012). Speech pathologists are a wonderful resource, as well as special education teachers and reading specialists. With the emphasis on the effects of behavior on academic learning in the RTI model, behavior intervention specialists, counselors, and social workers also may provide excellent suggestions for addressing student needs. Music educators should make every effort to attend available conferences and sessions about differentiation and behavior interventions, as well as music in-service training.

Keep in mind one very important difference between classroom and music instruction. It is the nature of music instruction to be "inclusive," meaning that all students are doing the same thing at the same time. Due to the "sound" nature of music activities, it is difficult for small groups of students to be working separately in making music (performing). It is much easier to plan for differentiation in the responding or describing category of music activities. Create tiered levels of music representation such as the following:

1. **Concrete level:** use of physical manipulatives (objects, popsicle sticks, blocks) or movements (enactive)
2. **Representational graphics** (icons): two-dimensional representations such as lines of varied lengths showing rhythm durations, drawings of melodic contours, or combinations such as listening maps
3. **Symbols:** actual music notation examples (symbolic) or vocabulary words (on cards or word walls)

By providing options for music representation, all students may respond at their level of understanding, even when grouped in the same class using the same audio musical examples.

It is in the actual music-making process (performance) where differentiation may be most difficult yet also may provide the most support for student learning. Music making provides its own positive rewards in real time. Group music making, when structured for individual success, brings forth inclusion naturally through physical and emotional synchrony (Burger et al., 2013; Olsson, Schéele, & Theorell, 2013; Patel, 2008).

Three-Tiered Instructional Hierarchy for Differentiation

To explore connections between music and language, it is helpful to consider features of sound common to both music and language and their implications for teaching literacy (Bernstorf, 2008). That publication provided descriptions for three aspects of sound (both music and language) that are important for instruction: global elements, segmented patterns, and distinct features of individual sounds (see Figure 12.3).

Figure 12.3. Hierarchy levels for sound feature differentiation.

In general, this three-level hierarchy relates to the science of sound (timbre, intensity, time, and frequency), the perceived boundaries that structure combined sounds (patterns), and the specific aspects that distinguish individual units of sound (phonemic awareness for language or "note-level" aural awareness for music). By guiding students through these stages of perception and production of sound (music), teachers can accommodate most learners at some point in the hierarchy. In figure 12.4 the most generic elements of sound are those that are often measured; these elements are easily visualized on an oscilloscope and also on many electronic audio devices. As musicians we can hear, see, and even "feel" the general envelop of sound (timbre), general recurring patterns (pitch or time), and how intensely sounds are offered (dynamics). Infants and many students with severe disabilities will automatically respond to the most obvious (global) changes in these sound features whether in speech (prosody) or in music (contour; McMullen & Saffran, 2004; Patel, 2008; Trehub & Hannon, 2006).

Most individuals will perceive and begin to recognize when various boundaries create words or other repeated patterns of sound (segments). Music educators want all students to learn to hear, see, and "read" the distinct pitches and duration of pitches (note values) that they want them to perceive, sing, and play. But realistically, the most prominent and repeated patterns are those that will actually stick. Figure 12.4 describes the common music elements as they relate to the sound features with three levels (global [G], segments [S], and distinct [D]).

Global

Begin with the "big ideas." Routinely start the lesson with brief, but whole, musical examples that can be perceived and responded to globally (generally by moving with gestural responses such as rocking/swaying, bilateral tapping, or simple arm movements). Even older students in ensembles can start class with some kind of global activity using the

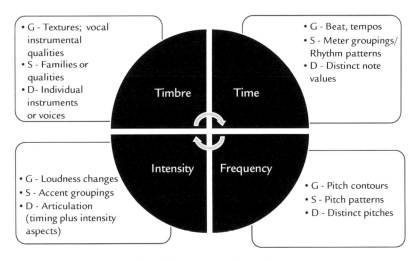

Figure 12.4. Sound features with global, segment, and distinct hierarchy examples.

music that they will later be singing or playing, or similar musical examples. Kodály, Orff, and Dalcroze programs routinely do this with group movement activities through games or creative movements using the macro beat or micro beat to reinforce global parameters that represent the musical form. Gross motor movements in response to tempo changes, dynamic changes, obvious sectional timbre changes, and pitch contour changes are appropriate global responses that virtually all students can experience in some way. Students may need the guidance of a paraprofessional or a peer to demonstrate. Props such as a scarf, parachute, puppet, or simple listening map can encourage all students to focus on the big ideas. Even if some students can go no further, virtually all students can maintain some type of global understanding and response to music. Form in music is often marked at this global level through broad changes in dynamics, tempos, meters, timbres, harmonic structures, or melodic contours. This enactive or kinesthetic mode of representation is, according to Bruner (1966), evidence of *authentic* learning. Teachers should always plan some time for engaging with appropriate global features of the music and then allow students who need this adaptation to continue responding to global features. Teachers should encourage learners to move toward segmented patterns and distinct features but allow them the dignity of being responders (National Coalition for Core Arts Standards [NCCAS], 2014), and not set them up to become silent and frozen observers by jumping too far ahead, too fast. The use of large motor props like streamers, parachutes, phrase pictures, and conducting movements are effective. How often we see toddlers conducting the global elements with great accuracy—we should take note.

Segment

Most students then can gradually move to the segment level. They can perceive patterns, hear them as same and different, categorize the patterns, and recognize specific patterns when they occur in new situations. Such is the same process for melodic patterns, rhythm patterns, and speech patterns such as vocabulary words, phrases, sentences, and all types of segments associated with both text meanings (vocabulary/semantics or grammar/syntax). McMullen and Saffron (2004) cited their own research and the research of others that indicates that infants have been shown to perceive cognitive boundaries for both music and language. Their studies indicated that infants first segment language sounds into words and then perceive the order of words (grammar), but that the infants always seem to prefer sentences that are grammatically correct.

We all have been in situations where we recognize words that we cannot pronounce yet. Many students will always need to respond to patterns by gesturing, pointing to visuals, choosing, matching, ordering, moving, and even dancing. Students with disabilities may have great difficulty in singing, playing, improvising, or creating the patterns, but they can function and learn at this "segment" level of understanding and should be encouraged to do so. This level of understanding is one where graphic representations (icons) and manipulatives can be especially helpful. Such is true in other subject areas as well. In addition to word walls that highlight specific musical terms, we might want to consider "pattern" walls with common melodic and rhythmic patterns. Many teachers in the Kodaly tradition use these types of patterns on long "flash cards" that students can order and manipulate as they recognize patterns visually and aurally. Many students who cannot sing or play these patterns accurately can still recognize, order, and respond to them. Many students can read and produce (chant or play) rhythm patterns more easily than pitch patterns, but they should continually be encouraged to try to respond to, perform, and create segments of music. Kodaly, Orff, Gordon's Music Learning Theory, and Comprehensive Musicianship focus on helping students learn these building blocks of music. It is the order in which we present the segments and the manner in which we manipulate the segments that will ultimately determine how inclusive our program appears to students. Obviously, this is somewhat simplistic, but the nature of pattern recognition in learning makes this level of experience vitally important for all students at all ages and stages in their musical development.

Distinct Features

Ultimately, our goal is for each individual to perceive, recognize, recall, read, sing, play, analyze, and create music. In this case, music may be defined as specific pitches produced for specific amounts of time using specific intensities produced by specific timbres. Combinations of these individual and distinct elements provide the articulated sounds that we call speech or music. Those who are fluent in such production are rewarded, whether they are skilled speakers, singers, or instrumentalists. We value the precision of such distinct sound productions. We become so aware of distinct sound production patterns that even everyday nonpitched sound sources (such as car motors) ultimately produce such *distinct* individual qualities that we can tell a mechanic when we hear a change in the "sounds of the engine." We may even notice a change in individual ticks of a small alarm clock and know we need to change the battery.

The majority of our students also perceive these distinct levels. Such perception is required for the sound-to-symbol associations of "phonemic-alphabetic awareness" and individual note recognition in music. But not all learners can do this automatically and may need direct instruction. Many students with disabilities find great difficulty in working at this level of precision, whether in *perceiving* the distinct levels of sounds (phonemes or musical sounds) or *reading* the symbols that represent the sounds, and especially in *producing* sounds from the symbols.

It is necessary to work at the most discreet levels—especially in the arts, where even the minutest aspects of each distinction (e.g., tuning, articulation, vowel blending, and precision of attack) makes a difference. Savant students often are able to perceive and reproduce sounds at very distinct levels but may not be able to describe, label, or classify such sound categories. Students with motor disorders such as cerebral palsy may understand every nuance of sound features yet be unable to respond to or perform them with accuracy, even if working at the global level of keeping a beat. The key is for teachers to not work exclusively at any one level, but to continually move between and among the sound features (global, segment, and distinct) and to use varying experiences that accommodate learners' abilities for content, process, and product (Tomlinson & Imbeau, 2010). The result is that different learners will find their individual places of understanding along the spiral curriculum (Bruner, 1960) that we call music education and then will most likely readily participate and succeed. Tomlinson's long-term research has demonstrated that schools that implement differentiation of instruction foster student success and retention. Two of the major areas where schools have established differentiation are student reading and behavior needs. The specific aspects of music literacy require direct instruction that balances growth in decoding (notation and text) with growth in comprehension (reading and musicology).

BALANCED INSTRUCTION

The regular curriculum may prove challenging and sometimes overwhelming for students with exceptionalities. When this happens, teachers look to RTI models to consider adaptations and accommodations. An adaptation may be applied to the regular curriculum and may involve planning, materials, activities, and assessments. In generating adaptations to current curriculums, the differentiation model of Tomlinson and Imbeau (2010) can be especially helpful. Table 12.2 uses their ideas to provide musical suggestions that might be helpful. The table is self-explanatory; however, one specific adaptation, the RAFT model, is especially applicable for music education. RAFT is an acronym that encourages differentiation of Role, Audience, Format, and Task. RAFT can be a great tool for music educators since they readily identify with the terms of role, audience, and task. Table 12.2 also provides suggestions for changing the nature, amount, and format of content representation (concrete, representational, or abstract [symbolic] have been described). Finally, Table 12.2 provides suggestions for musical tasks that are authentic musically but varied in the nature of perception and difficulty of performance (global, segmental, and distinct).

Suggestions in this chapter have described forms of differentiation based on the structure of music (content), the instructional design (process), and variety in demonstrations of learning (product). Tomlinson and Imbeau (2010) also discuss what they call *affect*, or "how students' emotions and feeling impact their learning" (p. 16). I have purposely left this as the concluding aspect of differentiation because this single parameter filters all else. The Core Arts Standards from the United States are based on student outcomes that give students the potential tasks to create, perform, respond, and connect (The College Board, 2014). I challenge that while these may be behavioral outcomes for music education, they are, essentially, the roles of a comprehensive musician. Thus, we encourage students to experience all four roles. Students usually are open to these roles depending on their music abilities and social comfort levels. But students should be encouraged to try all roles. We cannot continue to see the majority as responders, with some of the best as performers, and only the very top tier as creators.

Differentiation provides a golden opportunity for students to fulfill varied roles as they respond using lower-risk private responses (perhaps using personal manipulatives, answer clickers, or iPad applications), perform

Table 12.2 MUSIC EDUCATION DIFFERENTIATION BASED ON STUDENT NEED[a]

	Readiness	Interest	Learning Profile
Content	• Use materials of varied reading levels. • Provide different manipulatives using photos, graphic drawings (icons), stick notation, and regular notation depending on student level (e.g., picture exchange communication materials). • Front-load vocabulary with visual reminders (such as word walls). • Highlight single parts or important patterns. • Highlight text in one color and leave music white (or opposite). • Simplify content (give some students parts that have been altered for easier readability by alignment, fewer pitches, or simplified rhythms)	• Provide a range of materials. • Use interesting age-appropriate texts with simple musical structures (party songs are a good example). • Tie music to other learning themes in the school setting. • Provide a range of materials including examples that will be heard frequently in the real world (popular, patriotic, scores from video games, TV/movie themes). • Link to student interests (culture, favorite artists, interesting composers).	• Vary teaching modes (auditory is always present but add visual, kinesthetic, tactile). • Provide preteaching materials or extension materials that students can access in their classroom or library or online. • Video or audio notes may allow additional repetitions (e.g., digitally record public domain songs and burn to CDs so students can check them out for home repetition).
Process	• Tier activities: Allow nonspecific music responses (e.g., allow nonverbal gesture or tracing icons before requiring specific pitch/rhythm hand signs, playing, etc). • Provide direct instruction for new material, tasks, and skill sets. • Be flexible with use of time if possible. • Set up learning contracts that may help students monitor their success within the group.	• Encourage expert groups (good for high-level students and students with autism/Asperger's). • Create interest centers for classrooms, library, or online. • Suggest apps for independent study. • Allow independent learning on high-interest areas with encouraging support for areas that are difficult or low interest to the student.	• Allow choices (e.g., move alone or with a partner). • Design tasks around student's interests. • Provide RAFT options when possible. (RAFT—Role, Audience, Format, Topic). • Allow onlooker behavior until the student feels comfortable with demonstrating his/her skills. • Allow private demonstrations to a chosen peer or to the teacher only for shy students to reduce stress.

(*continued*)

Table 12.2 (CONTINUED)

	Readiness	Interest	Learning Profile
	• Explore use of para, teacher, therapist (speech-language pathology, physical therapist, occupational therapist [OT]) for interdisciplinary work—(e.g., OT works on grasp—ask OT to help student learn to use woodblock grasping mallet in one hand and block in the other).		• Encourage reflection and data collection so that students can understand their own learning profiles.
Product	• Encourage quality products. Strive for students to do their best within their ability level. • Encourage students to work for perfection of tasks where they show readiness. • Provide safe feedback and encourage students to risk mistakes on more difficult tasks.	• When possible, allow choices of product. Encourage students to persevere toward a completed product. • Provide support that can enhance students' products, but do not minimize or bury student work within "professional" products (e.g., adding light harmony for uncertain singers or allowing two peers to sing together, but not having students sing or play quietly while professionals or a recording carries the performance).	• Preserve student work to demonstrate varied types of learning. • Use e-portfolios to encourage students to use self-reflection. • Encourage students to gather samples of products that support their learning preferences (e.g., recordings, compositions, photos, etc.).

Student affect: Filtered by the system "mindset."

Note. © Elaine Bernstorf (2013a).
ᵃ Influenced by Tomlinson and Imbeau (2010).

privately using keyboards or iPad instruments with headphones, and create privately using composition software, apps, or other technology. For many students, allowing privacy as they are learning can reduce their stress level dramatically and keep them involved. Their audiences can be graduated from private (e.g., responding to technology), to working with an assistant, then to age peers in a small group, and ultimately to large situations. For some students, working with an older student or a college student mentor may be less stressful than responding, performing, or creating in front of age peers. While for many students, singing or playing with a group is enjoyable, for students with disabilities, having an opportunity to create a short composition in a private setting may yield a stronger demonstration of their true capabilities. Allowing students some choice of their role(s) and some variety of audience settings may be the only differentiation needed. After they have some success in private or smaller group settings, students may be comfortable with larger groups. After experiencing success as a responder, they may be willing to perform. On the other hand, after being encouraged to create, a more confident student may be willing to respond to others' creations. Almost every student has some affinity for music—but many students do not like "music education," especially if and when a "great" musical product is produced, but at the expense of an individual's public dignity (which can occur far too easily). Students with disabilities and students with exceptional abilities have radar for closed systems that are about product and not people, and they avoid them at all costs. If we truly are open minded about music education, every student will be affirmed in his or her role as a musician no matter whether that musician is a responder, performer, or creator. Only by providing students an open system that invites all students to safely experience forms of music literacy can we foster the literacy for music that leads to lifelong affinity and continued support. As Tomlinson and Imbeau state, "when a student has a positive affect regarding learning and himself or herself as a learner, it opens the door to academic growth. Conversely, a student's negative affect regarding learning or his or her own abilities as a learner shuts the door" (2010, p. 16). Music educators have seen too many students who shut the door on any role in music because of a system mindset that becomes fixed on a perfected performance to the exclusion of musical literacy growth for all learners.

NOTES

1. Those interested in understanding the specifics of reading acquisition may want to explore these focused materials available without cost at http://www.sedl.org.

2. Note: Research by Saffran and Griepentrog (2001) and Saffran (2003) suggested that mothers and other caregivers tend to use the same key and absolute pitches when singing to their infants, and that infants may be more attuned to absolute pitches whereas adults begin to broaden their categorizations of tonality to move toward relative pitch inclusions. This may explain the characteristic of some students with disabilities such as autism to demand that a song be played using exactly the same key and pitches. It also heightens the importance of in-tune playing and singing for music educators who work with students who have disabilities (in fact, for all students).

3. The use of "centers" to differentiate instruction is quite plausible, especially with the availability of iPads and other technology, but is not the focus of this chapter. Centers and small group adaptations may not be compatible across all music methodologies, nor easily made possible when teachers must teach using carts or in portable environments such as lunchrooms and stages.

REFERENCES

Atterbury, B. (1985). Musical differences in learning-disabled and normal-achieving readers, aged seven, eight, and nine. *Psychology of Music, 13*, 114–123. doi:10.1177/0305735685132005

Bartel, M. (2012). *Empathic critique*. Retrieved from http://bartelart.com/arted/critique08.html on 7/4/2013

Bernstorf, E. (2008). Music and language: Sound features for teaching literacy. *Kodály Envoy, 34*(2), 26–29.

Bernstorf, E. (2013a). Differentiation in music instruction: Implications of MTSS and Common Core for inclusion settings. *Kansas Music Review, 76*(3) Fall. Retrieved from http://kmr.ksmea.org/?issue=201314f&section=articles&page=differentiation

Bernstorf, E. (2013b). Reading acquisition in music and language: The cry for preschool music endures. *Kodály Envoy, 40*(1), 24–28.

Bernstorf, E., & Brenzikofer, K. (2013). *MTSS for music: A framework for Kansas music teachers*. Presentation to the Kansas Music Educators Association Board, Wichita, KS, August 2, 2013.

Bernstorf, E., & Kordonowy, J. (2013). Music literacy acquisition: A conceptual framework for comprehensive music learning. In *Kaleidoscope Music Curriculum*. Wichita, KS: Wichita State University Evelyn H. Cassatt Speech-Language Hearing Clinic.

Blair, D. (2009). Stepping aside: Teaching in a student-centered music classroom. *Music Educators Journal, 98*(3), 42–45.

Bruner, J. (1960). *The process of education*. Cambridge, MA: Harvard University Press.

Bruner, J. (1966). *Toward a theory of instruction*. Cambridge, MA: Harvard University Press.

Burger, B., Saarikallio, S., Luck, G., Thompson, M., & Toiviainen, P. (2013). Relationships between perceived emotions in music and music-induced movement. *Music Perception: An Interdisciplinary Journal, 30*(5), 517–533. Retrieved from http://www.jstor.org/stable/10.1525/m0.2013.30.5.517

The College Board. (2012). *Child development and arts education: A review of recent research and best practices*. New York, NY: Author. Retrieved from http://nccas.wikispaces.com/Child+Development+Research

Degé, F., & Schwarzer, G. (2011). The effect of a music program on phonological awareness in preschoolers. *Frontiers in Psychology, 2*(124), 1-7.

Fedorenko, E., Patel, A., Cassanto, D., Winawer, J., & Gibson, E. (2009). Structural integration in language and music: Evidence for a shared system. *Memory & Cognition, 37*(1), 1–9. doi:10.3758/MC.37.1.1

Gardner, H. (1983). *Frames of mind: The theory of multiple intelligences*. New York, NY: Basic Books.

Hall, S. (2013). Preparing music preservice teachers to enhance language arts reading skills in the elementary music classroom: A degree program and course content analysis. *Journal of Music Teacher Education, 20*(10), 1–14.

Hansen, D., Bernstorf, E., & Stuber, G. (2004). *The music and literacy connection*. Reston, VA: MENC.

Hansen, D., Bernstorf, E., & Stuber, G. (2014). *The music and literacy connection, 2nd edition*. Lantham, MD: Roman and Littlefield.

Jäncke, L. (2012). The relationship between music and language. *Frontiers in Psychology: Auditory Cognitive Neuroscience, 3*, 1–2. doi:103389/fpsyg.2012.00123

Lavoie, R. (1989). *F.A.T. City: How difficult can this be?* Greenwich, CT: Eagle Hill Foundation. Distributed by PBS Video.

McMullen, E., & Saffran, J. (2004). Music and language: A developmental comparison. *Music Perception: An Interdisciplinary Journal, 21*(3), 289–311. doi:10:1525/mp.2004.21.3.289

National Association of State Directors of Special Education. (2006). *Response to intervention: Policy considerations and implications.* Alexandria, VA: Author.

National Coalition for Core Arts Standards (2014). *National Core Arts Standards.* Rights administered by the State Education Agency Directors of Arts Education. Dover, DE. http://www.nationalartsstandards.org

National Reading Panel. (2000). *Teaching children to read: An evidence-based assessment of the scientific research literature on reading and its implications for reading instruction.* Washington, DC: National Institute of Child Health and Human Development.

Olsson, E., Schéele, B., & Theorell, T. (2013). Heart rate variability during choral singing. *Music and Medicine, 5*(1), 52–59.

Patel, A. (2003). Language, music, syntax and the brain. *Nature Neuroscience, 6*(7), 674–681.

Patel, A. (2008). *Music, language, and the brain.* New York, NY: Oxford University Press.

President's Committee on the Arts and the Humanities. (2011). *Reinvesting in arts education: Winning America's future through creative schools.* Washington, DC: Author. Retrieved from http://www.pcah.gov

Rautenberg, I. (2015). The effects of musical training on the decoding skills of German-speaking primary school children. *Journal of Research in Reading, 38*(1), 1–17. doi:10.1111/j4i4.12010.

Register, D., Darrow, A., Standley, J., & Swedberg, O. (2007). The use of music to enhance reading skills of second grade students and students with reading disabilities. *Journal of Music Therapy, 44*(1), 23–37.

Reis, S., Kaplan, S., Tomlinson, C., Westbern, K., Callahan, C., & Cooper, C. (1998). A response: Equal does not mean identical. *Educational Leadership, 56*(3), 74.

Saffran, J. (2003). Absolute pitch in infancy and adulthood: The role of tonal structure. *Developmental Science, 6*(1), 35–47.

Saffran, J. R., Griepentrog, G. J., Jenny R. S., & Gregory J. G. (2001). Absolute pitch in infant auditory learning: Evidence for developmental reorganization. *Developmental Psychology, 37*(1), 74.

Tomlinson, C. (1999). *The differentiated classroom: Responding to the needs of all learners.* Alexandria, VA: Association for Supervision and Curriculum Development.

Tomlinson, C., & Allan, S. (2000). *Leadership for differentiating schools and classrooms.* Alexandria, VA: Association for Supervision and Curriculum Development.

Tomlinson, C., & Imbeau, M. (2010). *Leading and managing a differentiated classroom.* Alexandria, VA: Association for Supervision and Curriculum Development.

Törmänen, M. (2010). *Auditory-visual matching in learning disabilities: Intervention studies from Finland and Sweden.* Research Report 315. Helsinki, Finland: University of Helsinki.

Trehub, S., & Hannon, E. (2006). Infant music perception: Domain-general or domain-specific mechanisms? *Cognition, 100,* 73–99. doi:10.1016/j.cognition.2005.11.006

Wolff, P. H. (2002). Timing precision and rhythm in developmental dyslexia. *Reading and Writing: An Interdisciplinary Journal, 15,* 179–206. doi:10.1023/A:1013880723925

Wren, S. (2000). *The cognitive foundations of learning to read: A framework.* Austin, TX: Southwest Educational Development Laboratory.

CHAPTER 13

Understanding the Individualized Education Program Model within the United States

KIMBERLY VANWEELDEN

The Individualized Education Program (IEP) has been in existence for almost 40 years in the United States; however, the document that is currently used has changed substantially since its introduction in 1975. Through multiple federal laws, today's IEP has become the primary tool for instructional planning to improve educational results for children with disabilities. Containing statements about present levels of academic achievement and functional performance, annual goals, services, and accommodations and modifications, the IEP document is one of the most important pieces of information music educators can have at their disposal. Due to the large amount of material contained within an IEP document, however, finding the needed information can be confusing and overwhelming. Several American authors within the area of special music education have described the IEP process (Adamek & Darrow, 2010; Atterbury, 1990; Hammel & Hourigan, 2011; Nocera, 1979; Sobol, 2008); thus, this chapter is meant to expand upon these previous works. Specifically, this chapter will outline the (1) history of the IEP document, (2) eligibility needed to develop an IEP document, (3) description and development of the IEP document, and (4) sections within an IEP document that should be utilized by music educators when working with students with disabilities in music.

THE HISTORY OF THE INDIVIDUALIZED EDUCATION PROGRAM

Before the 1970s, special education in the United States was in a dismal state. Children with disabilities did not often have access to public education, and most either were home schooled, did not receive any education at all, or were placed in institutions (Dray, 2009). In 1975, US Congress passed the Education for All Handicapped Children Act (Public Law [PL] 94-142), which mandated an IEP for every student with a disability. The law further required that the IEP include short- and long-term goals for the student and that the necessary services and resources be available to educate the child (US Department of Education [DOE], 2010). This law became the foundation of today's special education law.

In 1990, the Individuals with Disabilities Education Act (IDEA '90) reaffirmed PL 94-142's requirements of a free, appropriate public education through an IEP with related services and due process procedures. This law expanded the eligibility categories to include autism and traumatic brain injuries, required a transition plan to be a part of every IEP no later than the child's 16th birthday, and designated assistive technology devices as a related service on the IEP (DOE, 2010). These additions remain in place in the current law today.

In the late 1990s, the reauthorization of IDEA '90 as the Individuals with Disabilities Education Act Amendments of 1997 (IDEA '97) was an important step in the development of the IEP. Previous versions of the law were concerned with ensuring that students would not be excluded from school or from free and appropriate services at school (Rothstein & Johnson, 2009). With the passing of IDEA '97, US Congress started to actively address the *quality* of services children received by requiring schools to provide services that would allow them to progress *in* the general curriculum. This placed greater importance on state- and district-wide assessment programs for children with disabilities, which then placed greater importance on the child's IEP document (DOE, 2002). IDEA '97 also mandated the following (Mitchell, Morton, & Hornby, 2010; Wright, 2004):

- One regular education teacher must be a member of the child's IEP team if the child participates in the regular education environment.
- A child's IEP must be accessible to each teacher and service provider who is responsible for its implementation.
- An IEP must include statements of the child's present levels of educational performance, measurable annual goals, special education and related services, and modifications or supports provided.
- IEPs must be developed and implemented for every child with disabilities between the ages of 3 and 21.

These amendments increased the role of the IEP document as the primary tool for educational planning (Driscoll & Nagel, 2010).

The Individuals with Disabilities Education Improvement Act (IDEIA, or IDEA '04) is the law educators follow today. When US Congress enacted this law, it made significant changes meant to ensure that children with disabilities would receive a high-quality, free, and appropriate public education that would align with the standards within the No Child Left Behind Act. IDEA '04 requires that schools are accountable, children with disabilities are educated by highly qualified teachers, there are enhanced opportunities for parental involvement, and paperwork burdens are reduced for teachers, local school districts, and states (Newsline, 2005). With regard to the IEP, IDEA '04 both preserved and extended the language of IDEA '97 to clarify intent, such as replacing the words "educational performance" with "academic achievement and functional performance" (see Figure 13.1). While most of the changes within the IEP section may seem minor, these small differences, as well as the more significant changes made throughout the rest of IDEA '04, have brought us closer to meeting all the needs of children with disabilities within our educational system.

Figure 13.1 LANGUAGE CHANGES FROM THE INDIVIDUALS WITH DISABILITIES EDUCATION ACT 1997 TO THE INDIVIDUALS WITH DISABILITIES EDUCATION ACT 2004

IEP Content

In general, the term individualized education program or IEP means a written statement for each child with a disability that is developed, reviewed, and revised in accordance with this section and that includes—

IDEA 1997	IDEA 2004
I. A statement of the child's present levels of educational performance, including—	I. A statement of the child's present levels of academic achievement and functional performance, including—
a. how the child's disability affects the child's involvement and progress in the general curriculum;	a. how the child's disability affects the child's involvement and progress in the general education curriculum;
b. for preschool children, as appropriate, how the disability affects the child's participation in appropriate activities;	b. for preschool children, as appropriate, how the disability affects the child's participation in appropriate activities; and
	c. for children with disabilities who take alternative assessments aligned to alternative achievement standards, a description of benchmarks or short-term objectives;

(continued)

Figure 13.1 (CONTINUED)

IDEA 1997	IDEA 2004
II. A statement of measurable annual goals, including benchmarks or short-term objectives, related to—	II. A statement of measurable annual goals, including <u>academic and functional goals, designed to—</u>
a. meet the child's needs that result from the child's disability to enable the child to be involved in and progress in the general education curriculum; and	a. meet the child's needs that result from the child's disability to enable the child to be involved in and <u>make</u> progress in the general education curriculum; and
b. meet each of the child's other education needs that result from the child's disability;	b. meet each of the child's other education needs that result from the child's disability;
III. N/A	III. <u>A description of how the child's progress toward</u> meeting the annual goals described in subclause (II) will be measured and when periodic reports on the progress the child is making toward meeting the annual goals (such as through the use of quarterly <u>or other periodic reports, concurrent with the issurance of report cards) will be provided;</u>
IV. A statement of the special education and related services and supplementary aids and services, to be provided to the child, or on behalf of the child, and a statement of the program modifications or supports for school personnel that will be provided for the child;	IV. A statement of the special education and related services and supplementary aids and services, based on peer-reviewed research to the extent practicable, to be provided to the child, or on behalf of the child, and a statement of the program modifications or supports for school personnel that will be provided for the child;
a. to advance appropriately toward attaining the annual goals;	a. to advance appropriately toward attaining the annual goals;
b. to be involved in and progress in the general education curriculum in accordance with subclause (I) and to participate in extracurriculuar and other nonacademic activities; and	b. to be involved in and <u>make</u> progress in the general education curriculum in accordance with subclause (I) and to participate in extracurriculuar and other nonacademic activities; and
c. to be educated and participate with other children with disabilities and nondisabled children in the activities described in this subparagraph;	c. to be educated and participate with other children with disabilities and nondisabled children in the activities described in this subparagraph;

(*continued*)

Figure 13.1 (CONTINUED)

IDEA 1997	IDEA 2004
V. An explanation of the extent, if any, to which the child will not participate with nondisabled children in the regular class and in the activities described in subclause (IV)(c);	V. An explanation of the extent, if any, to which the child will not participate with nondisabled children in the regular class and in the activities described in subclause (IV)(c);
VI. N/A	VI. A statement of any individual appropriate accommodations that are necessary to measure the academic achievement and functional performance of the child on State and districtwide assessments; and a. if the IEP Team determines that the child shall take an alternative assessment on a particular State or districtwide assessment of student achievement, a statement of why— i. the child cannot participate in the regular assesssment; and ii. the particular alternative assessment selected is appropriate for the child;
VII. The projected date for the beginning of the services and modifications described in subclause (IV), and the anticipated frequency, location, and duration of those services and modifications; and	VII. The projected date for the beginning of the services and modifications described in subclause (IV), and the anticipated frequency, location, and duration of those services and modifications; and
VIII.	VIII. Beginning not later than the first IEP to be in effect when the child is 16, and updated annually thereafter— a. appropriate measurable postsecondary goals based upon age appropriate transition assessments related training, education, employment, and where appropriate, independent living skills; b. the transition services (including courses of study) needed to assist the child in reaching those goals; and
c. beginning not later than 1 year before the child reaches the age of majority under State law, a statement that the child has been informed of the child's rights under this title, if any, that will tranfer to the child on reaching the age of majority inder section 615(m)	c. beginning not later than 1 year before the child reaches the age of majority under State law, a statement that the child has been informed of the child's rights under this title, if any, that will tranfer to the child on reaching the age of majority inder section 615(m)

Note. Underlined words are changes to the language within IDEA 2004.

INDIVIDUALIZED EDUCATION
PROGRAM ELIGIBILITY

A child with a disability is not automatically eligible to receive an IEP document within the United States (Wright & Wright, 2007). To become eligible, a child must first undergo a full and individual evaluation by the school district. The purpose of this evaluation is to (1) determine if the child has a disability, as defined under IDEA; (2) gather information about the child's educational needs; and (3) provide guidance for appropriate educational programming (National Dissemination Center for Children with Disabilities [NICHCY], 2010b). IDEA requires the use of a variety of assessment tools and strategies during this evaluation to gather relevant functional, developmental, and academic information about the child, including information provided by the parent (DOE, 2006). Specifically, the evaluation will include assessments of the child's health, vision and hearing, social and emotional status, general intelligence, academic performance, communicative status, and motor abilities (NICHCY, 2010b). Additionally, IDEA requires that the assessments used be proven valid and reliable through research and be administered by trained professionals within each area (DOE, 2006).

IDEA lists different disability categories under which a child may be found eligible for special education and related services and thus receive an IEP document. These categories are as follows (DOE, Office of Special Education and Rehabilitative Services, Office of Special Education Programs, 2006):

- Autism
- Deafness
- Deaf-blindness
- Developmental delay (optional for states)
- Emotional disturbance
- Hearing impairment
- Intellectual disability
- Multiple disabilities
- Orthopedic impairment
- Other health impairment
- Specific learning disability
- Speech or language impairment
- Traumatic brain injury
- Visual impairment, including blindness

The law further requires that the child's disability is to the extent that he or she *needs* special education and related services (DOE, Office of

Special Education and Rehabilitative Services, Office of Special Education Programs, 2006; NICHCY, 2010b). Only children meeting both of these criteria are eligible to have an IEP document written for them.

DESCRIPTION AND DEVELOPMENT OF THE INDIVIDUALIZED EDUCATION PROGRAM

An IEP is a written document developed for each child who is eligible to receive special education services by his or her local public school district. It is a working document describing the educational program that will address a child's unique needs and can be written or revised at any time during the school year. Once the IEP document is written and signed, it becomes a legal contract between the child's parent/legal guardian and the school district regarding the services that will be provided to the child during the school year. While each school district and/or state may have a different IEP format, federal law mandates that all IEP documents must include the following information (NICHCY, 2010a, para. 3):

1. A statement of the child's present levels of academic achievement and functional performance
2. A statement of measurable annual goals, including academic and functional goals
3. A description of how the child's progress toward meeting the annual goals will be measured
4. A statement of the special education and related services and supplementary aids and services to be provided to the child
5. A statement of the program modifications or supports for school personnel that will be provided to the child
6. An explanation of the extent, if any, to which the child will not participate with nondisabled children in the regular class and in extracurricular and nonacademic activities
7. A statement of any individual accommodations that are necessary for the child on state- and district-wide assessments
8. The projected date for the beginning of the services and modifications, including the frequency, location, and duration of those services and modifications

IDEA '04 also requires a child's IEP to include statements about transitional services designed to help prepare the child for life after high school by no later than the student's 16th birthday. These include the following (NICHCY, 2010a, para. 4):

1. Measurable postsecondary goals based on age-appropriate transition assessments related to training, education, employment, and, where appropriate, independent living skills
2. Transition services, including courses of study, needed to assist the child in reaching those goals
3. A statement that a child has been informed of his or her rights upon reaching the age of majority by no later than one year before the child reaches the age of majority

A group of individuals referred to as the IEP team writes, maintains, and updates a child's IEP document. Members of the IEP team consist of the child's parents, special education teacher(s), regular education teacher(s), and other school staff and experts that are knowledgeable about the child and/or special education (see Figure 13.2 for IDEA '04 IEP team member requirements). The purpose of the team is to combine their knowledge, expertise, and experience to design an educational program to help the child be involved and make positive improvement in the general education curriculum. Of particular interest to this chapter is the role of the regular education teacher on the team. IDEA '04 states that regular education teachers must, to the extent appropriate, determine:

- appropriate positive behavioral interventions and supports and other strategies for the child (DOE, 2006, §300.324(a)(3)(i));
- which supplementary aids and services, program modifications, and support for school personnel are needed to help the child:

  o progress toward attaining the annual goals;
  o be involved in and make progress in the general education curriculum; participate in extracurricular activities and other nonacademic activities; and
  o be educated and participate with other children with disabilities and those who are not disabled (DOE, 2006, §300.324(a)(3)(ii) and §300.320(a)(4)).

Federal law requires an IEP team to meet annually; however, they may also meet at other times during the year as needed (DOE, Office of Special Education and Rehabilitative Services, Office of Special Education Programs, 2006). At the annual meeting, the team determines the educational program designed to address a child's unique needs for the year, including the written portions required by law listed previously. The IEP team will also meet if revisions to the child's IEP are required between annual meetings. Team members may be excused from later meetings

Figure 13.2 THE INDIVIDUALIZED EDUCATION PLAN TEAM

The IEP Team is a group of individuals composed of:

I.   The parents of a child with a disability;

II.   Not less than 1 regular education teacher of such child (if the child is, or may be, participating in the regular education environment);

III. Not less than 1 special education teacher, or where appropriate, not less than 1 special education provider of such child;

IV.   A representative of the local education agency who:

    a. is qualified to provide, or supervise the provision of, specially designed instruction to meet the unique needs of children with disabilities;

    b. is knowledgeable about the general education curriculum; and

    c. is knowledgeable about the availability of resources of the local education agency;

V.   An individual who can interpret the instructional implications of evaluation results, who may be a member of the team described in clauses (II) through (VI)

VI.   At the discretion of the parent or the agency, other individuals who have knowledge or special expertise regarding the child, including related services personnel as appropriate; and

VII. Whenever appropriate, the child with a disability. (DOE, 2006b, §300.321)

if both the parent and the district agree in writing that (1) the member's area of curriculum or related service is not being modified or discussed at the meeting or (2) due to a scheduling conflict, the member will submit his or her written input to the IEP prior to the meeting (DOE, Office of Special Education and Rehabilitative Services, Office of Special Education Programs, 2006). IDEA '04 also allows revisions to be made to a child's IEP document without the actual IEP team meeting together if (1) the parent and school district agree to this approach and (2) any revisions or modifications to the IEP document are made in writing and the rest of the IEP team is informed of the changes (DOE, 2006, §300.324(a)(4)–(6)).

After the IEP team writes the document and the child's parent(s) sign it, the school is responsible for providing the child with the special education and related services listed.

According to IDEA '04, these services must begin as soon as possible; however, no specific amount of time between finishing the development of and beginning the services described in the IEP is given (DOE, Office of Special Education and Rehabilitative Services, Office of Special Education Programs, 2006, §300.323(c)(2)). Federal law does mandate that a child's IEP be in effect at the beginning of each school year (DOE, Office of Special Education and Rehabilitative Services, Office of Special Education Programs, 2006, §300.323). IDEA '04 also requires that the school ensure that all teachers and service providers responsible for implementing the child's IEP (1) have access to the IEP document; (2) are informed of their specific responsibilities; and (3) are informed of specific accommodations, modifications, and supports to be provided to the child in accordance with the IEP (DOE, Office of Special Education and Rehabilitative Services, Office of Special Education Programs, 2006, §300.323(d)).

THE INDIVIDUALIZED EDUCATION PLAN AND THE MUSIC EDUCATOR
Individualized Education Plan Document

A child's IEP document rarely contains music education information; however, there are several points that are relevant to music educators. Specifically, four statements within the document could help create a successful environment for a child with a disability in a music class or ensemble. These include the student's (1) present levels of academic achievement and functional performance; (2) annual goals, including academic and functional goals; (3) special education and related services and supplementary aids and services; and (4) program modifications or supports for school personnel. To follow are short explanations of each statement, as well as how music educators could use the information when working with a student with a disability in music.

Present levels of academic achievement and functional performance. This section of the IEP describes what the student can currently do both academically and functionally (see Figure 13.3 for examples). Academic achievement refers to the academic subjects a child studies in school (e.g., reading, math, science) and the skills to be mastered in each (DOE, Office of Special Education and Rehabilitative Services, Office of Special Education Programs, 2006). Functional performance refers to "skills or activities that are not considered academic or related to a child's academic achievement" (DOE, 2006, §300.320(a)(1)), such as dressing oneself, walking up and down stairs, or making friends. This section will include a student's most current evaluation/assessment results, as well as statements concerning his or

Figure 13.3 PRESENT LEVELS OF ACADEMIC ACHIEVEMENT
AND FUNCTIONAL PERFORMANCE EXAMPLES

- Jacob works better in a small group or one-on-one where he can verbally answer questions instead of writing them down.
- Katie needs a quiet place to work so she will not be distracted.
- Michael is currently on a behavior chart where the paraprofessional and/or teacher periodically rates his behavior throughout the day.
- Emma requires frequent breaks when working on long tests and assignments.

her learning characteristics, social development, physical development, and management needs.

Knowing this information could be helpful to music educators. The use of the word *could* is deliberate, because knowing what a student can do in other situations does not always equate to what he or she can do in music. However, this information may be particularly helpful to music educators if they do not know the student, especially concerning his or her placement in the appropriate music class, or to begin planning for any accommodations and modifications the student will need to participate.

Annual goals, including academic and functional goals. The purpose of this section is to address the needs identified in the student's present levels of academic achievement and functional performance statement (see Figure 13.4 for examples). Determined by the IEP team, this section lists what a student with a disability can reasonably be expected to achieve both academically and functionally over the course of a year. Each goal within this portion of the IEP document should include at least three components: (1) a clear and understandable statement of each skill or behavior in need of change, (2) conditions under which each skill or behavior is to occur and be evaluated, and (3) method of measurement of what constitutes an acceptable level of performance of each skill or behavior (NICHCY, 2010a). While IDEA '04 requires that the goals must enable the student to "make progress in the general education curriculum" (Wright, 2004, p. 30), federal law does not require goals to be written for each specific discipline (DOE, Office of Special Education and Rehabilitative Services, Office of Special Education Programs, 2006).

Even though music goals are not usually included in the student's IEP, federal law requires that *all* general education teachers who have that child in their classes, including music educators, actively work on the child's annual goals where applicable. Of course, it is not possible to work on every annual goal in a music education class because some do not apply (e.g., learning multiplication facts). However, it is important for music educators to realize they are responsible for working on the goals that can be incorporated into their curriculum, such as helping a student increase his or her skills in reading left to right, following directions, or maintaining good behavior.

Figure 13.4 ANNUAL GOALS, INCLUDING ACADEMIC
AND FUNCTIONAL GOAL EXAMPLES

- Madison will increase being on task from 50% of the time to 70% of the time by the end of the year.
- Noah will increase his knowledge of multiplication facts from 5 up to 9.
- William will increase from going to class without his necessary materials and textbooks to being prepared for class 80% of the time.

Special education and related services and supplementary aids and services. This section contains several types of services that are important to meet a student's academic and functional needs (see Figure 13.5 for examples). Special education refers to the accommodations and modifications within the instruction that are specially designed to meet the unique needs of a child with a disability. Related services describe who will provide services to the child (e.g., special education teacher, paraprofessional, occupational therapist), what services these professionals will provide, and how often the services will be provided. Supplementary aids and services are defined as "aids, services, and other supports that are provided in regular education classes, other education-related settings, and in extracurricular and nonacademic settings, that will enable the child with a disability to be educated with children without disabilities to the greatest extent appropriate" (DOE, 2006, §300.42). These include accommodations and modifications to the student's curriculum or the presentation and measurement of

---

Figure 13.5 EXAMPLES OF SPECIAL EDUCATION AND RELATED SERVICES
AND SUPPLEMENTARY AIDS AND SERVICES

Special Education is instruction specially designed to meet the unique needs of a child with a disability.

Accommodations

- Olivia will be able to leave class 2-3 minutes early so that she can avoid the hallway rush and get to her next class on time.
- John will be able to take frequent breaks to reduce anxiety and behavior problems.
- Jack will be given extra time to complete assignments or tests.

Modifications

- Alex will go to the resource room for reading so he can work in a small group who is at his reading level.
- Abby will master 5 of the 20 spelling words assigned to the class each week.

Related Services help provide to a child with a disability so they may benefit from their special education.

- Paraprofessional
- Speech-Language pathology and audiology services
- Interpreting services
- Physical or Occupational therapy
- Mobility services

Supplementary Aids and Services can included accommodations and modifications but also include:

- Planned seating on the bus, in the classroom, at lunch etc.
- Computer software
- Teaching study skills
- Home set of materials

---

the content, specialized equipment needs, and support and training for staff working with the child (NICHCY, 2010a).

This section of the IEP is probably the most useful for music educators because it can assist in making accommodations and modifications to the music curriculum and determining how to present and measure the material. Often included in this section are accommodations and modifications that specifically address the following (NICHCY, 2013, para. 7):

- Environmental needs—preferential and/or planned seating; altered physical room arrangement
- Staff support needs—classroom companion; paraprofessional
- Pacing of instruction needs—frequent breaks; more time given to complete tasks; a set of materials given for use at home
- Presentation of the subject matter needs—taped lectures; sign language; paired reading and writing
- Materials needed—large print or Braille; assistive technology; shared note taking
- Assignment modification needs—shorter assignments; taped lessons; instructions broken down into smaller steps
- Self-management needs—calendars; study skills
- Testing adaptation needs—tests read to the child; test format modified; the child given more time to complete the test
- Social interaction needs—circle of friends provided; cooperative learning groups used

Oftentimes the accommodations and modifications listed in this section transfer to the music class as is or with slight alterations. However, if the student requires a specific supplementary aid or support to participate in music and it is not listed in this section, such as specialized equipment, music educators should talk to a member of the child's IEP team to have that information included in the IEP.

Program modifications or supports for school personnel. This section lists the supports required by teachers and other staff to help the child be successful in school. Supports within this section could include attending a conference or training related to the student's needs, getting help from another staff member or administrative person, having an aide in the classroom to help the student with course content, or getting special equipment or teaching materials to help the student participate as fully as possible within a course (NICHCY, 2010a). The IEP team is responsible for determining all needed supports and specifying these on the IEP document. Music educators could utilize this section of a child's IEP to request (1) in-service training on how to work with children with disabilities in music, (2) a paraprofessional to accompany the student during music, or (3) teaching materials and resources to better prepare and plan for working with the student.

Knowing the information within the four sections of a child's IEP discussed earlier can be very beneficial; however, music educators may also find it helpful to create their own form that asks the special education teacher to suggest accommodations, modifications, and supplementary aids that would be useful to the student when participating in music activities. Figure 13.6 is an example of a form created by McCord (2006) that could serve this purpose and be adapted to any level of music class or ensemble. Notice how the first column lists the music skills and behaviors that are particular to the child's music class, while the second column is left blank for the special education teacher to list ideas on how to help the child participate as fully as possible with each.

Figure 13.6 CHILD ASSESSMENT FORM

General Music Grade _____

Student Name_____

Music Skills or Behaviors	Suggested Accommodations, Modifications or Supports
Movement with legs, arms and hands	
Sing	
Read music notation	
Read lyrics/text	
Play instruments with one hand	
Play instruments with both hands	
Play instruments that require physical support	
Play instruments that require holes to be covered with fingers	
Play instruments with varied physical force	
Play instruments that required articulating with tongue	
Play instruments that require hearing exact pitch	

Note. This form was created by Dr. Kimberly McCord (2006).

Individualized Education Plan Team

Music educators may or may not be on a child's IEP team. This is usually dependent on how many other regular education classes the child attends. If a music educator is a part of the IEP team in the role of a regular education teacher, his or her responsibilities would fall under those discussed previously within this chapter, such as determining the supplementary aids and services needed in *any* regular education class or extracurricular activity the child may be involved in, not just music class, and attending a student's annual IEP meeting, since he or she will assist in devising the portions of the document that pertain to the general education of the child. Music educators in this role may have difficulty, however, attending subsequent meetings due to scheduling conflicts. Excusal from these latter meetings is possible if the procedures described in this chapter are followed.

When music educators are not part of a student's IEP team, knowing who is a member is equally important. Since team members know the student best, music educators should contact the special education teacher(s), regular education teacher(s), and/or paraprofessional or other support staff members of the child's IEP team if they have any questions or concerns on how to work with the student in music. Furthermore, if a student requires specific supports, supplementary aids, and/or services to fully participate in the music class, music educators should take their requests to a member of the student's IEP team.

Individualized Education Plan Implementation

Music educators are responsible for implementing the child's annual goals within the music class/ensemble where applicable. While theoretically this seems appropriate, the reality of serving so many students with disabilities, often in one class, and having so little time can make this task seem overwhelming. Therefore, it is important that music educators take proactive steps to help themselves and their students.

First, music educators should make sure they have access to each student's IEP document, which is a guaranteed right according to US federal law (DOE, Office of Special Education and Rehabilitative Services, Office of Special Education Programs, 2006, §300.323(d)). Once the documents are accessed, music educators should note which annual goals can be addressed in the music class. Oftentimes there are many goals written in a student's IEP document that are easily implemented within a music class or ensemble because they are already a part of normal music education practice. Next, music educators should note which specific accommodations, modifications, and supports will be provided to the child in accordance with the IEP. Some of these techniques and supports will transfer to the music class; others will not. While it is not good educational practice to ignore all the accommodations, modifications, and supports listed in this section, the nature of the music class is unique and may require music educators to apply additional thought on how to apply the techniques and supports within the music education curriculum. Consulting the special education teachers, as they are often a wonderful resource, may help with this process. Finally, it is entirely possible that a student with a disability will require specialized equipment or materials to attain the music goals of the class. Therefore, music educators should note what specific supplementary aids or supports the child will need to participate in music that are not listed in this section and talk to the child's IEP team so these additional supports can be provided.

A RECAP OF THE MUSIC EDUCATOR'S RIGHTS AND RESPONSIBILITIES

Almost 40 years after the passage of PL 94-142, music educators are still learning how to include and work with students with disabilities in their classrooms. And while many music educators admit they received little or no training in teaching music to students with disabilities (VanWeelden & Whipple, in press) and are rarely involved in the IEP process (Rose, 2005), it is important to remember that students with disabilities are in music because they want to participate and learn about music. Therefore, it is the music educator's responsibility to ensure that the student's time spent in the music class is as successful an experience as possible.

The child's IEP document is one of the most important and useful pieces of information music educators can have at their disposal to help create a successful environment for students with disabilities in their music classes and ensembles. Specifically, music educators should know the following statements within a student's IEP document:

- Current levels of academic achievement and functional performance
- Annual goals, including academic and functional goals
- Special education and related services and supplementary aids and services
- Program modifications or supports for school personnel

These sections of the IEP document are vital to ensuring that the student receives the necessary supports needed to learn and progress within the music curriculum.

Additionally, music educators should know their rights and responsibilities regarding the IEP process. Specifically, music educators should know they are:

- allowed access to the student's IEP document if that child is in their music class;
- responsible for implementing the student's annual goals within the music class or ensemble where applicable;
- responsible for consulting with a member of the student's IEP team if they are unclear on how to apply the techniques and supports listed within the IEP in the music education curriculum;
- allowed to request additional music-specific supports, materials, and/or training to help work with the student in their music class; and
- responsible for determining the supplementary aids and services needed in *any* regular education class or extracurricular activity the student may be involved in, not just music class, if they are a member of the IEP team.

REFERENCES

Adamek, M. S., & Darrow, A. A. (2010). *Music in special education* (2nd ed.). Silver Springs, MD: American Music Therapy Association.

Atterbury, B. W. (1990). *Mainstreaming exceptional learners in music.* Englewood Cliffs, NJ: Prentice Hall.

Dray, B. J. (2009). Special education, history of. In E. F. Provenzo, Jr. (Ed.), *Encyclopedia of the social and cultural foundations of education* (Vol. 3, pp. 744–747). Thousand Oaks, CA: Sage.

Driscoll, A., & Nagel, N. G. (2010). *Individuals with Disabilities Education Act.* Retrieved from http://www.education.com/reference/article/individuals-disabilities-education-act/

Hammel, A. M., & Hourigan, R. M. (2011). *Teaching music to students with special needs: A label-free approach.* New York, NY: Oxford University Press.

McCord, K. A. (2006). Collaboration and access for our students: Music educators and special educators together. *Music Educators Journal, 92*(4), 26–34.

Mitchell, D., Morton, M., & Hornby, G. (2010). IEPs: Origins, purposes and critiques. In *Review of literature on individual education plans: Report to the New Zealand Ministry of Education.* Retrieved from http://www.educationcounts.govt.nz/publications/literacy/literature-review

National Dissemination Center for Children with Disabilities (NICHCY). (2010a). *Contents of an IEP?* Retrieved from http://nichcy.org/schoolage/iep/iepcontents

National Dissemination Center for Children with Disabilities (NICHCY). (2010b). *Evaluating children for disability.* Retrieved from http://nichcy.org/schoolage/evaluation

National Dissemination Center for Children with Disabilities (NICHCY). (2013). *Supplementary aids and services.* Retrieved from http://nichcy.org/schoolage/iep/iepcontents/

Newsline. (2005). Major changes to IDEA 2004. *Newsline: Newsletter of the Federation for Children with Special Needs*, 25(4), 1, 4–6.

Nocera, S. D. (1979). *Reaching the special learner through music*. Morristown, NJ: Silver Burdett Company.

Rose, L. (2005). A proactive strategy for working with children who have special needs. *General Music Today*, 19(1), 35. doi:10.1177/10483713050190010110

Rothstein, L. F., & Johnson, S. F. (2009). *Special education law* (4th ed.). Thousand Oaks, CA: Sage Publications.

Sobol, E. S. (2008). *An attitude and approach for teaching music to special learners* (2nd ed.). Lanham, MD: R&L Education.

US Department of Education. (2002). *IDEA'97 the law*. Retrieved from http://www2.ed.gov/offices/OSERS/Policy/IDEA/index.html

US Department of Education. (2006, August). *71 Federal Register 46662, § 300.320(a) (1)*. Retrieved from http://www.wrightslaw.com/idea/comment/46661-46688.reg.320-328.ieps.pdf

US Department of Education. (2010). *Thirty-five years of progress in educating children with disabilities through IDEA*. Retrieved from http://www2.ed.gov/about/offices/list/osers/idea35/history/index_pg10.html

US Department of Education. (n.d.). *Child with a disability*. Retrieved from http://idea.ed.gov/explore/view/p/,root,regs,300,A,300%252E8

US Department of Education, Office of Special Education and Rehabilitative Services, Office of Special Education Programs. (2006, April). *26th annual (2004) report to Congress on the implementation of the Individuals with Disabilities Education Act* (Vol. 1). Washington, DC: Government Printing Office.

VanWeelden, K., & Whipple, J. (2014). Music educators' perceptions of preparation and supports available for inclusion. *Journal of Music Teacher Education*, 23, 33-51. doi:10.1177/1057083713484585

Wright, P. W. D. (2004). *The Individuals with Disabilities Education Act of 2004 overview explanation and comparison IDEA 2004 v. IDEA 97*. Retrieved from http://www.wrightslaw.com/idea/idea.2004.all.pdf

Wright, P. W. D., & Wright, P. D. (2007). *Wrightslaw: Special education law* (2nd ed.). Hartfield, VA: Harbor House Law Press.

CHAPTER 14

Special Education and Special Music Education Outside of the United States

KIMBERLY McCORD

Exceptional children and exceptional pedagogy exist across the globe. This collection of chapters from leading researchers and educators demonstrates some of the best ideas for including students in music. All of the authors have been active members of the International Society for Music Education (ISME) Commission on Special Music Education and Music Therapy, including six chairs of the commission. The commission meets every two years prior to the ISME World Conference. Here, commissioners share their research and teaching strategies for special music education and music therapy. Inclusion in music is a shared concern, and commission members discuss special music education in their respective countries. Countries approach inclusion for students with disabilities differently depending on their laws and the way schools are set up to support students with disabilities.

Most countries use the Convention on the Rights of Persons with Disabilities[1] as a guiding document (August 2006). An explanation of what the countries that commit to the convention agree to do can be found in Article 4 of the document:

> Countries that join in the Convention engage themselves to develop and carry out policies, laws and administrative measures for securing the rights recognized in the Convention and abolish laws, regulations, customs and practices that constitute discrimination.

Approximately 1 billion people around the world live with a disability of some type (Kendrick, 2014). The United Nations document attempts, in particular, to provide guidance for developing countries where civil rights for people with disabilities are not yet guaranteed. Many children do not have a right to education or any sort of support for learning. Indeed, the term *handicapped* is thought to originate from children and adults with disabilities who were reduced to begging, thus *hand in cap*. Many individuals with disabilities are homeless or become prostitutes in countries that do not provide educational opportunities that prepare the person for an adult life. In some countries, babies born with disabilities are still left to starve and die by parents who adhere to outdated thinking that there are no possibilities for people with disabilities to live meaningful and productive lives.

To date, 138 countries have signed and ratified the UN Treaty, including Taiwan and Austria. It is interesting that the United States, Finland, and Ireland have all signed the treaty but have not ratified it. Countries that have signed but not ratified the treaty are often concerned that more comprehensive current laws will weakened by signing the treaty. Other concerns are linked to Article 23, which states:

> Persons with disabilities shall have equal opportunity to experience parenthood, to marry and to found a family, to decide the number and spacing of children, to have access to reproductive and family planning education and means, and to enjoy equal rights and responsibilities regarding guardianship, wardship, trusteeship and adoption of children.

The United States has strong differing opinions about reproductive rights. Some members of Congress object to family planning because it implies legal abortion on demand. Reproductive rights were at the heart of the US Senate's inability to pass the treaty even though President Obama signed it.

Once a country signs and ratifies the treaty, the country develops a document that addresses how the treaty will be implemented. In Austria, that document is called the Nationaler Aktionsplan Behindung 2012–2020. Austria ratified the convention in 2008. As a result, the format of education in Austria is evolving by phasing out separate special schools for students with disabilities in favor of more inclusive regular schools. The Nationaler Aktionsplan Behindung document is an excellent example of how to thoughtfully adapt the UN guidelines to ensure accessibility for all. The UN treaty specifically speaks to the importance of arts education, addressing "the development by persons with disabilities of their personality, talents and creativity, as well as their mental and physical abilities, to their fullest potential" (Article 24).

Teachers should explore Article 24 for specific recommendations on how the education of all students should be supported through their schools and governments. Article 24 states that all persons with disabilities have the right to an education and that each country "shall ensure an inclusive education system at all levels. . . ." Indeed, the focus of this book is how to achieve inclusive music education experiences for all students. That said, we recognize that special schools do exist across the globe. These include schools for children who are deaf, are blind, have physical disabilities, have intellectual disabilities, or have emotional disturbance.

We asked the authors represented in this text from outside the United States to provide us with information on how students with disabilities receive a music education in their countries. Realizing that all but Austria and Taiwan are reviewing ratification or developing their own response to the treaty, a brief overview of each country represented in this book is provided here. Chapter 14 covers the United States' Individualized Education Plan (IEP) and the law that guides the development of the IEP. In many countries, a collaborative approach to classifying and developing a plan for education is done much like the IEP process in the United States. The Austrian document certainly emphasizes the importance of collaboration in developing an educational plan for children with disabilities.

AUSTRIA

Music is a compulsory subject for children ages 6 through 15. Most music classes meet one to two times per week. There are some secondary schools that have a music emphasis that provide up to four music classes per week. Most students who want to learn an instrument attend lessons or classes outside of the school day for which they are charged a fee. It is difficult to get into these music schools because there are not enough teachers to meet the demand and most students with disabilities are not selected; thus, these special music schools are not inclusive.

Music classes in primary and secondary schools are inclusive and often cotaught with special educators. Primary school classroom teachers teach all subjects except religion and handicrafts including the required music and movement classes in the national curriculum. Music educators teach at the secondary level (often with special education coteachers), because few have had training in educating children with disabilities. This will soon change in Austria with new required courses in music education on inclusion of students with disabilities.

FINLAND

Finland has not yet ratified the UN agreement, but it is and always has been a leader in education and in the education of persons with disabilities. The Finnish see inclusion for people with disabilities in society as a matter of social justice. Indeed, cutting-edge methods of inclusion like coteaching can be traced back decades to the Finnish schools.

Classroom teachers teach music in primary (elementary) schools. The classroom teachers are well trained and many are members of the Finland Orff Association. Music specialists teach in secondary and upper secondary schools (middle and high school). The curriculum is focused on general music, music theory, and occasionally ensembles that are typically rock bands. Finnish students who want to take instrumental music lessons or perform in large ensembles must do that outside of the school system in private conservatories.

Special schools exist for children with severe disabilities, and music therapists primarily teach music education in these settings. Music therapy is very advanced and is an accepted resource for students with disabilities in Finland.

Music educators are not required to take course work on teaching children with disabilities, although in many music education training schools there are elective courses in special music education. Inclusion is very accepted in Finnish schools; Finnish teachers believe in the value of inclusion and consider it a basic educational right of all students.

IRELAND

Ireland has also not ratified the UN treaty but has been working on inclusion for children with disabilities since 1993. Music is compulsory in primary schools but not in secondary schools. As in Austria, students who wish to participate in ensembles or learn an instrument need to pursue lessons and classes outside of the regular school day.

Training for teachers is very limited depending on the university. Most teachers are not prepared to fully include children with disabilities in music classes, and with cutbacks in assistants for children with disabilities, there is poor overall support.

Like Finland, Ireland uses a social model of disability perspective. Laws may use a medical model of disability that defines the individual according to his or her disability. When a person with hearing loss is labeled, special educators and other specialists in the school develop a plan to help the student function successfully in school and be prepared to independently participate in the community. Disability rights advocates have rejected the medical model because it is limiting and "fails to capture an equally important part of possessing a disability: what is feels like to 'be disabled' in society today" (Abramo, 2012, p. 40).

A social model views the environment, rather than the individual's disability, as the disabling factor. Consider musical instruments—individuals with disabilities have long struggled with how to play instruments that are difficult to access because of their disability. It is not the person's fault that musical instruments are not easily accessible. As teachers, we can help bridge the gap by finding ways to adapt instruments or adapt the environment to allow for instruments to be played in a less traditional way. For example, students with hearing loss might play louder than typical students in a performing ensemble; music teachers can help to adapt the environment to be more accepting of a musician who hears differently. However, there exists a gap between what Ireland believes inclusive education should be and what it can afford to do.

TAIWAN

Taiwan has ratified the UN treaty and is moving toward more inclusive music education. Currently, parents have the option of sending their children to special schools if they want more focused special education or to regular schools, which have less support for students with disabilities. In Taiwan, some parents prefer that their children are not labeled with a disability and thus send their child to the regular schools to avoid their child being categorized.

Special educators are generally more prepared to teach music to students with disabilities than are music educators. Special educators are required in most universities to take music education courses, but music educators are not required to take special education courses. Some universities in Taiwan are just beginning to offer special music education courses.

If parents want their children to attend special schools, they have to pay tuition for children younger than kindergarten but are offered free education once their children reach kindergarten age. A collaborative team similar to the IEP team in the United States works together on testing and identification of children with disabilities.

IN SUMMARY

Ideally, communities across the world would be able to offer music education in inclusive settings taught by trained music educators who are prepared to teach all children. Communities would not only offer general music but also offer opportunities to participate in ensembles and study instruments. The Resonaari School in Helsinki, Finland, is an excellent example of how passionate, socially conscious music educators develop the skills of musicians with intellectual disabilities who are eventually able to work as professional musicians in their communities. Chaoyang University of Technology in Taichung, Taiwan, not only trains teachers to teach music to children with disabilities but also models how to engage children with severe disabilities in music that develops social and academic skills in ways that are often a challenge to the special educator. SoundOUT in Cork City, Ireland, provides a community-based music program that teaches people with severe physical disabilities to play virtual and electronic instruments. Ball State University in Indiana provides music classes for local children with autism who may or may not have an opportunity to learn music at their regular school.

Music teachers can use these models of exemplary educators who, in the spirit of inclusion and accessibility, have found meaningful ways to reach individuals with disabilities. They represent the ideal of offering opportunities for the development of musical expression and creativity for everyone.

NOTE

1. See http://www.un.org/disabilities/convention/convention.shtml.

REFERENCES

Abramo, J. (2012). Disability in the classroom: Current trends and impacts on music education. *Music Educators Journal, 99*(39), 40.

Convention on the Rights of Persons with Disabilities. (n.d.). *The convention in brief.* Retrieved from http://www.un.org/disabilities/convention/convention.shtml

CRS report for Congress prepared for members and committees of Congress. Retrieved from http://www.un.org/disabilities/convention/conventionfull.shtml

Kendrick, D. (2014). This time around, let's ratify U.N. treaty on disabilities. *Columbus Dispatch,* August 11. Retrieved from http://www.dispatch.com/content/stories/editorials/2014/08/11/this-time-around-lets-ratify-u-n--treaty-on-disabilities.html

United Nations enable draft convention on the rights of persons with disabilities. Article 24-Education. Ad Hoc Committee on a Comprehensive and Integral International Convention on the Protection and Promotion of the Rights and Dignity of Persons with Disabilities Eighth Session, New York, NY, August 14–25, 2006. Retrieved from http://www.un.org/esa/socdev/enable/rights/ahc8adart.htm#art24

INDEX

8648885R00200

Printed in Germany
by Amazon Distribution
GmbH, Leipzig